Hot Gimmick

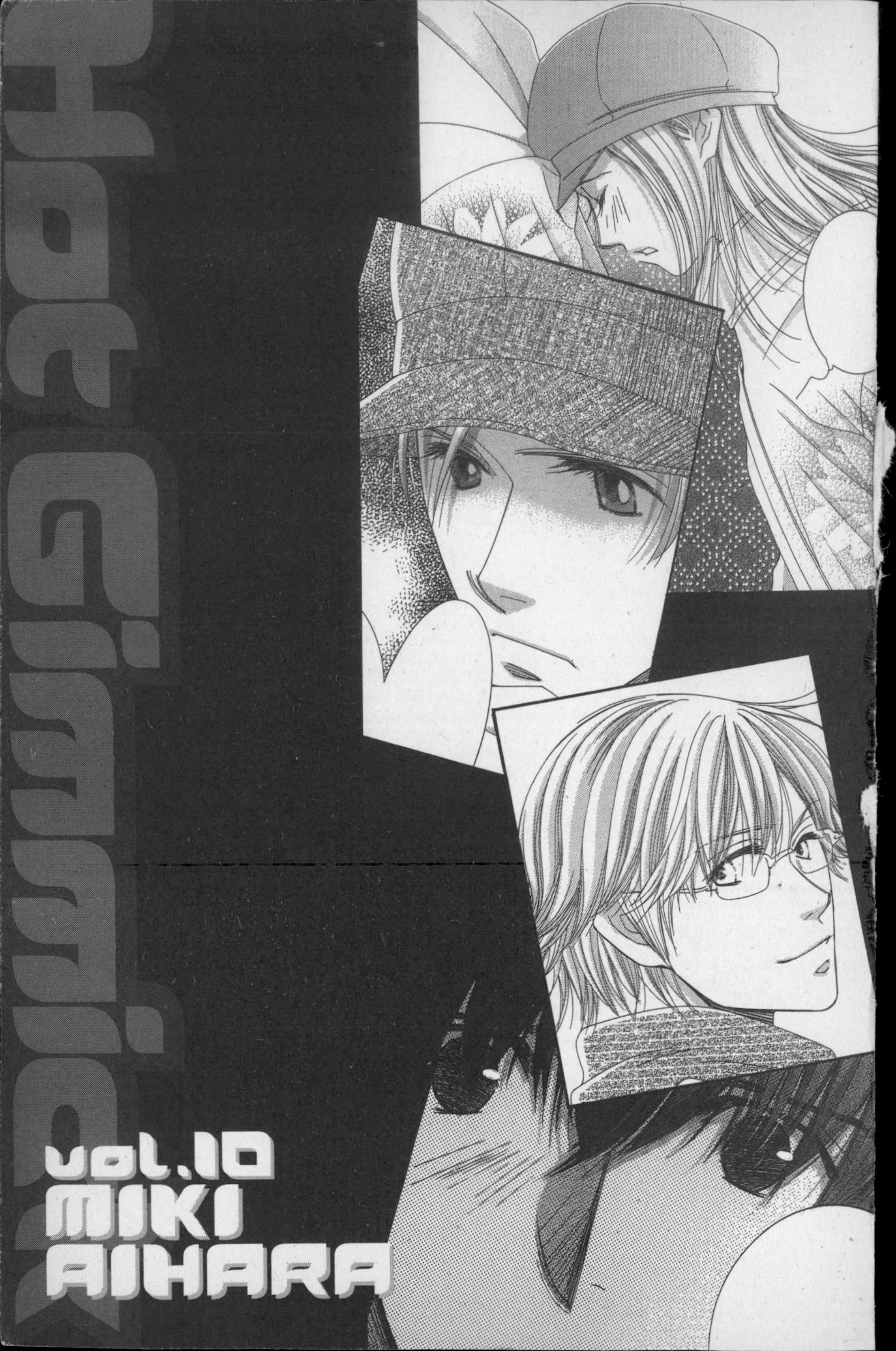

vol.10
MIKI
AIHARA

HOT GIMMICK
CONTENTS

Chapter 42

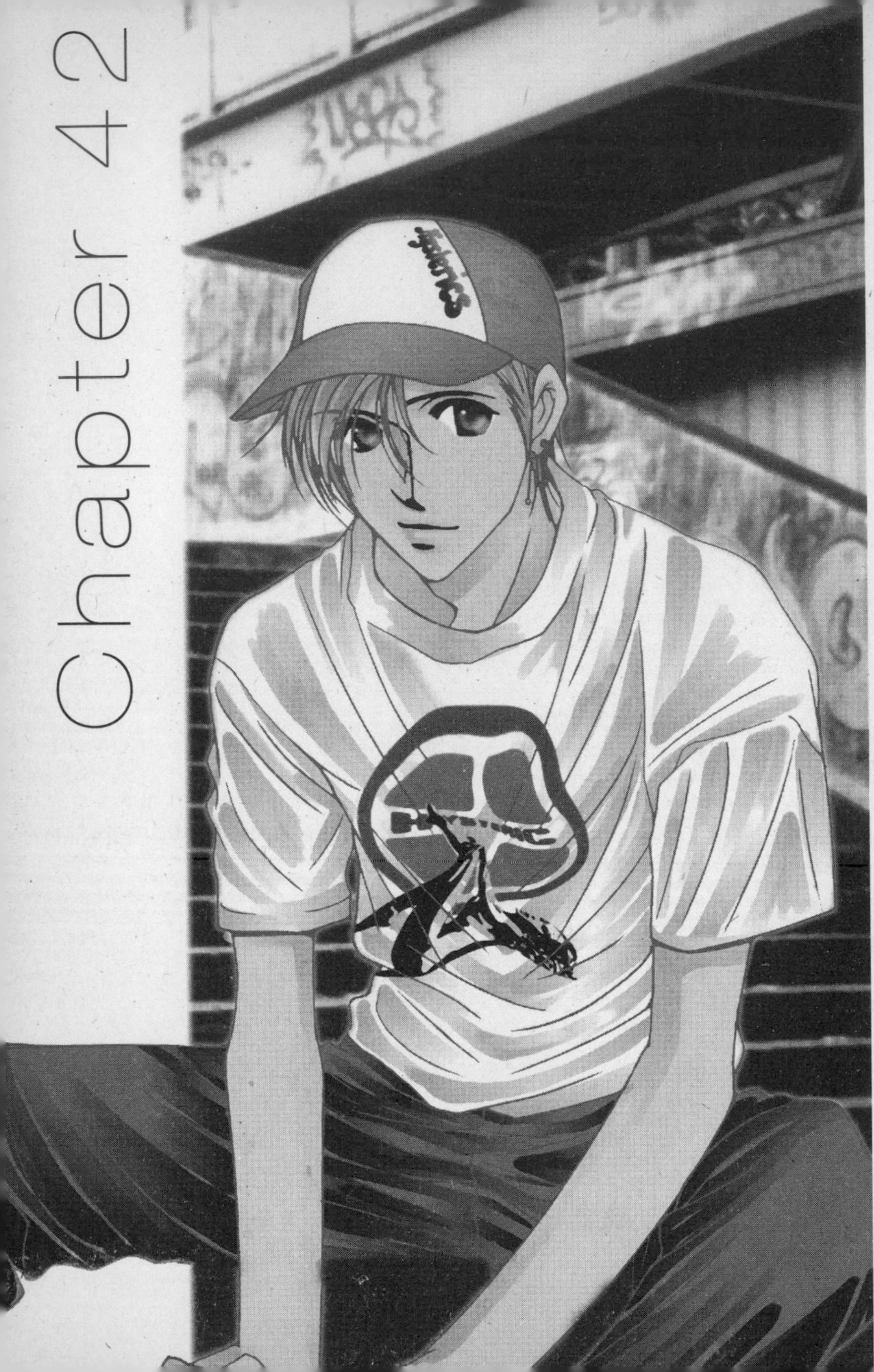

hot gimmick

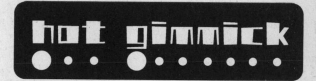

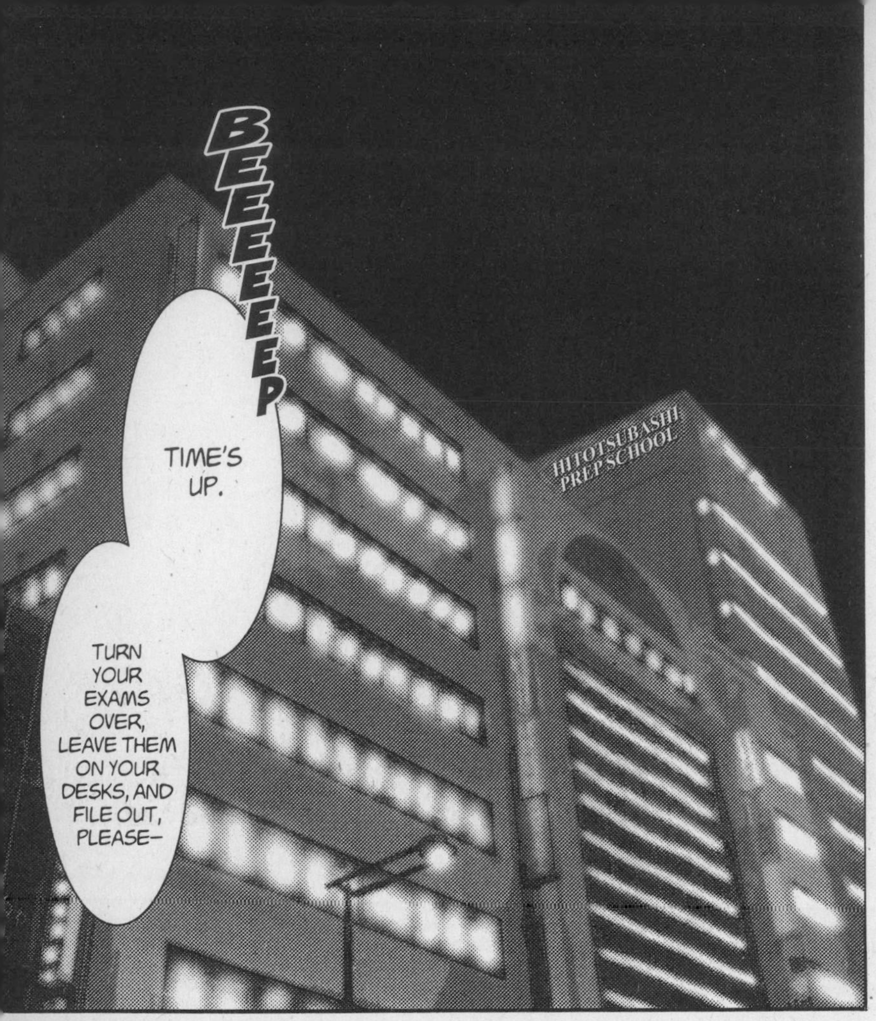
BEEEEEEP
HITOTSUBASHI PREP SCHOOL
TIME'S UP.
TURN YOUR EXAMS OVER, LEAVE THEM ON YOUR DESKS, AND FILE OUT, PLEASE–

hot gimmick

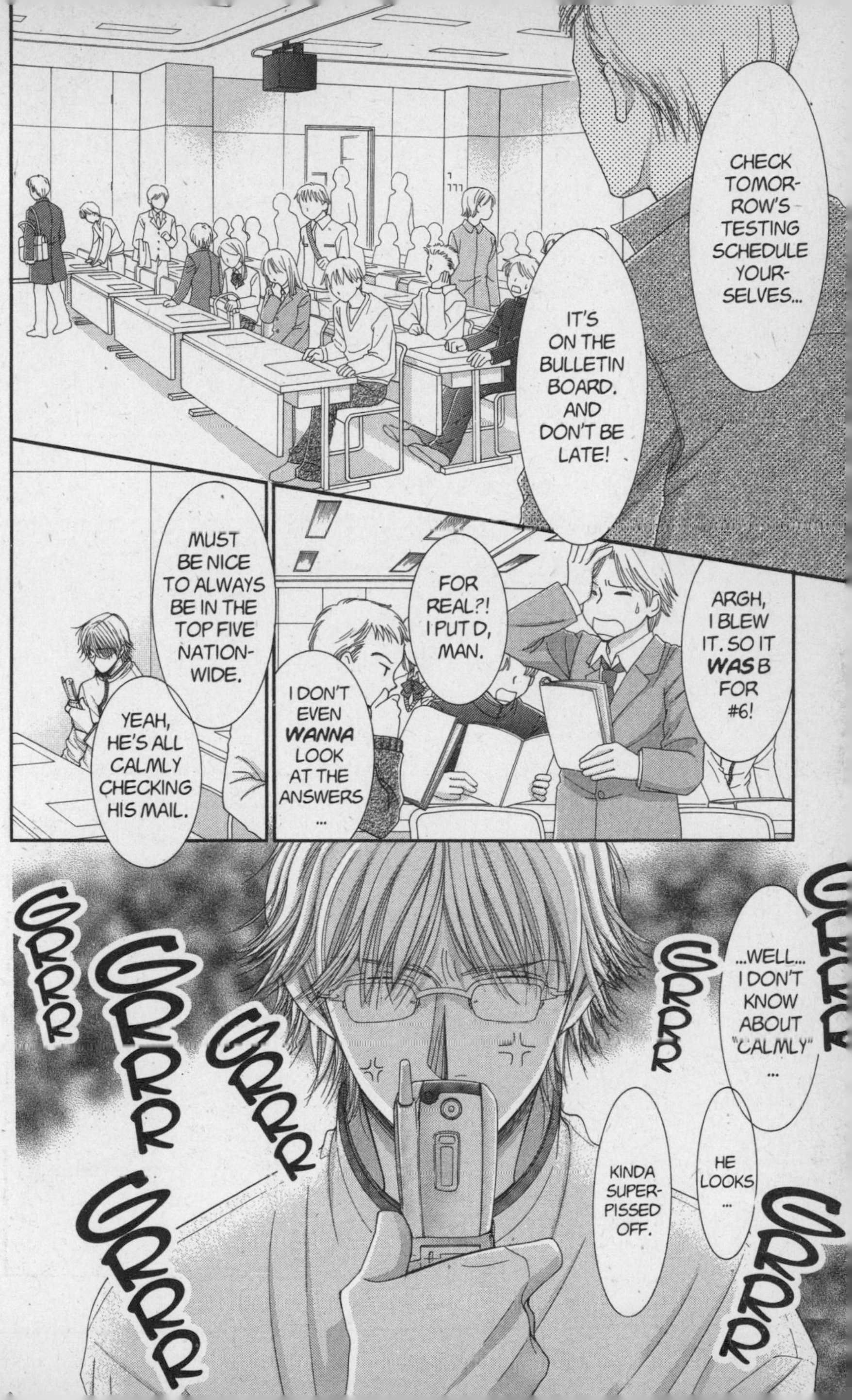
CHECK TOMOR-ROW'S TESTING SCHEDULE YOUR-SELVES...
IT'S ON THE BULLETIN BOARD. AND DON'T BE LATE!
ARGH, I BLEW IT. SO IT **WAS** B FOR #6!
FOR REAL?! I PUT D, MAN.
I DON'T EVEN **WANNA** LOOK AT THE ANSWERS ...
MUST BE NICE TO ALWAYS BE IN THE TOP FIVE NATION-WIDE.
YEAH, HE'S ALL CALMLY CHECKING HIS MAIL.
GRRR
GRRR
...WELL... I DON'T KNOW ABOUT "CALMLY" ...
HE LOOKS ...
KINDA SUPER-PISSED OFF.
GRRR
GRRR
GRRR
GRRR
GRRR
GRRR

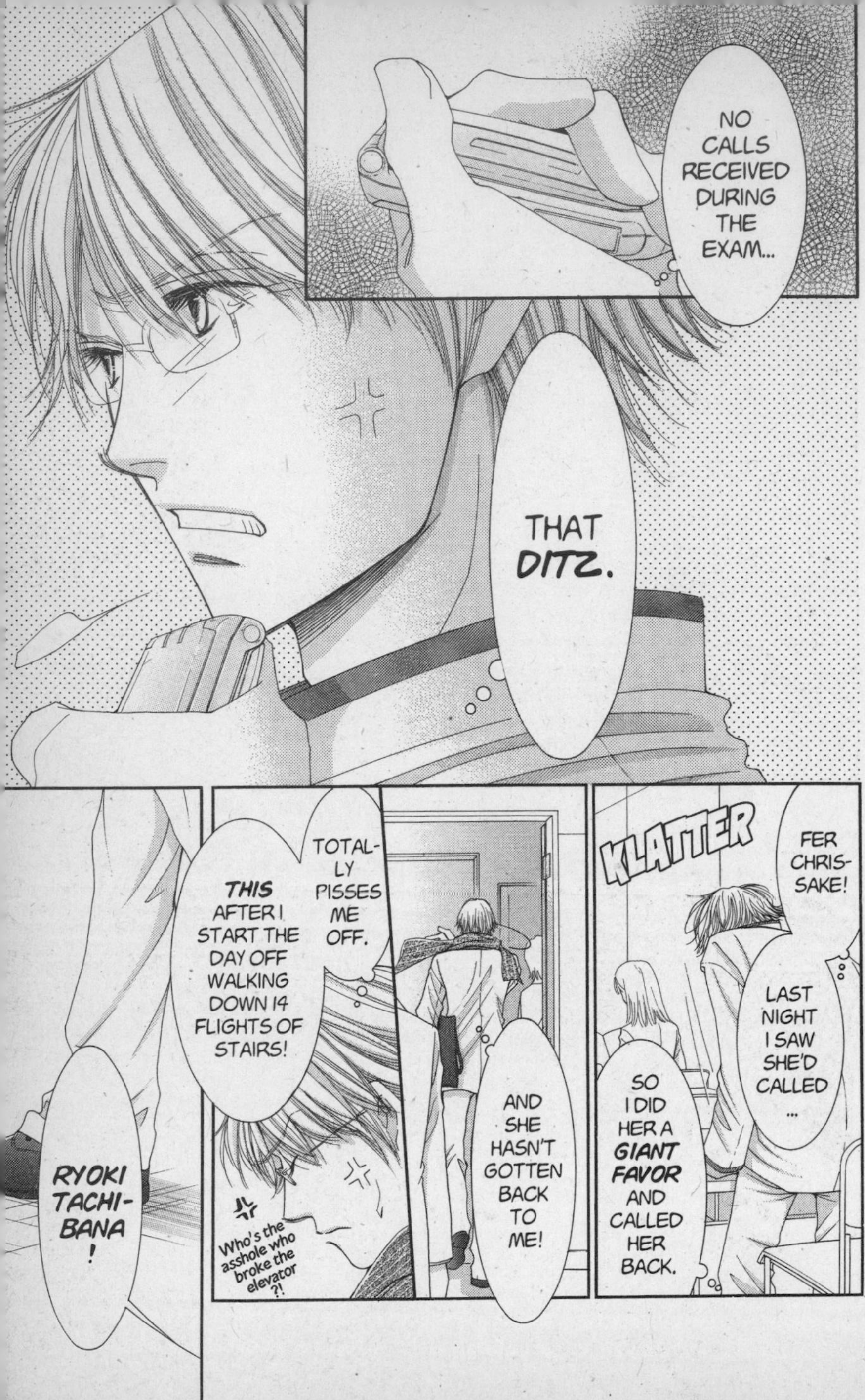

NO CALLS RECEIVED DURING THE EXAM...
THAT DITZ.
KLATTER
FER CHRIS-SAKE!
LAST NIGHT I SAW SHE'D CALLED ...
SO I DID HER A GIANT FAVOR AND CALLED HER BACK.
AND SHE HASN'T GOTTEN BACK TO ME!
TOTAL-LY PISSES ME OFF.
THIS AFTER I START THE DAY OFF WALKING DOWN 14 FLIGHTS OF STAIRS!
Who's the asshole who broke the elevator ?!
RYOKI TACHI-BANA !

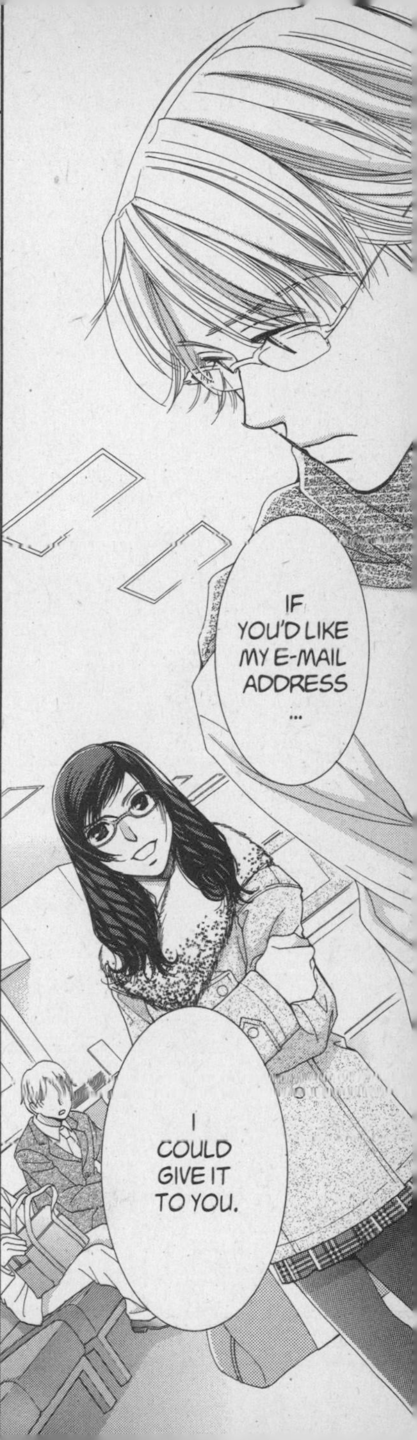
IF YOU'D LIKE MY E-MAIL ADDRESS ...
I COULD GIVE IT TO YOU.

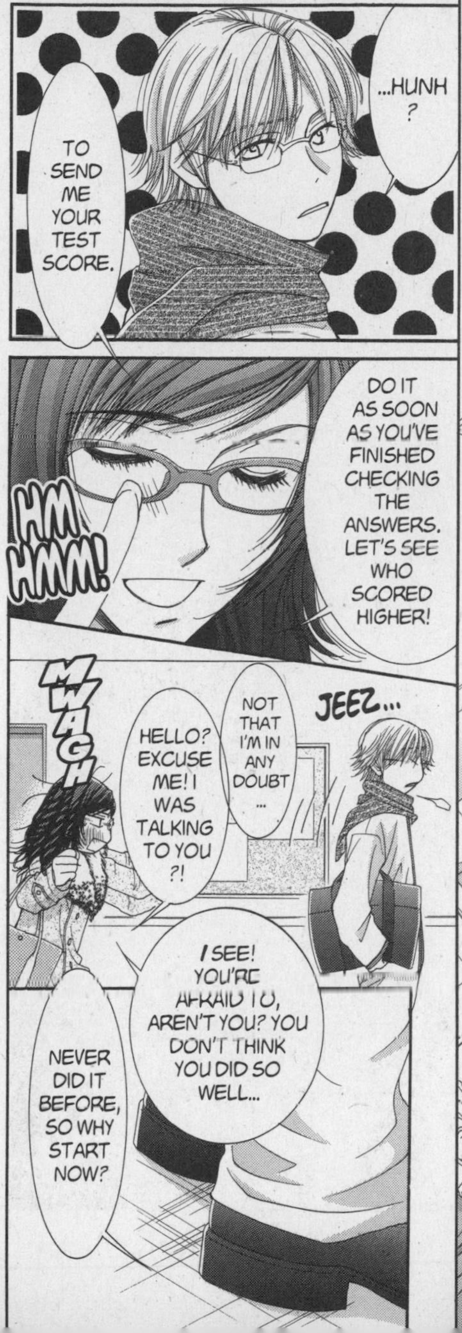
...HUNH ?
TO SEND ME YOUR TEST SCORE.
DO IT AS SOON AS YOU'VE FINISHED CHECKING THE ANSWERS. LET'S SEE WHO SCORED HIGHER!
HM HMM!
JEEZ...
NOT THAT I'M IN ANY DOUBT ...
HELLO? EXCUSE ME! I WAS TALKING TO YOU ?!
MWAGH
I SEE! YOU'RE AFRAID TO, AREN'T YOU? YOU DON'T THINK YOU DID SO WELL...
NEVER DID IT BEFORE, SO WHY START NOW?

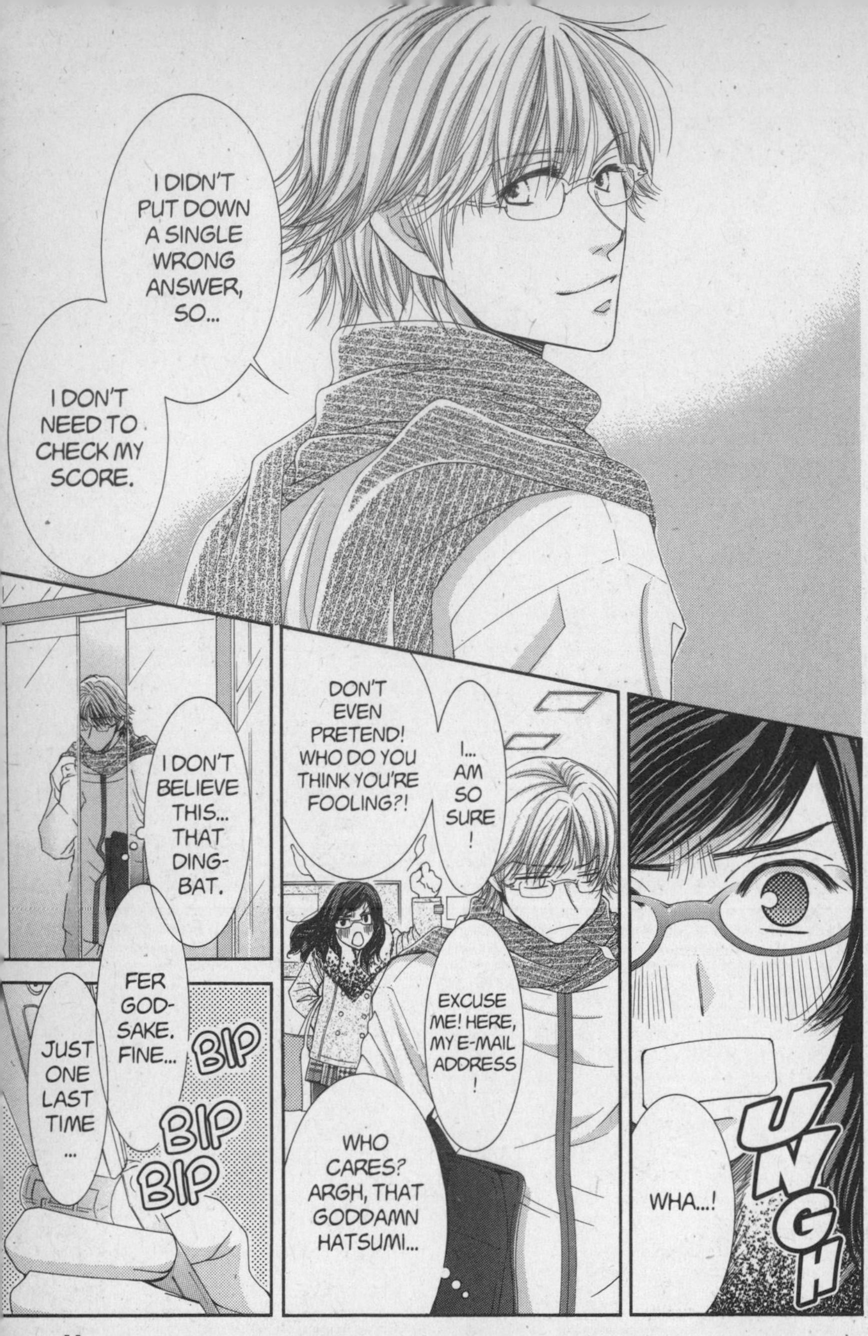
I DIDN'T PUT DOWN A SINGLE WRONG ANSWER, SO...
I DON'T NEED TO CHECK MY SCORE.
WHA...!
UNGH
I... AM SO SURE!
DON'T EVEN PRETEND! WHO DO YOU THINK YOU'RE FOOLING?!
EXCUSE ME! HERE, MY E-MAIL ADDRESS!
WHO CARES? ARGH, THAT GODDAMN HATSUMI...
I DON'T BELIEVE THIS... THAT DING-BAT.
FER GOD-SAKE. FINE...
BIP
BIP
BIP
JUST ONE LAST TIME...

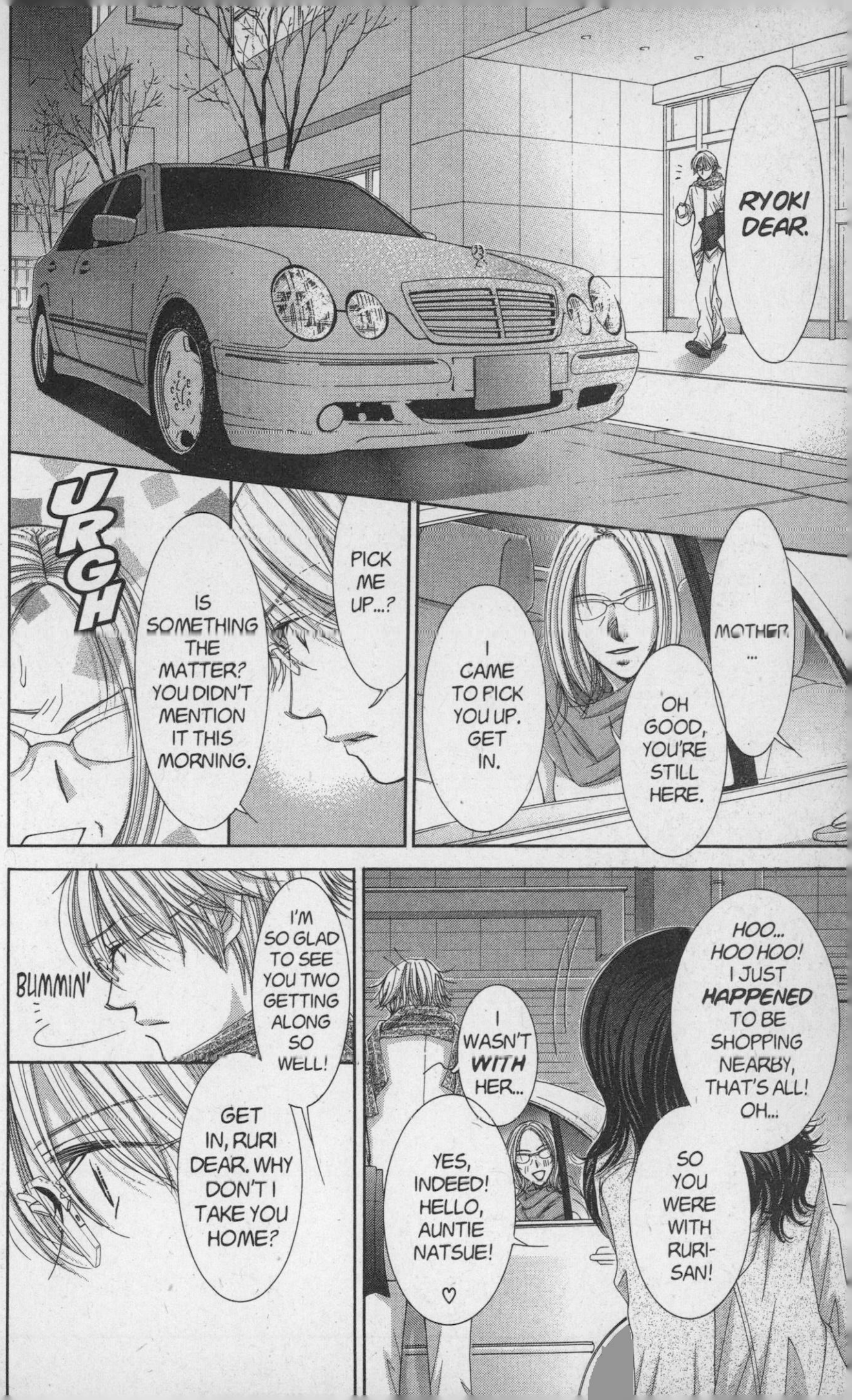
RYOKI DEAR.
MOTHER...
OH GOOD, YOU'RE STILL HERE.
I CAME TO PICK YOU UP. GET IN.
PICK ME UP...?
IS SOMETHING THE MATTER? YOU DIDN'T MENTION IT THIS MORNING.
URGH
HOO... HOO HOO! I JUST **HAPPENED** TO BE SHOPPING NEARBY, THAT'S ALL! OH...
SO YOU WERE WITH RURI-SAN!
I WASN'T **WITH** HER...
YES, INDEED! HELLO, AUNTIE NATSUE! ♡
I'M SO GLAD TO SEE YOU TWO GETTING ALONG SO WELL!
BUMMIN'
GET IN, RURI DEAR. WHY DON'T I TAKE YOU HOME?

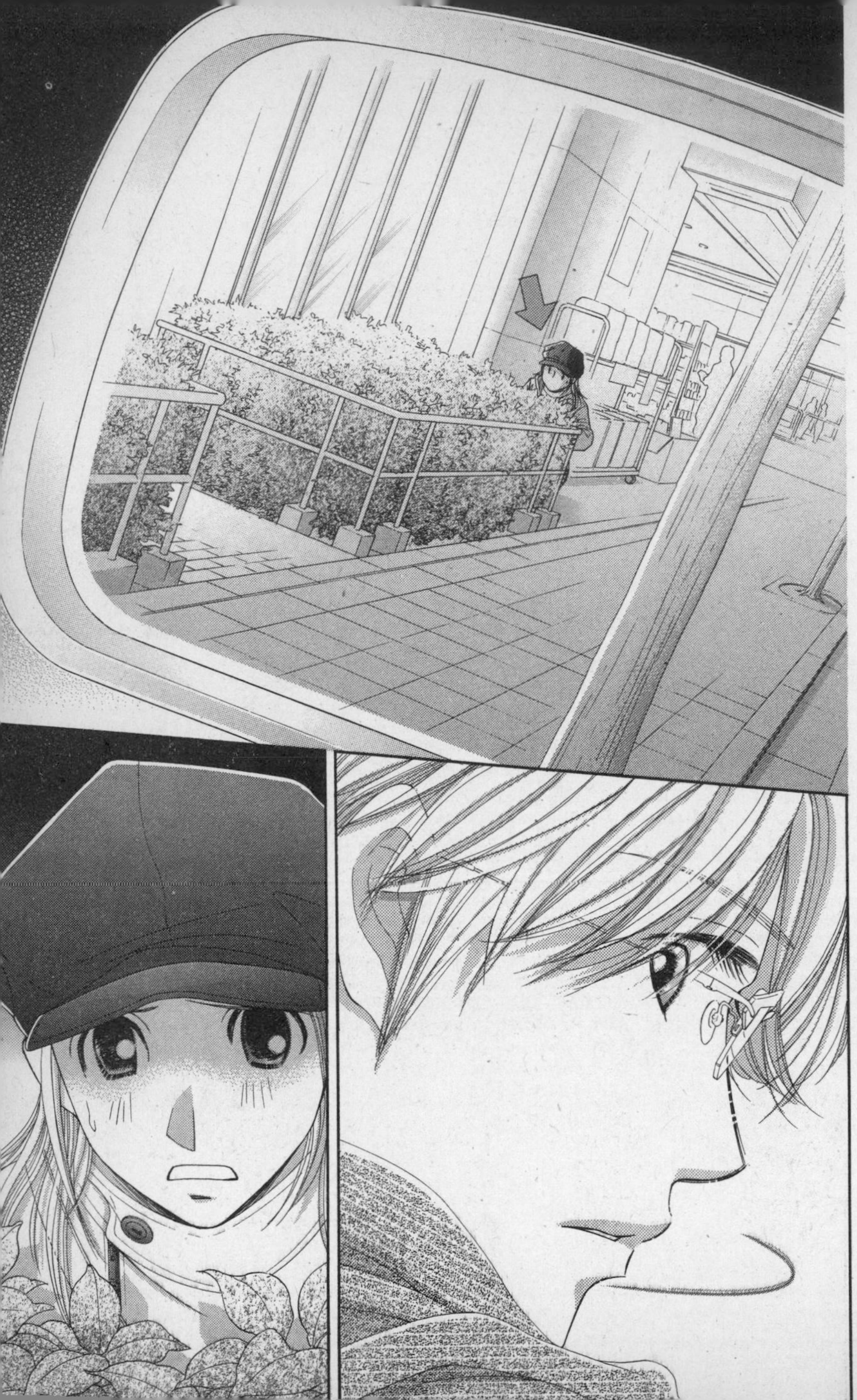

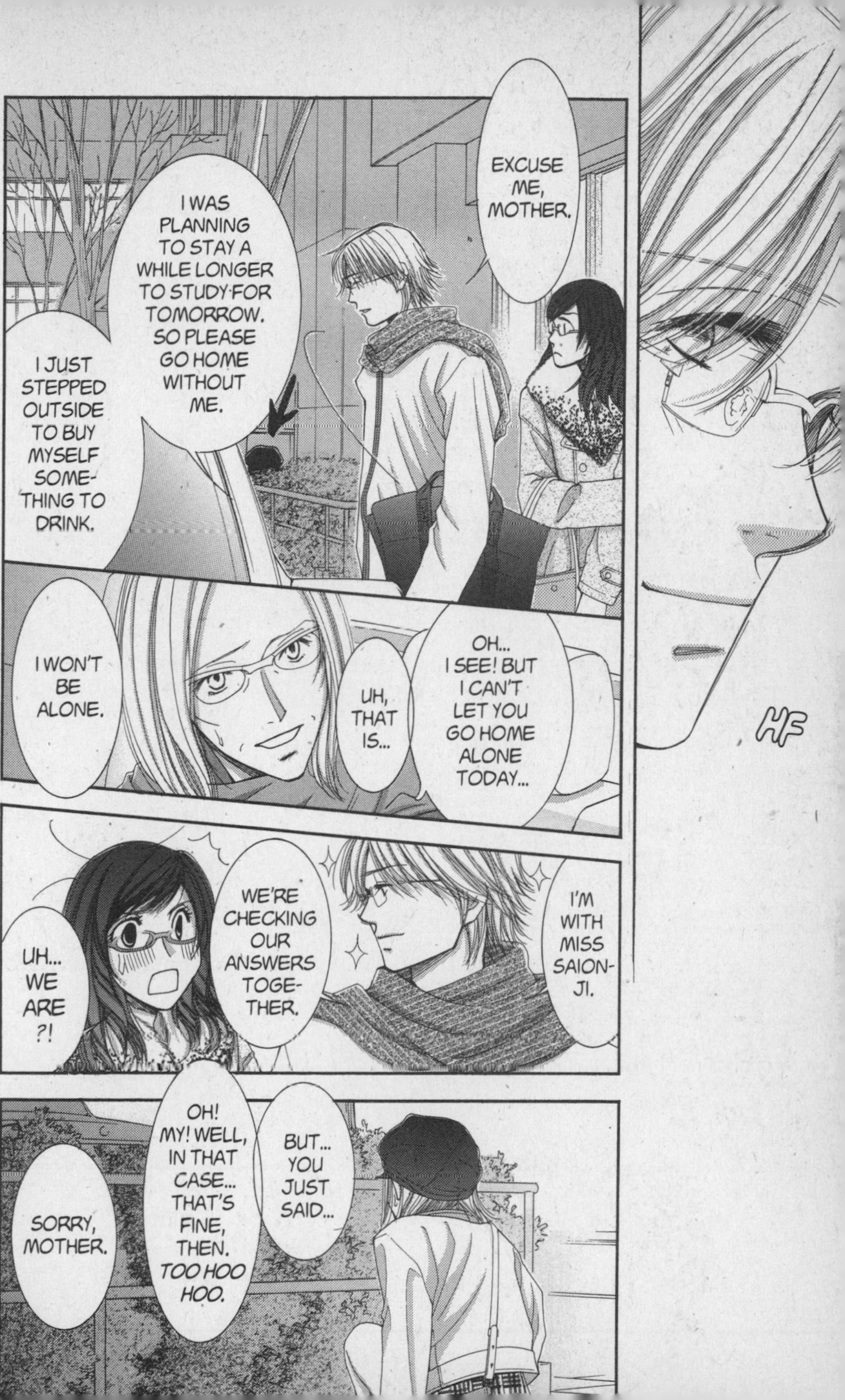
HF
EXCUSE ME, MOTHER.
I WAS PLANNING TO STAY A WHILE LONGER TO STUDY FOR TOMORROW. SO PLEASE GO HOME WITHOUT ME.
I JUST STEPPED OUTSIDE TO BUY MYSELF SOME-THING TO DRINK.
OH... I SEE! BUT I CAN'T LET YOU GO HOME ALONE TODAY...
UH, THAT IS...
I WON'T BE ALONE.
I'M WITH MISS SAION-JI.
WE'RE CHECKING OUR ANSWERS TOGE-THER.
UH... WE ARE ?!
BUT... YOU JUST SAID...
OH! MY! WELL, IN THAT CASE... THAT'S FINE, THEN. *TOO HOO HOO.*
SORRY, MOTHER.

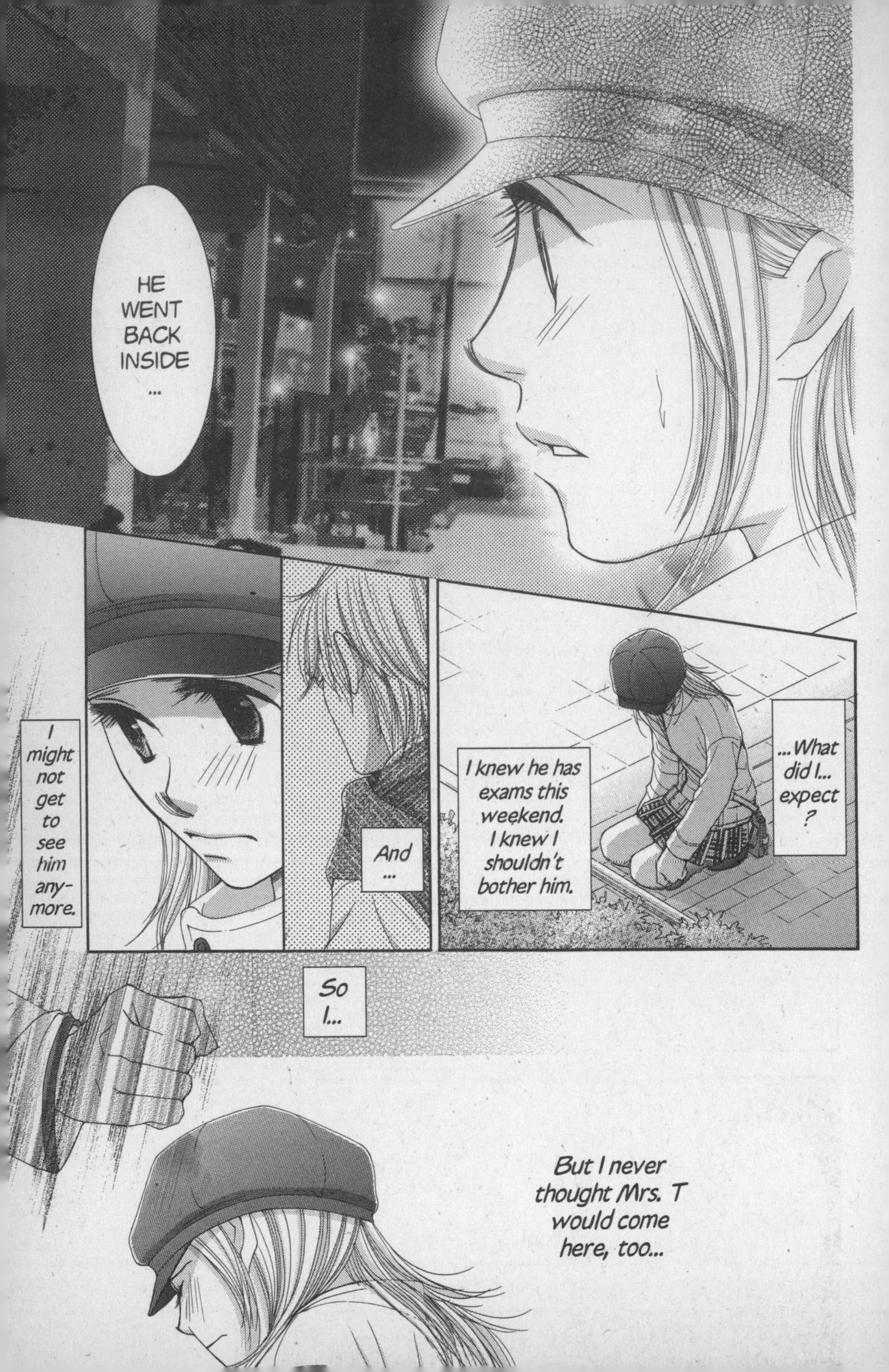
HE WENT BACK INSIDE ...
...What did I... expect?
I knew he has exams this weekend. I knew I shouldn't bother him.
And ...
I might not get to see him anymore.
So I...
But I never thought Mrs. T would come here, too...

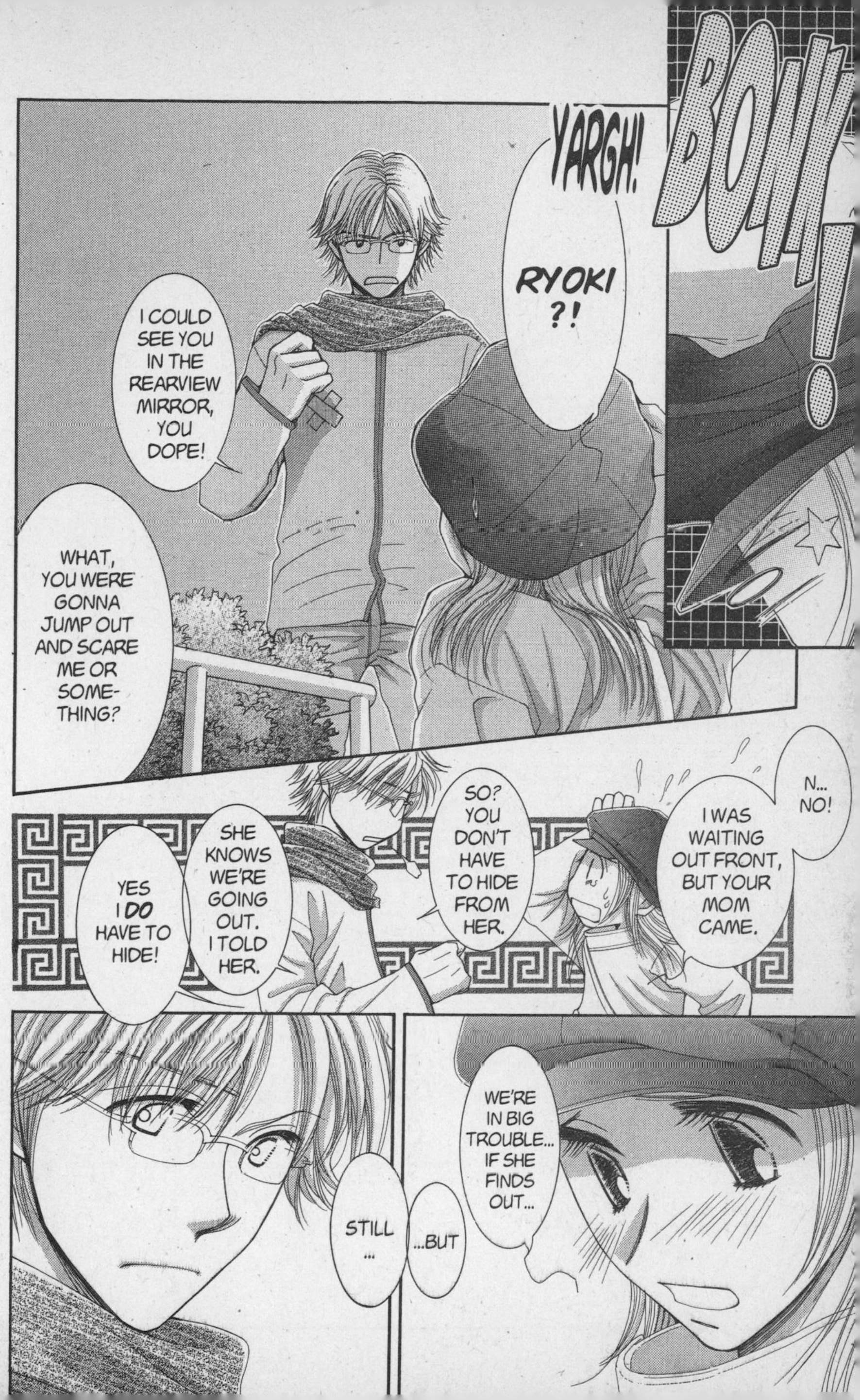
BONK!
YARGH!
RYOKI?!
I COULD SEE YOU IN THE REARVIEW MIRROR, YOU DOPE!
WHAT, YOU WERE GONNA JUMP OUT AND SCARE ME OR SOME-THING?
N... NO!
I WAS WAITING OUT FRONT, BUT YOUR MOM CAME.
SO? YOU DON'T HAVE TO HIDE FROM HER.
SHE KNOWS WE'RE GOING OUT. I TOLD HER.
YES I DO HAVE TO HIDE!
WE'RE IN BIG TROUBLE... IF SHE FINDS OUT...
...BUT
STILL ...

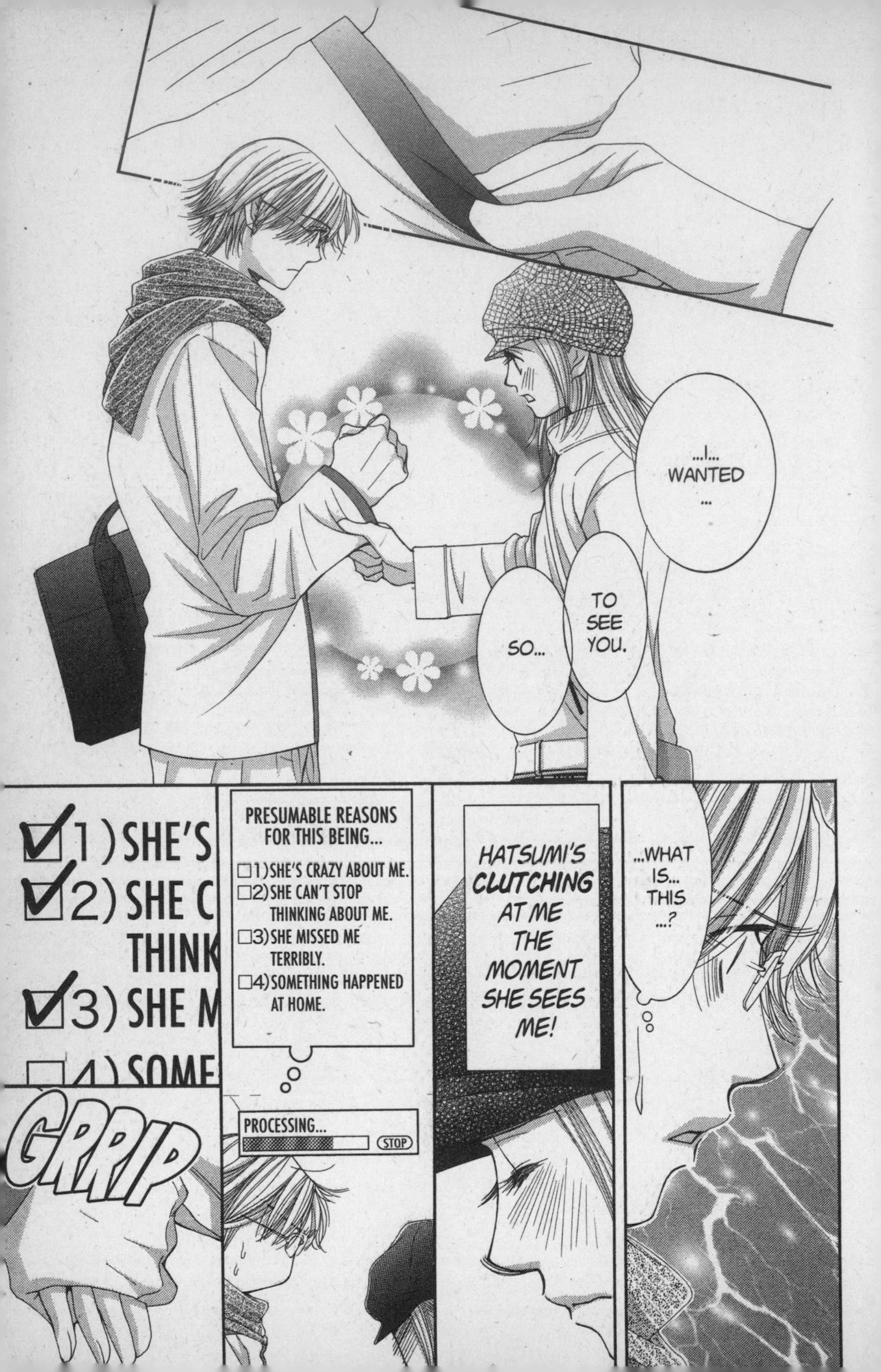
...I... WANTED ...
TO SEE YOU.
SO...
...WHAT IS... THIS ...?
HATSUMI'S CLUTCHING AT ME THE MOMENT SHE SEES ME!
PRESUMABLE REASONS FOR THIS BEING...
1) SHE'S CRAZY ABOUT ME.
2) SHE CAN'T STOP THINKING ABOUT ME.
3) SHE MISSED ME TERRIBLY.
4) SOMETHING HAPPENED AT HOME.
PROCESSING...
STOP
1) SHE'S
2) SHE C
THINK
3) SHE M
4) SOME
GRRIP

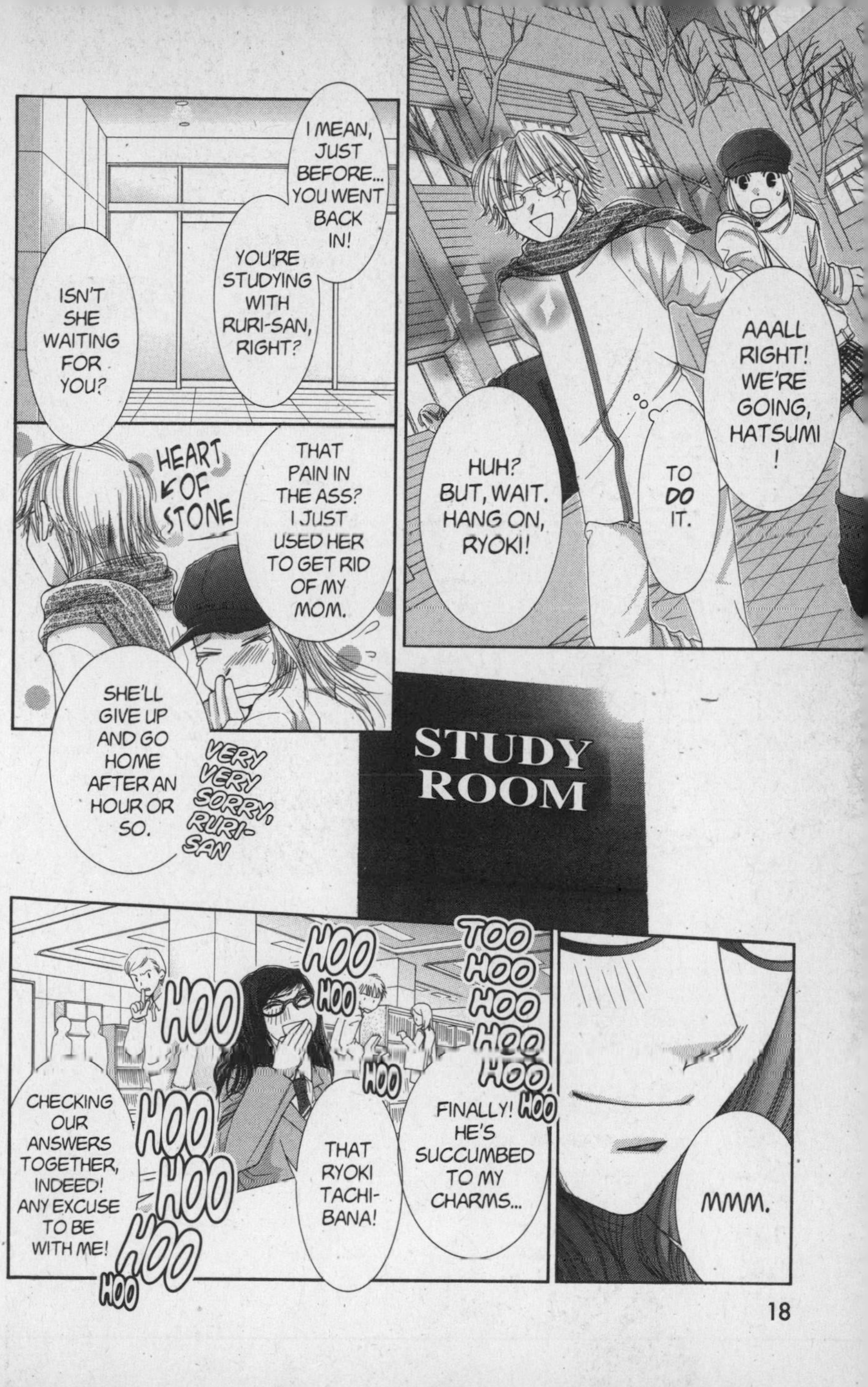
AAALL RIGHT! WE'RE GOING, HATSUMI!
TO DO IT.
HUH? BUT, WAIT. HANG ON, RYOKI!
I MEAN, JUST BEFORE... YOU WENT BACK IN!
YOU'RE STUDYING WITH RURI-SAN, RIGHT?
ISN'T SHE WAITING FOR YOU?
THAT PAIN IN THE ASS? I JUST USED HER TO GET RID OF MY MOM.
HEART OF STONE
SHE'LL GIVE UP AND GO HOME AFTER AN HOUR OR SO.
VERY VERY SORRY, RURI-SAN
STUDY ROOM
MMM.
TOO HOO HOO HOO HOO HOO
FINALLY! HE'S SUCCUMBED TO MY CHARMS...
HOO HOO HOO
THAT RYOKI TACHIBANA!
CHECKING OUR ANSWERS TOGETHER, INDEED! ANY EXCUSE TO BE WITH ME!
HOO HOO HOO HOO HOO

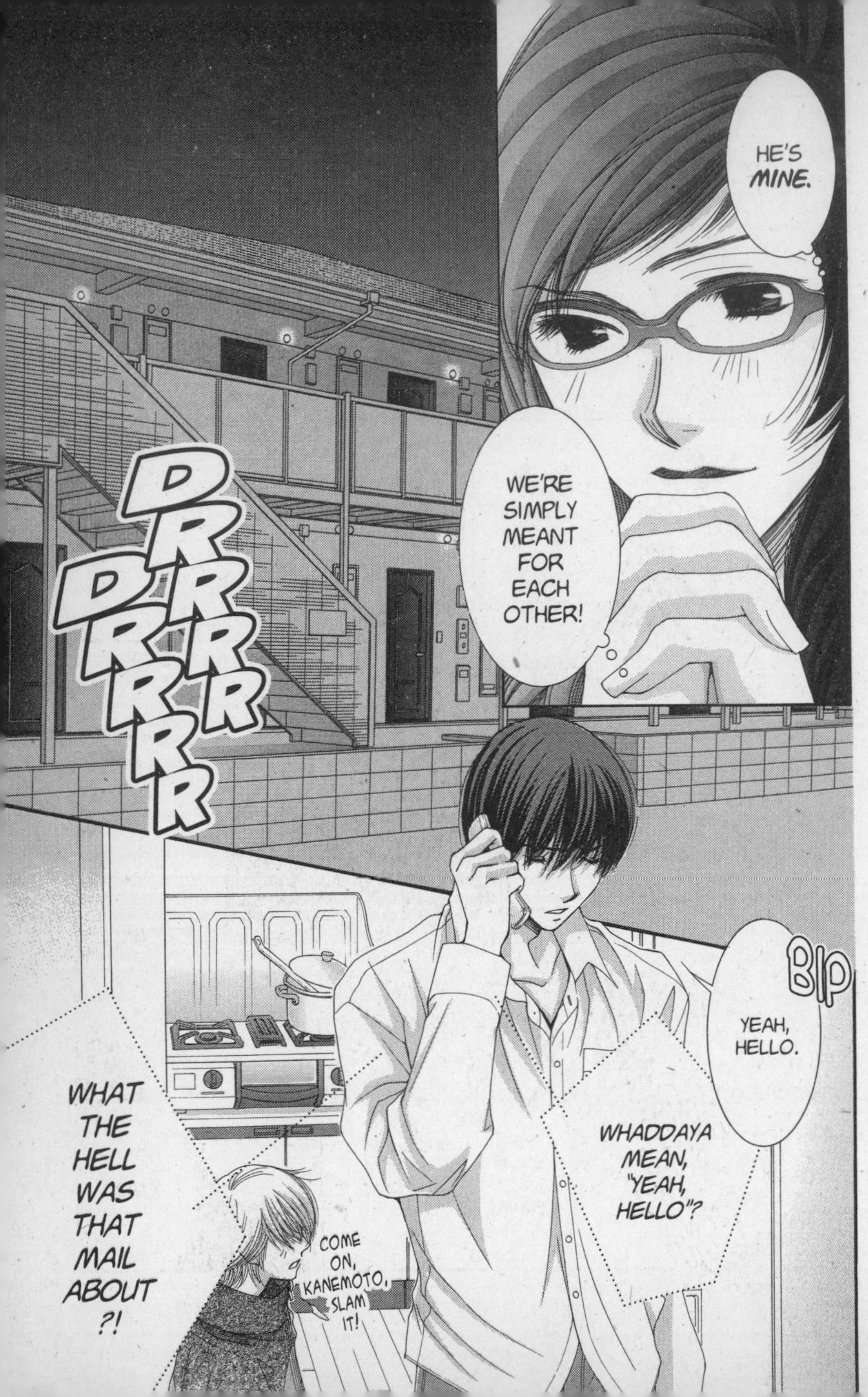
HE'S MINE.
WE'RE SIMPLY MEANT FOR EACH OTHER!
DRRRR
DRRRR
BIP
YEAH, HELLO.
WHADDAYA MEAN, "YEAH, HELLO"?
WHAT THE HELL WAS THAT MAIL ABOUT ?!
COME ON, KANEMOTO, SLAM IT!

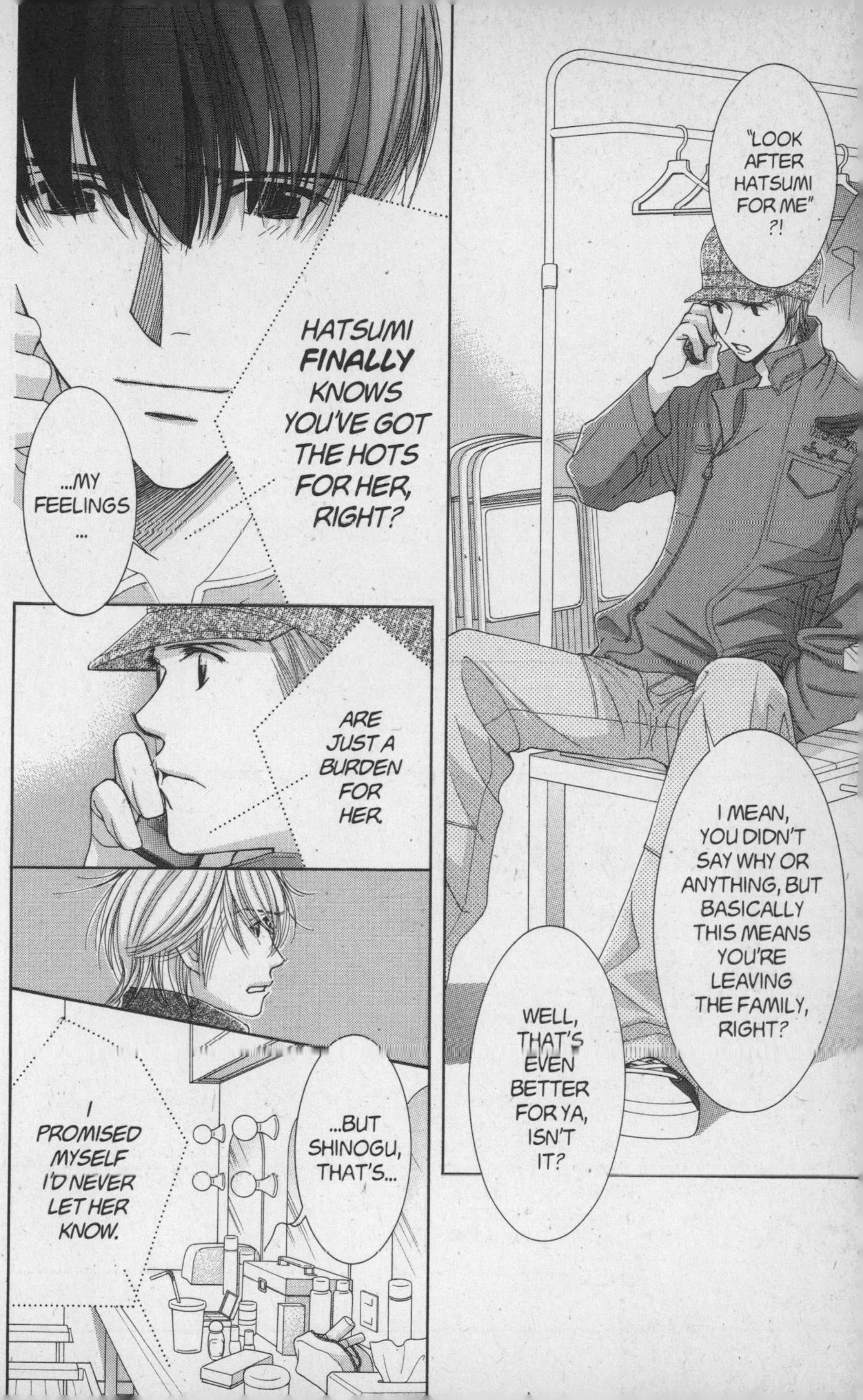
"LOOK AFTER HATSUMI FOR ME" ?!
I MEAN, YOU DIDN'T SAY WHY OR ANYTHING, BUT BASICALLY THIS MEANS YOU'RE LEAVING THE FAMILY, RIGHT?
WELL, THAT'S EVEN BETTER FOR YA, ISN'T IT?
HATSUMI **FINALLY** KNOWS YOU'VE GOT THE HOTS FOR HER, RIGHT?
...MY FEELINGS ...
ARE JUST A BURDEN FOR HER.
...BUT SHINOGU, THAT'S...
I PROMISED MYSELF I'D NEVER LET HER KNOW.

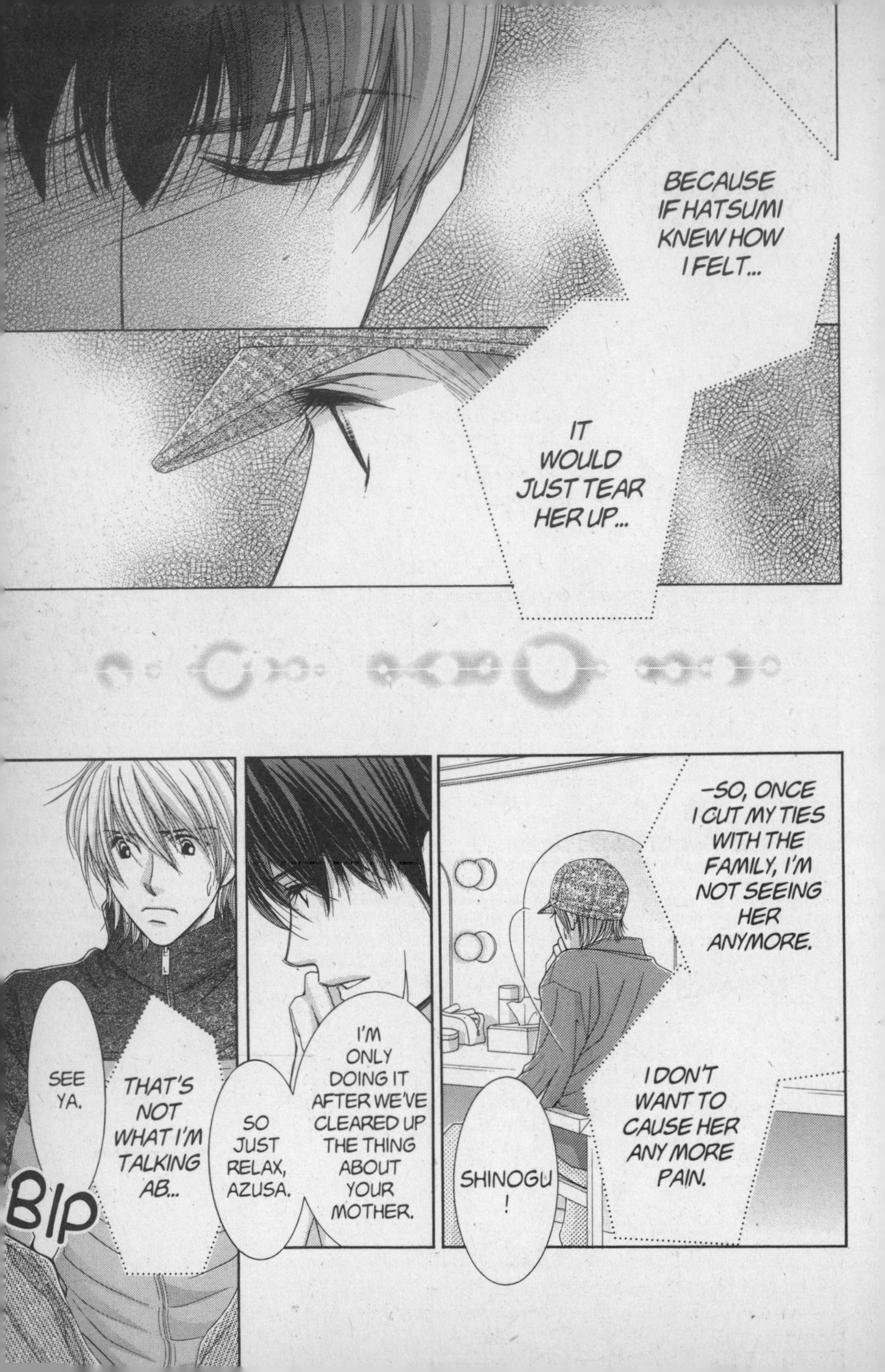
BECAUSE IF HATSUMI KNEW HOW I FELT...
IT WOULD JUST TEAR HER UP...
—SO, ONCE I CUT MY TIES WITH THE FAMILY, I'M NOT SEEING HER ANYMORE.
I DON'T WANT TO CAUSE HER ANY MORE PAIN.
SHINOGU!
I'M ONLY DOING IT AFTER WE'VE CLEARED UP THE THING ABOUT YOUR MOTHER.
SO JUST RELAX, AZUSA.
THAT'S NOT WHAT I'M TALKING AB...
SEE YA.
BIP

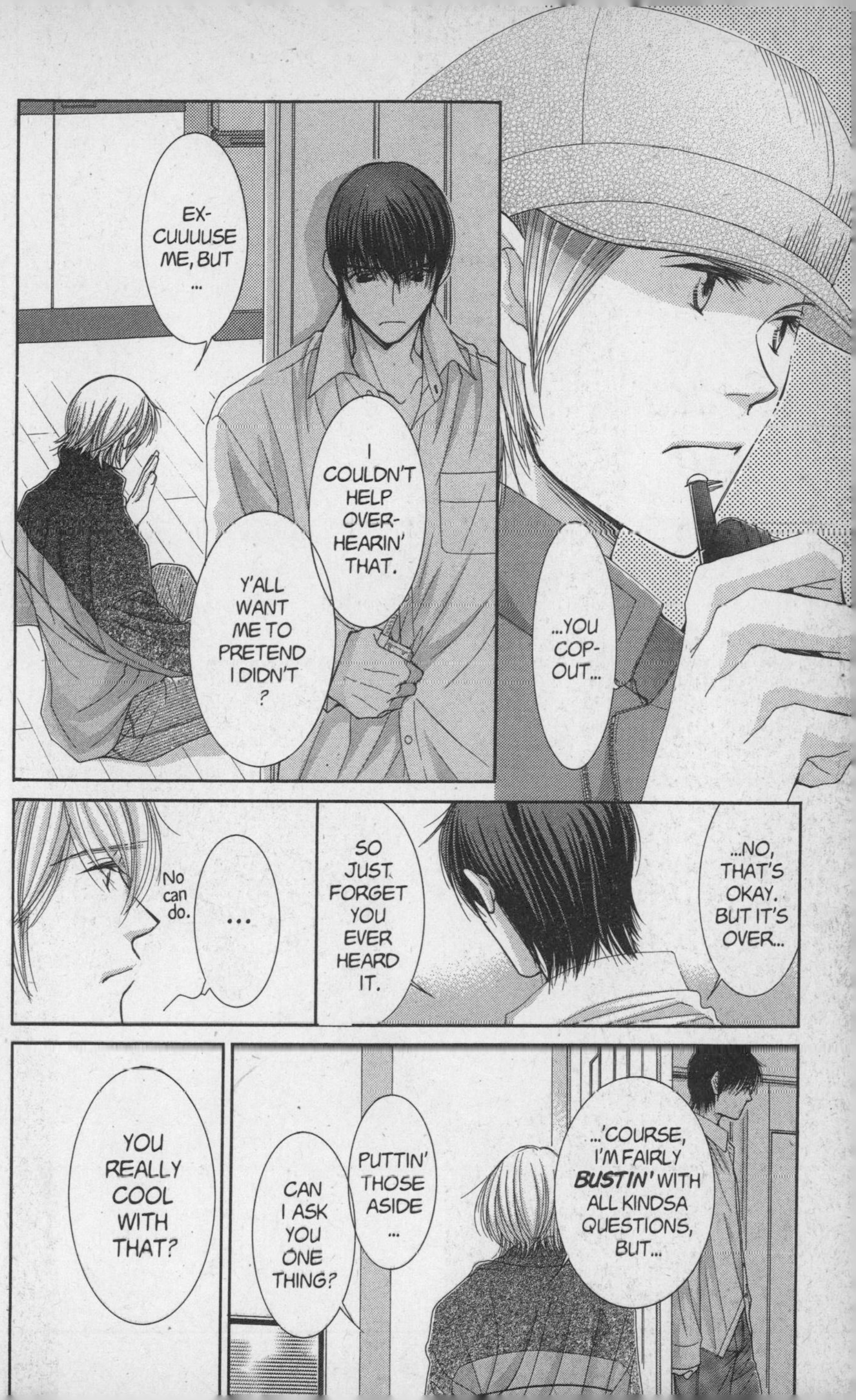
...YOU COP-OUT...
EX-CUUUUSE ME, BUT ...
I COULDN'T HELP OVER-HEARIN' THAT.
Y'ALL WANT ME TO PRETEND I DIDN'T?
...NO, THAT'S OKAY. BUT IT'S OVER...
SO JUST FORGET YOU EVER HEARD IT.
...
No can do.
...'COURSE, I'M FAIRLY **BUSTIN'** WITH ALL KINDSA QUESTIONS, BUT...
PUTTIN' THOSE ASIDE ...
CAN I ASK YOU ONE THING?
YOU REALLY COOL WITH THAT?

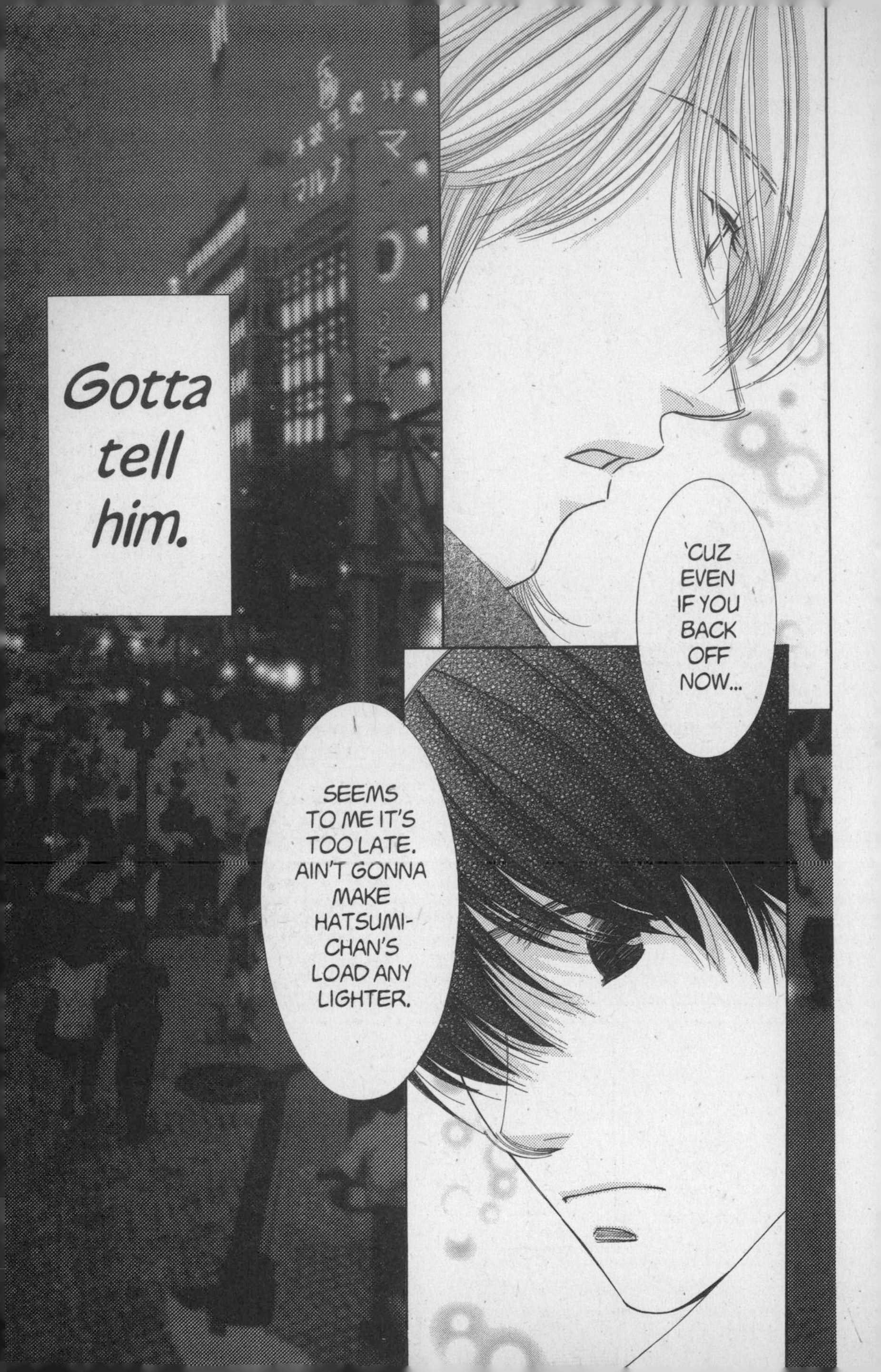
'CUZ EVEN IF YOU BACK OFF NOW...
SEEMS TO ME IT'S TOO LATE. AIN'T GONNA MAKE HATSUMI-CHAN'S LOAD ANY LIGHTER.
Gotta tell him.

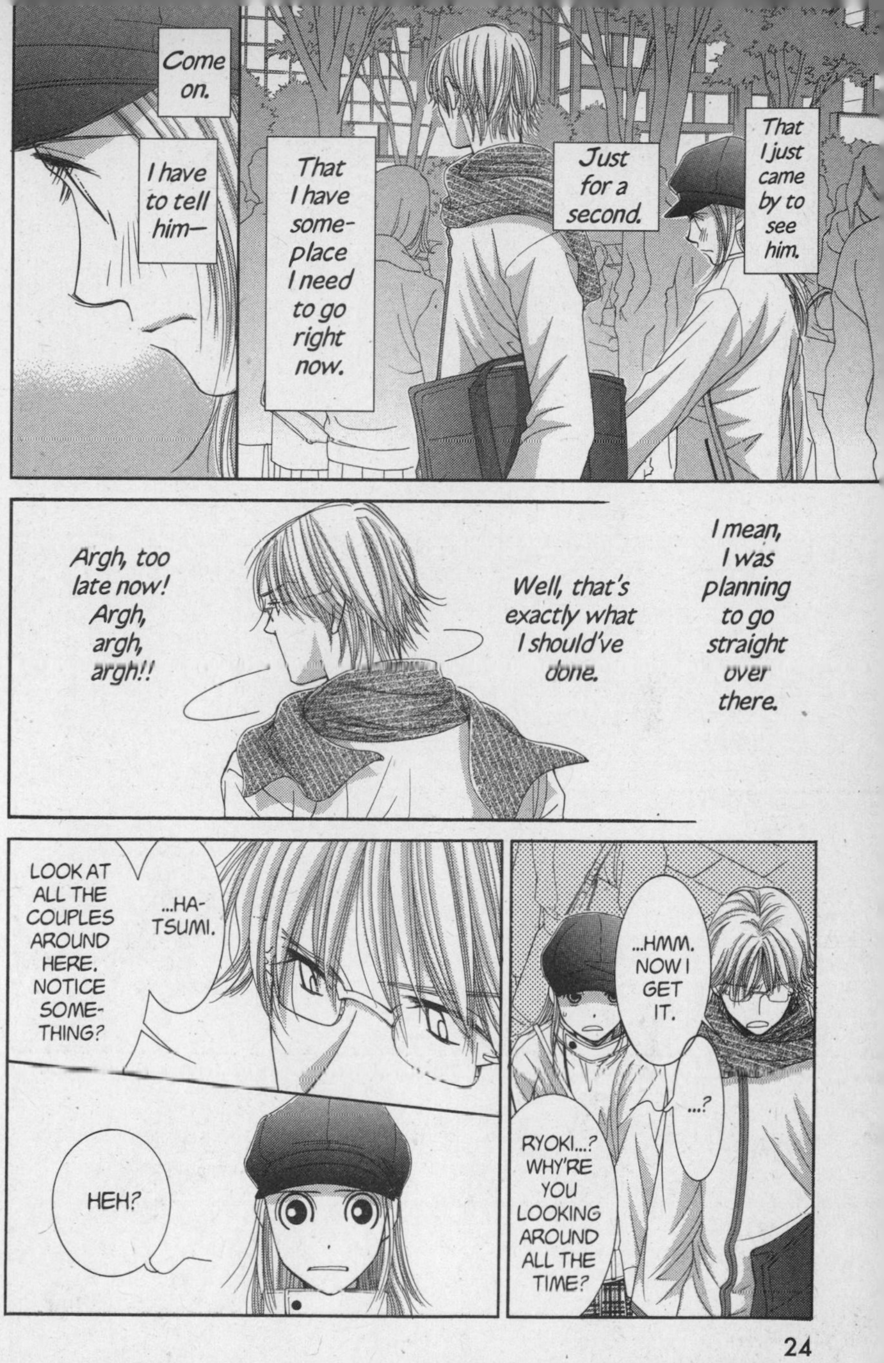
That I just came by to see him.
Just for a second.
That I have some-place I need to go right now.
Come on.
I have to tell him—
I mean, I was planning to go straight over there.
Well, that's exactly what I should've done.
Argh, too late now! Argh, argh, argh!!
...HMM. NOW I GET IT.
...?
RYOKI...? WHY'RE YOU LOOKING AROUND ALL THE TIME?
...HA-TSUMI.
LOOK AT ALL THE COUPLES AROUND HERE. NOTICE SOME-THING?
HEH?

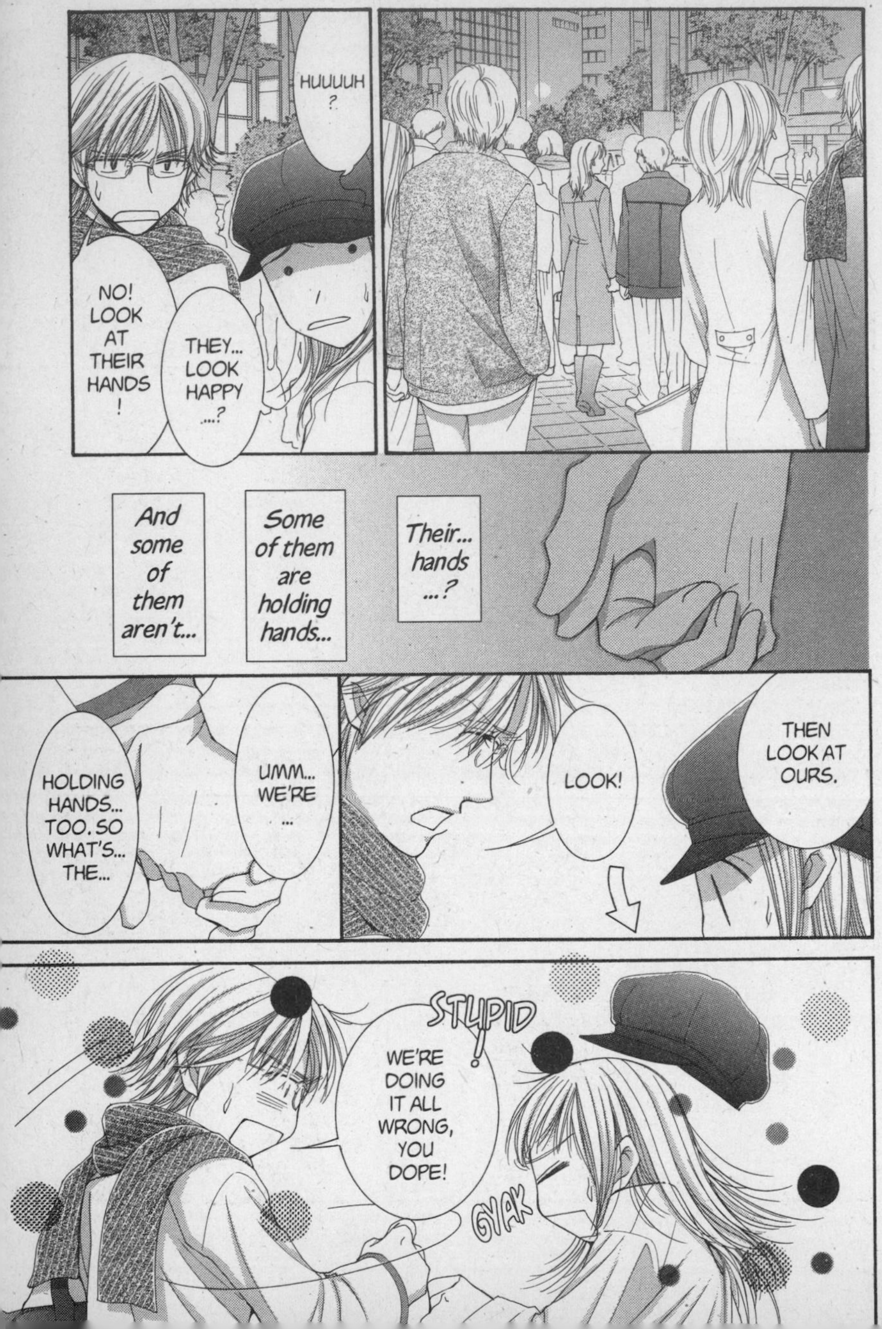
HUUUUH?
THEY... LOOK HAPPY ...?
NO! LOOK AT THEIR HANDS!
Their... hands ...?
Some of them are holding hands...
And some of them aren't...
THEN LOOK AT OURS.
LOOK!
UMM... WE'RE ...
HOLDING HANDS... TOO. SO WHAT'S... THE...
STUPID!
WE'RE DOING IT ALL WRONG, YOU DOPE!
GYAK

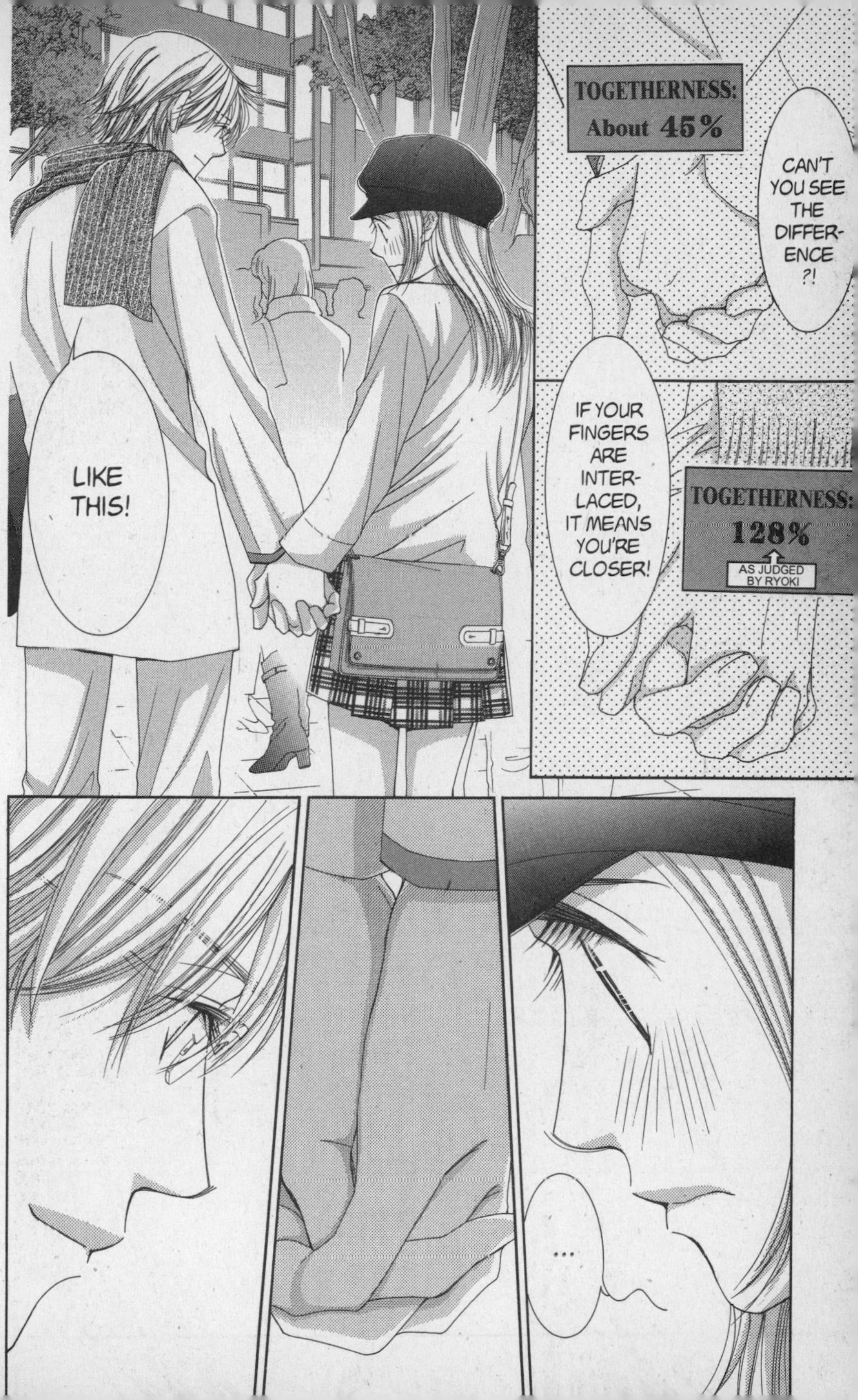
TOGETHERNESS: About 45%
CAN'T YOU SEE THE DIFFERENCE?!
IF YOUR FINGERS ARE INTERLACED, IT MEANS YOU'RE CLOSER!
TOGETHERNESS: 128%
AS JUDGED BY RYOKI
LIKE THIS!
...

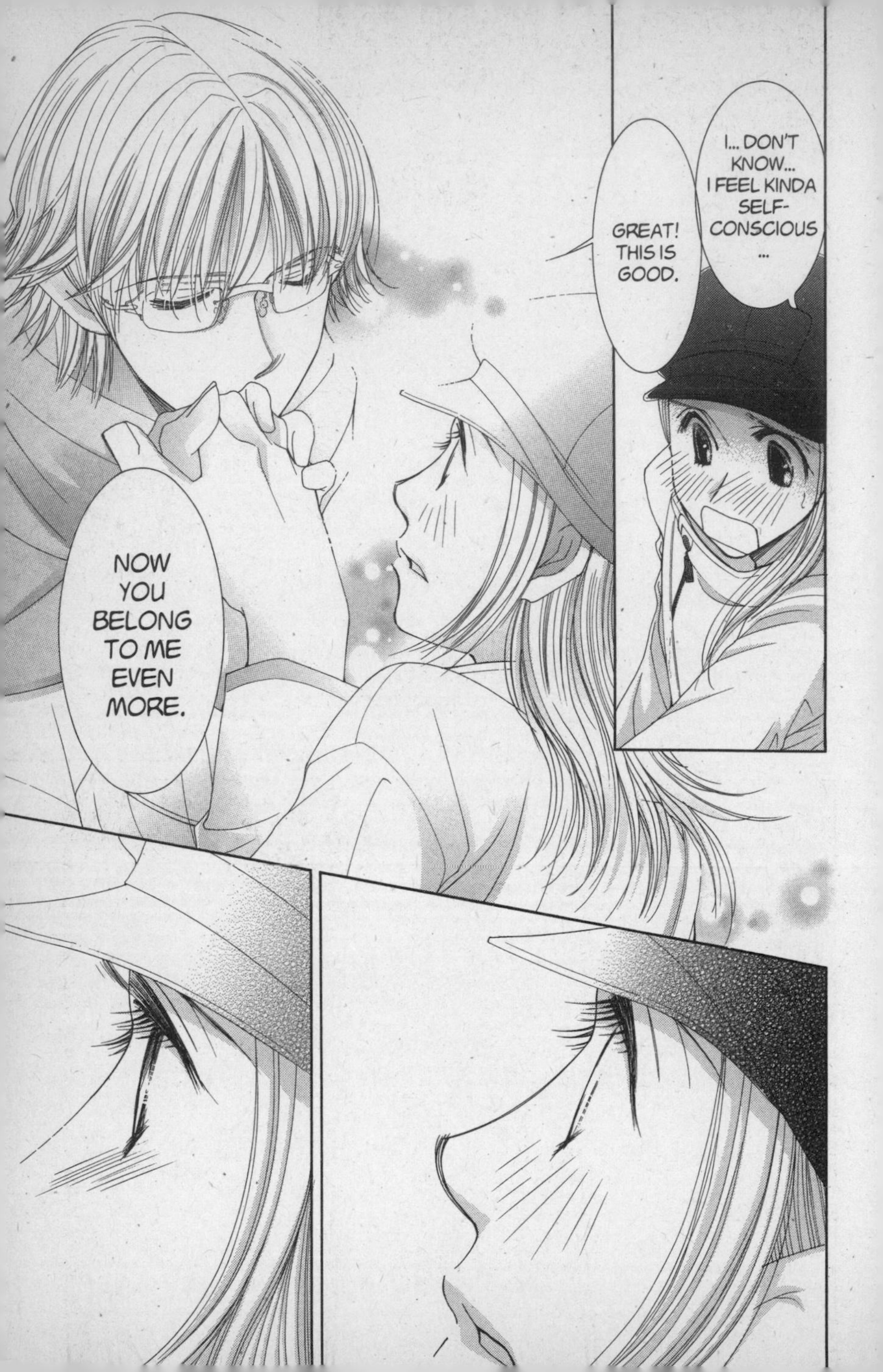
I... DON'T KNOW... I FEEL KINDA SELF-CONSCIOUS ...
GREAT! THIS IS GOOD.
NOW YOU BELONG TO ME EVEN MORE.

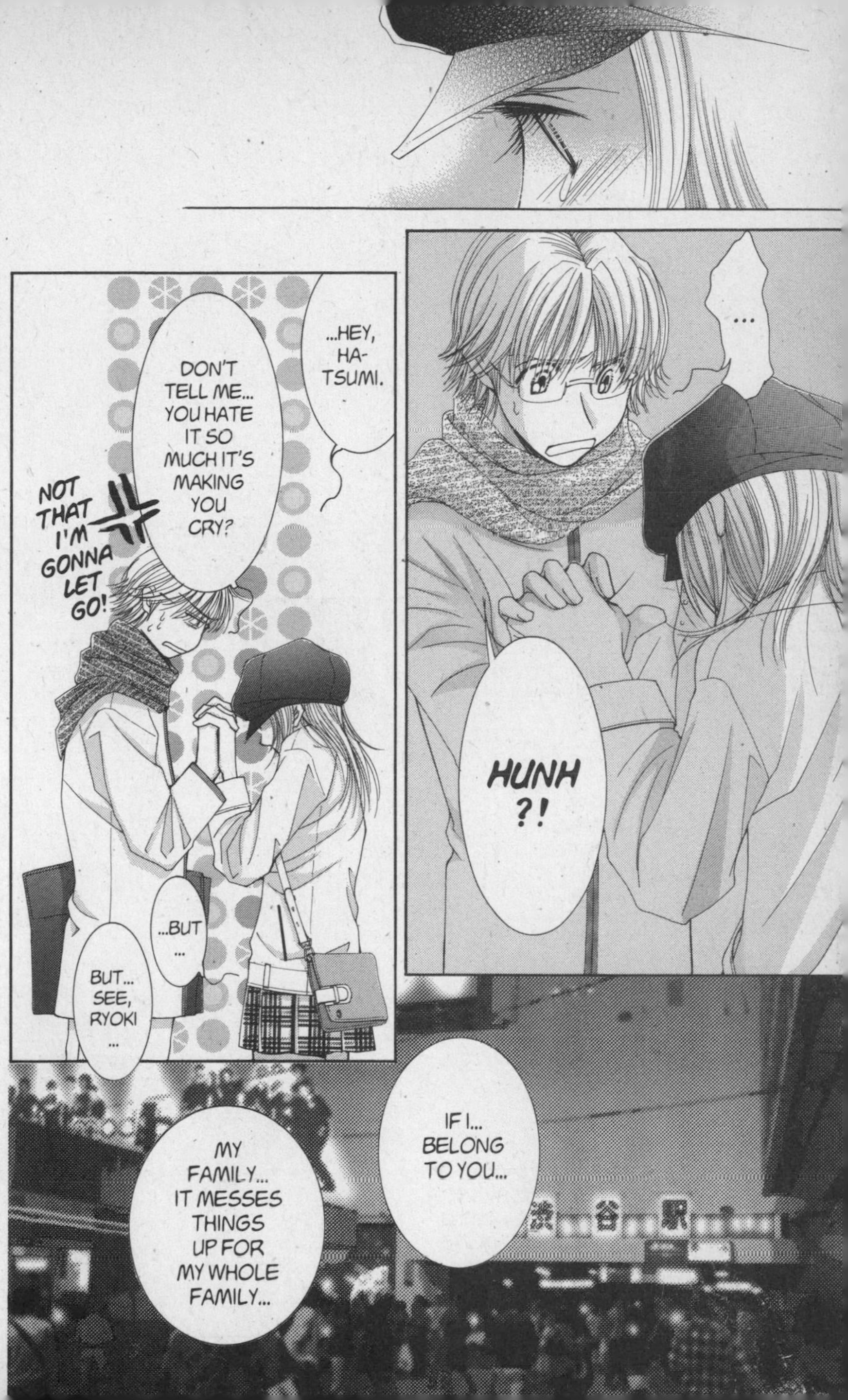
...
HUNH?!
...HEY, HATSUMI.
DON'T TELL ME... YOU HATE IT SO MUCH IT'S MAKING YOU CRY?
NOT THAT I'M GONNA LET GO!
...BUT...
BUT... SEE, RYOKI...
IF I... BELONG TO YOU...
MY FAMILY... IT MESSES THINGS UP FOR MY WHOLE FAMILY...
渋谷駅

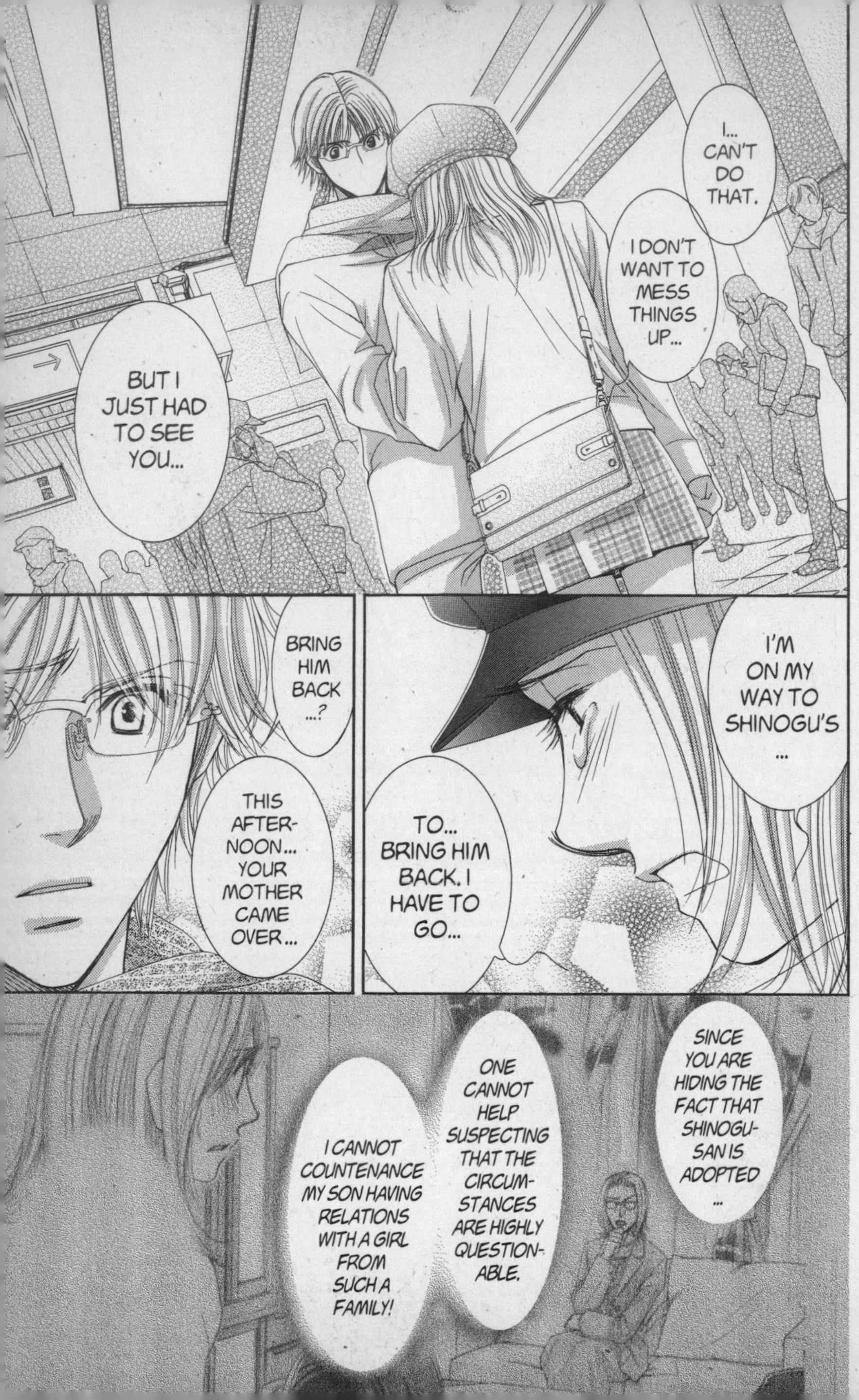
I... CAN'T DO THAT.
I DON'T WANT TO MESS THINGS UP...
BUT I JUST HAD TO SEE YOU...
I'M ON MY WAY TO SHINOGU'S ...
TO... BRING HIM BACK. I HAVE TO GO...
BRING HIM BACK ...?
THIS AFTERNOON... YOUR MOTHER CAME OVER...
SINCE YOU ARE HIDING THE FACT THAT SHINOGU-SAN IS ADOPTED ...
ONE CANNOT HELP SUSPECTING THAT THE CIRCUMSTANCES ARE HIGHLY QUESTIONABLE.
I CANNOT COUNTENANCE MY SON HAVING RELATIONS WITH A GIRL FROM SUCH A FAMILY!

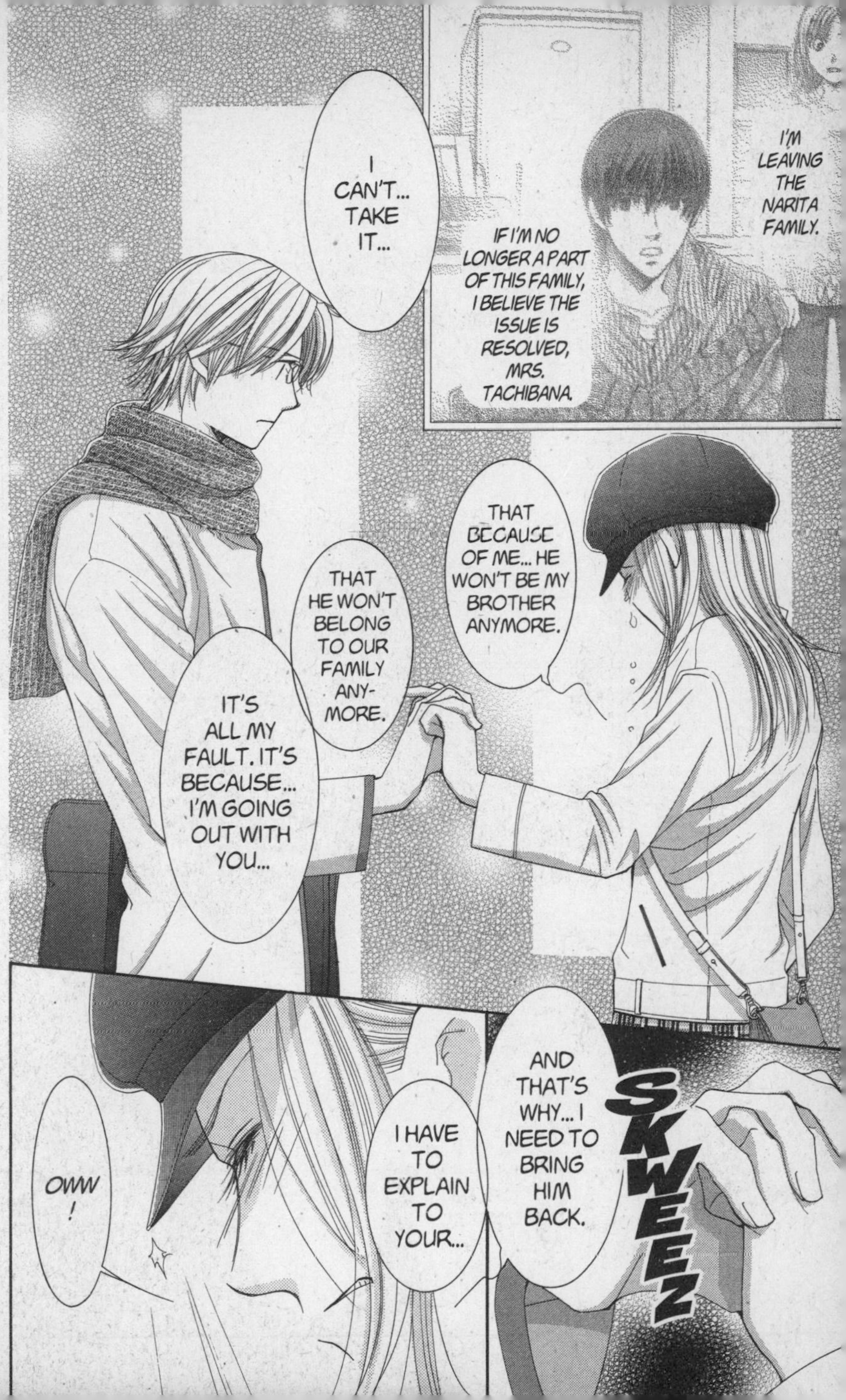
I'M LEAVING THE NARITA FAMILY.
IF I'M NO LONGER A PART OF THIS FAMILY, I BELIEVE THE ISSUE IS RESOLVED, MRS. TACHIBANA.
I CAN'T... TAKE IT...
THAT BECAUSE OF ME... HE WON'T BE MY BROTHER ANYMORE.
THAT HE WON'T BELONG TO OUR FAMILY ANY-MORE.
IT'S ALL MY FAULT. IT'S BECAUSE... I'M GOING OUT WITH YOU...
SKWEEZ
AND THAT'S WHY... I NEED TO BRING HIM BACK.
I HAVE TO EXPLAIN TO YOUR...
OWW!

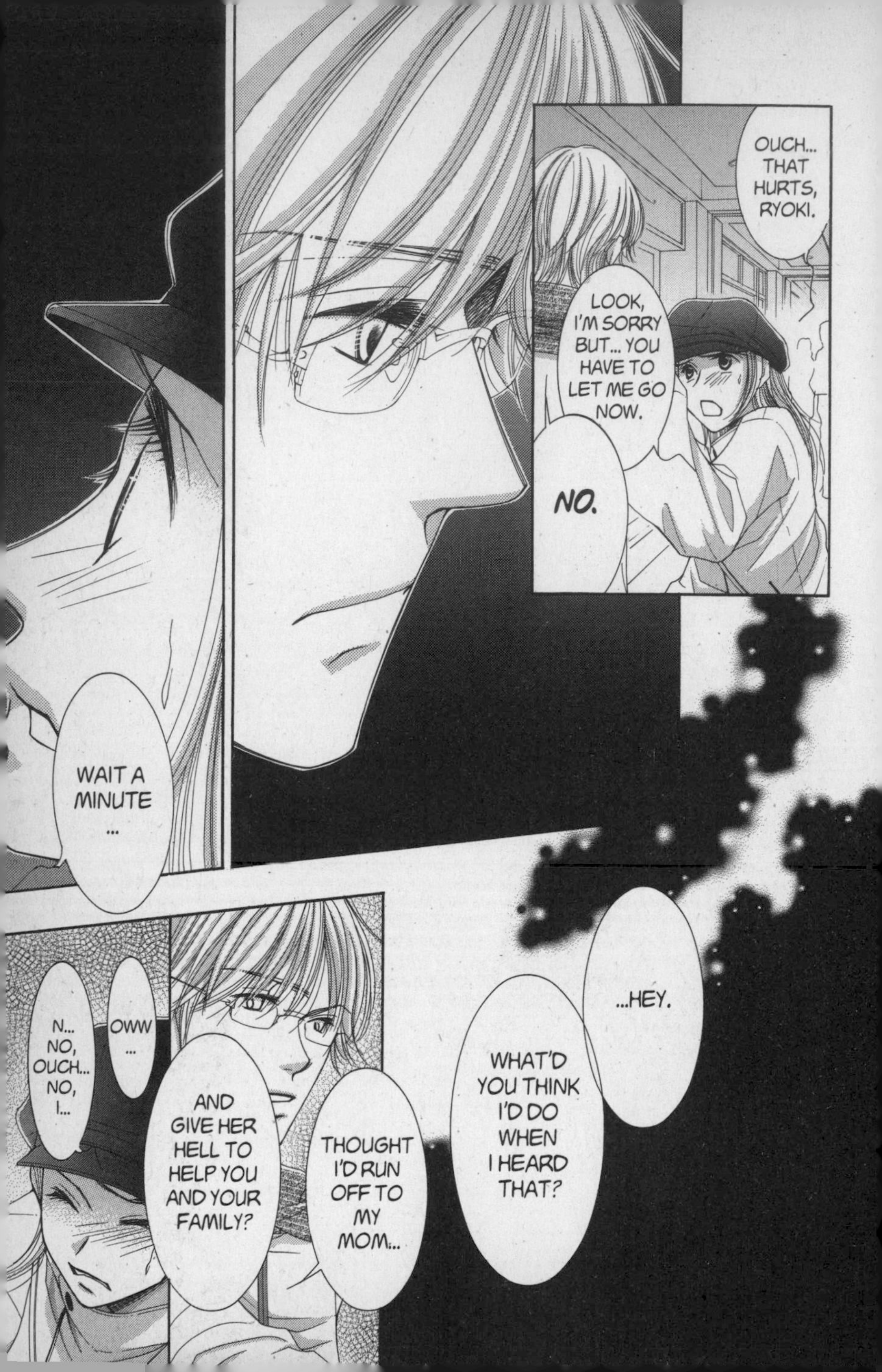
OUCH... THAT HURTS, RYOKI.
LOOK, I'M SORRY BUT... YOU HAVE TO LET ME GO NOW.
NO.
WAIT A MINUTE ...
...HEY.
WHAT'D YOU THINK I'D DO WHEN I HEARD THAT?
THOUGHT I'D RUN OFF TO MY MOM...
AND GIVE HER HELL TO HELP YOU AND YOUR FAMILY?
OWW ...
N... NO, OUCH... NO, I...

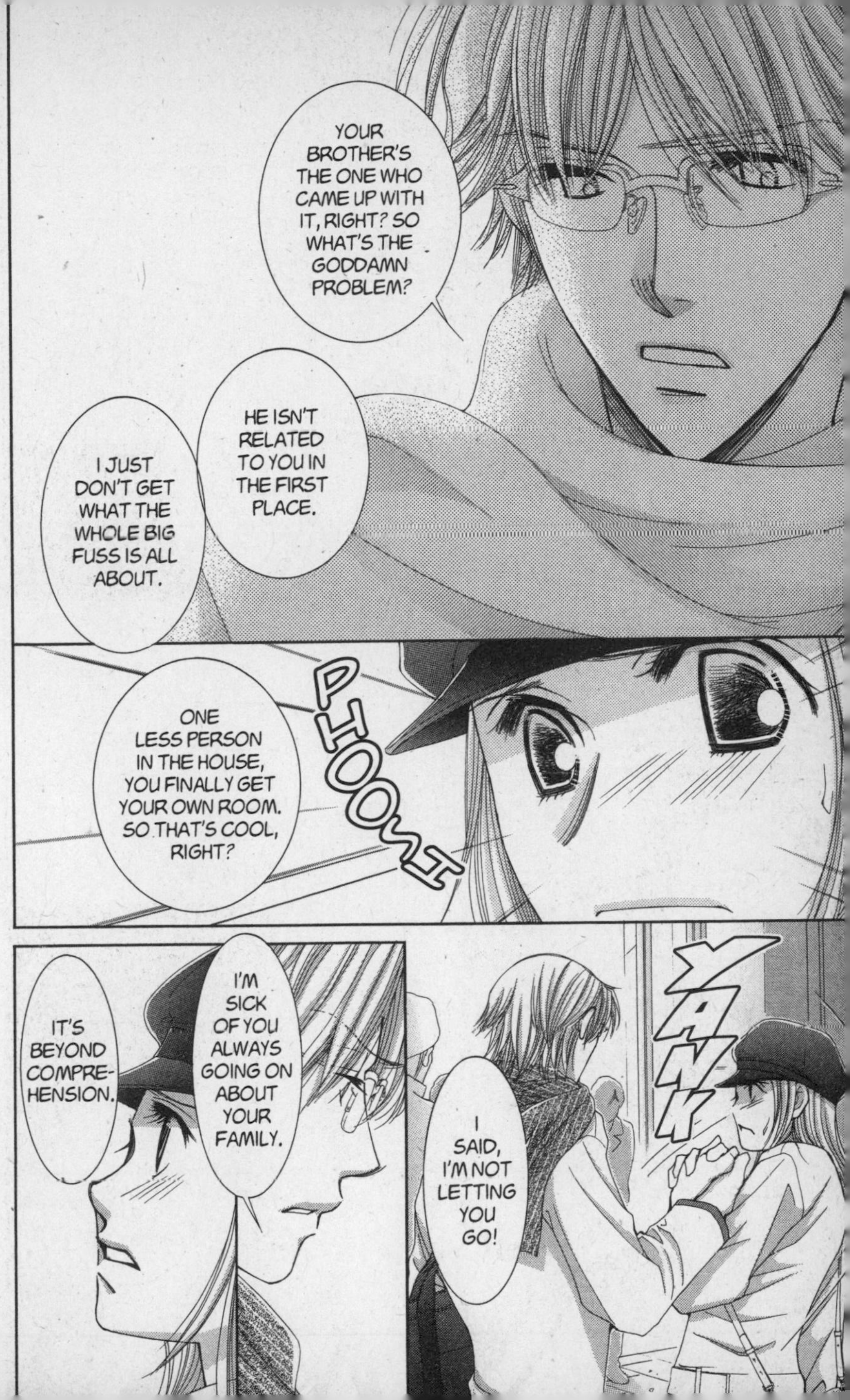
YOUR BROTHER'S THE ONE WHO CAME UP WITH IT, RIGHT? SO WHAT'S THE GODDAMN PROBLEM?
HE ISN'T RELATED TO YOU IN THE FIRST PLACE.
I JUST DON'T GET WHAT THE WHOLE BIG FUSS IS ALL ABOUT.
PHOOSH
ONE LESS PERSON IN THE HOUSE, YOU FINALLY GET YOUR OWN ROOM. SO THAT'S COOL, RIGHT?
YANK
I SAID, I'M NOT LETTING YOU GO!
I'M SICK OF YOU ALWAYS GOING ON ABOUT YOUR FAMILY.
IT'S BEYOND COMPRE-HENSION.

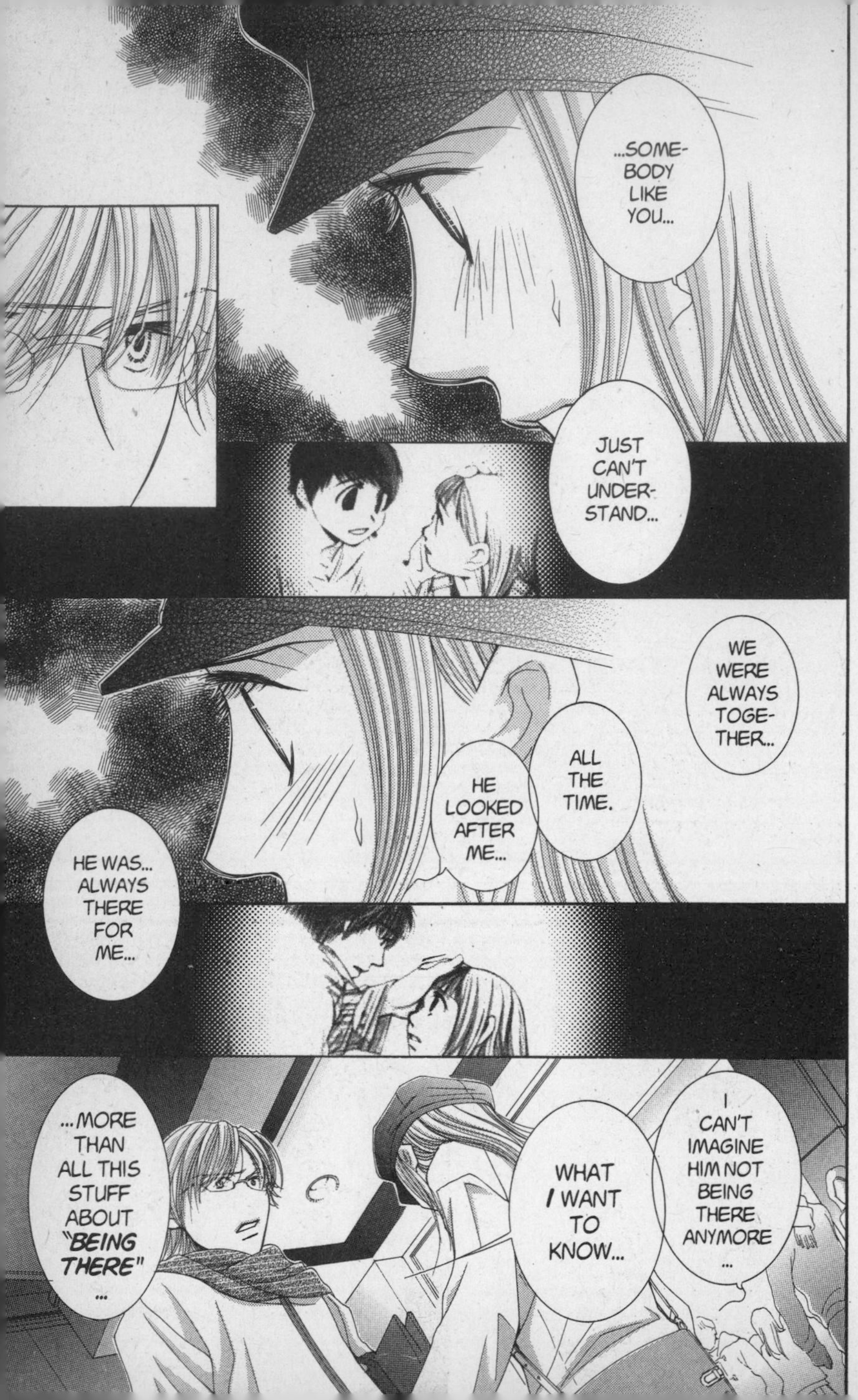
...SOMEBODY LIKE YOU...
JUST CAN'T UNDERSTAND...
WE WERE ALWAYS TOGETHER...
ALL THE TIME.
HE LOOKED AFTER ME...
HE WAS... ALWAYS THERE FOR ME...
I CAN'T IMAGINE HIM NOT BEING THERE ANYMORE...
WHAT *I* WANT TO KNOW...
...MORE THAN ALL THIS STUFF ABOUT "***BEING THERE***"...

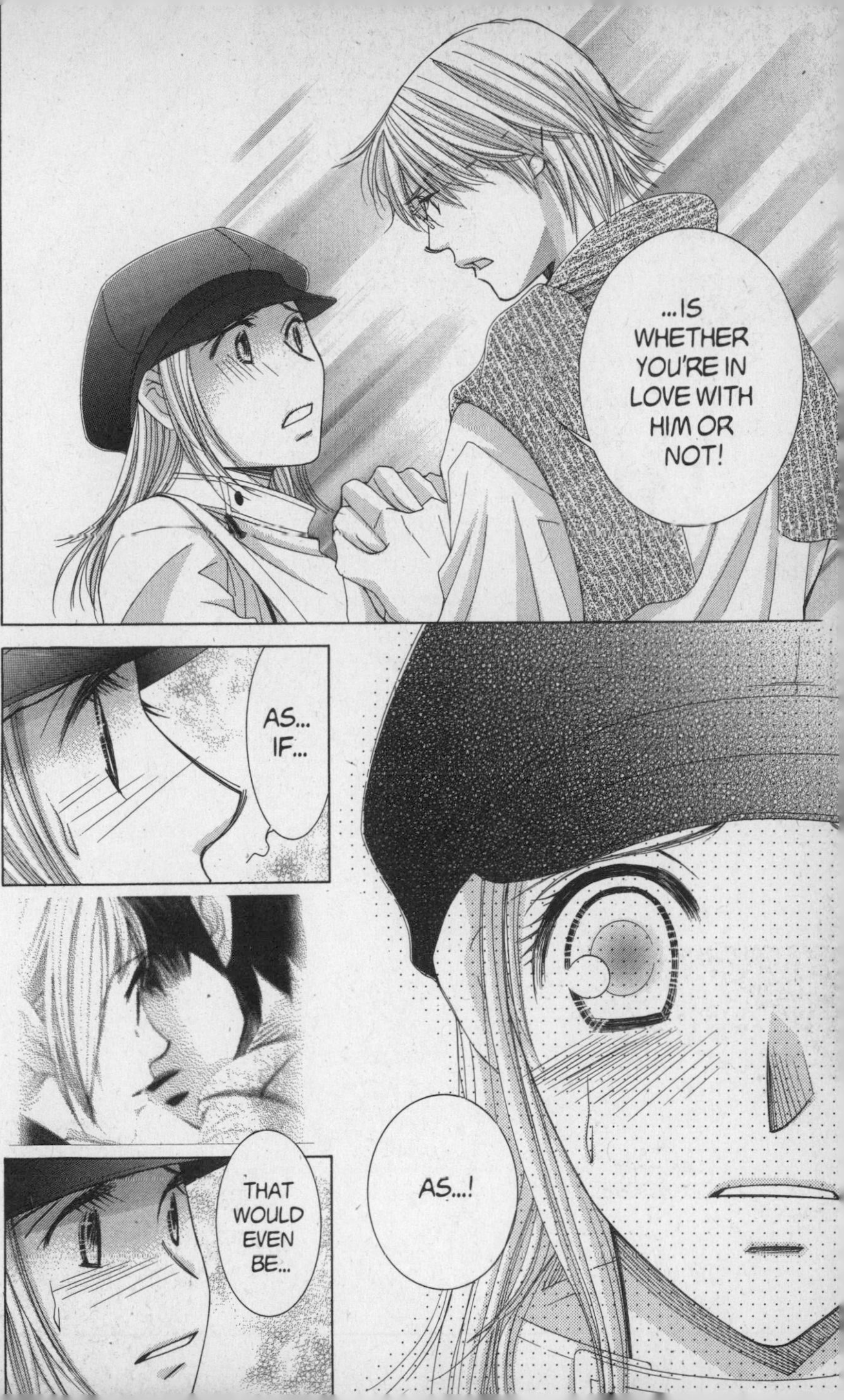
...IS WHETHER YOU'RE IN LOVE WITH HIM OR NOT!
AS...!
AS... IF...
THAT WOULD EVEN BE...

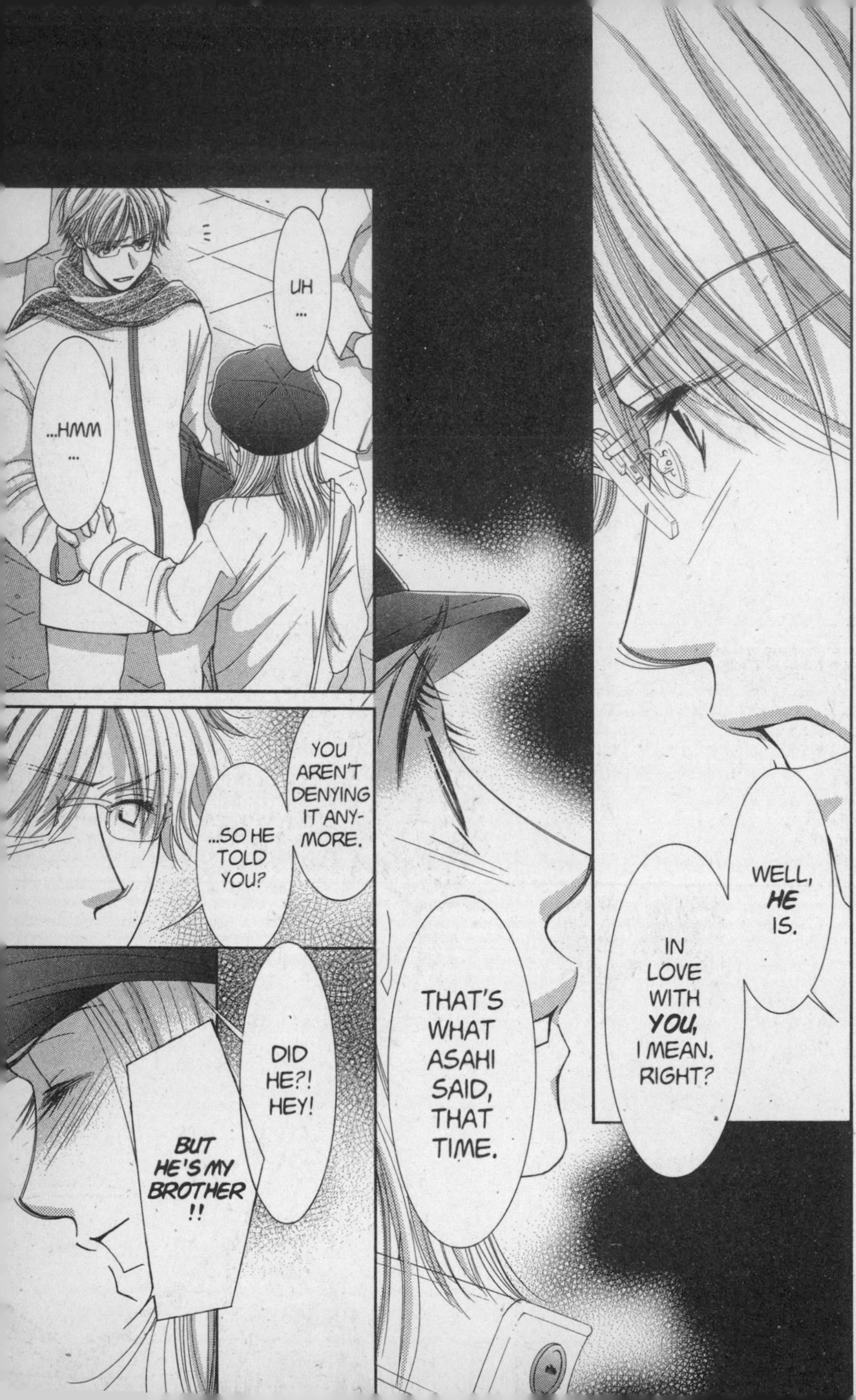
WELL, HE IS.
IN LOVE WITH YOU, I MEAN. RIGHT?
THAT'S WHAT ASAHI SAID, THAT TIME.
UH ...
...HMM ...
YOU AREN'T DENYING IT ANY-MORE.
...SO HE TOLD YOU?
DID HE?! HEY!
BUT HE'S MY BROTHER !!

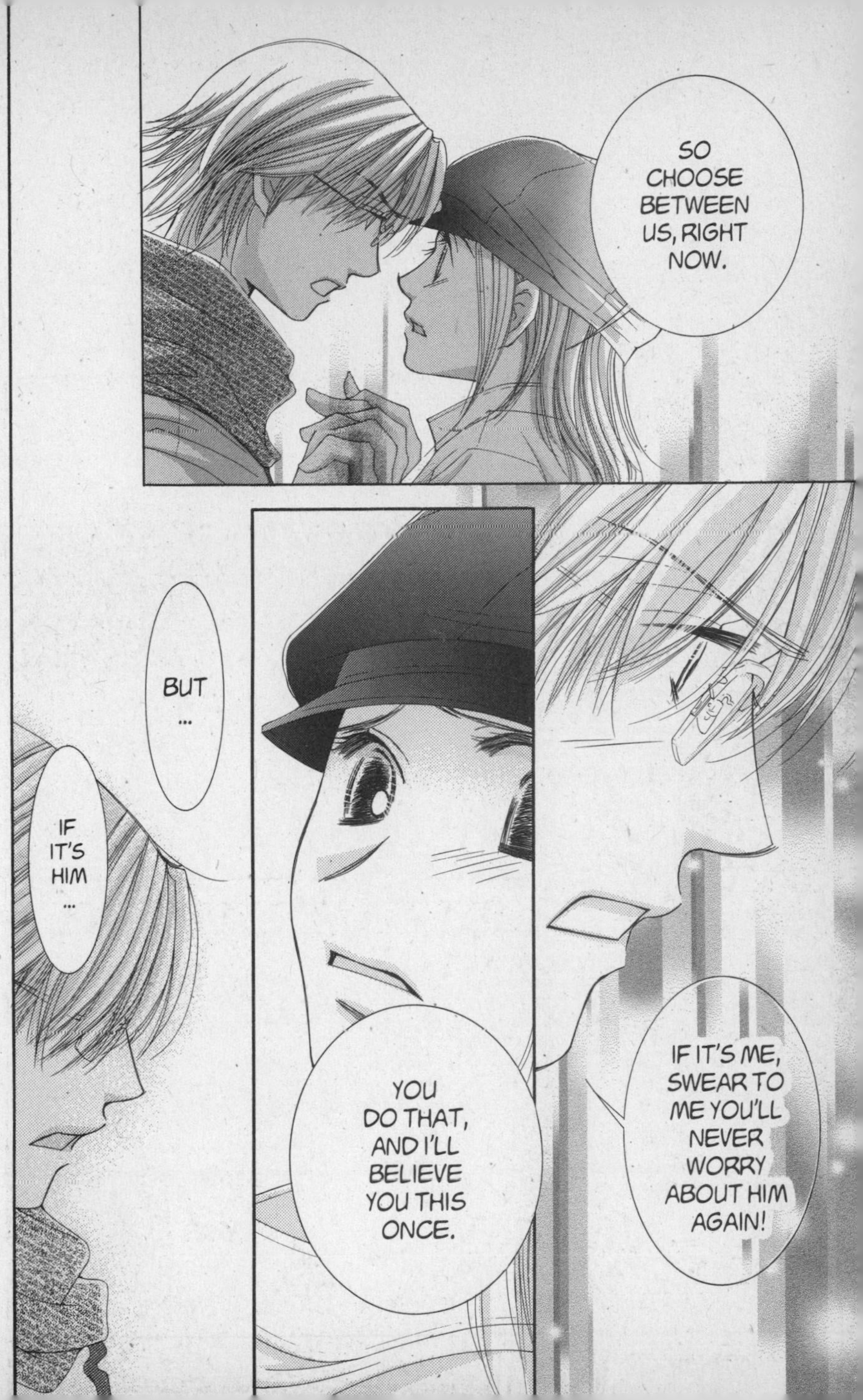
SO CHOOSE BETWEEN US, RIGHT NOW.
IF IT'S ME, SWEAR TO ME YOU'LL NEVER WORRY ABOUT HIM AGAIN!
YOU DO THAT, AND I'LL BELIEVE YOU THIS ONCE.
BUT ...
IF IT'S HIM ...

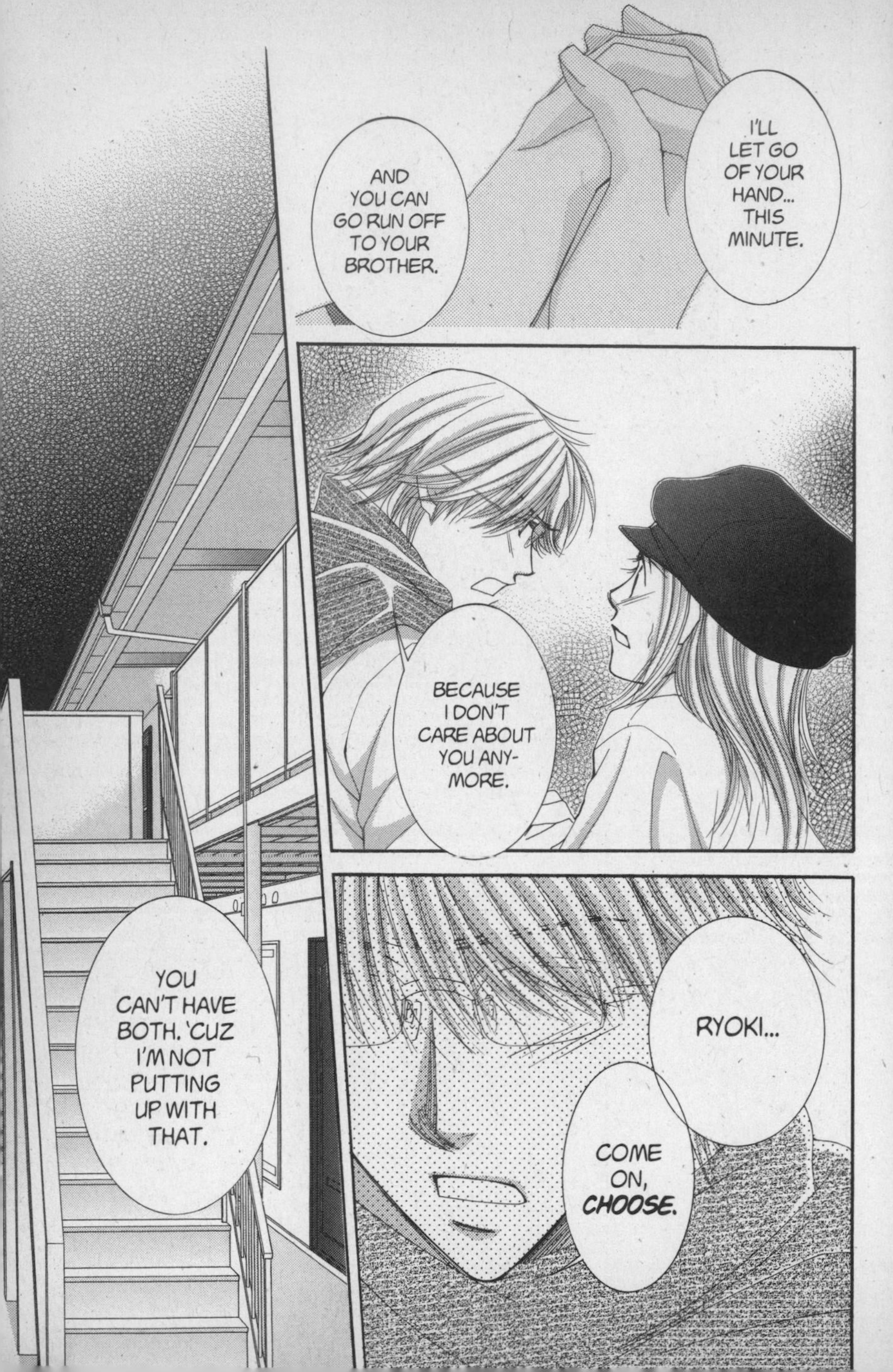
I'LL LET GO OF YOUR HAND... THIS MINUTE.
AND YOU CAN GO RUN OFF TO YOUR BROTHER.
BECAUSE I DON'T CARE ABOUT YOU ANY-MORE.
RYOKI...
COME ON, *CHOOSE.*
YOU CAN'T HAVE BOTH. 'CUZ I'M NOT PUTTING UP WITH THAT.

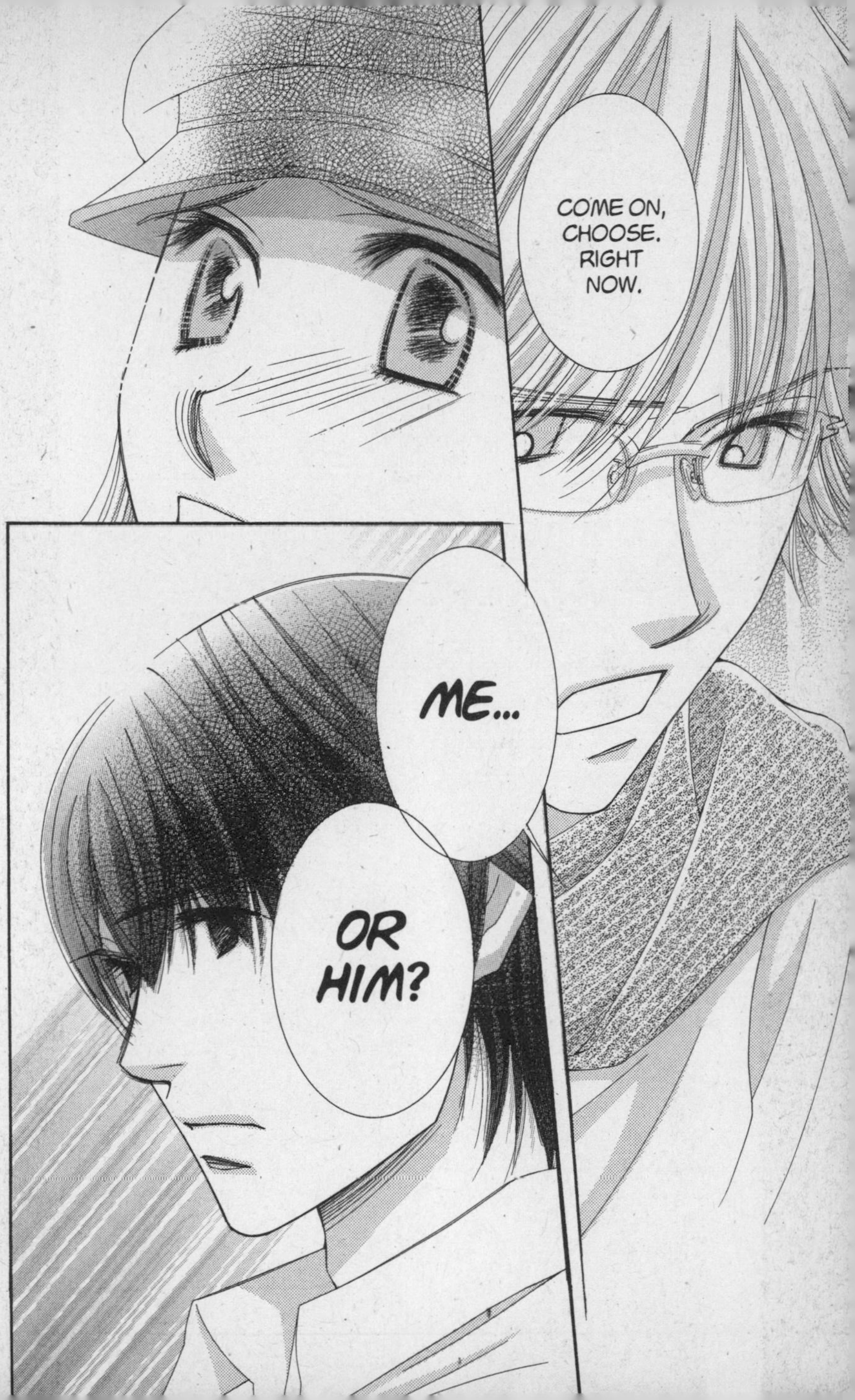
COME ON, CHOOSE. RIGHT NOW.
ME...
OR HIM?

Chapter 43

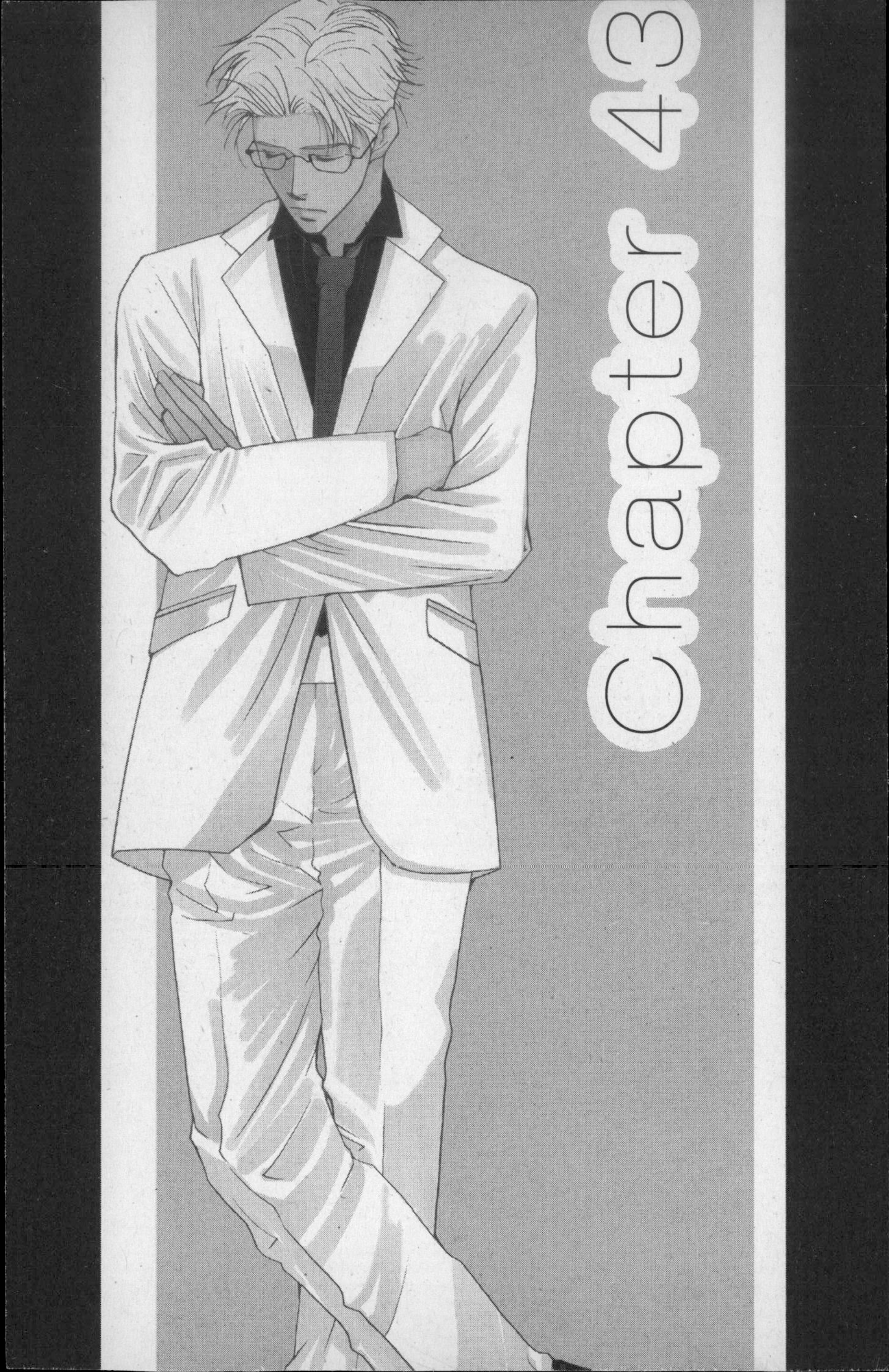

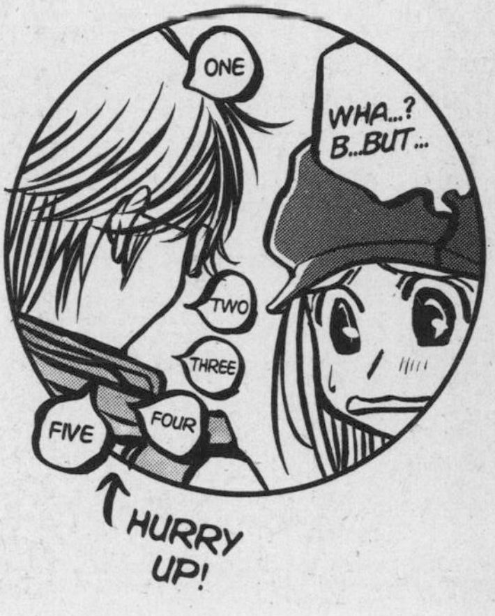
WHA...?
B...BUT...
ONE
TWO
THREE
FOUR
FIVE
HURRY UP!

CHAPTER 42 CONTINUED (PART 1)

HEY, I KNEW Y'ALL WERE REAL SWEET ON HATSUMI-CHAN, BUT...
LORDY... **NOT** THAT SWEET, FOR SURE. I MEAN, NOT LIKE THAT...
HOO-BOY. I'M STILL KINDA STUNNED ...

hot gimmick

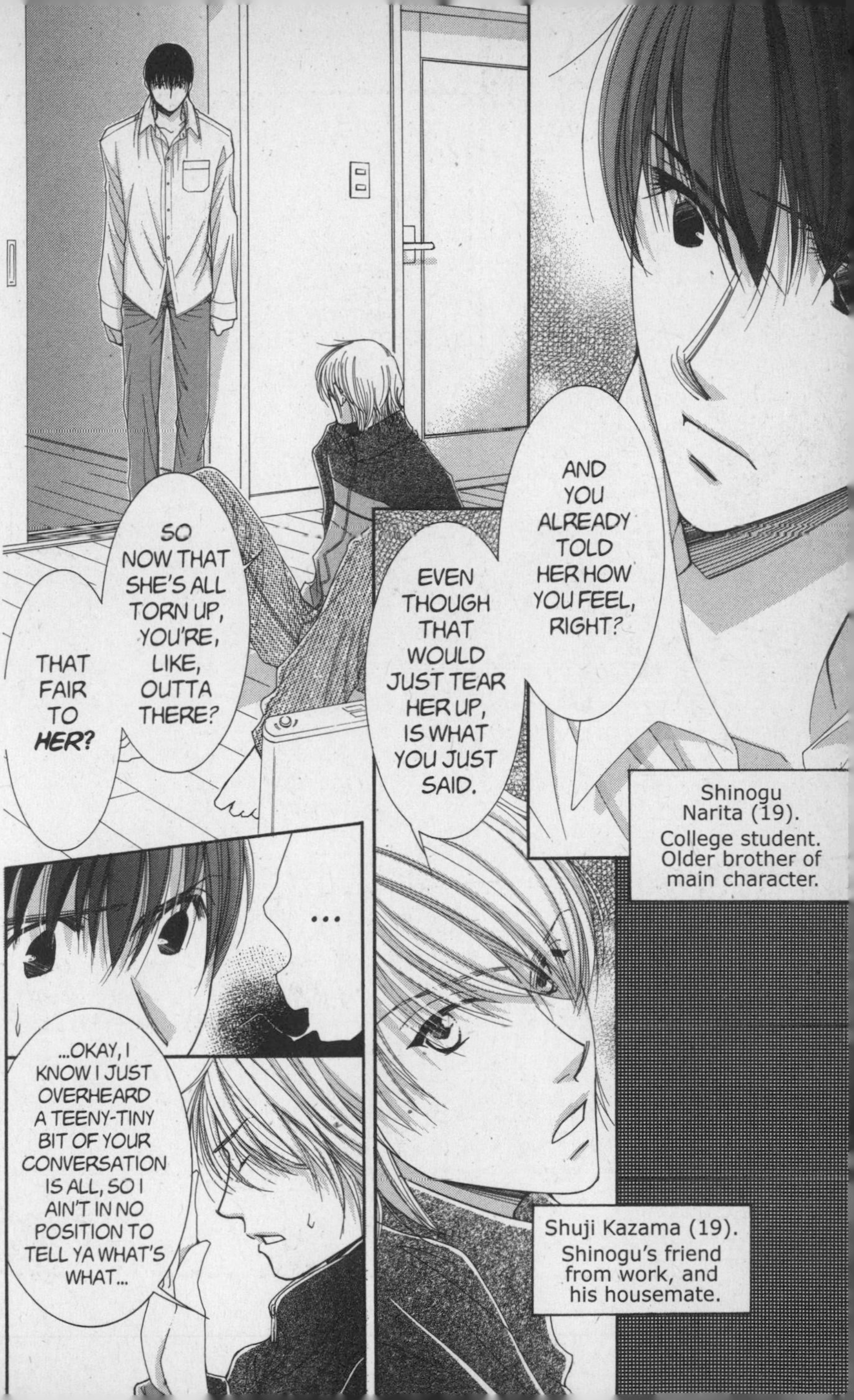
Shinogu Narita (19). College student. Older brother of main character.
AND YOU ALREADY TOLD HER HOW YOU FEEL, RIGHT?
EVEN THOUGH THAT WOULD JUST TEAR HER UP, IS WHAT YOU JUST SAID.
Shuji Kazama (19). Shinogu's friend from work, and his housemate.
SO NOW THAT SHE'S ALL TORN UP, YOU'RE, LIKE, OUTTA THERE?
THAT FAIR TO *HER?*
...
...OKAY, I KNOW I JUST OVERHEARD A TEENY-TINY BIT OF YOUR CONVERSATION IS ALL, SO I AIN'T IN NO POSITION TO TELL YA WHAT'S WHAT...

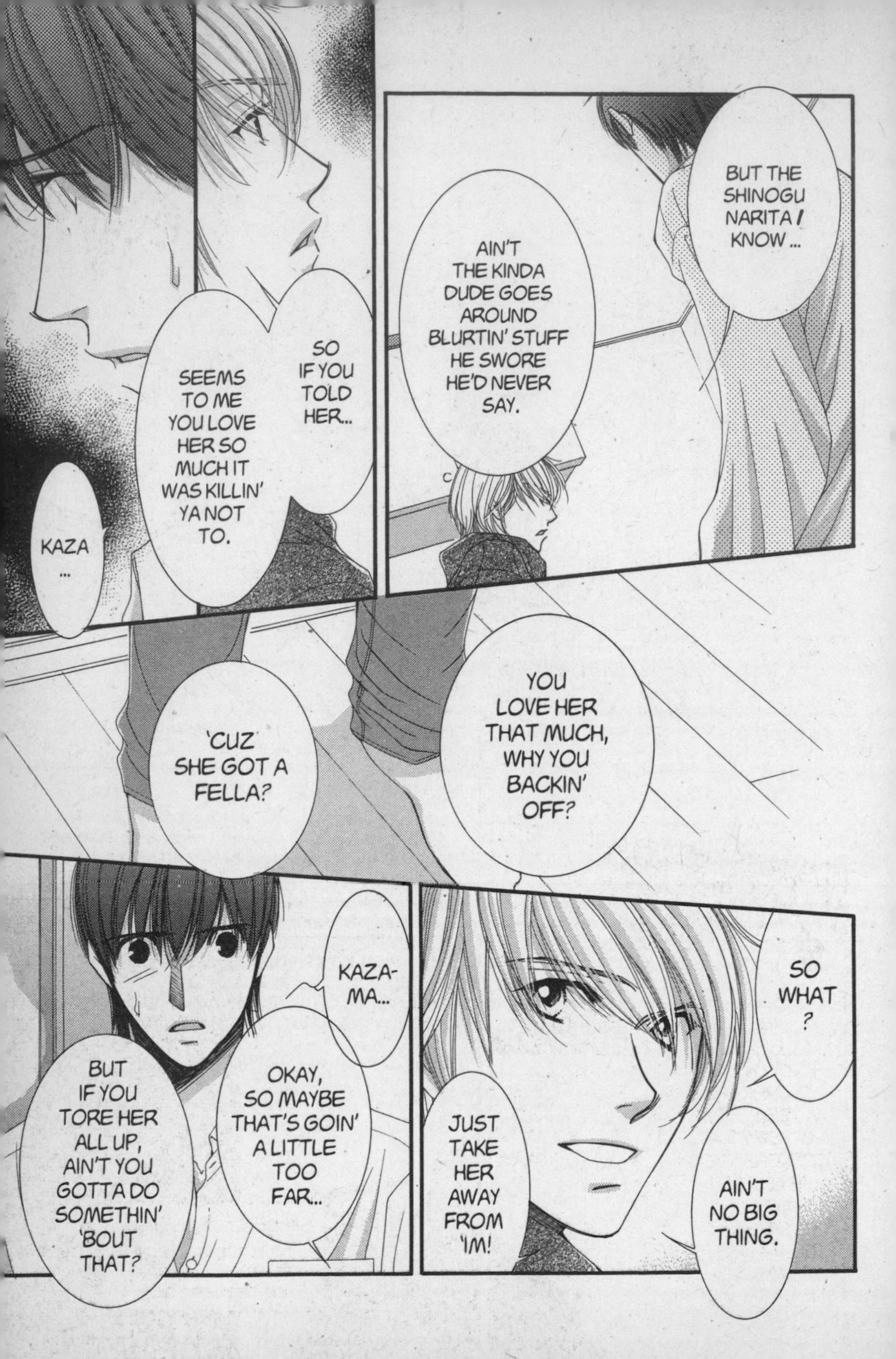
BUT THE SHINOGU NARITA I KNOW...
AIN'T THE KINDA DUDE GOES AROUND BLURTIN' STUFF HE SWORE HE'D NEVER SAY.
SO IF YOU TOLD HER...
SEEMS TO ME YOU LOVE HER SO MUCH IT WAS KILLIN' YA NOT TO.
KAZA...
YOU LOVE HER THAT MUCH, WHY YOU BACKIN' OFF?
'CUZ SHE GOT A FELLA?
SO WHAT?
AIN'T NO BIG THING.
JUST TAKE HER AWAY FROM 'IM!
KAZAMA...
OKAY, SO MAYBE THAT'S GOIN' A LITTLE TOO FAR...
BUT IF YOU TORE HER ALL UP, AIN'T YOU GOTTA DO SOMETHIN' 'BOUT THAT?

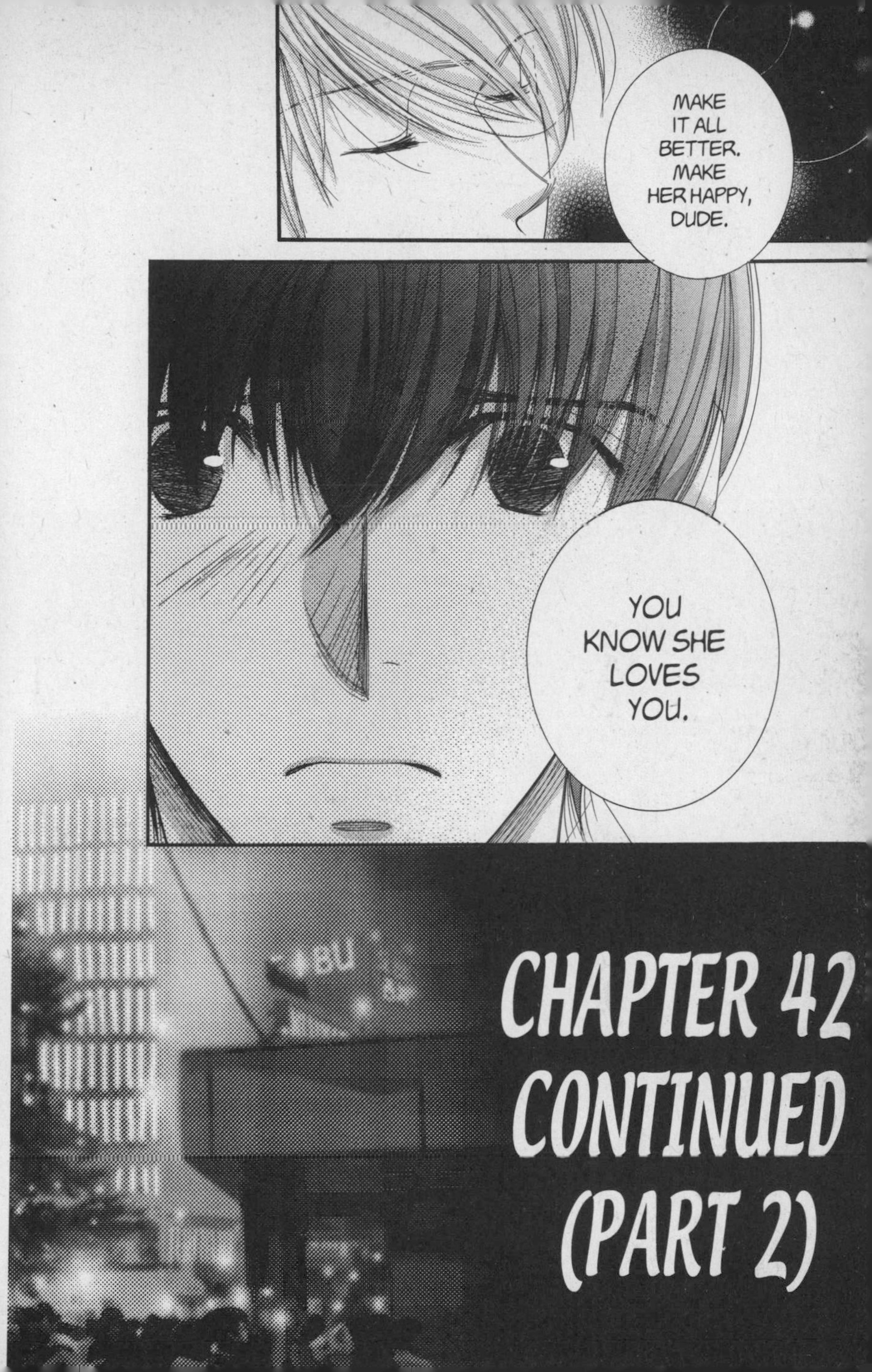
MAKE IT ALL BETTER. MAKE HER HAPPY, DUDE.
YOU KNOW SHE LOVES YOU.
CHAPTER 42 CONTINUED (PART 2)

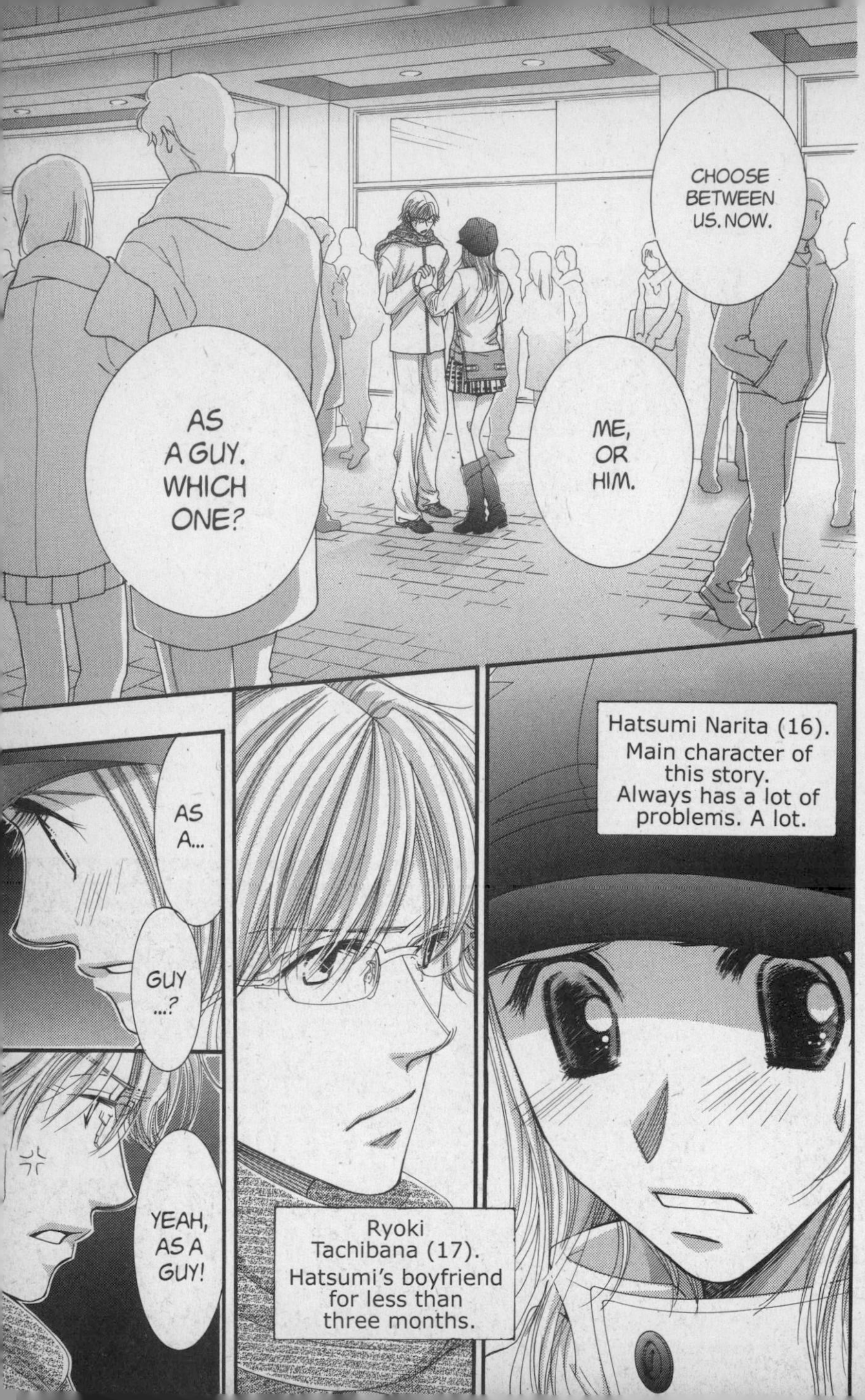
CHOOSE BETWEEN US. NOW.
ME, OR HIM.
AS A GUY. WHICH ONE?
Hatsumi Narita (16). Main character of this story. Always has a lot of problems. A lot.
Ryoki Tachibana (17). Hatsumi's boyfriend for less than three months.
AS A...
GUY ...?
YEAH, AS A GUY!

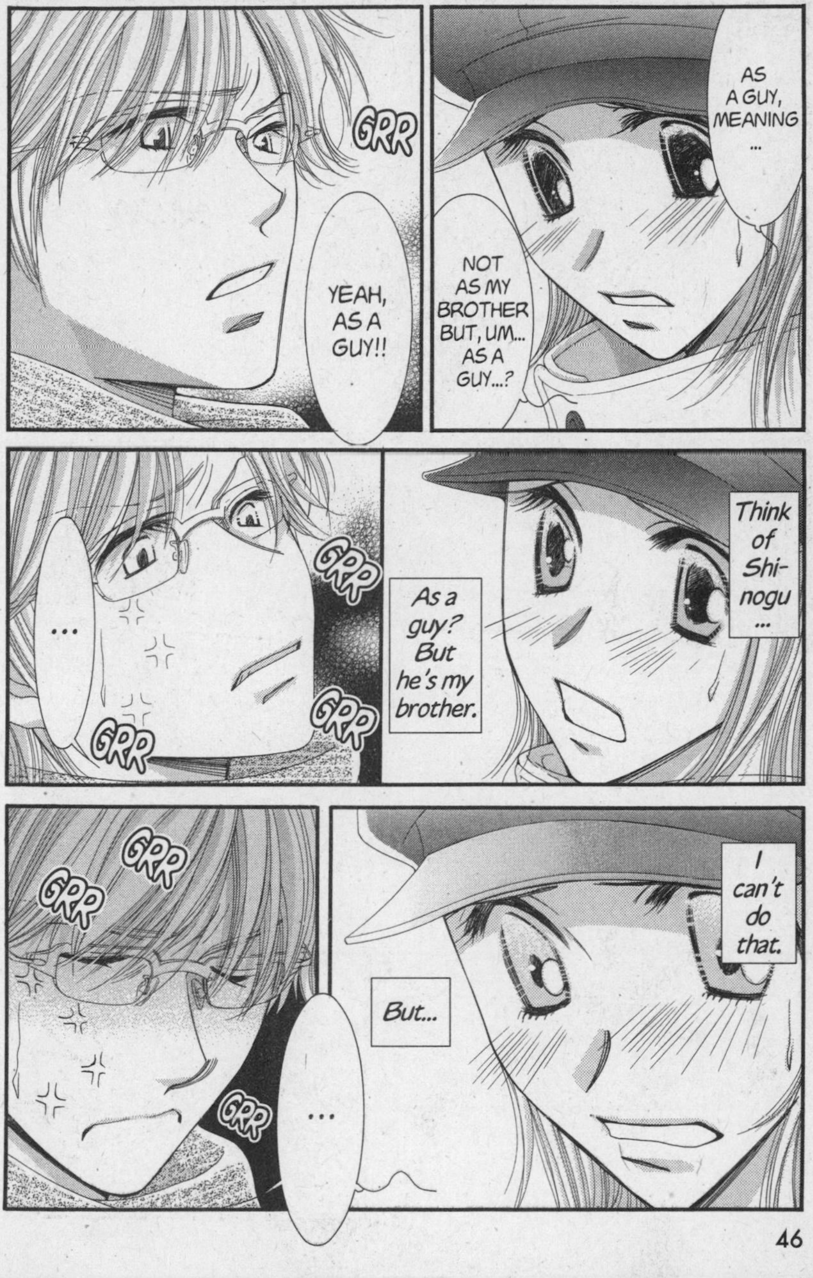
AS A GUY, MEANING ...
NOT AS MY BROTHER BUT, UM... AS A GUY...?
GRR
YEAH, AS A GUY!!
Think of Shi-nogu ...
As a guy? But he's my brother.
GRR
GRR
GRR
...
I can't do that.
But...
GRR
GRR
...
GRR

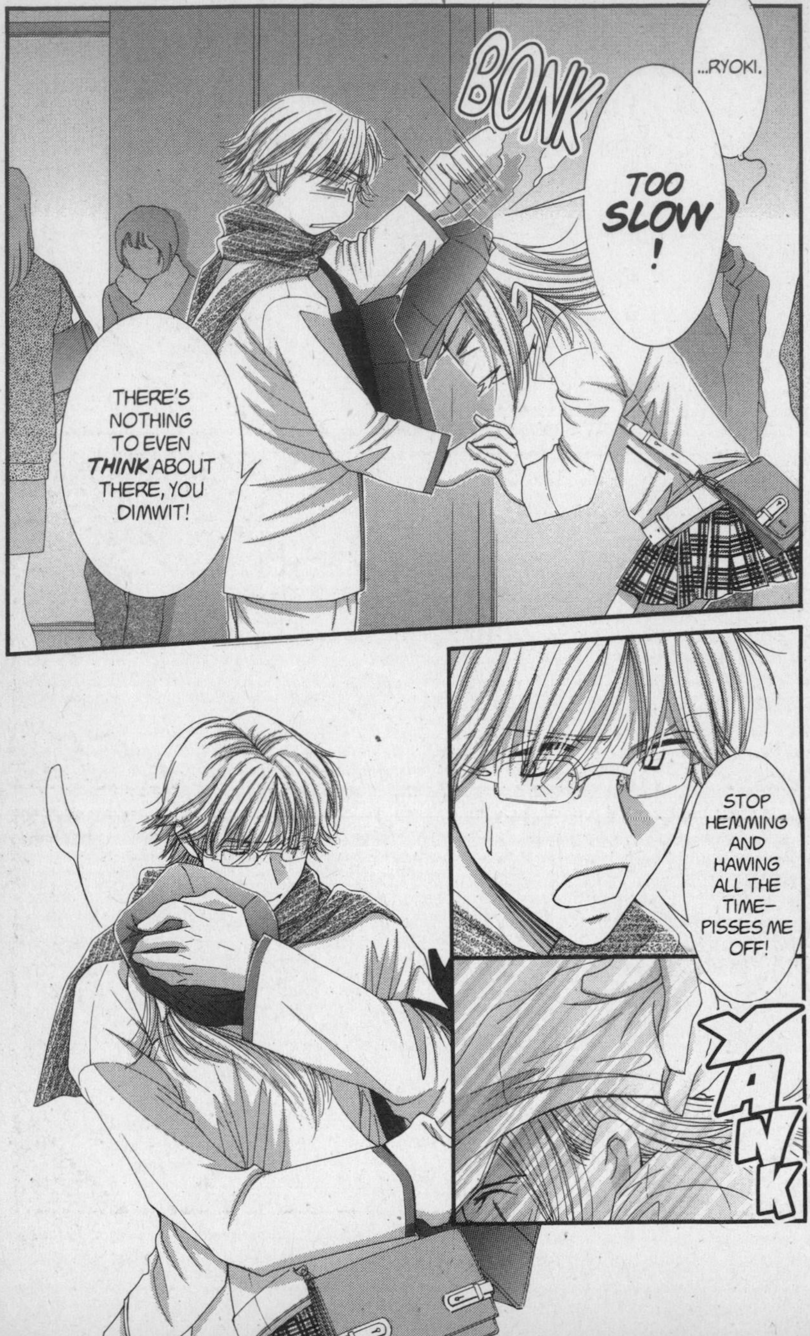
...RYOKI.
TOO SLOW!
BONK
THERE'S NOTHING TO EVEN THINK ABOUT THERE, YOU DIMWIT!
STOP HEMMING AND HAWING ALL THE TIME–PISSES ME OFF!
YANK

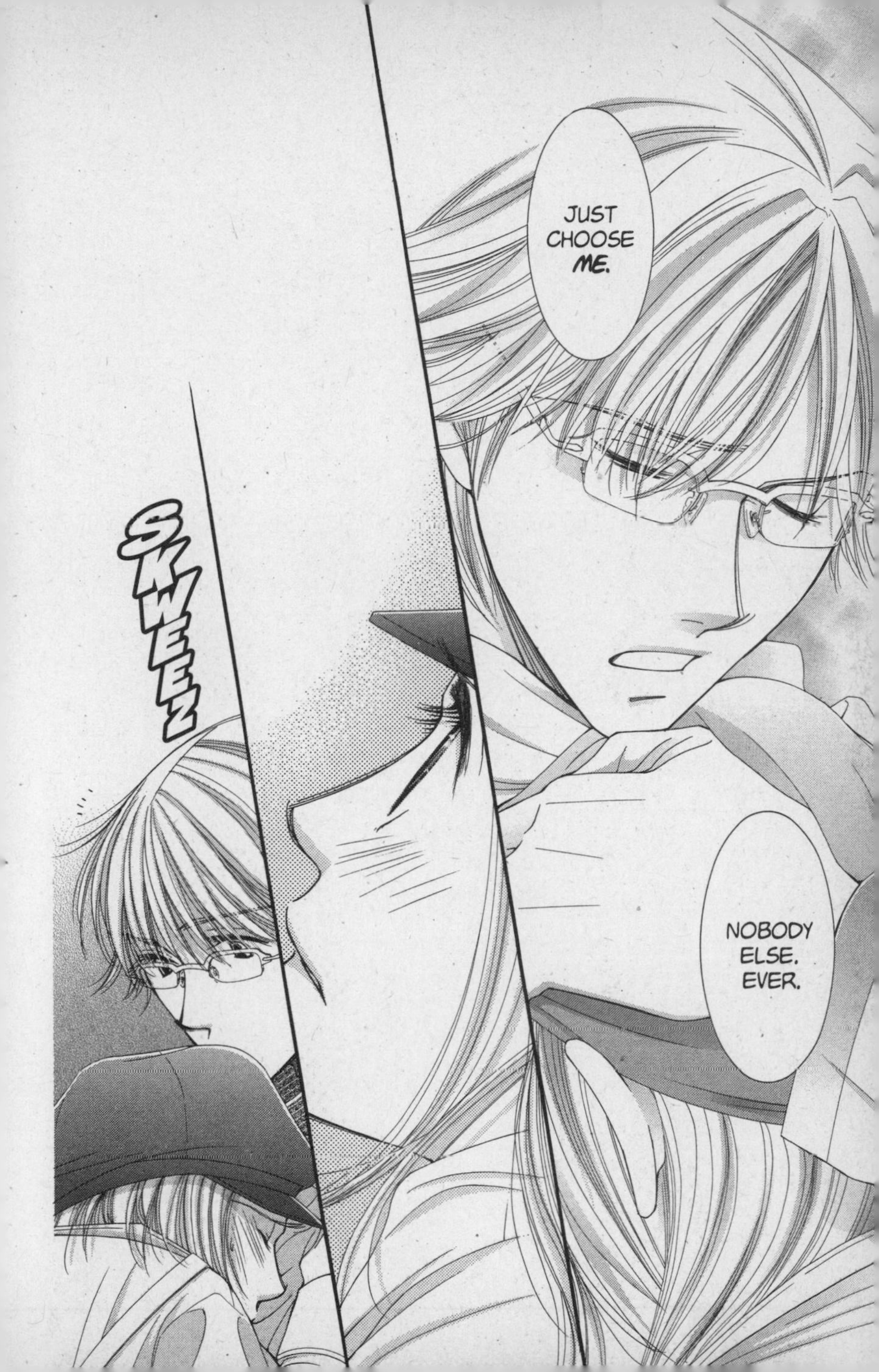
JUST CHOOSE ME.
NOBODY ELSE. EVER.
SKWEEZ

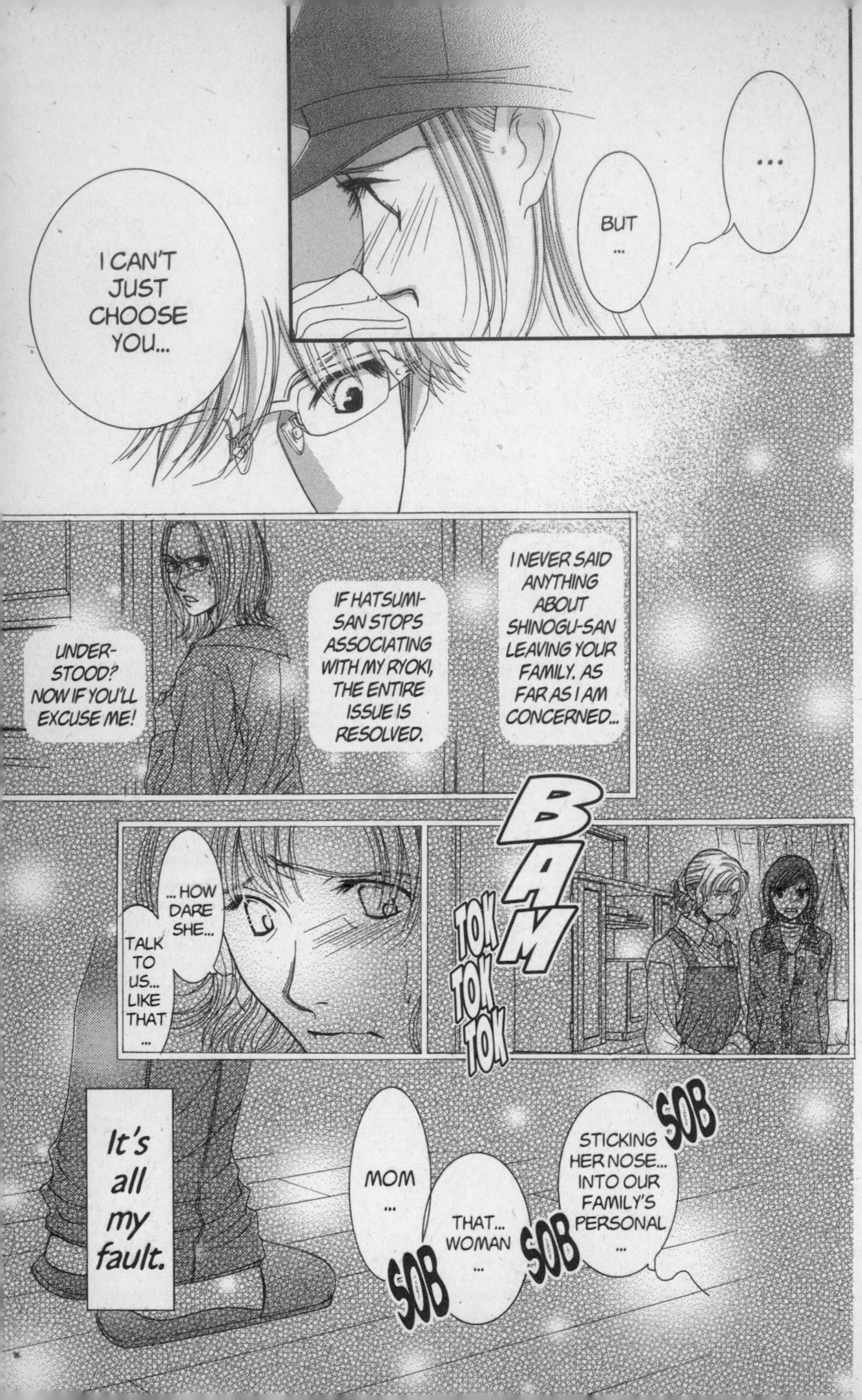
...
BUT ...
I CAN'T JUST CHOOSE YOU...
I NEVER SAID ANYTHING ABOUT SHINOGU-SAN LEAVING YOUR FAMILY. AS FAR AS I AM CONCERNED...
IF HATSUMI-SAN STOPS ASSOCIATING WITH MY RYOKI, THE ENTIRE ISSUE IS RESOLVED.
UNDER-STOOD? NOW IF YOU'LL EXCUSE ME!
BAM
TOK TOK TOK
... HOW DARE SHE...
TALK TO US... LIKE THAT ...
SOB
STICKING HER NOSE... INTO OUR FAMILY'S PERSONAL ...
SOB
THAT... WOMAN ...
MOM ...
SOB
It's all my fault.

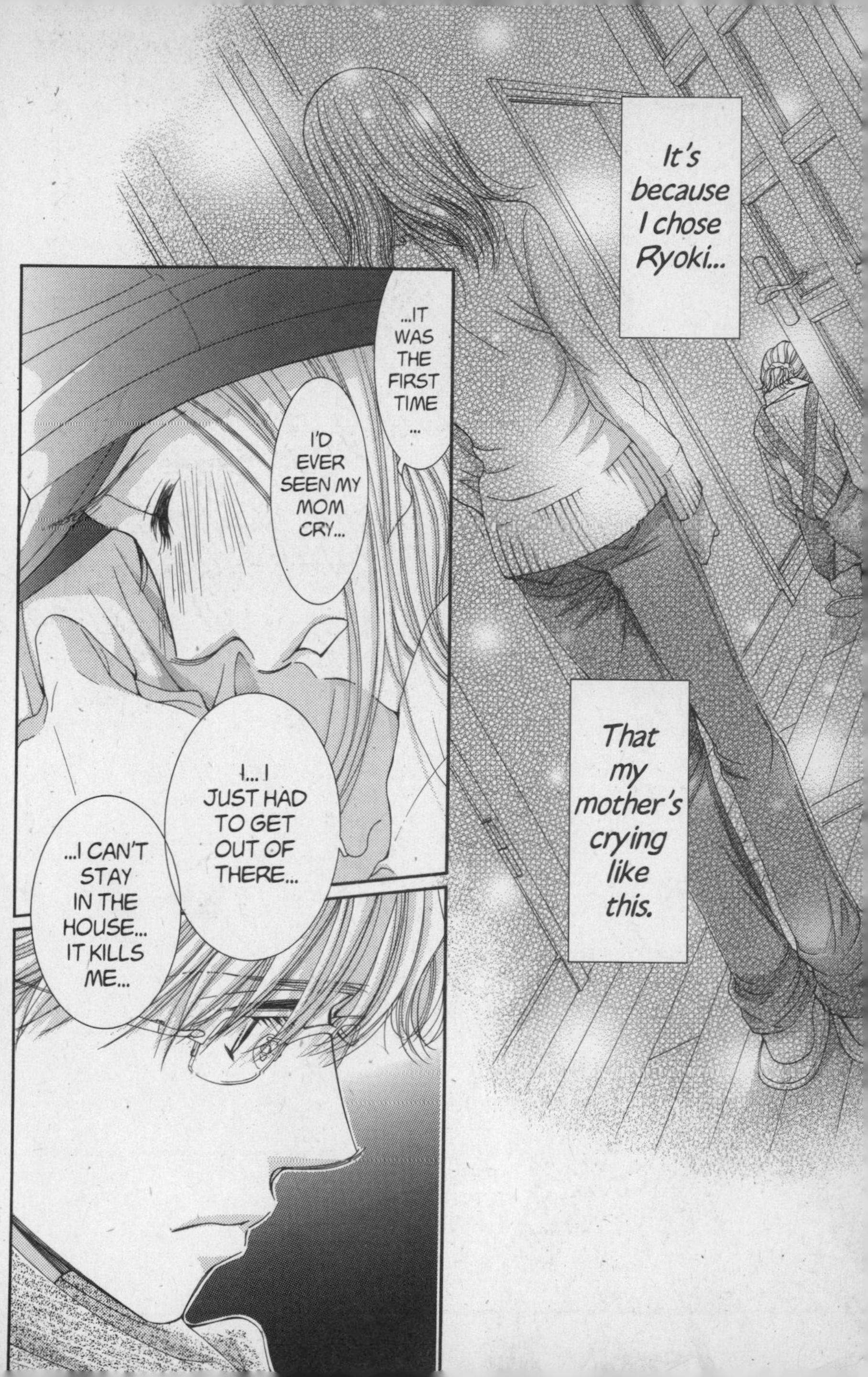
It's because I chose Ryoki...
That my mother's crying like this.
...IT WAS THE FIRST TIME...
I'D EVER SEEN MY MOM CRY...
I... I JUST HAD TO GET OUT OF THERE...
...I CAN'T STAY IN THE HOUSE... IT KILLS ME...

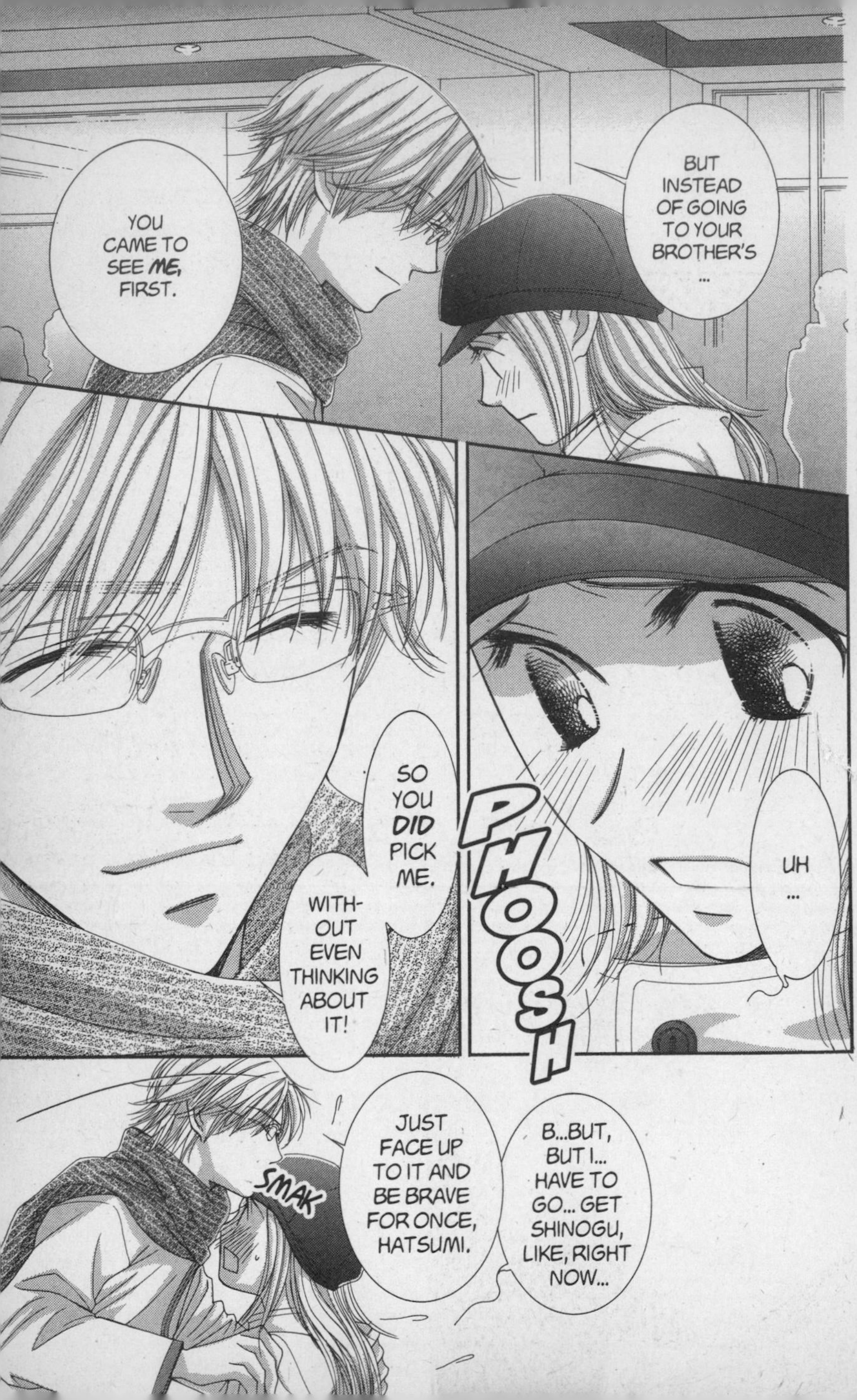

BUT INSTEAD OF GOING TO YOUR BROTHER'S ...
YOU CAME TO SEE ME, FIRST.
UH ...
PHOOSH
SO YOU DID PICK ME.
WITH-OUT EVEN THINKING ABOUT IT!
B...BUT, BUT I... HAVE TO GO... GET SHINOGU, LIKE, RIGHT NOW...
JUST FACE UP TO IT AND BE BRAVE FOR ONCE, HATSUMI.
SMAK

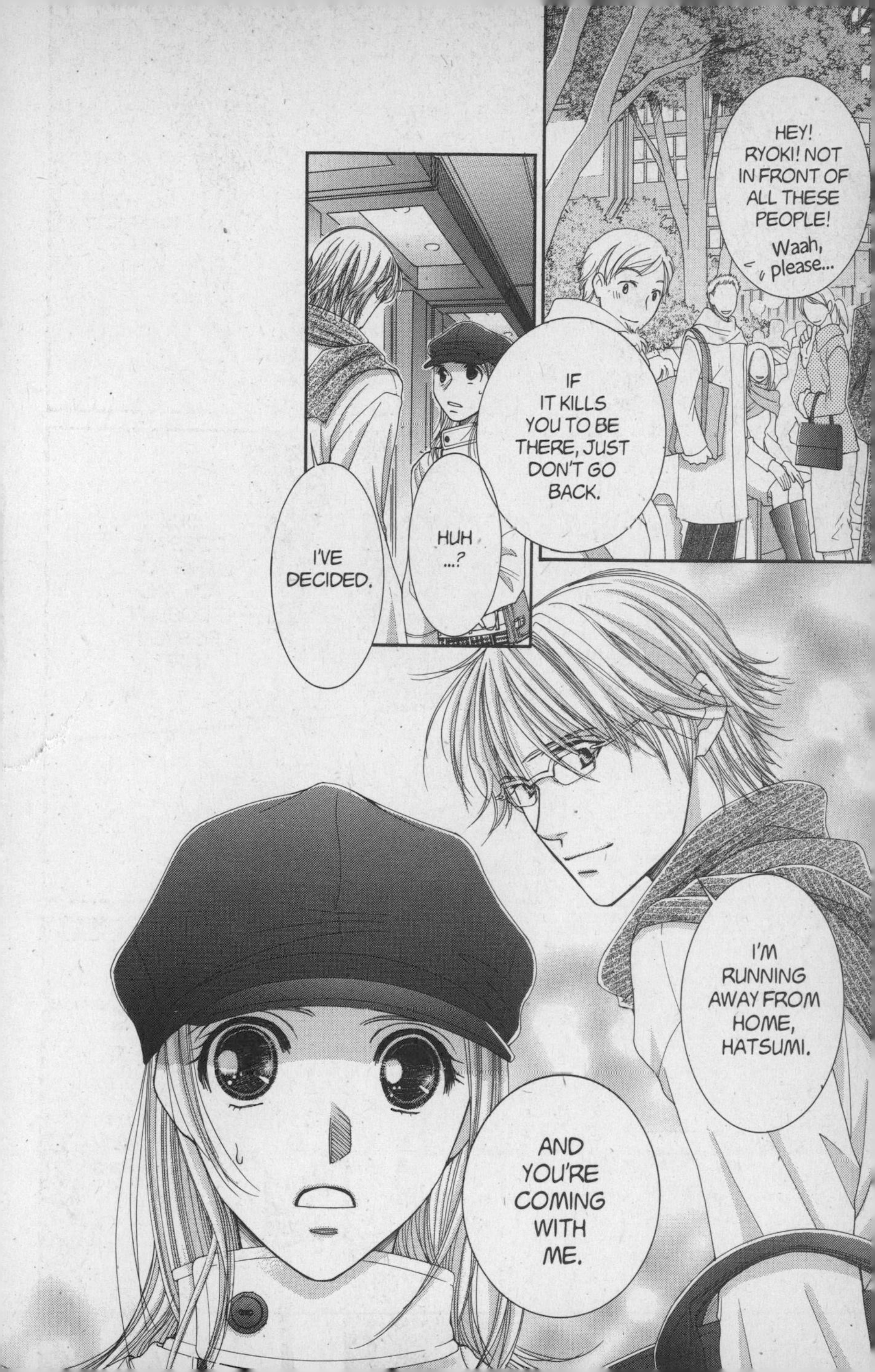
HEY! RYOKI! NOT IN FRONT OF ALL THESE PEOPLE!
Waah, please...
IF IT KILLS YOU TO BE THERE, JUST DON'T GO BACK.
HUH ...?
I'VE DECIDED.
I'M RUNNING AWAY FROM HOME, HATSUMI.
AND YOU'RE COMING WITH ME.

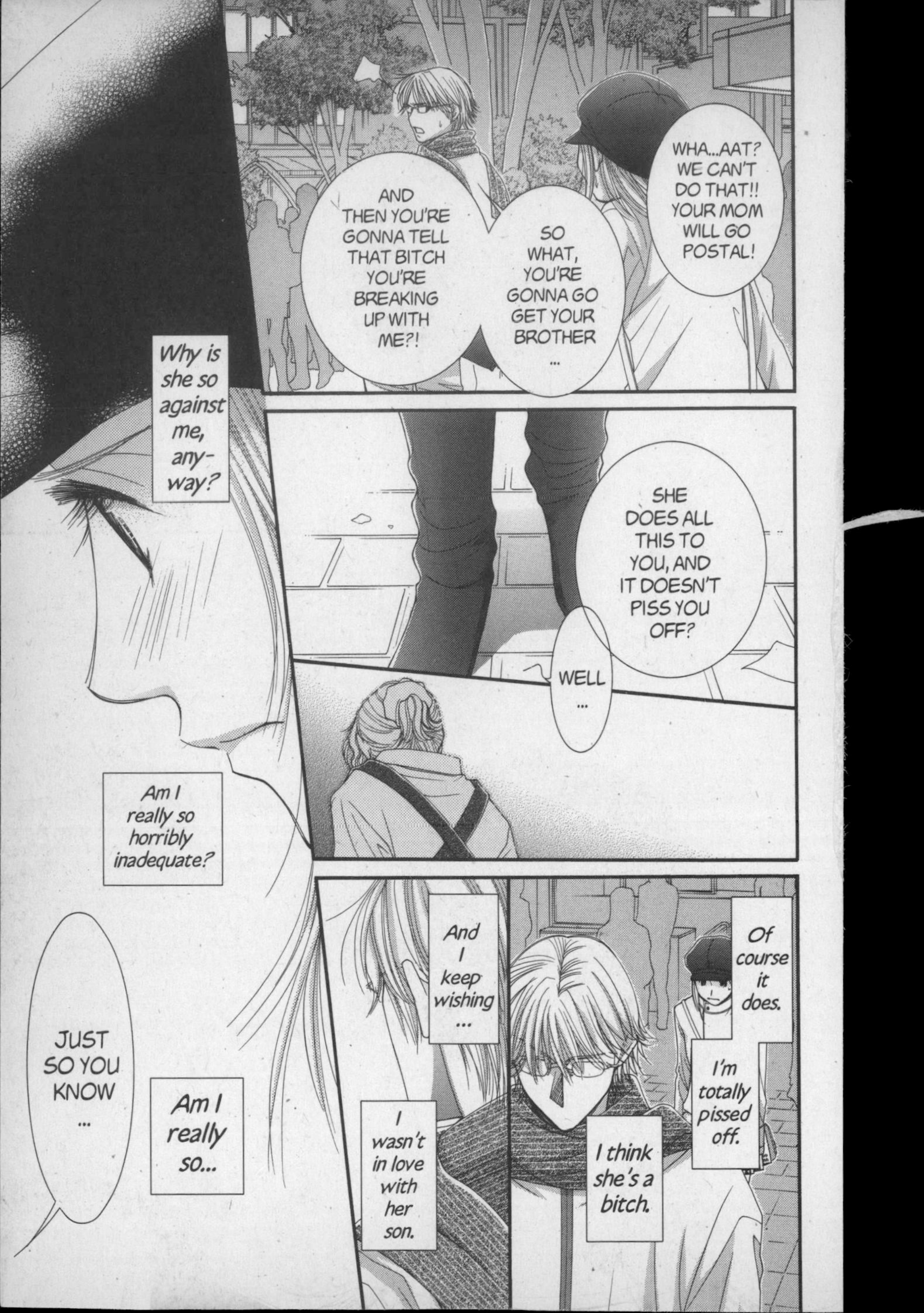
WHA...AAT? WE CAN'T DO THAT!! YOUR MOM WILL GO POSTAL!
SO WHAT, YOU'RE GONNA GO GET YOUR BROTHER ...
AND THEN YOU'RE GONNA TELL THAT BITCH YOU'RE BREAKING UP WITH ME?!
SHE DOES ALL THIS TO YOU, AND IT DOESN'T PISS YOU OFF?
WELL ...
Of course it does.
I'm totally pissed off.
I think she's a bitch.
And I keep wishing ...
I wasn't in love with her son.
Why is she so against me, any-way?
Am I really so horribly inadequate?
Am I really so...
JUST SO YOU KNOW ...

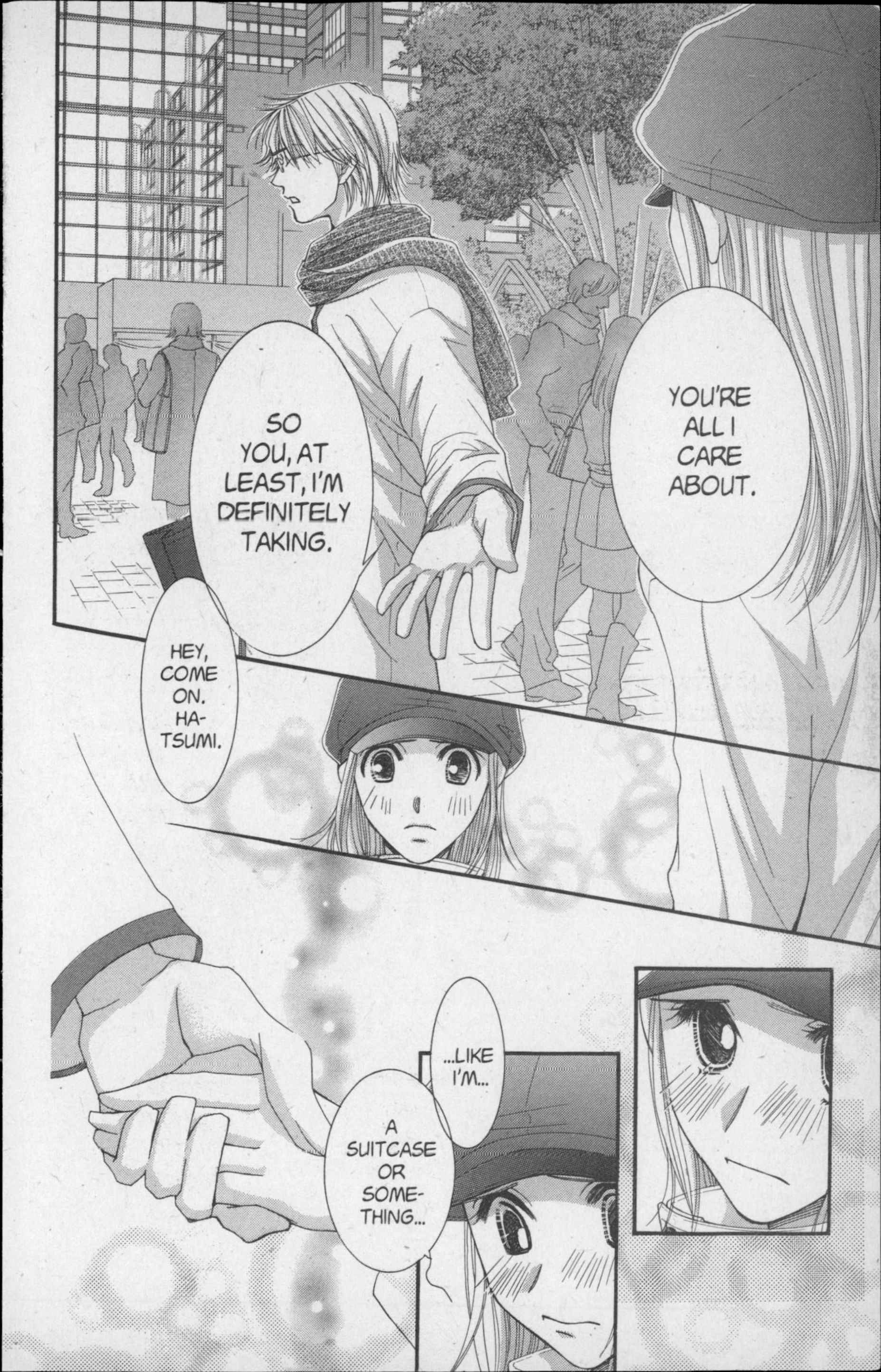
YOU'RE ALL I CARE ABOUT.
SO YOU, AT LEAST, I'M DEFINITELY TAKING.
HEY, COME ON. HA-TSUMI.
...LIKE I'M...
A SUITCASE OR SOMETHING...

hotgimmick

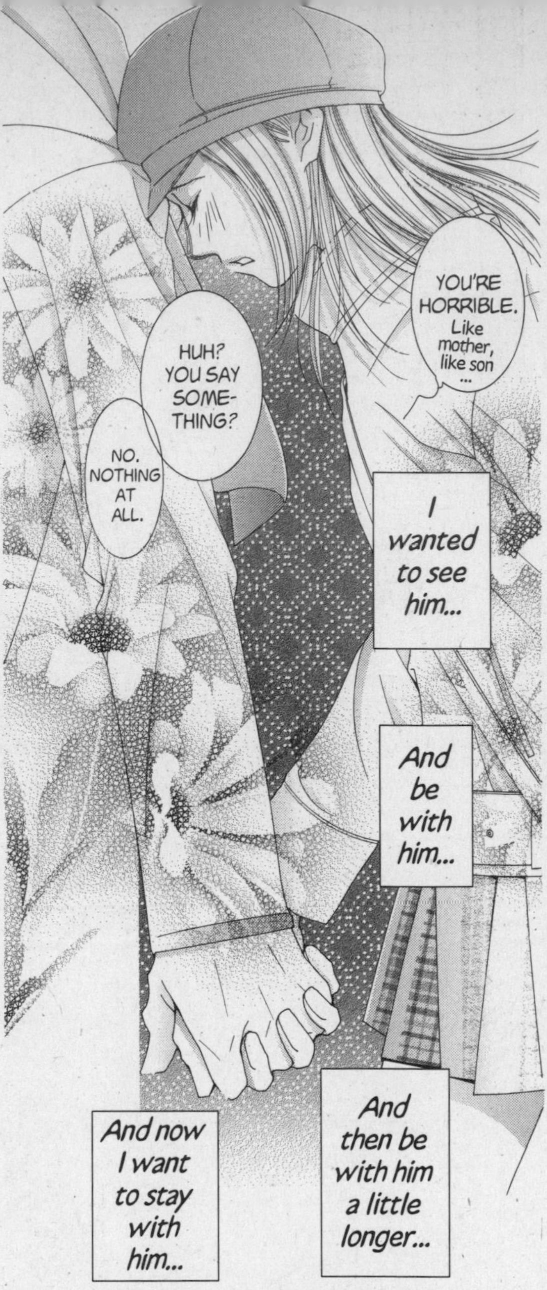

YOU'RE HORRIBLE. Like mother, like son ...
HUH? YOU SAY SOMETHING?
NO. NOTHING AT ALL.
I wanted to see him...
And be with him...
And then be with him a little longer...
And now I want to stay with him...

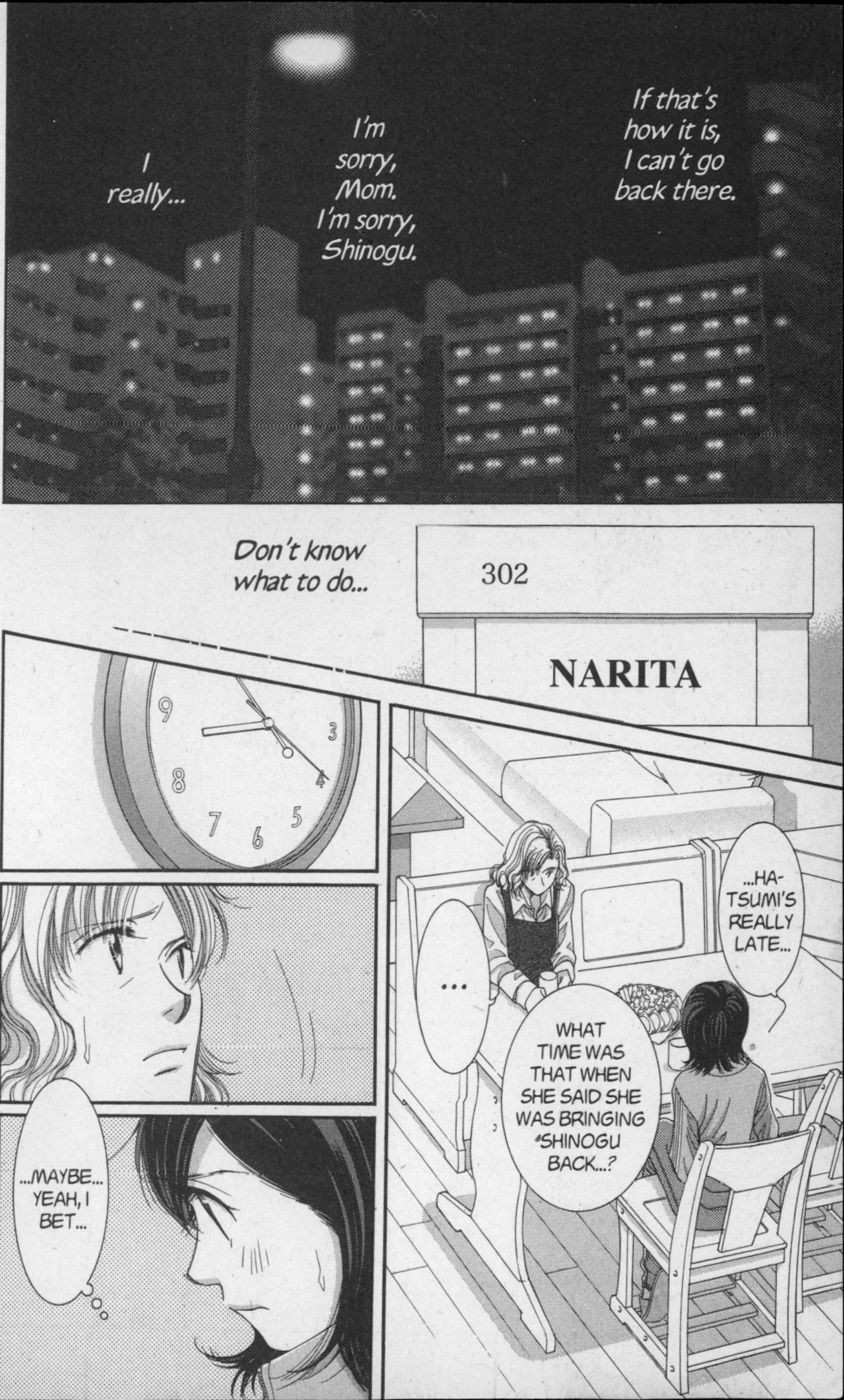
If that's how it is, I can't go back there.
I'm sorry, Mom. I'm sorry, Shinogu.
I really...
302
NARITA
Don't know what to do...
...HATSUMI'S REALLY LATE...
WHAT TIME WAS THAT WHEN SHE SAID SHE WAS BRINGING SHINOGU BACK...?
...
...MAYBE... YEAH, I BET...

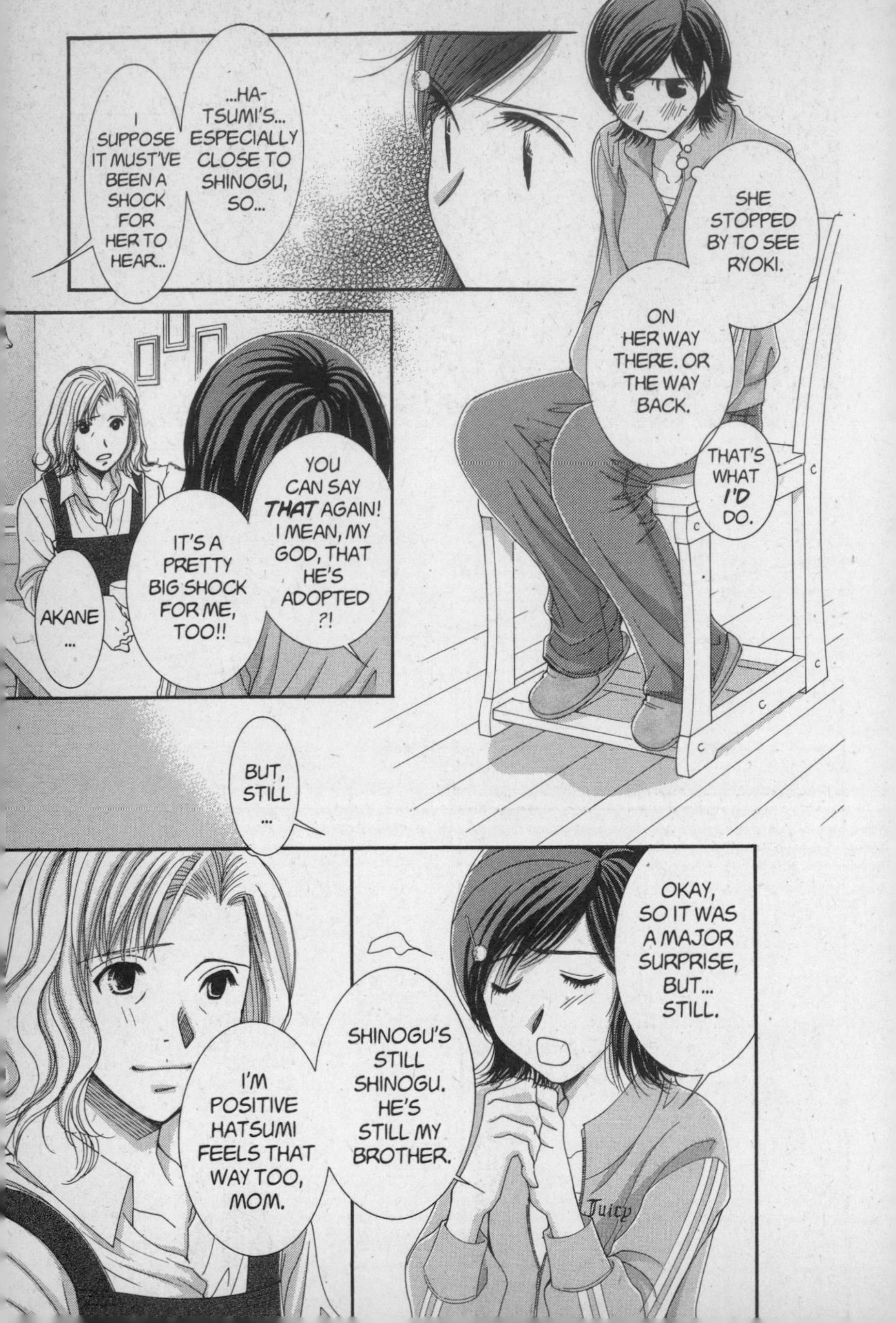
SHE STOPPED BY TO SEE RYOKI.
ON HER WAY THERE. OR THE WAY BACK.
THAT'S WHAT ***I'D*** DO.
...HA-TSUMI'S... ESPECIALLY CLOSE TO SHINOGU, SO...
I SUPPOSE IT MUST'VE BEEN A SHOCK FOR HER TO HEAR..
YOU CAN SAY ***THAT*** AGAIN! I MEAN, MY GOD, THAT HE'S ADOPTED ?!
IT'S A PRETTY BIG SHOCK FOR ME, TOO!!
AKANE ...
BUT, STILL ...
OKAY, SO IT WAS A MAJOR SURPRISE, BUT... STILL.
SHINOGU'S STILL SHINOGU. HE'S STILL MY BROTHER.
I'M POSITIVE HATSUMI FEELS THAT WAY TOO, MOM.
Juicy

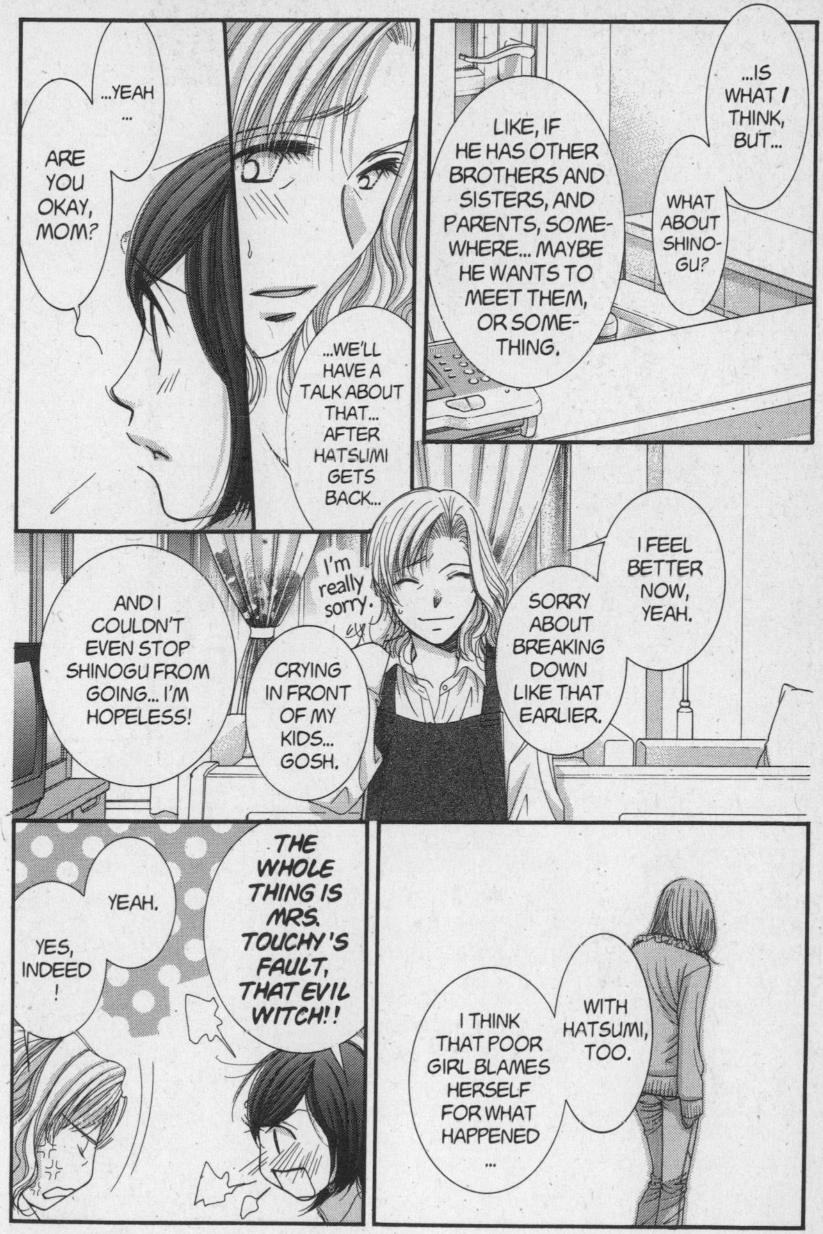
...IS WHAT I THINK, BUT...
WHAT ABOUT SHINOGU?
LIKE, IF HE HAS OTHER BROTHERS AND SISTERS, AND PARENTS, SOMEWHERE... MAYBE HE WANTS TO MEET THEM, OR SOMETHING.
...WE'LL HAVE A TALK ABOUT THAT... AFTER HATSUMI GETS BACK...
...YEAH ...
ARE YOU OKAY, MOM?
I FEEL BETTER NOW, YEAH.
SORRY ABOUT BREAKING DOWN LIKE THAT EARLIER.
I'm really sorry.
CRYING IN FRONT OF MY KIDS... GOSH.
AND I COULDN'T EVEN STOP SHINOGU FROM GOING... I'M HOPELESS!
WITH HATSUMI, TOO.
I THINK THAT POOR GIRL BLAMES HERSELF FOR WHAT HAPPENED ...
THE WHOLE THING IS MRS. TOUCHY'S FAULT, THAT EVIL WITCH!!
YEAH.
YES, INDEED!

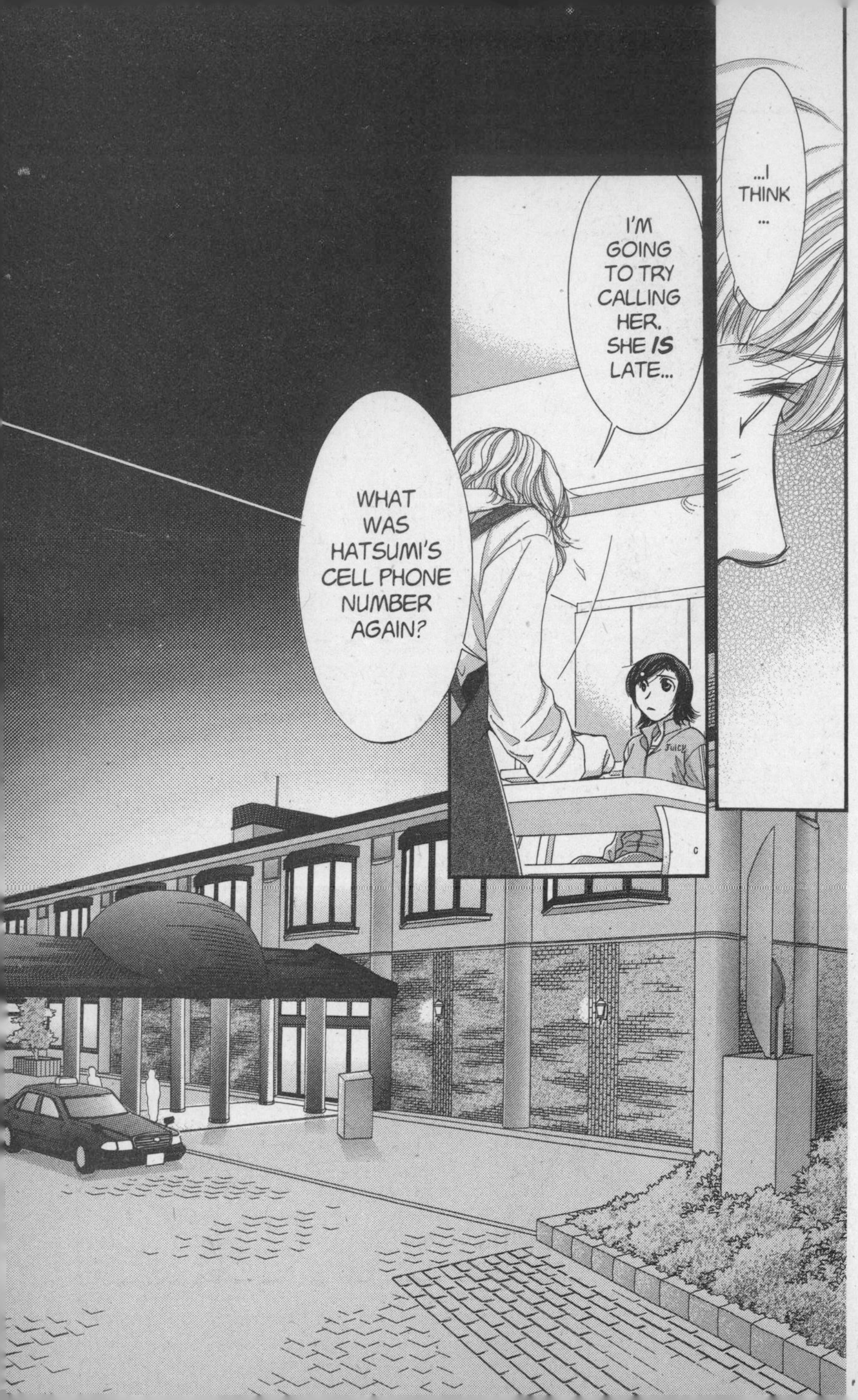
...I THINK ...
I'M GOING TO TRY CALLING HER. SHE IS LATE...
WHAT WAS HATSUMI'S CELL PHONE NUMBER AGAIN?

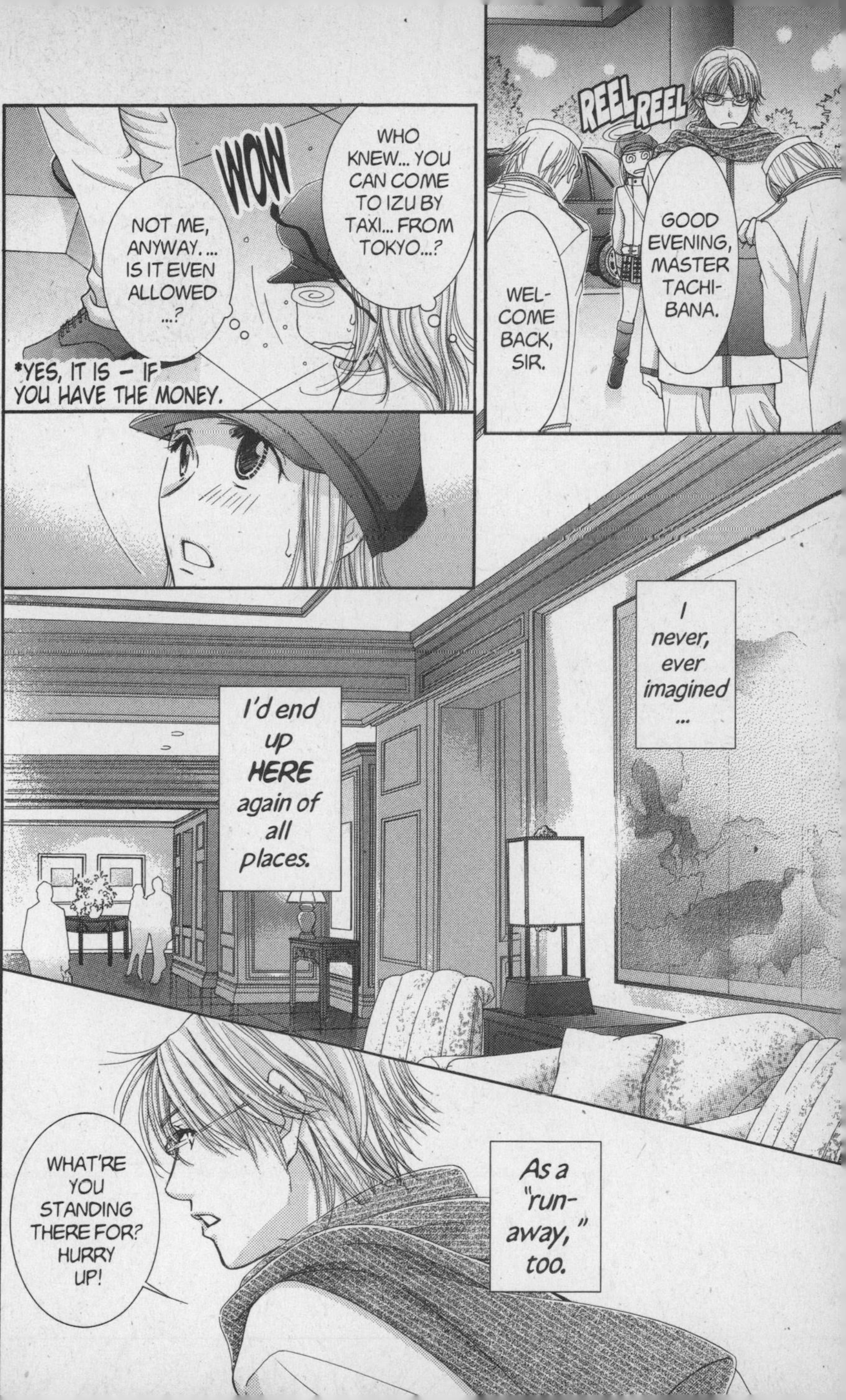
REEL REEL
GOOD EVENING, MASTER TACHIBANA.
WELCOME BACK, SIR.
WOW
WHO KNEW... YOU CAN COME TO IZU BY TAXI... FROM TOKYO...?
NOT ME, ANYWAY. ... IS IT EVEN ALLOWED ...?
*YES, IT IS — IF YOU HAVE THE MONEY.
I never, ever imagined ...
I'd end up HERE again of all places.
As a "run-away," too.
WHAT'RE YOU STANDING THERE FOR? HURRY UP!

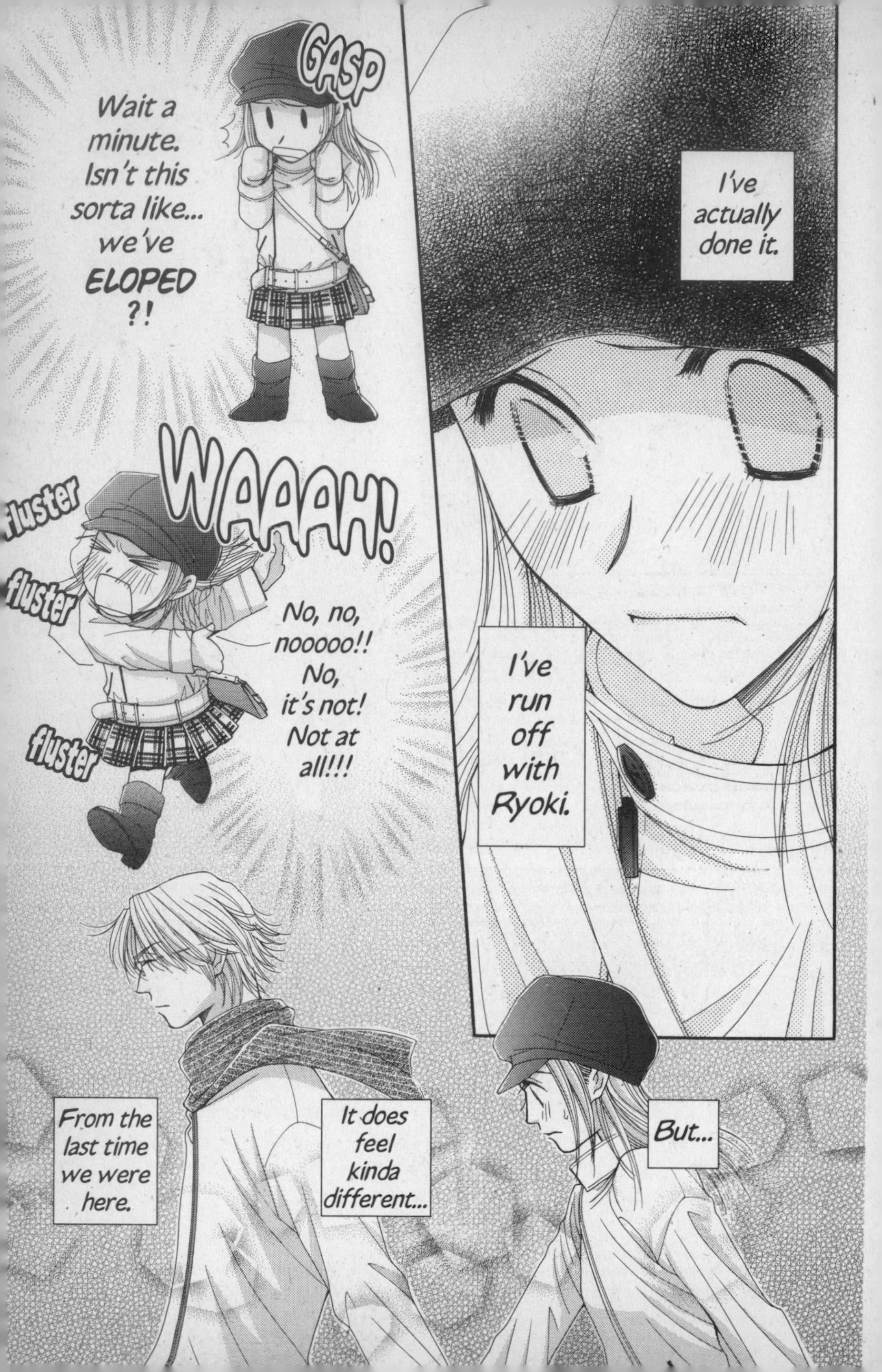
I've actually done it.
I've run off with Ryoki.
GASP
Wait a minute. Isn't this sorta like... we've ELOPED ?!
WAAAH!
fluster
fluster
fluster
No, no, nooooo!! No, it's not! Not at all!!!
But...
It does feel kinda different...
From the last time we were here.

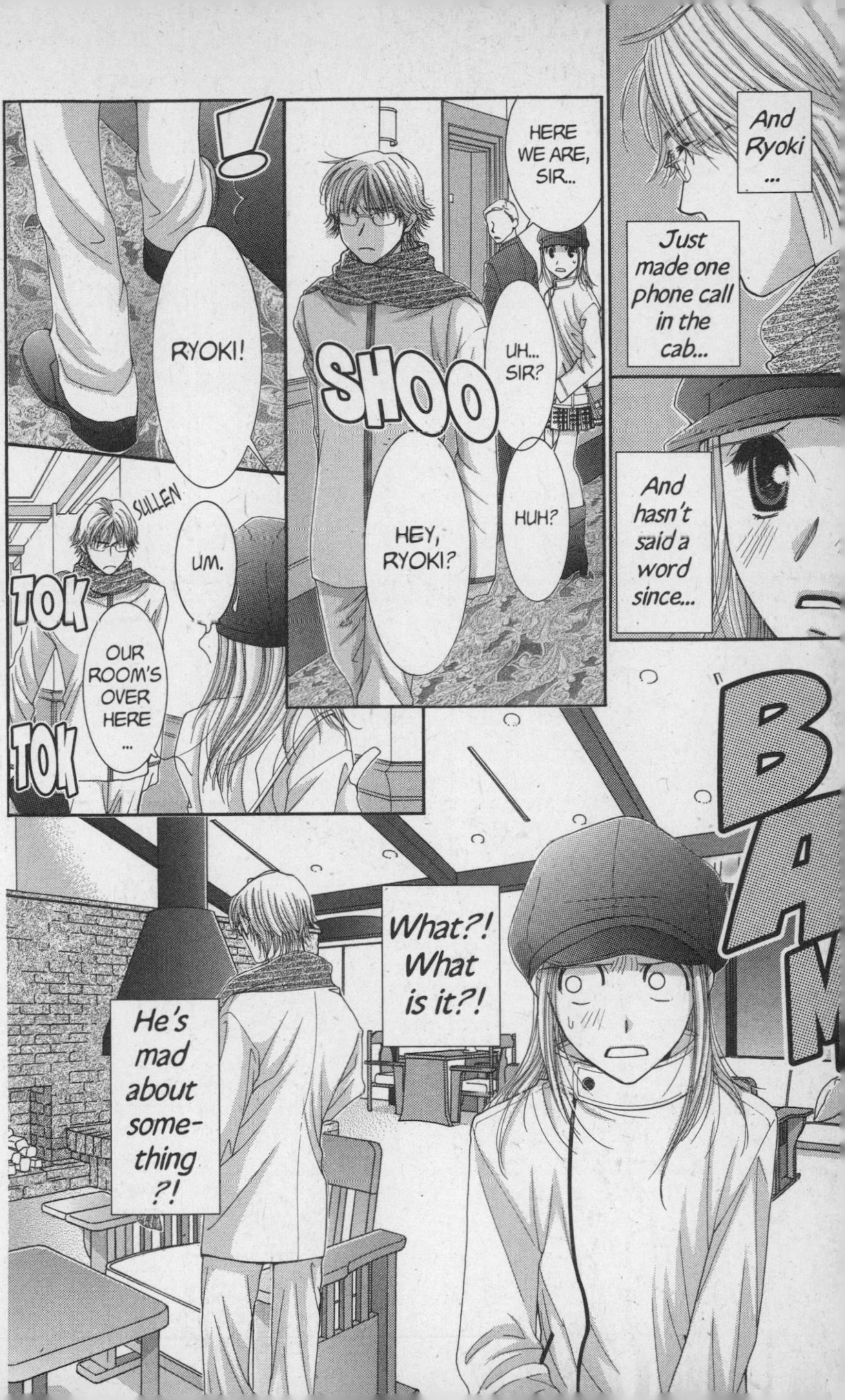
And Ryoki ...
Just made one phone call in the cab...
And hasn't said a word since...
HERE WE ARE, SIR...
UH... SIR?
SHOO
HUH?
HEY, RYOKI?
!
RYOKI!
SULLEN
UM.
TOK
OUR ROOM'S OVER HERE ...
TOK
BAM
What?! What is it?!
He's mad about something?!

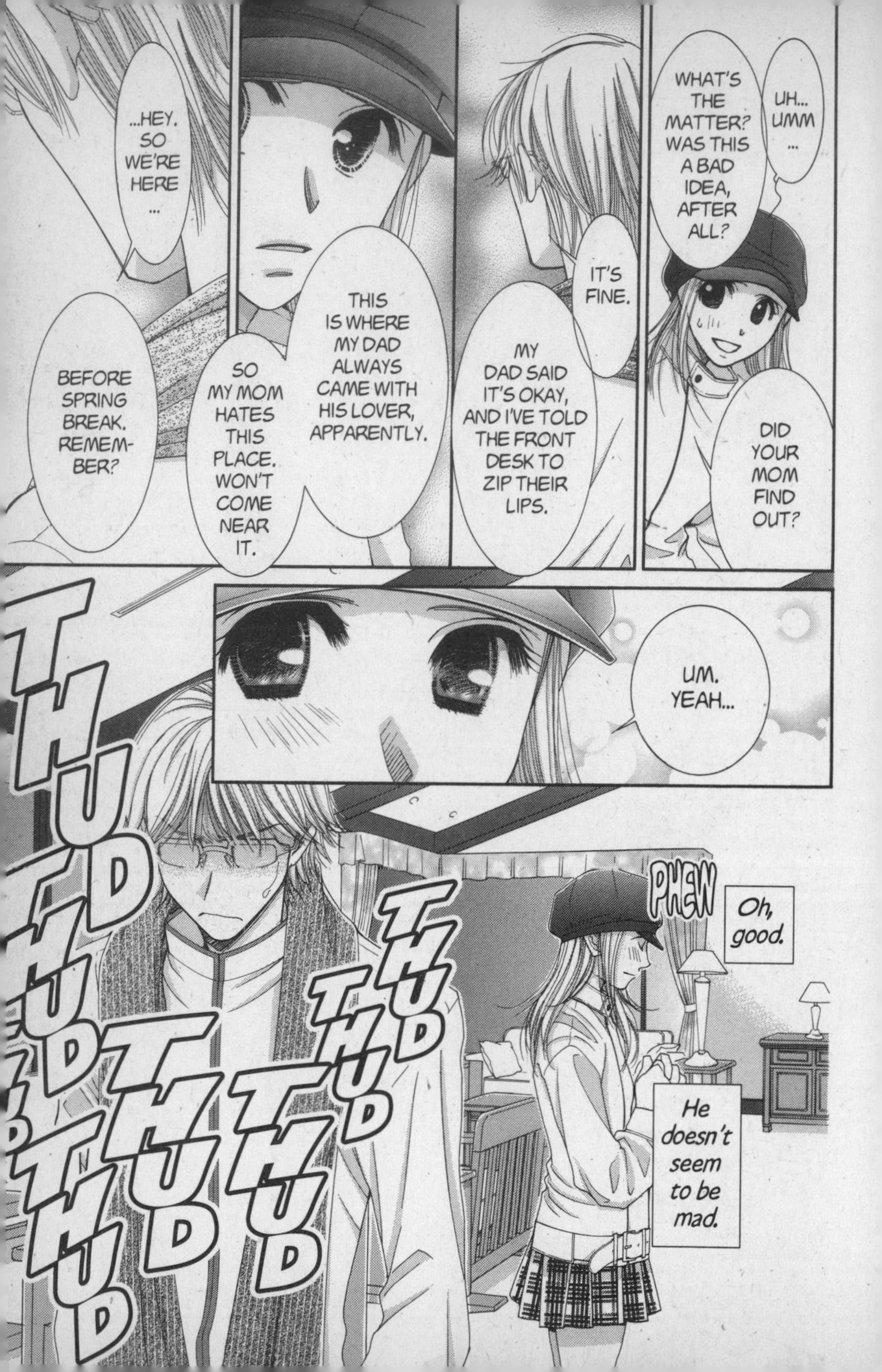
UH... UMM ...
WHAT'S THE MATTER? WAS THIS A BAD IDEA, AFTER ALL?
DID YOUR MOM FIND OUT?
IT'S FINE.
MY DAD SAID IT'S OKAY, AND I'VE TOLD THE FRONT DESK TO ZIP THEIR LIPS.
THIS IS WHERE MY DAD ALWAYS CAME WITH HIS LOVER, APPARENTLY.
SO MY MOM HATES THIS PLACE. WON'T COME NEAR IT.
...HEY. SO WE'RE HERE ...
BEFORE SPRING BREAK. REMEMBER?
UM. YEAH...
PHEW
Oh, good.
He doesn't seem to be mad.
THUD THUD THUD THUD THUD THUD THUD

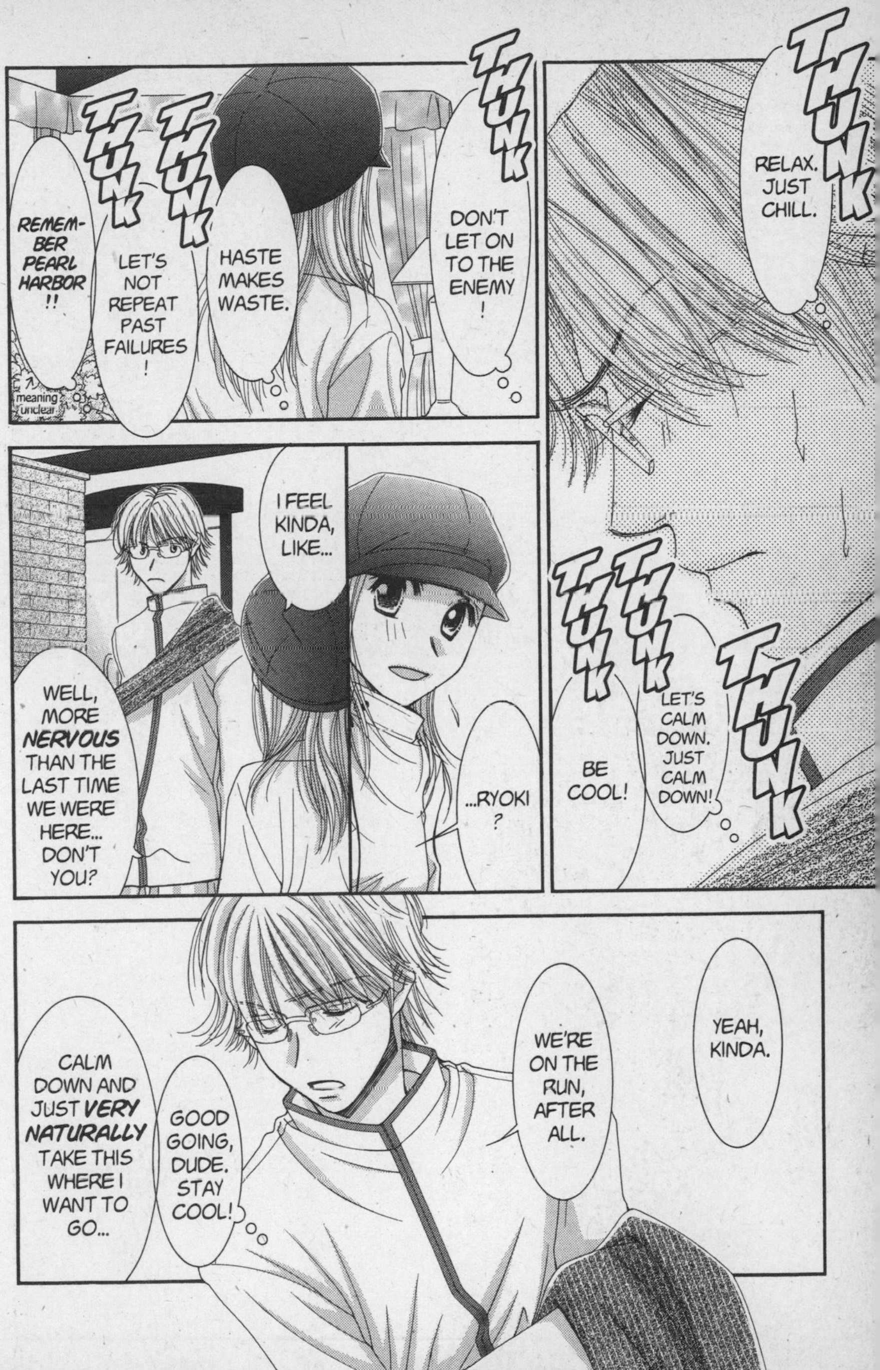
THUNK
RELAX. JUST CHILL.
THUNK
THUNK
THUNK
LET'S CALM DOWN. JUST CALM DOWN!
BE COOL!
THUNK
DON'T LET ON TO THE ENEMY!
HASTE MAKES WASTE.
THUNK
LET'S NOT REPEAT PAST FAILURES!
THUNK
REMEMBER PEARL HARBOR!!
meaning unclear
...RYOKI?
I FEEL KINDA, LIKE...
WELL, MORE NERVOUS THAN THE LAST TIME WE WERE HERE... DON'T YOU?
YEAH, KINDA.
WE'RE ON THE RUN, AFTER ALL.
GOOD GOING, DUDE. STAY COOL!
CALM DOWN AND JUST VERY NATURALLY TAKE THIS WHERE I WANT TO GO...

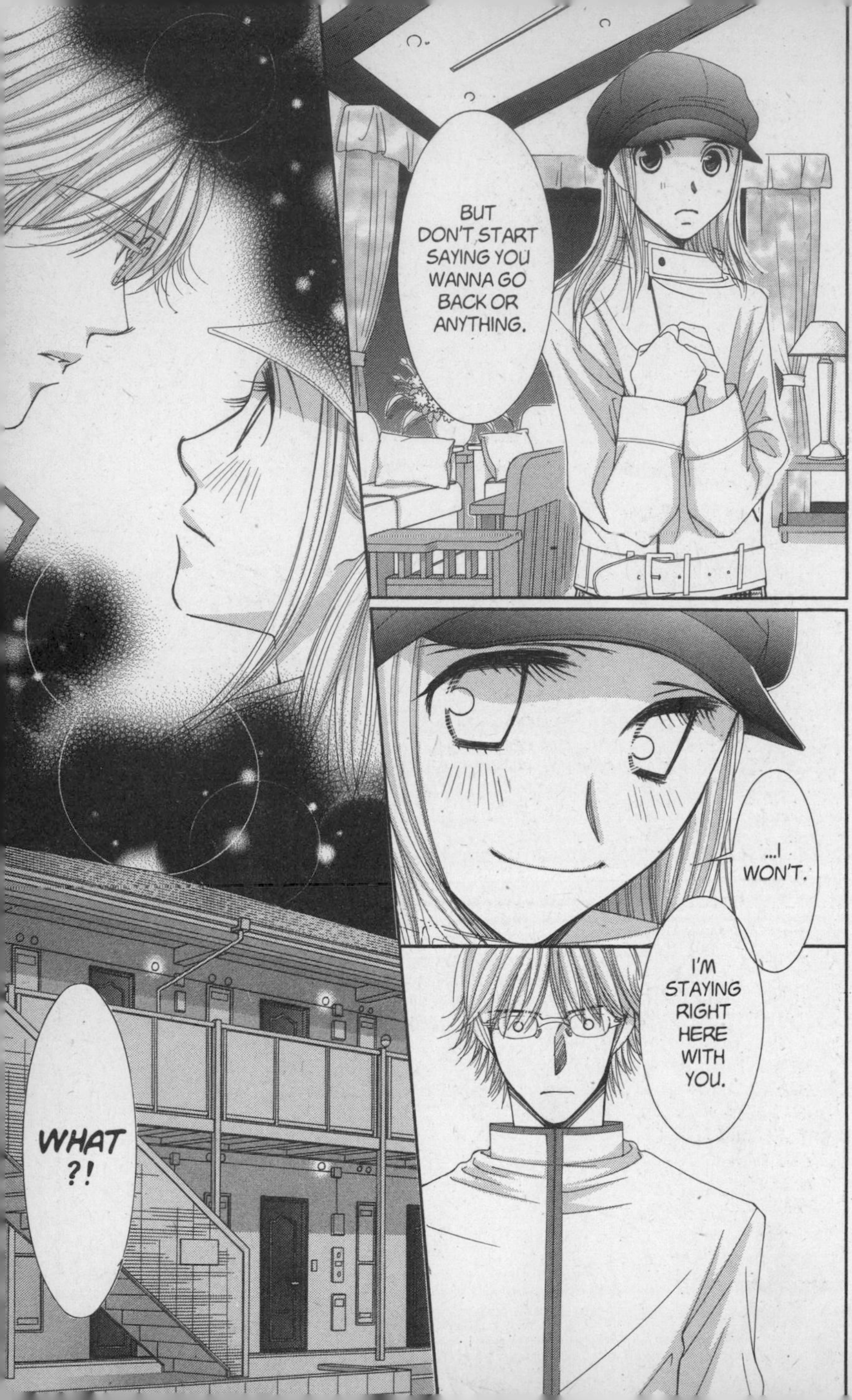
BUT DON'T START SAYING YOU WANNA GO BACK OR ANYTHING.
...I WON'T.
I'M STAYING RIGHT HERE WITH YOU.
WHAT ?!

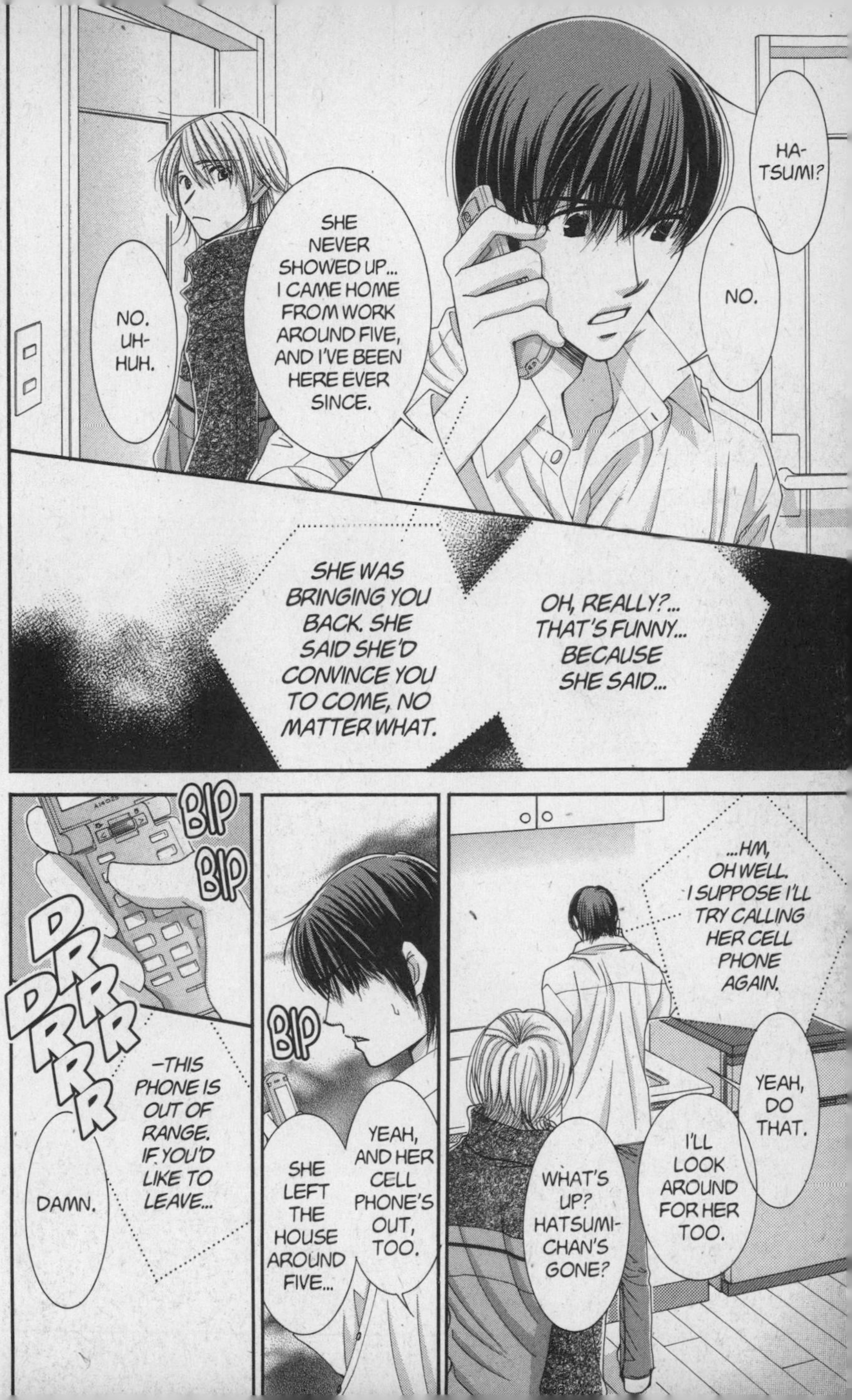
HA-TSUMI?
NO.
SHE NEVER SHOWED UP... I CAME HOME FROM WORK AROUND FIVE, AND I'VE BEEN HERE EVER SINCE.
NO. UH-HUH.
OH, REALLY?... THAT'S FUNNY... BECAUSE SHE SAID...
SHE WAS BRINGING YOU BACK. SHE SAID SHE'D CONVINCE YOU TO COME, NO MATTER WHAT.
...HM, OH WELL. I SUPPOSE I'LL TRY CALLING HER CELL PHONE AGAIN.
YEAH, DO THAT.
I'LL LOOK AROUND FOR HER TOO.
WHAT'S UP? HATSUMI-CHAN'S GONE?
BIP
YEAH, AND HER CELL PHONE'S OUT, TOO.
SHE LEFT THE HOUSE AROUND FIVE...
BIP
BIP
DRRRR
DRRRR
—THIS PHONE IS OUT OF RANGE. IF YOU'D LIKE TO LEAVE...
DAMN.

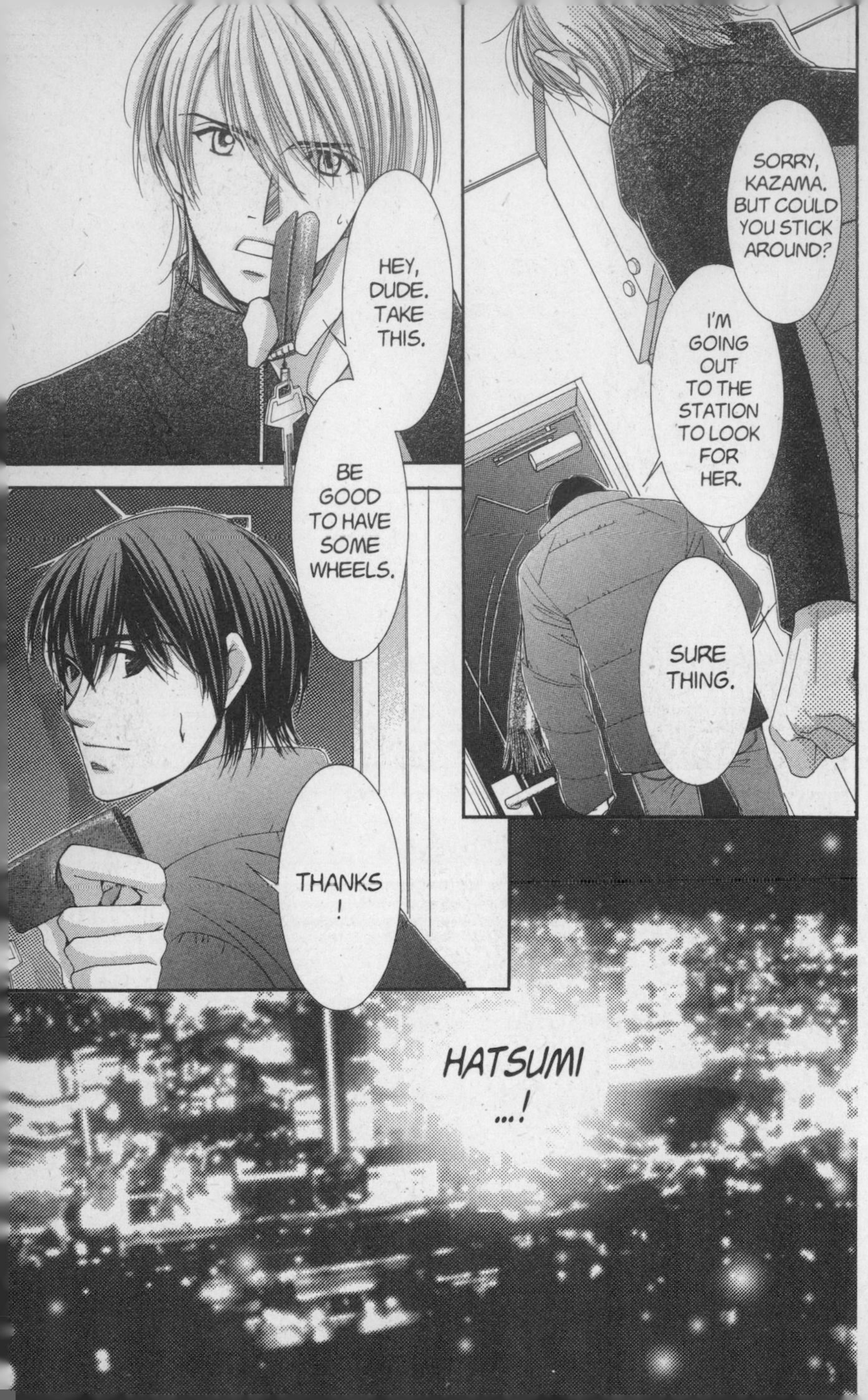
SORRY, KAZAMA. BUT COULD YOU STICK AROUND?
I'M GOING OUT TO THE STATION TO LOOK FOR HER.
SURE THING.
HEY, DUDE. TAKE THIS.
BE GOOD TO HAVE SOME WHEELS.
THANKS!
HATSUMI ...!

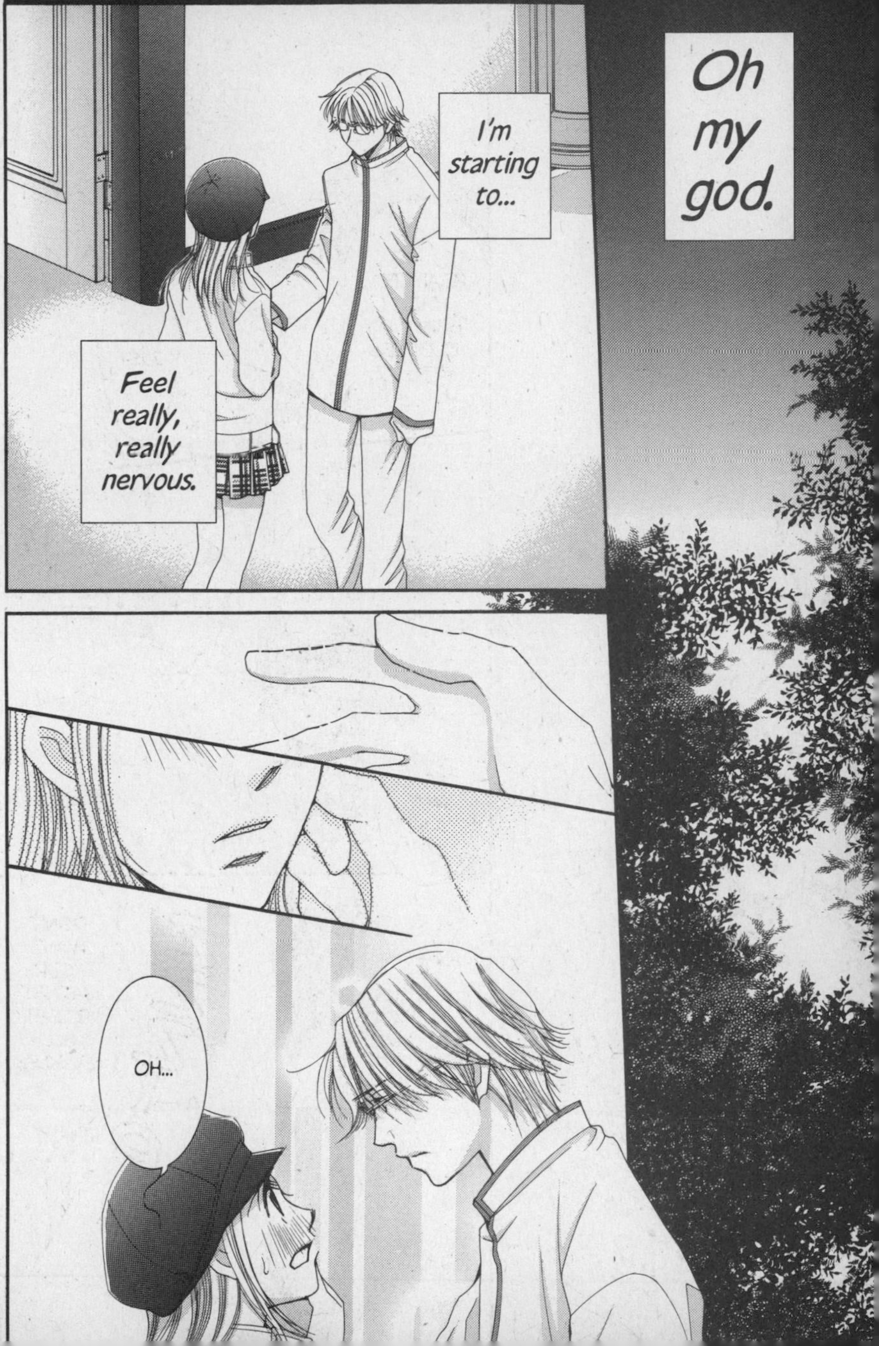
Oh my god.
I'm starting to...
Feel really, really nervous.
OH...

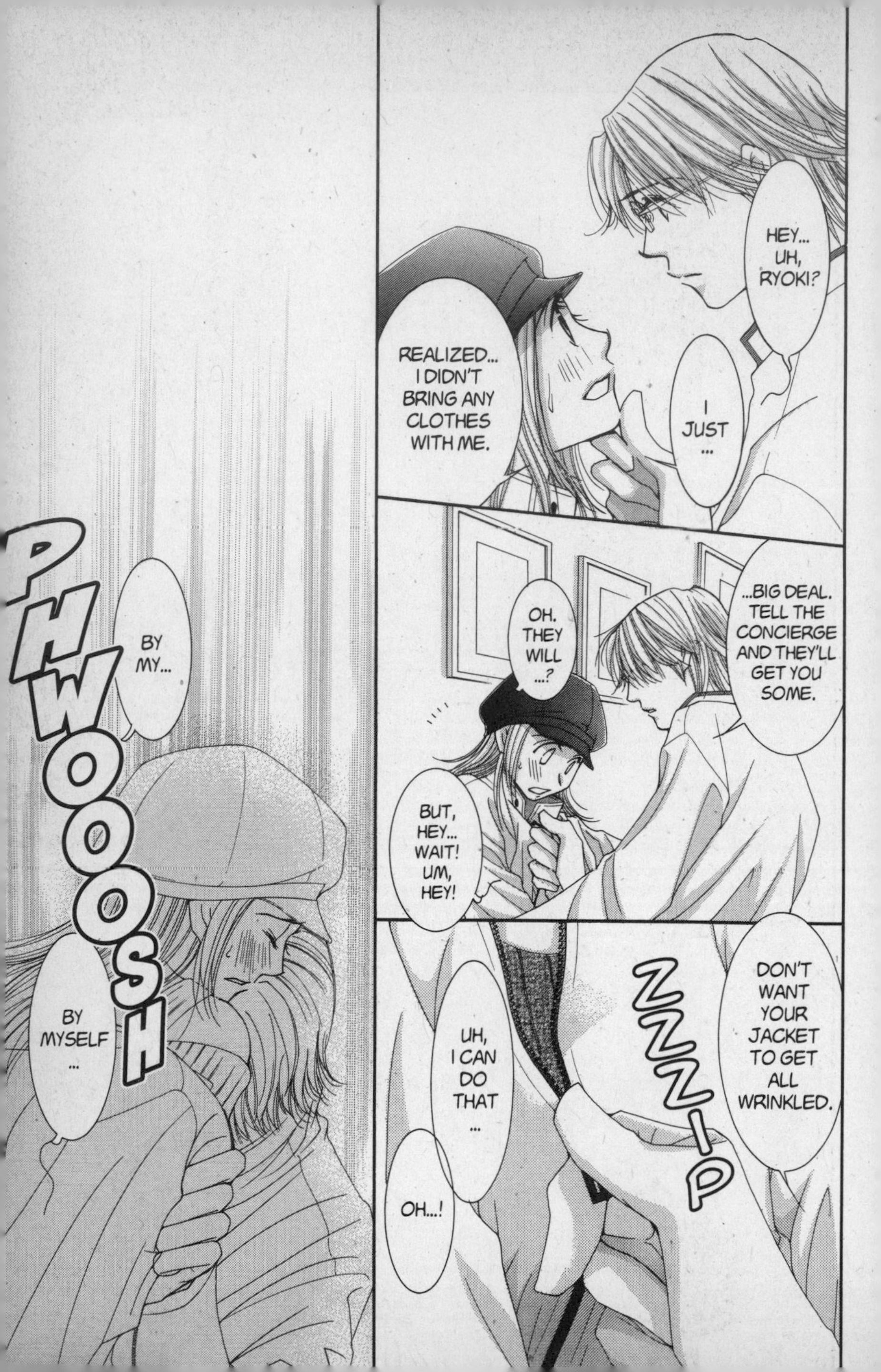
HEY... UH, RYOKI?
I JUST ...
REALIZED... I DIDN'T BRING ANY CLOTHES WITH ME.
...BIG DEAL. TELL THE CONCIERGE AND THEY'LL GET YOU SOME.
OH. THEY WILL ...?
BUT, HEY... WAIT! UM, HEY!
DON'T WANT YOUR JACKET TO GET ALL WRINKLED.
ZZZIP
UH, I CAN DO THAT ...
OH...!
PHWOOOSH
BY MY...
BY MYSELF ...

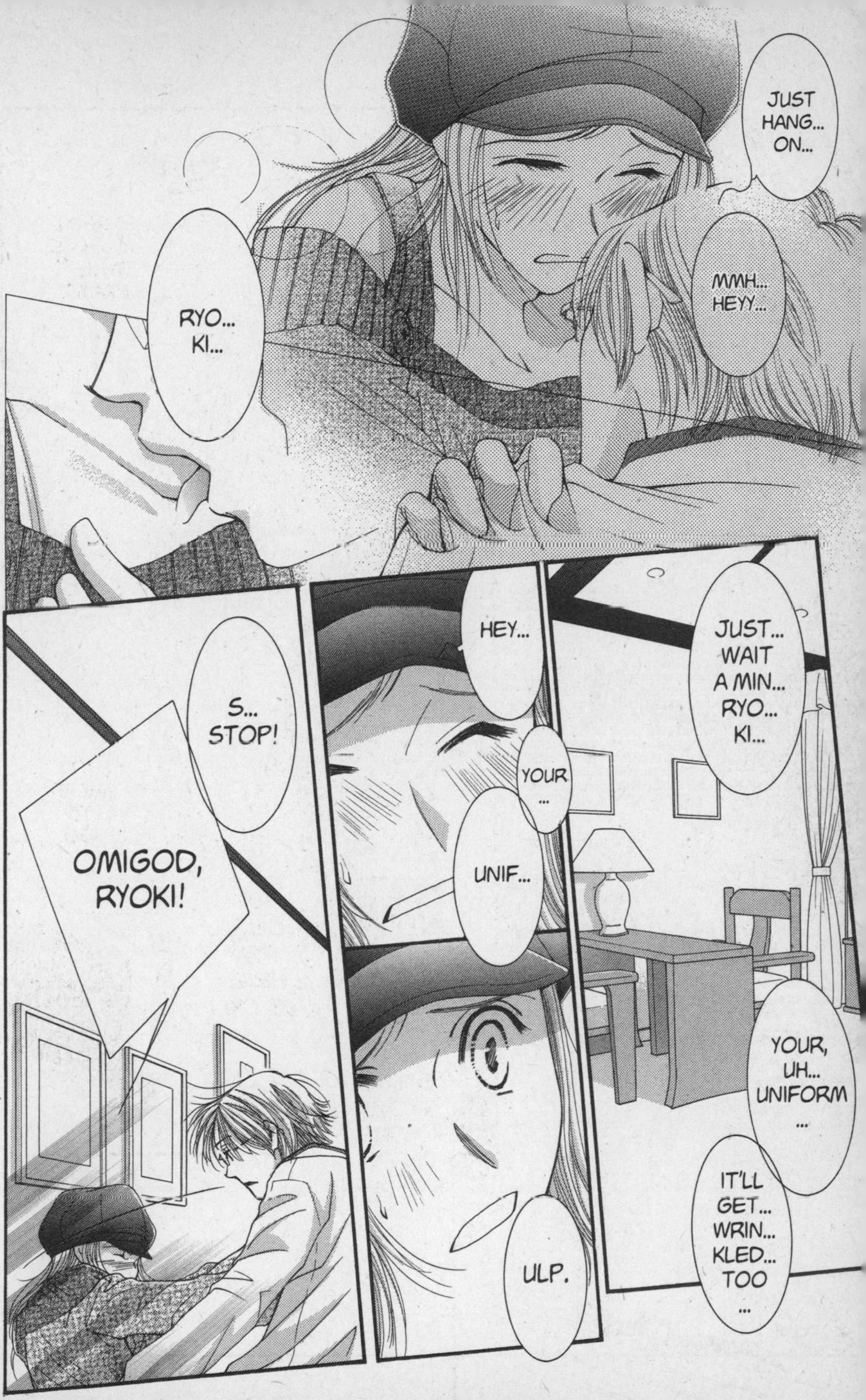
JUST HANG... ON...
MMH... HEYY...
RYO... KI...
JUST... WAIT A MIN... RYO... KI...
YOUR, UH... UNIFORM ...
IT'LL GET... WRIN... KLED... TOO ...
HEY...
YOUR ...
UNIF...
ULP.
S... STOP!
OMIGOD, RYOKI!

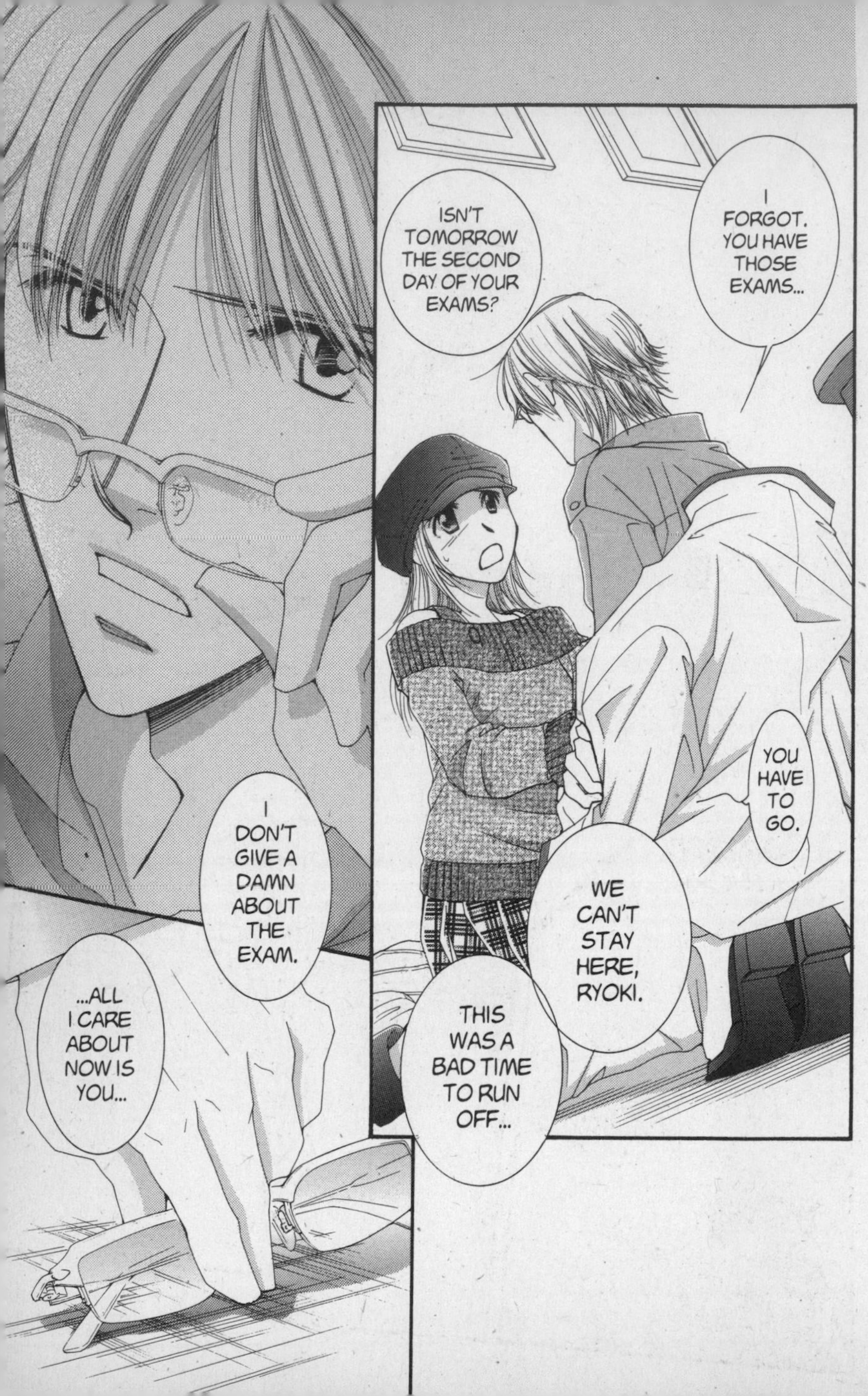
I FORGOT. YOU HAVE THOSE EXAMS...
ISN'T TOMORROW THE SECOND DAY OF YOUR EXAMS?
YOU HAVE TO GO.
WE CAN'T STAY HERE, RYOKI.
THIS WAS A BAD TIME TO RUN OFF...
I DON'T GIVE A DAMN ABOUT THE EXAM.
...ALL I CARE ABOUT NOW IS YOU...

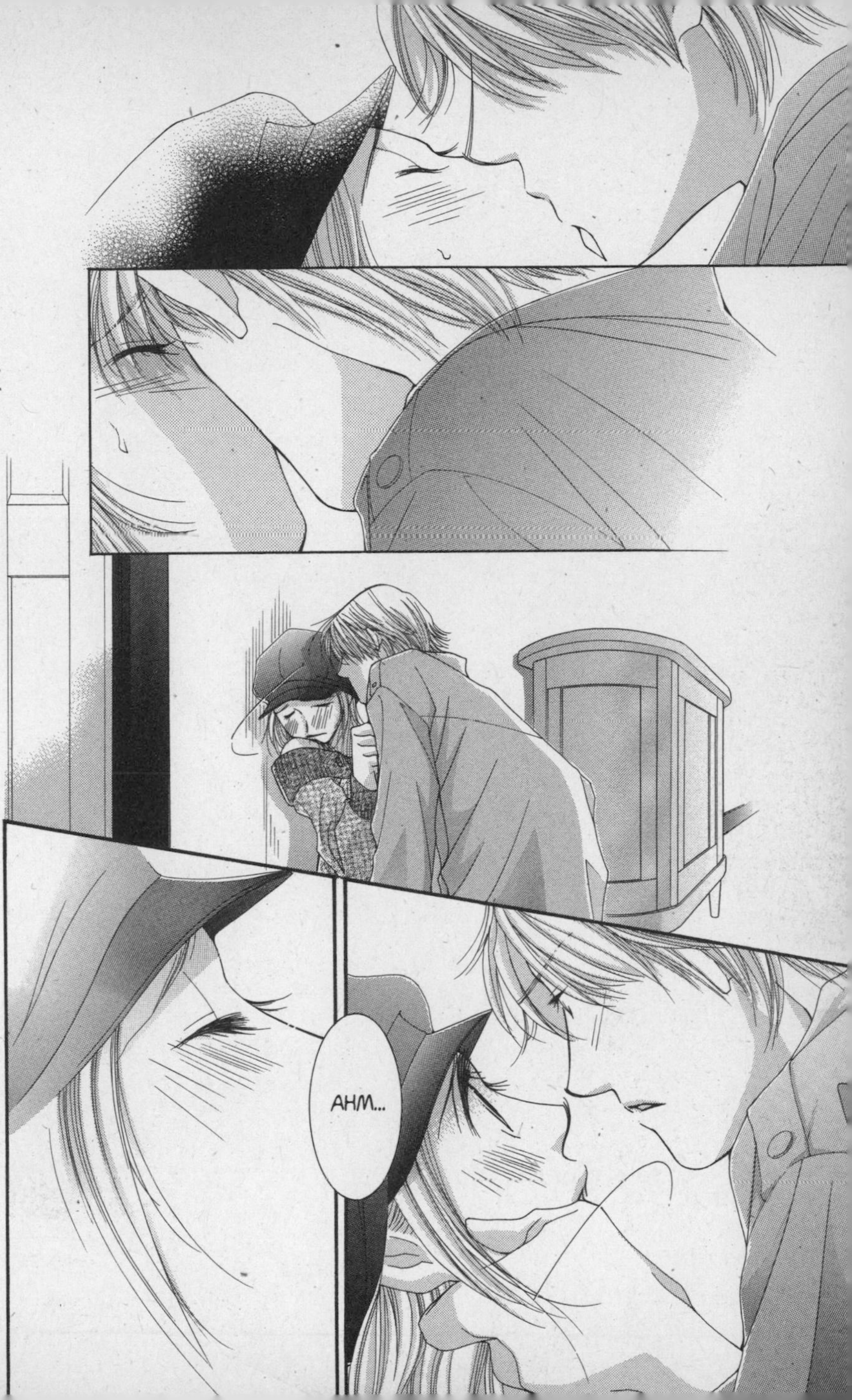
AHM...

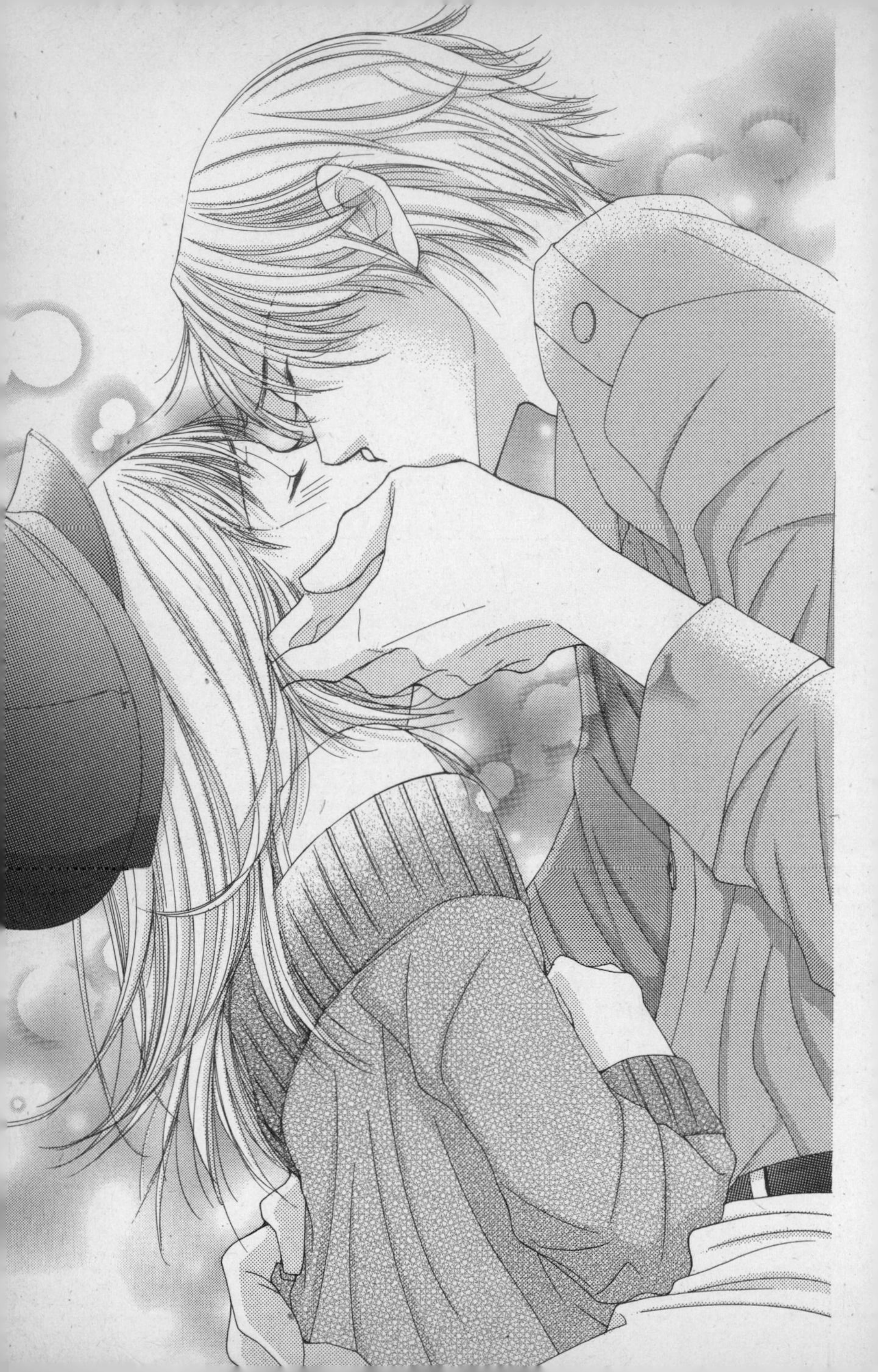

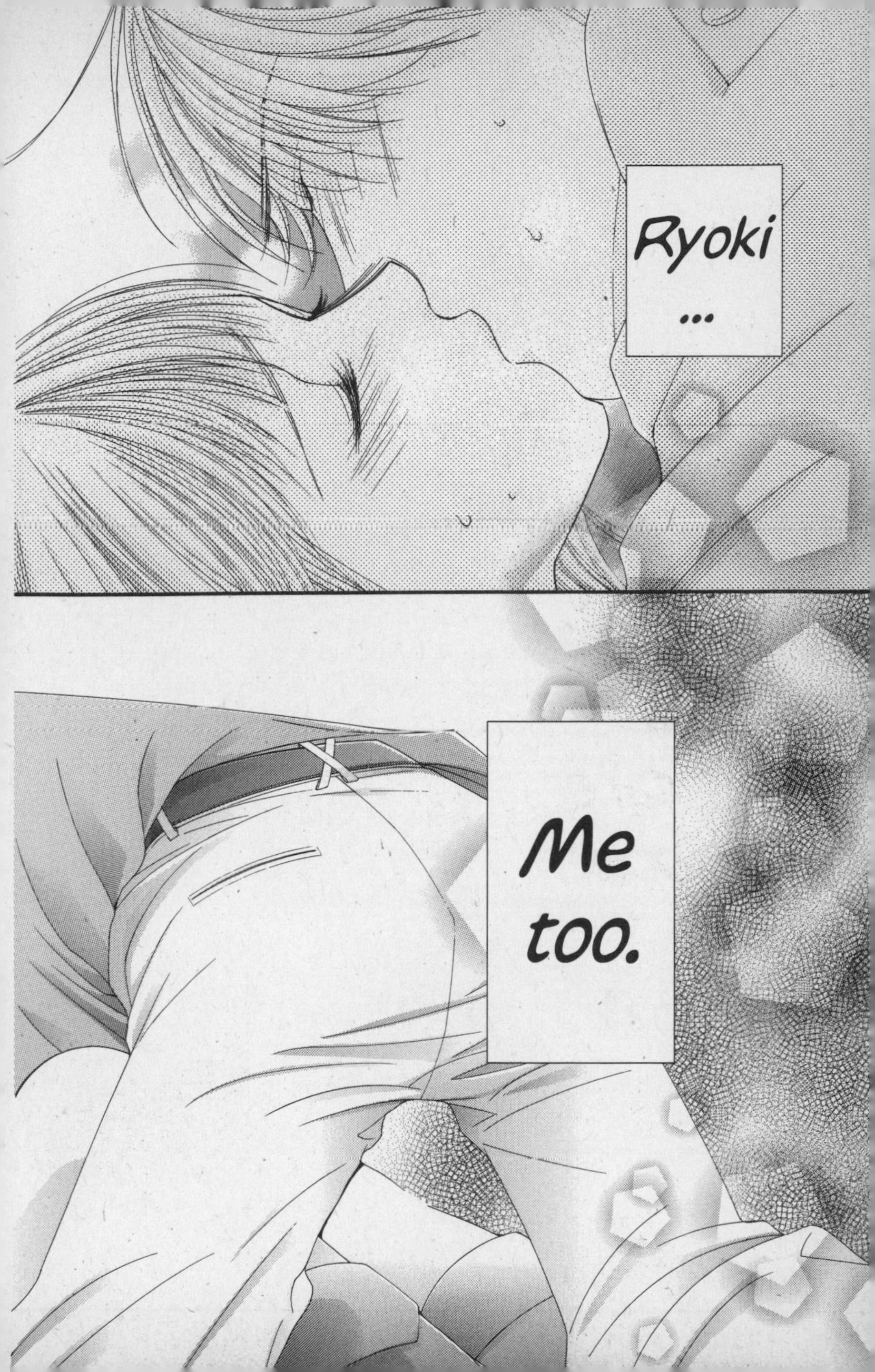
Ryoki ...
Me too.

Right now...

You're all I care about.

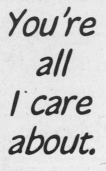

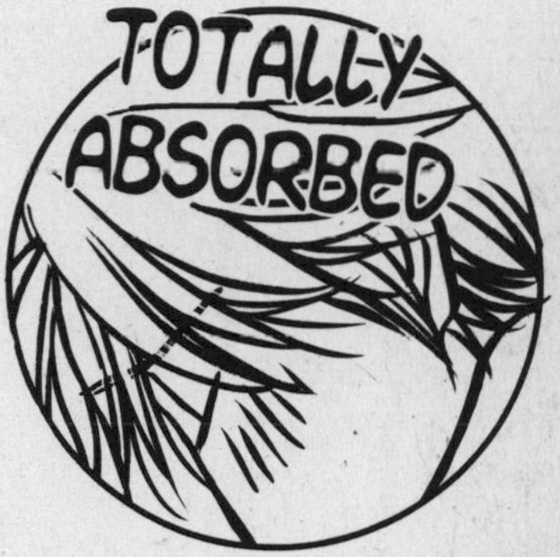
TOTALLY ABSORBED

Chapter 44

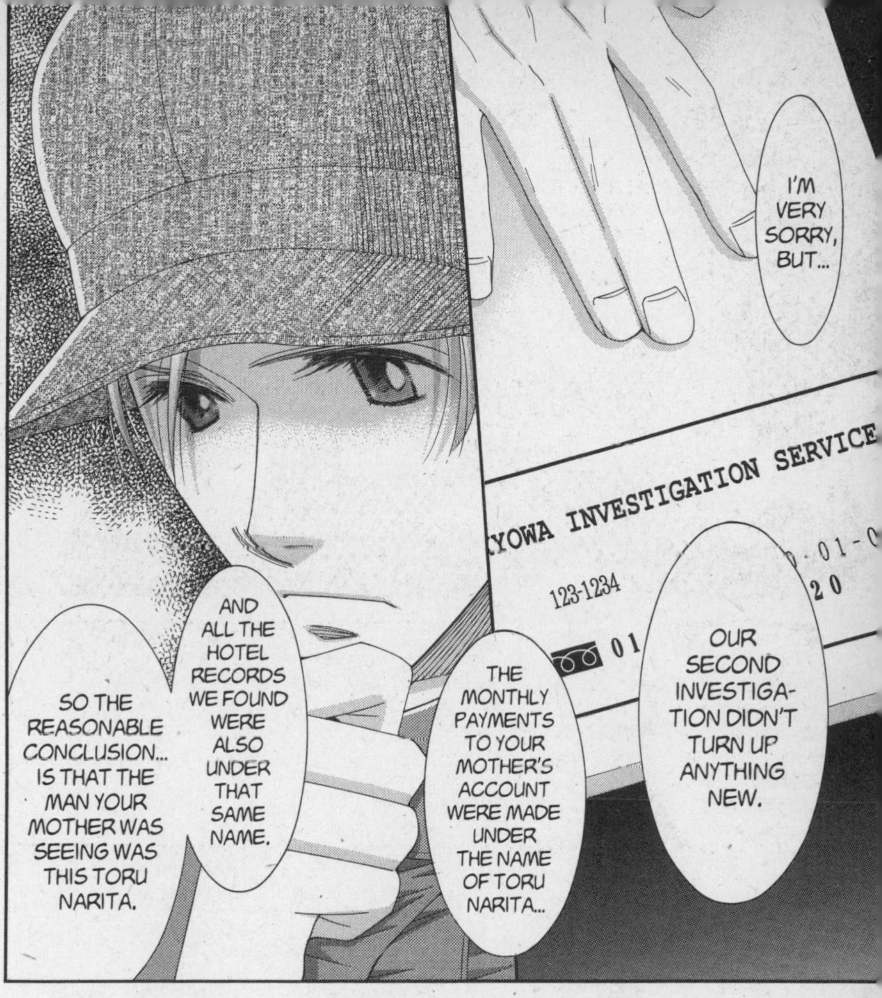
I'M VERY SORRY, BUT...
KYOWA INVESTIGATION SERVICE
123-1234
OUR SECOND INVESTIGATION DIDN'T TURN UP ANYTHING NEW.
THE MONTHLY PAYMENTS TO YOUR MOTHER'S ACCOUNT WERE MADE UNDER THE NAME OF TORU NARITA...
AND ALL THE HOTEL RECORDS WE FOUND WERE ALSO UNDER THAT SAME NAME.
SO THE REASONABLE CONCLUSION... IS THAT THE MAN YOUR MOTHER WAS SEEING WAS THIS TORU NARITA.

hot gimmick

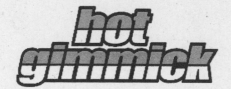

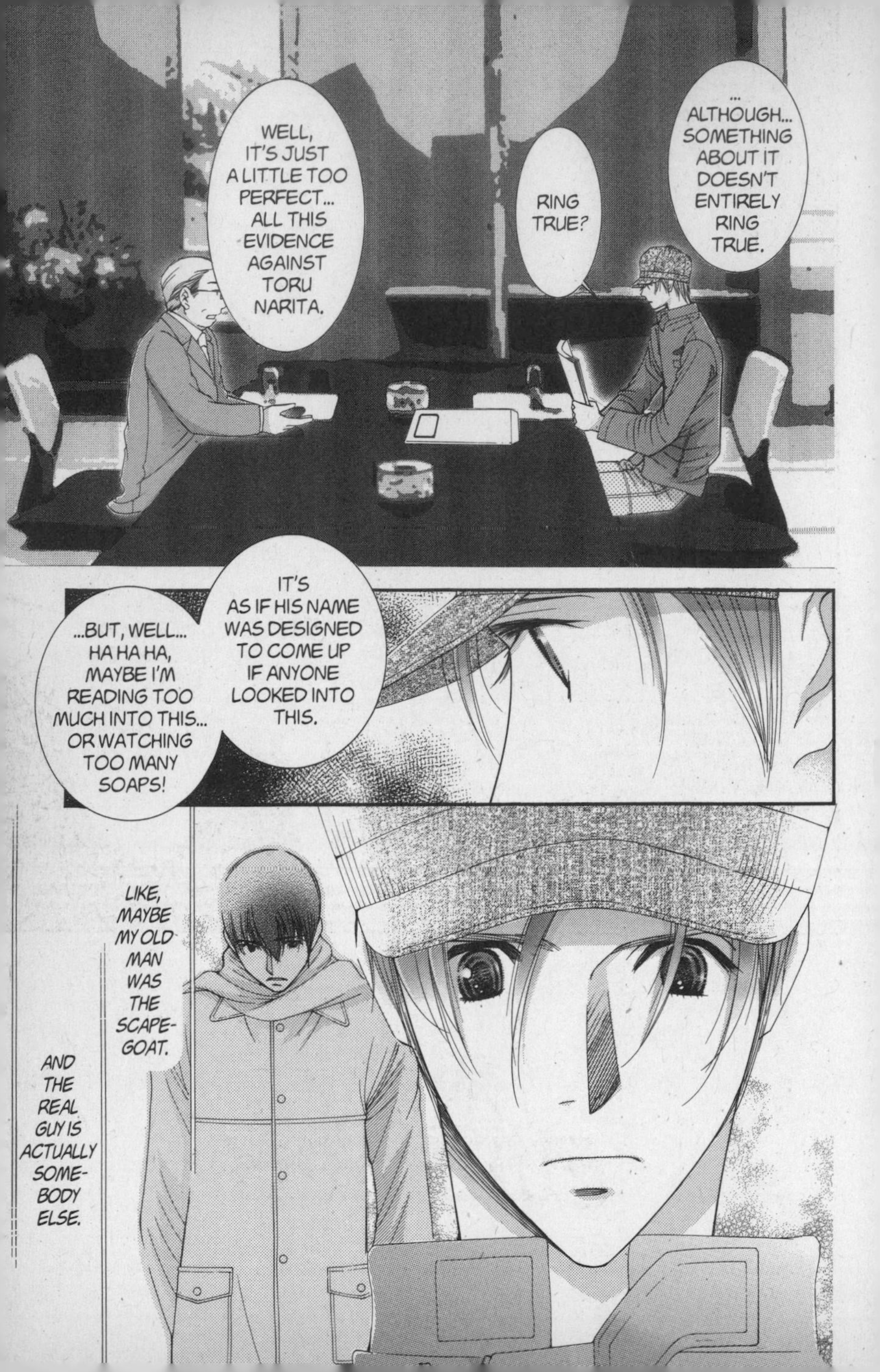
... ALTHOUGH... SOMETHING ABOUT IT DOESN'T ENTIRELY RING TRUE.
RING TRUE?
WELL, IT'S JUST A LITTLE TOO PERFECT... ALL THIS EVIDENCE AGAINST TORU NARITA.
IT'S AS IF HIS NAME WAS DESIGNED TO COME UP IF ANYONE LOOKED INTO THIS.
...BUT, WELL... HA HA HA, MAYBE I'M READING TOO MUCH INTO THIS... OR WATCHING TOO MANY SOAPS!
LIKE, MAYBE MY OLD MAN WAS THE SCAPE-GOAT.
AND THE REAL GUY IS ACTUALLY SOME-BODY ELSE.

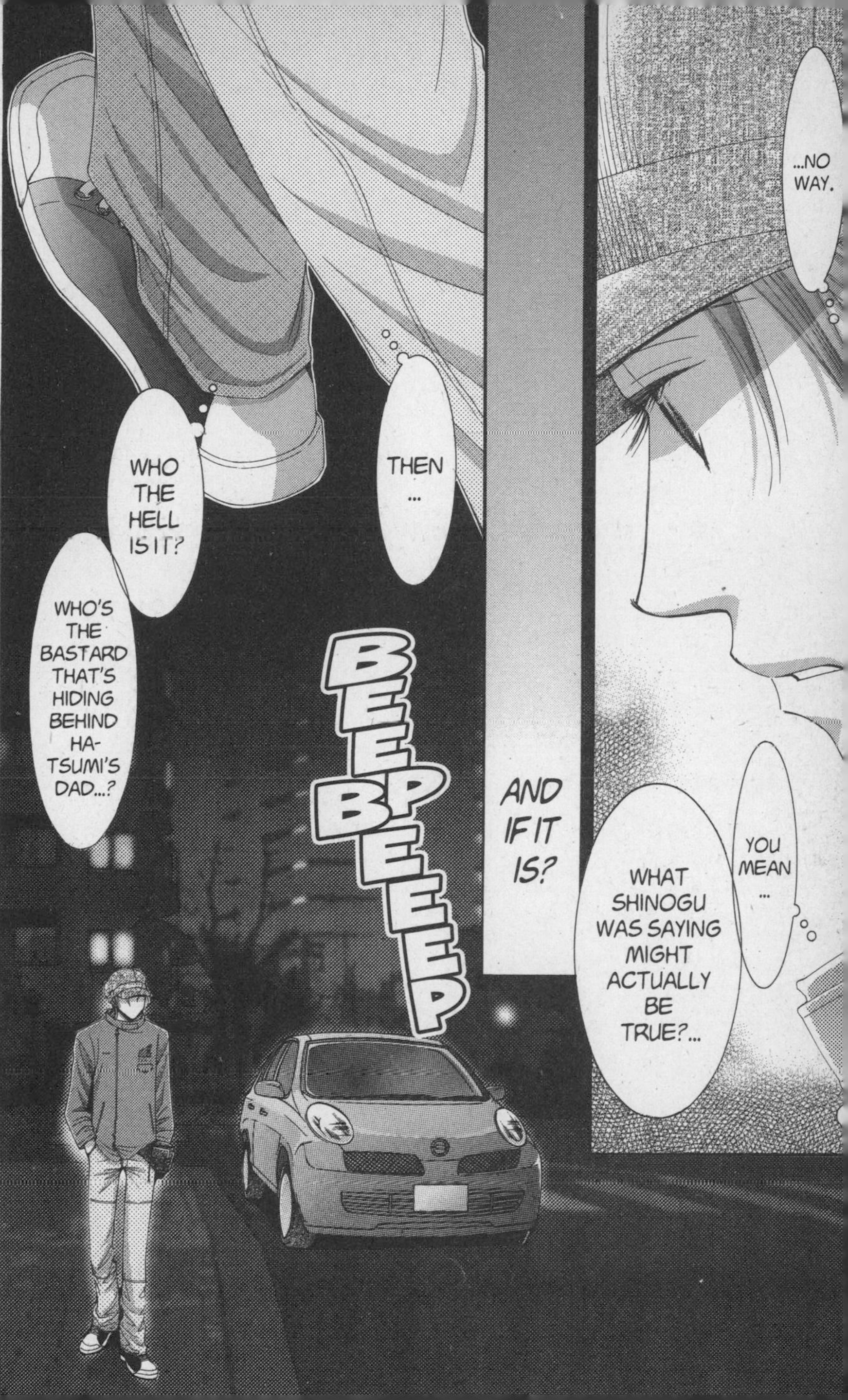
...NO WAY.
YOU MEAN ...
WHAT SHINOGU WAS SAYING MIGHT ACTUALLY BE TRUE?...
AND IF IT IS?
THEN ...
WHO THE HELL IS IT?
WHO'S THE BASTARD THAT'S HIDING BEHIND HA-TSUMI'S DAD...?
BEEP BEEEEP

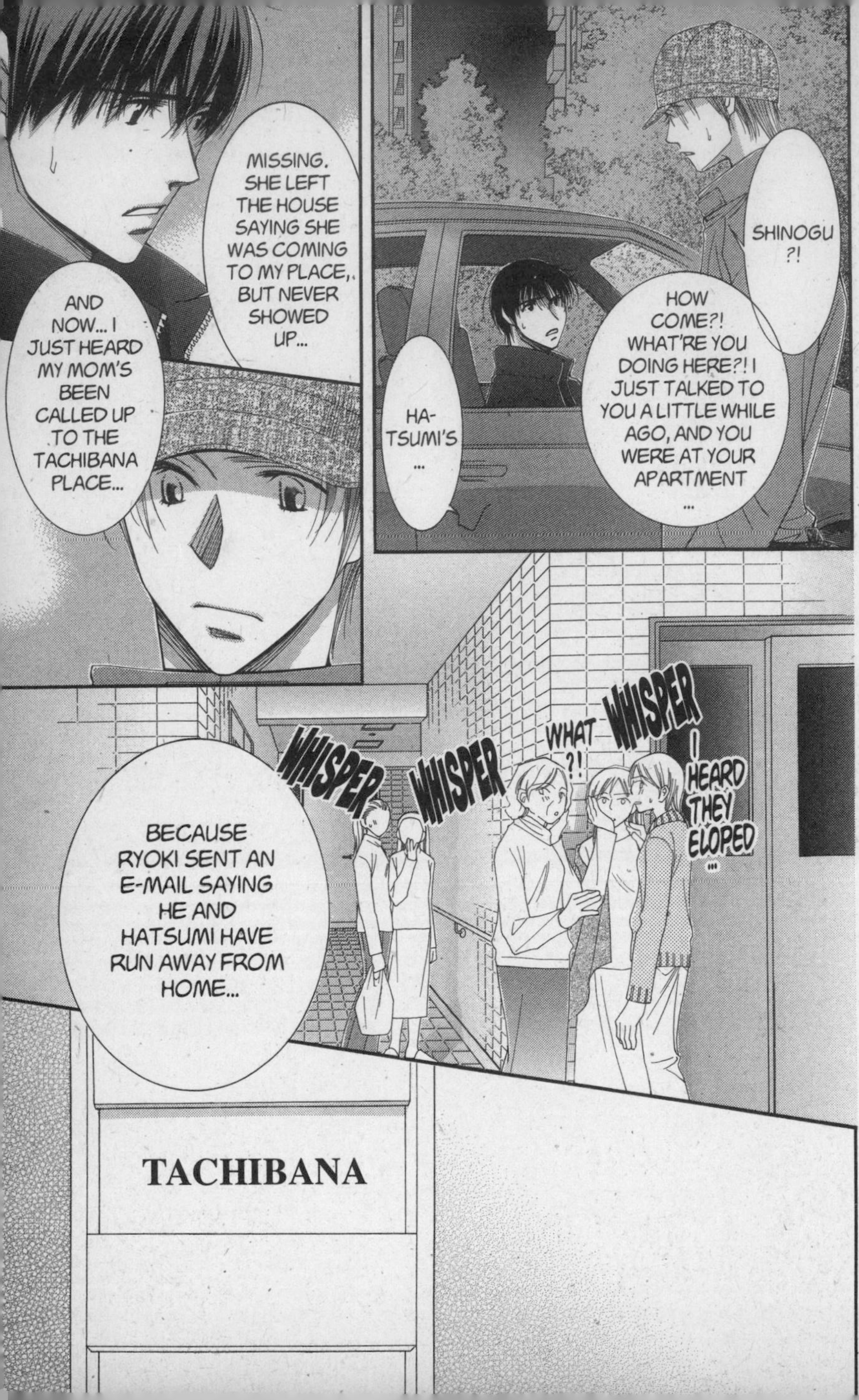
SHINOGU ?!
HOW COME?! WHAT'RE YOU DOING HERE?! I JUST TALKED TO YOU A LITTLE WHILE AGO, AND YOU WERE AT YOUR APARTMENT ...
HA-TSUMI'S ...
MISSING. SHE LEFT THE HOUSE SAYING SHE WAS COMING TO MY PLACE, BUT NEVER SHOWED UP...
AND NOW... I JUST HEARD MY MOM'S BEEN CALLED UP TO THE TACHIBANA PLACE...
I HEARD THEY ELOPED ...
WHISPER
WHAT ?!
WHISPER
WHISPER
BECAUSE RYOKI SENT AN E-MAIL SAYING HE AND HATSUMI HAVE RUN AWAY FROM HOME...
TACHIBANA

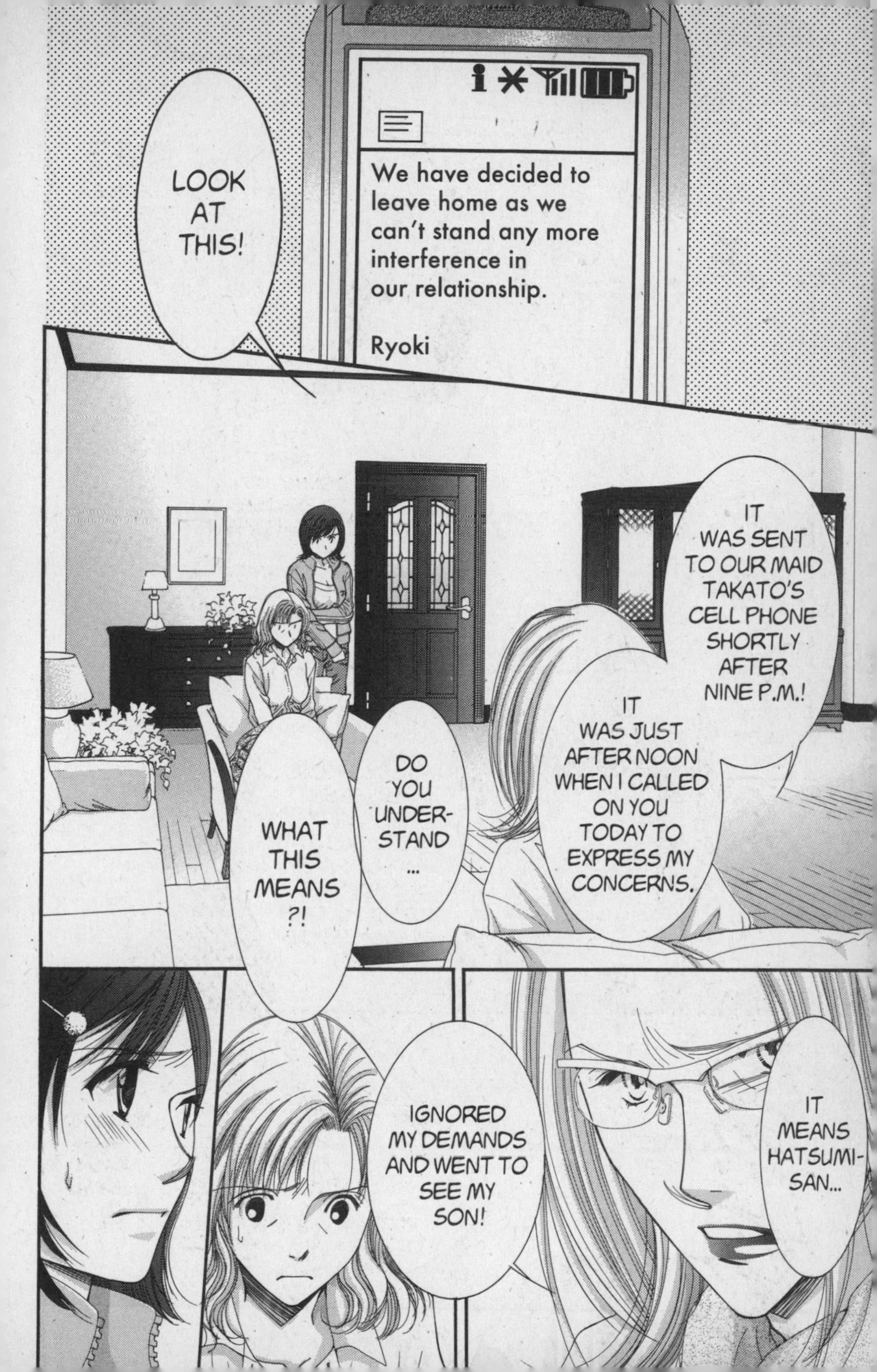
We have decided to leave home as we can't stand any more interference in our relationship.
Ryoki
LOOK AT THIS!
IT WAS SENT TO OUR MAID TAKATO'S CELL PHONE SHORTLY AFTER NINE P.M.!
IT WAS JUST AFTER NOON WHEN I CALLED ON YOU TODAY TO EXPRESS MY CONCERNS.
DO YOU UNDERSTAND...
WHAT THIS MEANS?!
IT MEANS HATSUMI-SAN...
IGNORED MY DEMANDS AND WENT TO SEE MY SON!

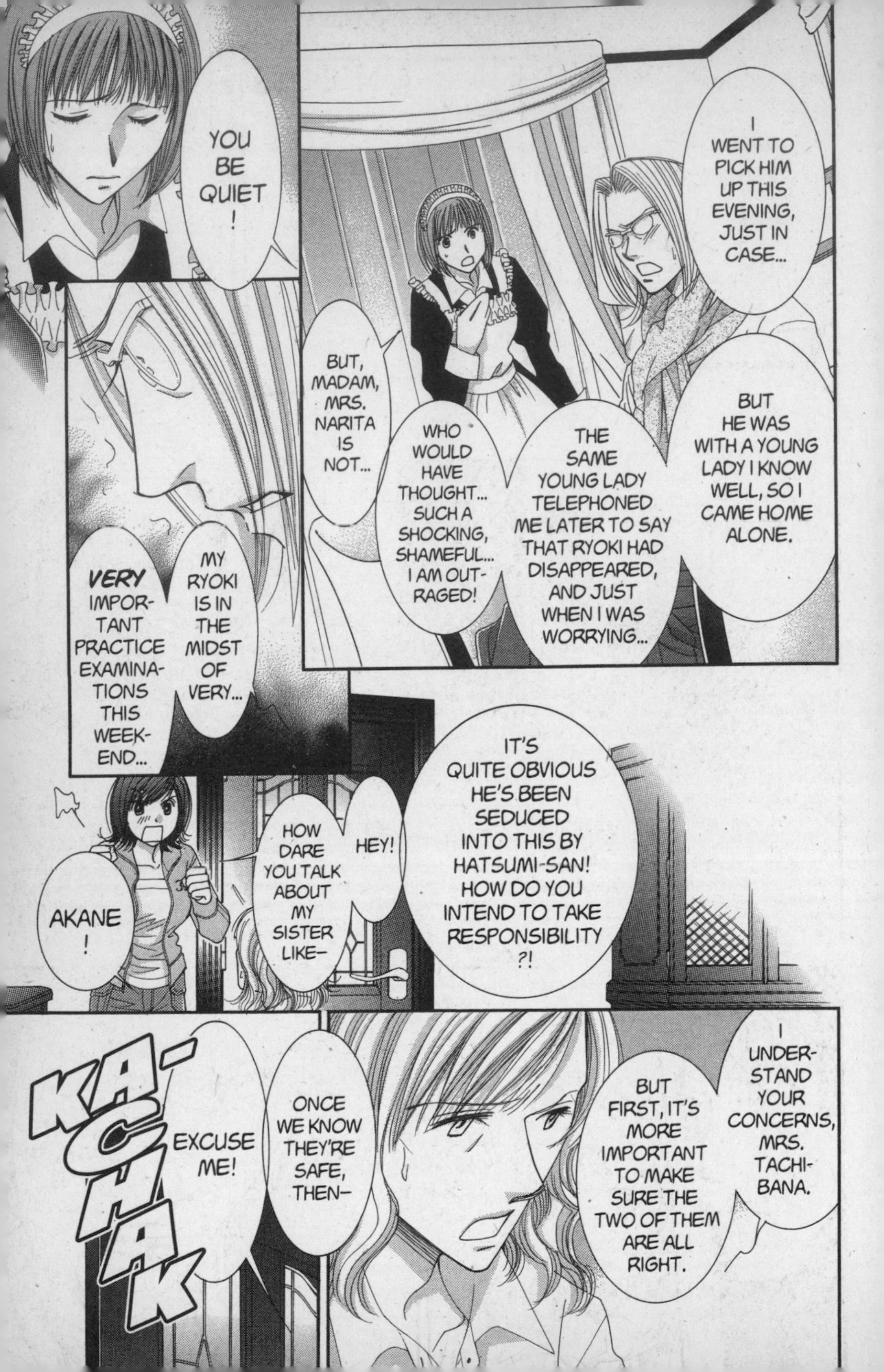
I WENT TO PICK HIM UP THIS EVENING, JUST IN CASE...
BUT HE WAS WITH A YOUNG LADY I KNOW WELL, SO I CAME HOME ALONE.
THE SAME YOUNG LADY TELEPHONED ME LATER TO SAY THAT RYOKI HAD DISAPPEARED, AND JUST WHEN I WAS WORRYING...
WHO WOULD HAVE THOUGHT... SUCH A SHOCKING, SHAMEFUL... I AM OUT-RAGED!
BUT, MADAM, MRS. NARITA IS NOT...
YOU BE QUIET!
MY RYOKI IS IN THE MIDST OF VERY...
VERY IMPORTANT PRACTICE EXAMINATIONS THIS WEEKEND...
IT'S QUITE OBVIOUS HE'S BEEN SEDUCED INTO THIS BY HATSUMI-SAN! HOW DO YOU INTEND TO TAKE RESPONSIBILITY?!
HEY!
HOW DARE YOU TALK ABOUT MY SISTER LIKE–
AKANE!
I UNDERSTAND YOUR CONCERNS, MRS. TACHIBANA.
BUT FIRST, IT'S MORE IMPORTANT TO MAKE SURE THE TWO OF THEM ARE ALL RIGHT.
ONCE WE KNOW THEY'RE SAFE, THEN–
EXCUSE ME!
KA-CHAK

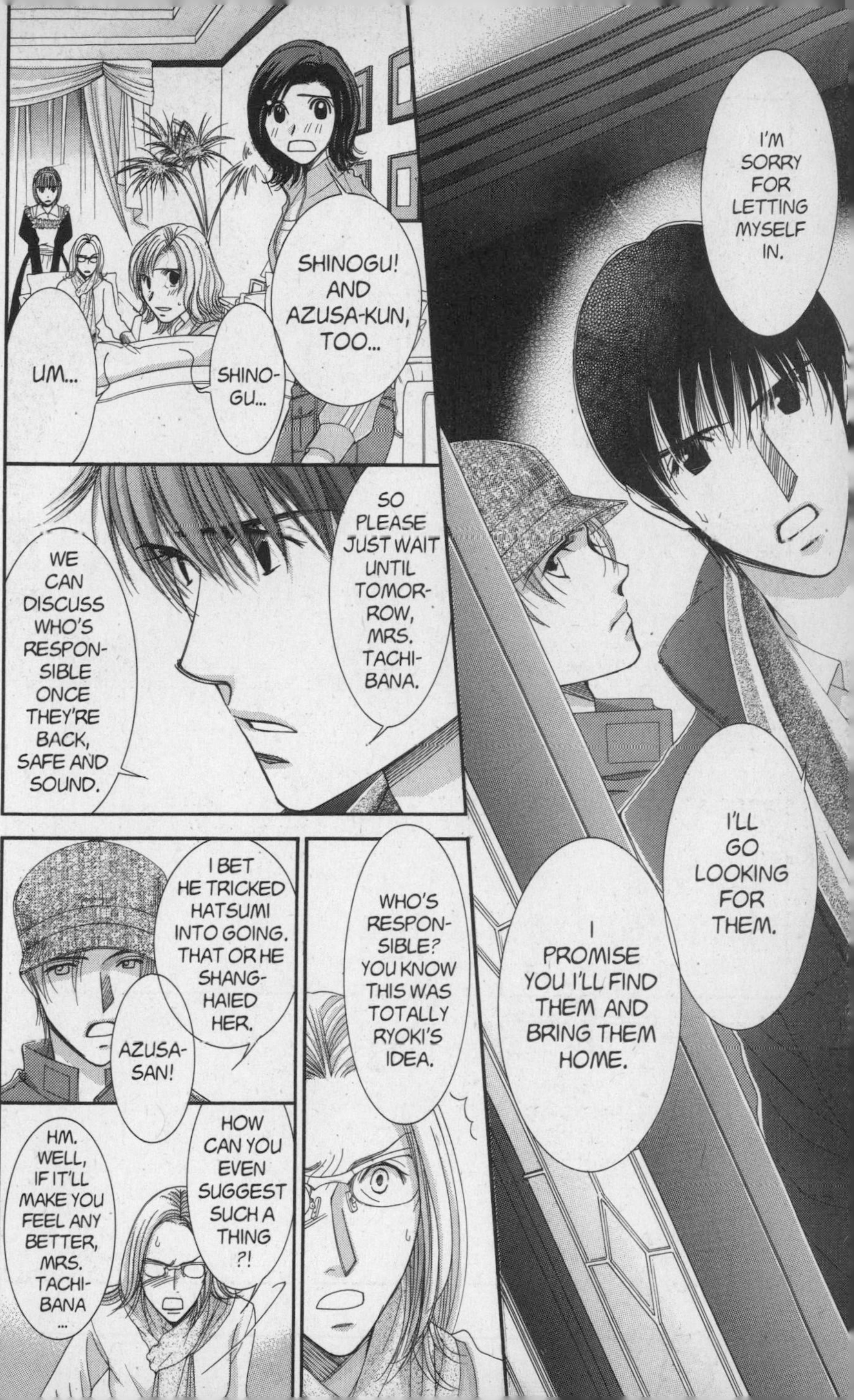
I'M SORRY FOR LETTING MYSELF IN.
I'LL GO LOOKING FOR THEM.
I PROMISE YOU I'LL FIND THEM AND BRING THEM HOME.
SHINOGU! AND AZUSA-KUN, TOO...
SHINOGU...
UM...
SO PLEASE JUST WAIT UNTIL TOMORROW, MRS. TACHIBANA.
WE CAN DISCUSS WHO'S RESPONSIBLE ONCE THEY'RE BACK, SAFE AND SOUND.
WHO'S RESPONSIBLE? YOU KNOW THIS WAS TOTALLY RYOKI'S IDEA.
I BET HE TRICKED HATSUMI INTO GOING. THAT OR HE SHANGHAIED HER.
AZUSA-SAN!
HOW CAN YOU EVEN SUGGEST SUCH A THING?!
HM. WELL, IF IT'LL MAKE YOU FEEL ANY BETTER, MRS. TACHIBANA...

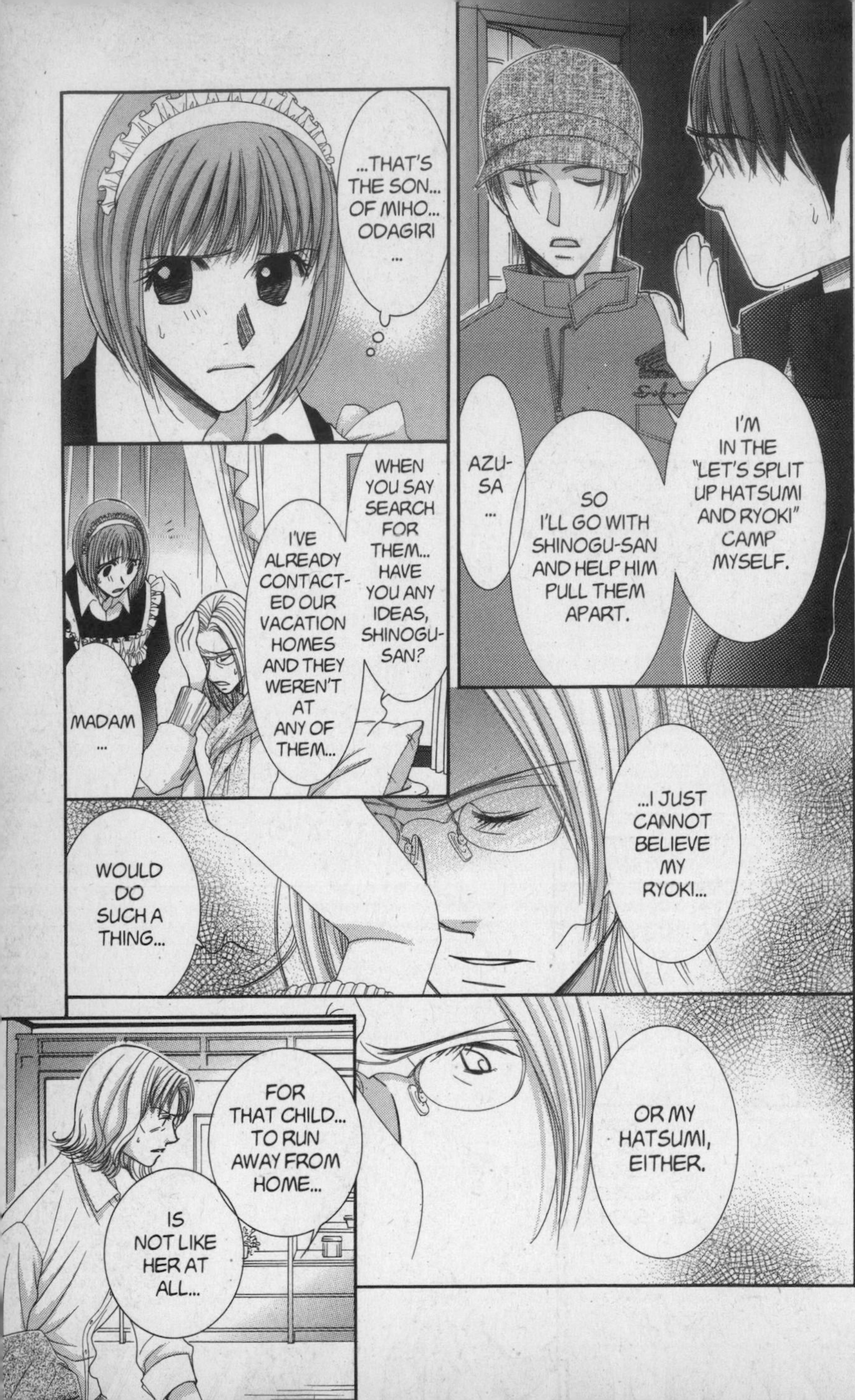
I'M IN THE "LET'S SPLIT UP HATSUMI AND RYOKI" CAMP MYSELF.
SO I'LL GO WITH SHINOGU-SAN AND HELP HIM PULL THEM APART.
AZUSA...
...THAT'S THE SON... OF MIHO... ODAGIRI...
WHEN YOU SAY SEARCH FOR THEM... HAVE YOU ANY IDEAS, SHINOGU-SAN?
I'VE ALREADY CONTACTED OUR VACATION HOMES AND THEY WEREN'T AT ANY OF THEM...
MADAM...
...I JUST CANNOT BELIEVE MY RYOKI...
WOULD DO SUCH A THING...
OR MY HATSUMI, EITHER.
FOR THAT CHILD... TO RUN AWAY FROM HOME...
IS NOT LIKE HER AT ALL...

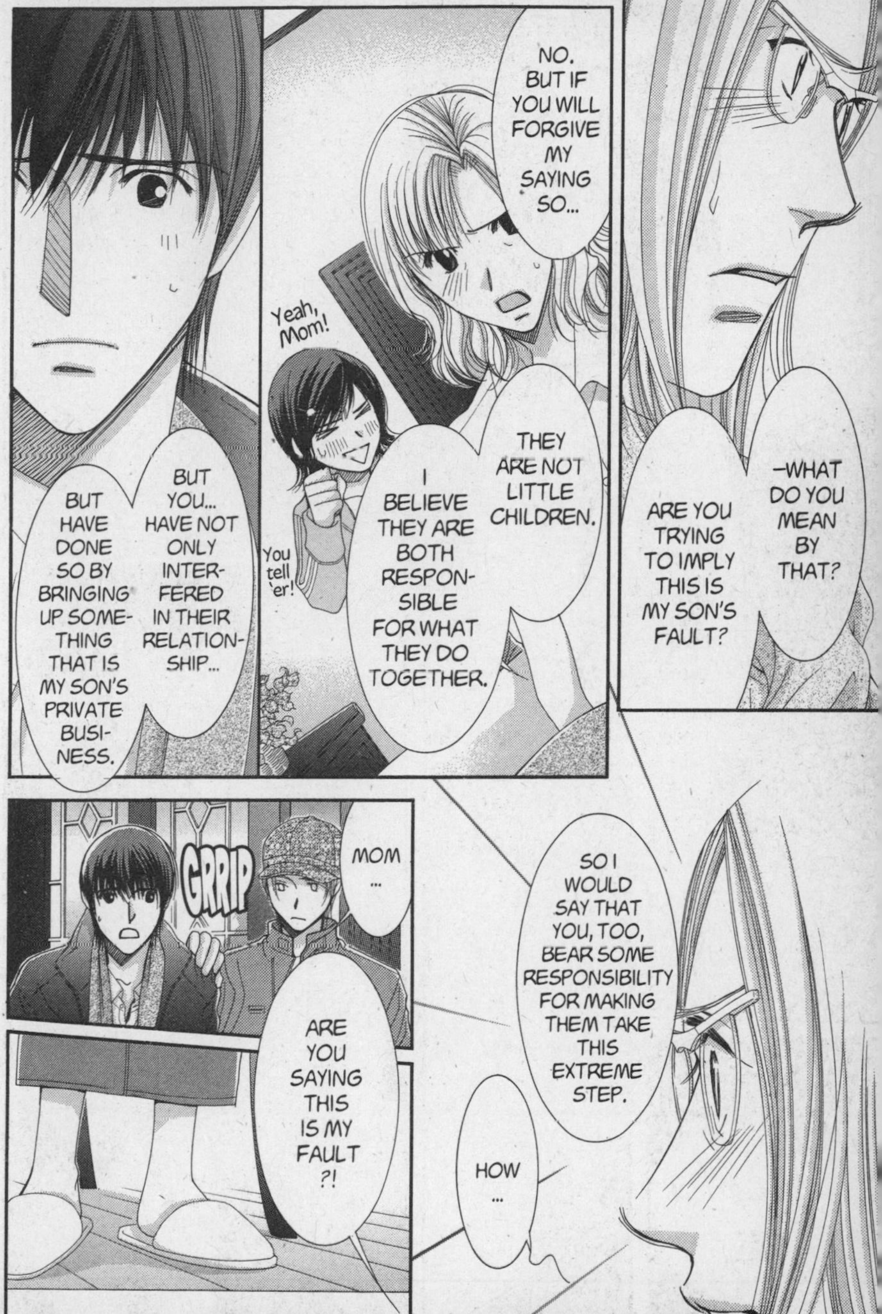
—WHAT DO YOU MEAN BY THAT?
ARE YOU TRYING TO IMPLY THIS IS MY SON'S FAULT?
NO. BUT IF YOU WILL FORGIVE MY SAYING SO...
THEY ARE NOT LITTLE CHILDREN.
I BELIEVE THEY ARE BOTH RESPONSIBLE FOR WHAT THEY DO TOGETHER.
Yeah, Mom!
You tell 'er!
BUT YOU... HAVE NOT ONLY INTERFERED IN THEIR RELATIONSHIP...
BUT HAVE DONE SO BY BRINGING UP SOMETHING THAT IS MY SON'S PRIVATE BUSINESS.
SO I WOULD SAY THAT YOU, TOO, BEAR SOME RESPONSIBILITY FOR MAKING THEM TAKE THIS EXTREME STEP.
HOW ...
GRRIP
MOM ...
ARE YOU SAYING THIS IS MY FAULT ?!

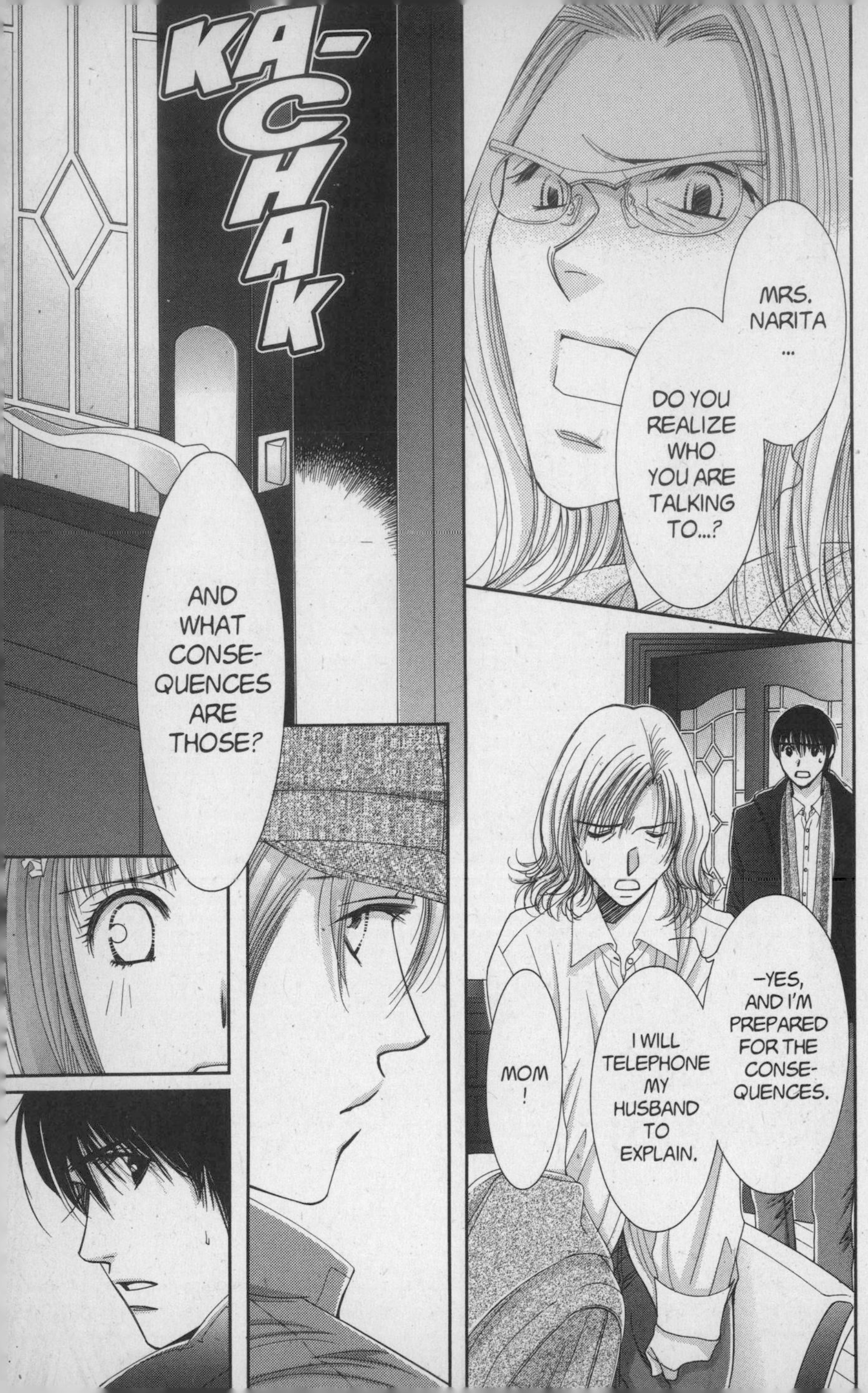
MRS. NARITA ...
DO YOU REALIZE WHO YOU ARE TALKING TO...?
KA-CHAK
AND WHAT CONSE-QUENCES ARE THOSE?
—YES, AND I'M PREPARED FOR THE CONSE-QUENCES.
I WILL TELEPHONE MY HUSBAND TO EXPLAIN.
MOM!

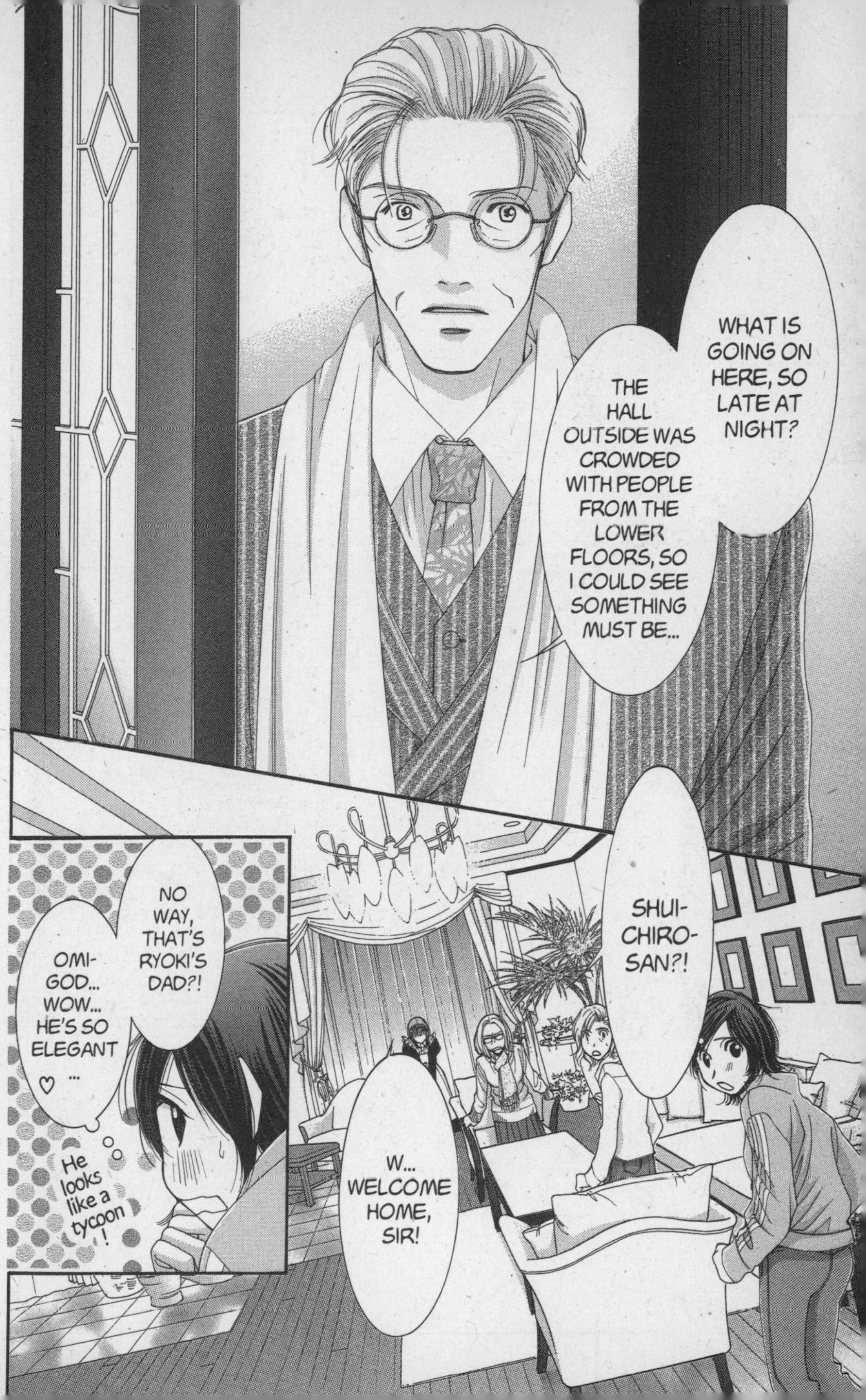
WHAT IS GOING ON HERE, SO LATE AT NIGHT?
THE HALL OUTSIDE WAS CROWDED WITH PEOPLE FROM THE LOWER FLOORS, SO I COULD SEE SOMETHING MUST BE...
SHUI-CHIRO-SAN?!
W... WELCOME HOME, SIR!
NO WAY, THAT'S RYOKI'S DAD?!
OMI-GOD... WOW... HE'S SO ELEGANT ♡ ...
He looks like a tycoon!

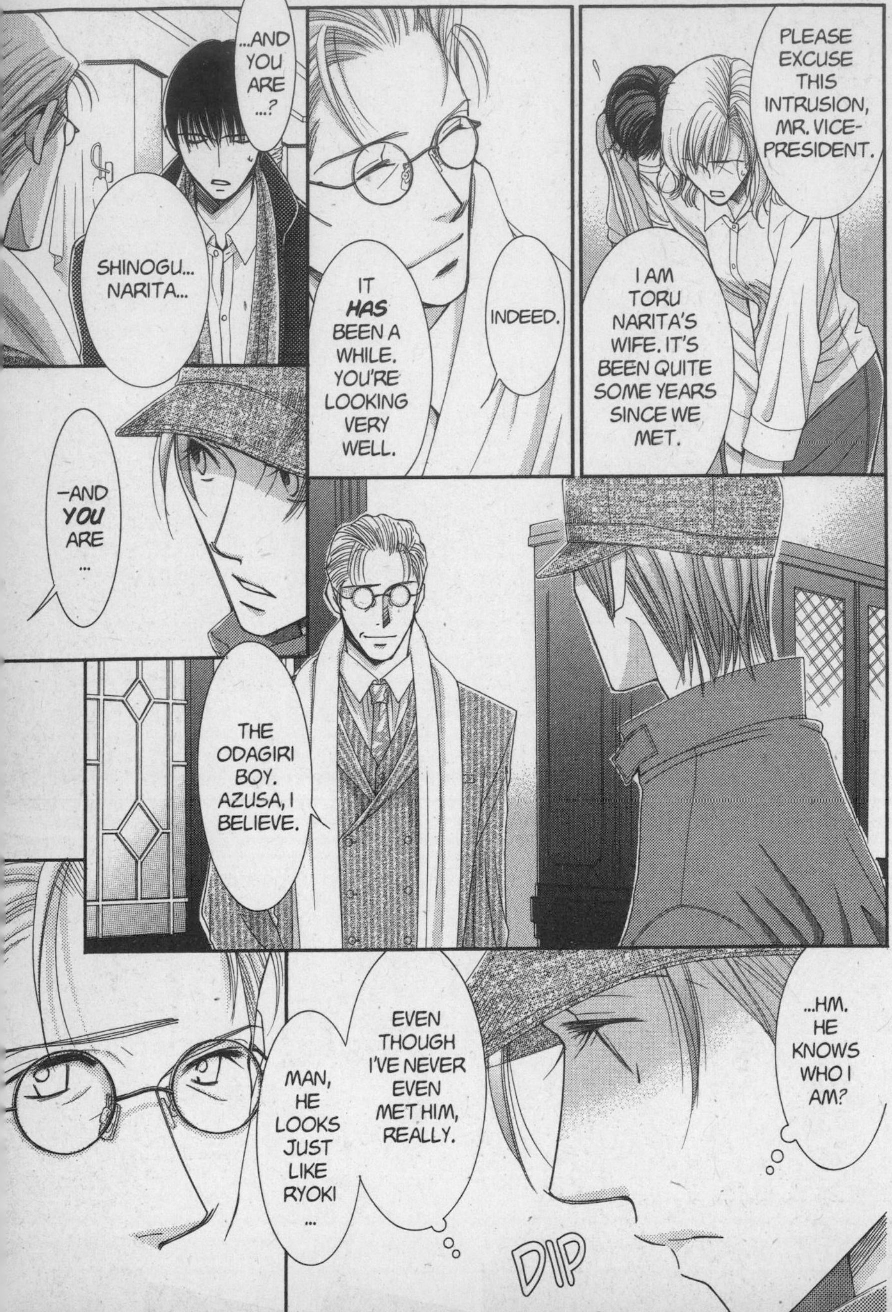
PLEASE EXCUSE THIS INTRUSION, MR. VICE-PRESIDENT.
I AM TORU NARITA'S WIFE. IT'S BEEN QUITE SOME YEARS SINCE WE MET.
INDEED.
IT *HAS* BEEN A WHILE. YOU'RE LOOKING VERY WELL.
...AND YOU ARE ...?
SHINOGU... NARITA...
–AND *YOU* ARE ...
THE ODAGIRI BOY. AZUSA, I BELIEVE.
...HM. HE KNOWS WHO I AM?
EVEN THOUGH I'VE NEVER EVEN MET HIM, REALLY.
MAN, HE LOOKS JUST LIKE RYOKI ...
DIP

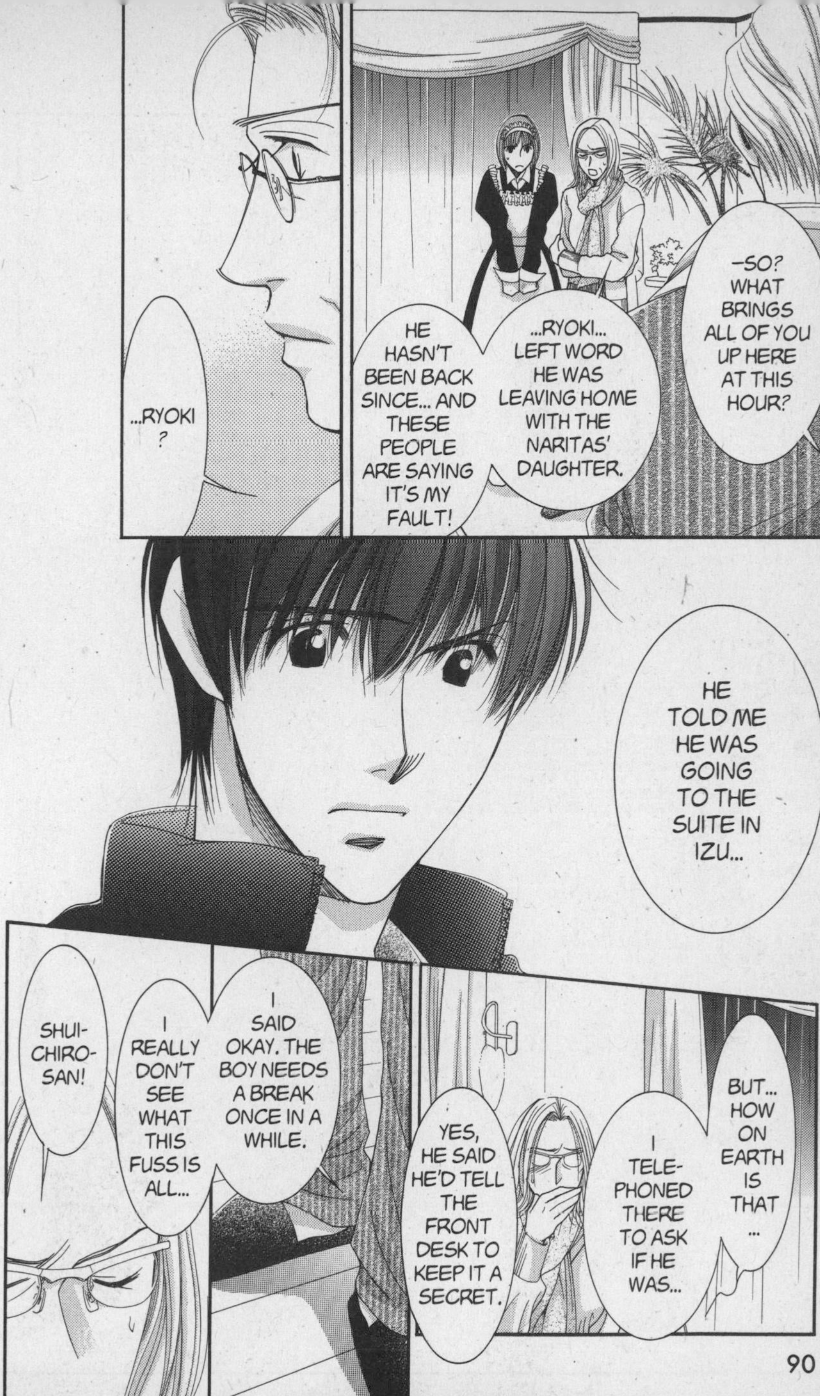
—SO? WHAT BRINGS ALL OF YOU UP HERE AT THIS HOUR?
...RYOKI... LEFT WORD HE WAS LEAVING HOME WITH THE NARITAS' DAUGHTER.
HE HASN'T BEEN BACK SINCE... AND THESE PEOPLE ARE SAYING IT'S MY FAULT!
...RYOKI ?
HE TOLD ME HE WAS GOING TO THE SUITE IN IZU...
BUT... HOW ON EARTH IS THAT ...
I TELE-PHONED THERE TO ASK IF HE WAS...
YES, HE SAID HE'D TELL THE FRONT DESK TO KEEP IT A SECRET.
I SAID OKAY. THE BOY NEEDS A BREAK ONCE IN A WHILE.
I REALLY DON'T SEE WHAT THIS FUSS IS ALL...
SHUI-CHIRO-SAN!

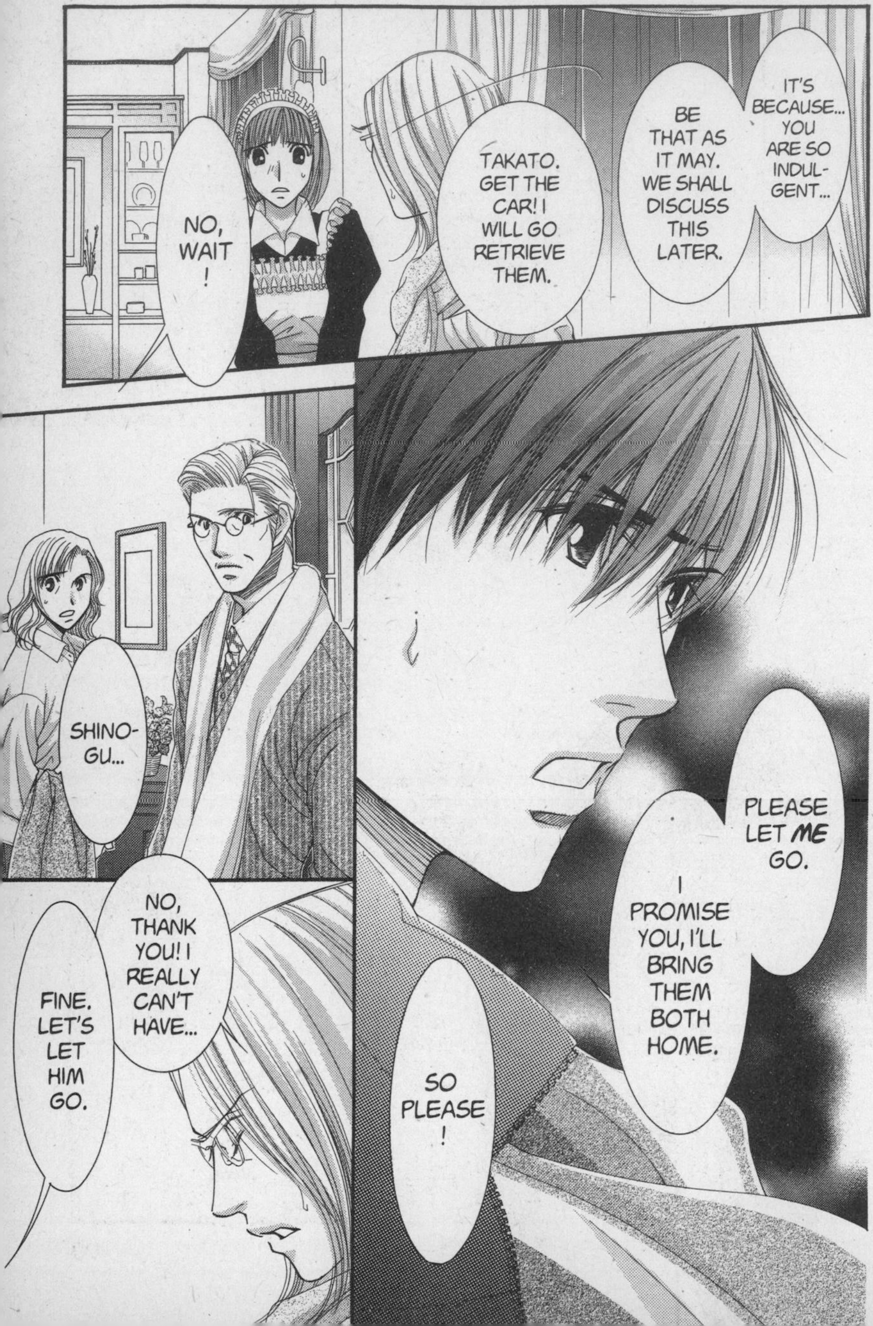
IT'S BECAUSE... YOU ARE SO INDUL-GENT...
BE THAT AS IT MAY. WE SHALL DISCUSS THIS LATER.
TAKATO. GET THE CAR! I WILL GO RETRIEVE THEM.
NO, WAIT!
PLEASE LET *ME* GO.
I PROMISE YOU, I'LL BRING THEM BOTH HOME.
SO PLEASE!
SHINO-GU...
NO, THANK YOU! I REALLY CAN'T HAVE...
FINE. LET'S LET HIM GO.

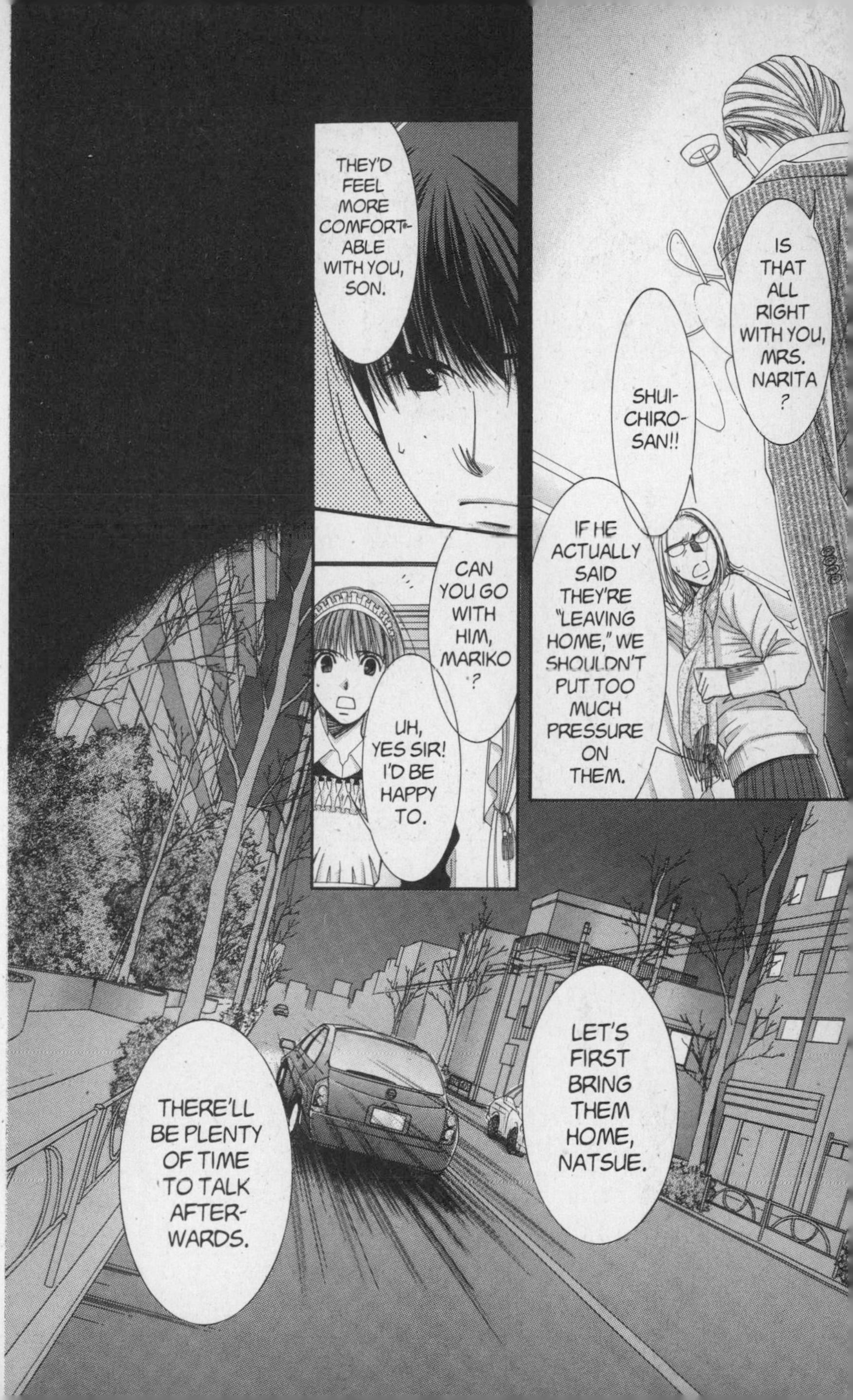
IS THAT ALL RIGHT WITH YOU, MRS. NARITA?
SHUI-CHIRO-SAN!!
IF HE ACTUALLY SAID THEY'RE "LEAVING HOME," WE SHOULDN'T PUT TOO MUCH PRESSURE ON THEM.
THEY'D FEEL MORE COMFORT-ABLE WITH YOU, SON.
CAN YOU GO WITH HIM, MARIKO?
UH, YES SIR! I'D BE HAPPY TO.
LET'S FIRST BRING THEM HOME, NATSUE.
THERE'LL BE PLENTY OF TIME TO TALK AFTER-WARDS.

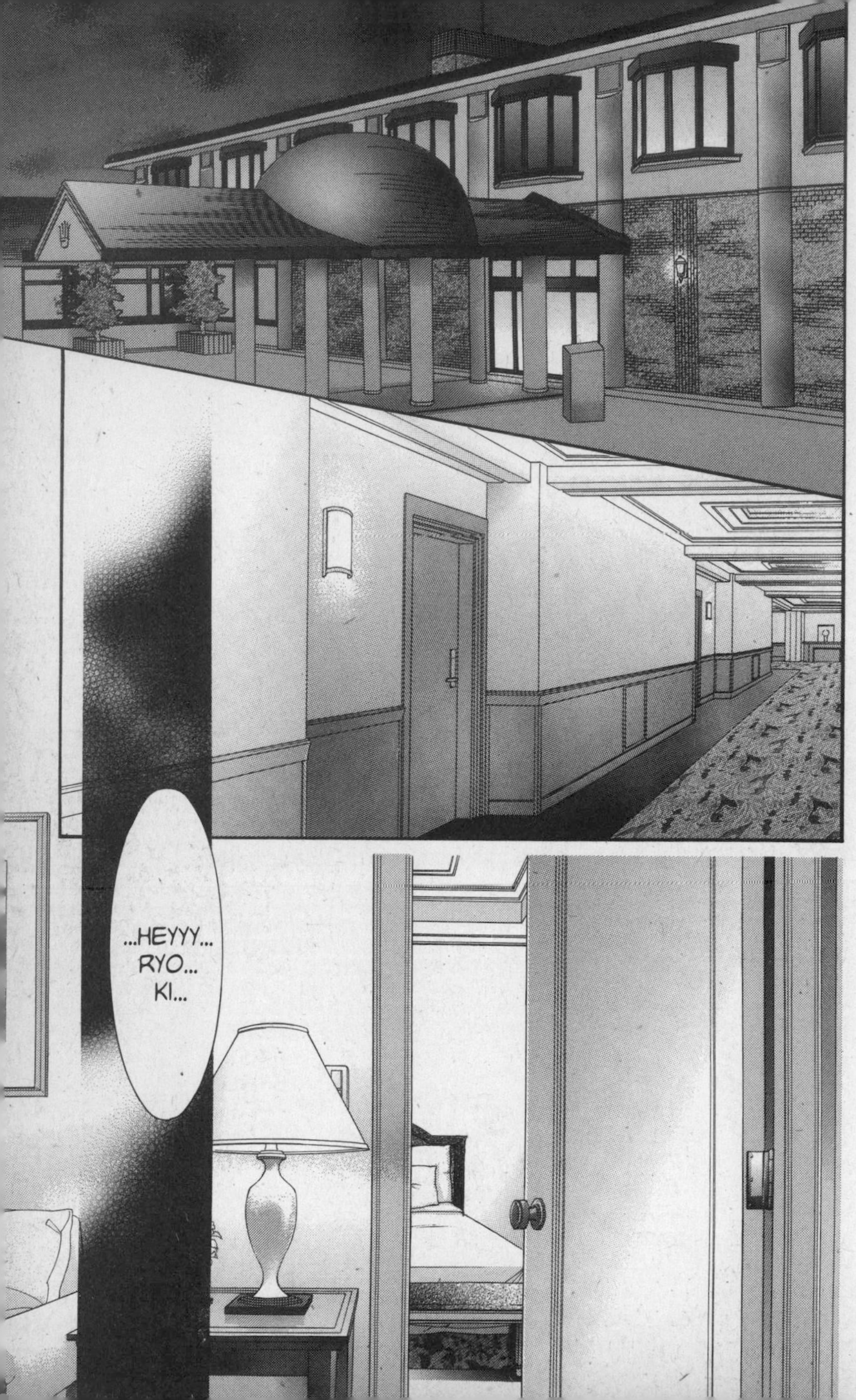
...HEYYY... RYO... KI...

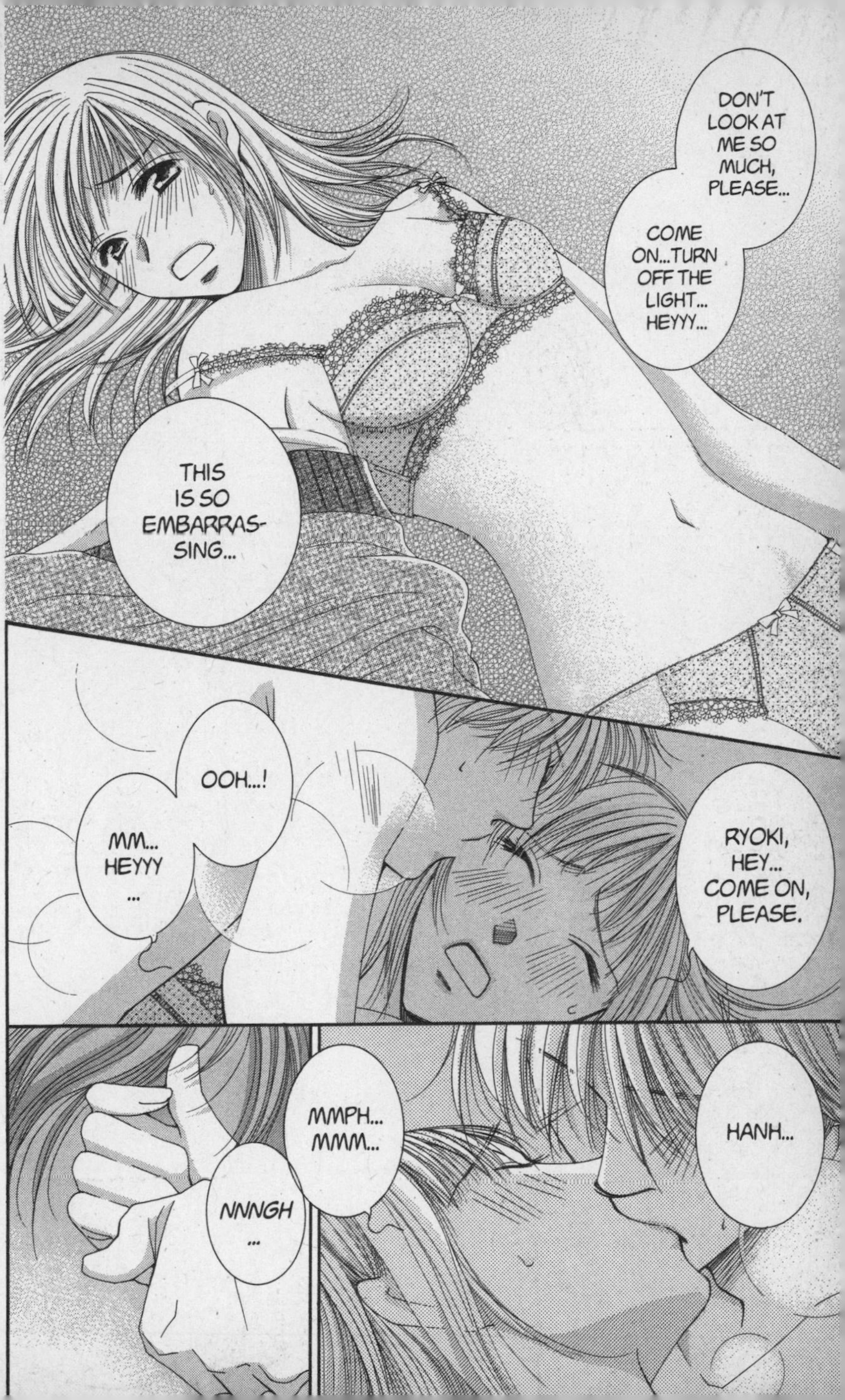
DON'T LOOK AT ME SO MUCH, PLEASE...
COME ON...TURN OFF THE LIGHT... HEYYY...
THIS IS SO EMBARRAS-SING...
RYOKI, HEY... COME ON, PLEASE.
OOH...!
MM... HEYYY ...
HANH...
MMPH... MMM...
NNNGH ...

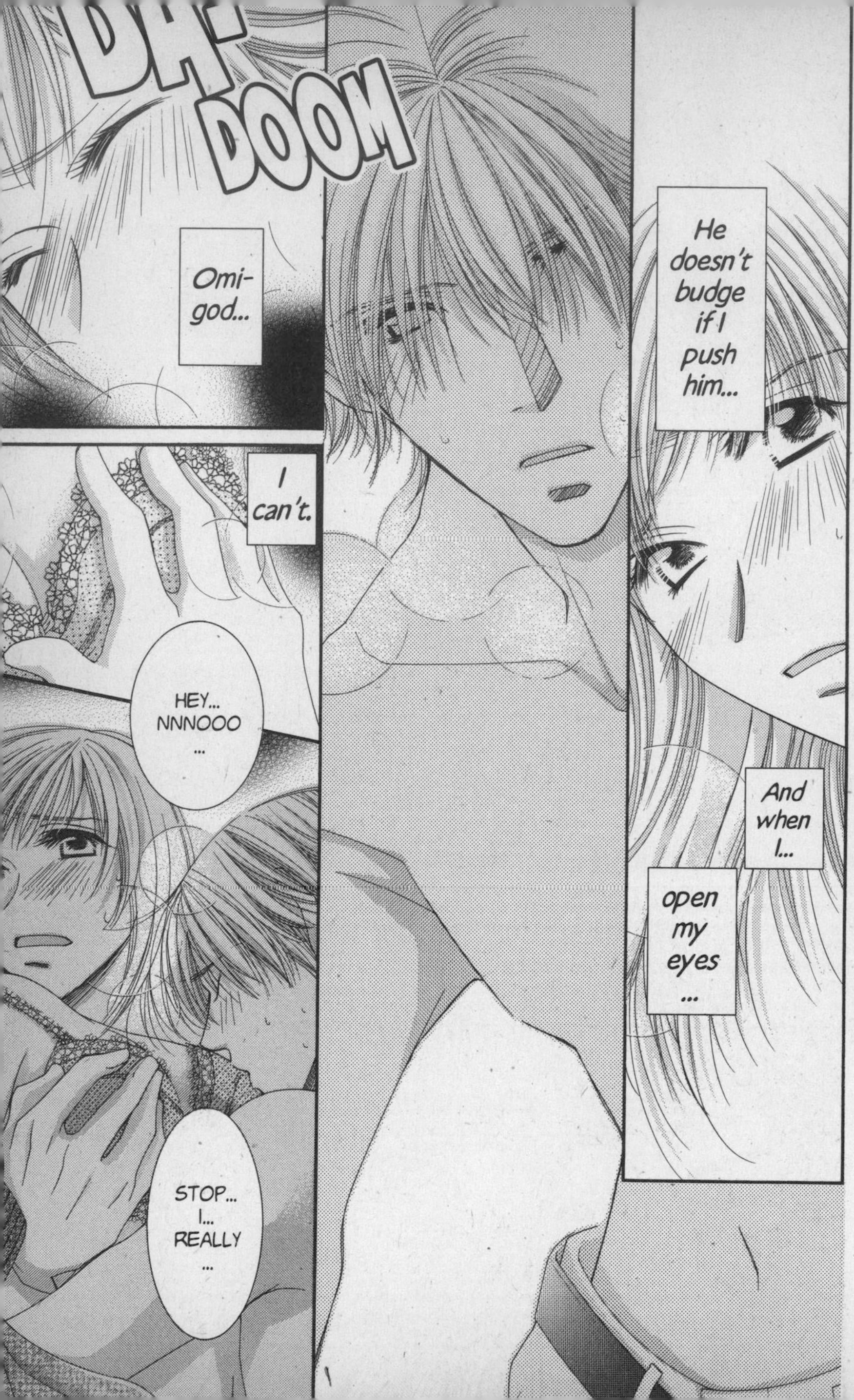
He doesn't budge if I push him...
And when I...
open my eyes ...
DA-DOOM
Omi-god...
I can't.
HEY... NNNOOO ...
STOP... I... REALLY ...

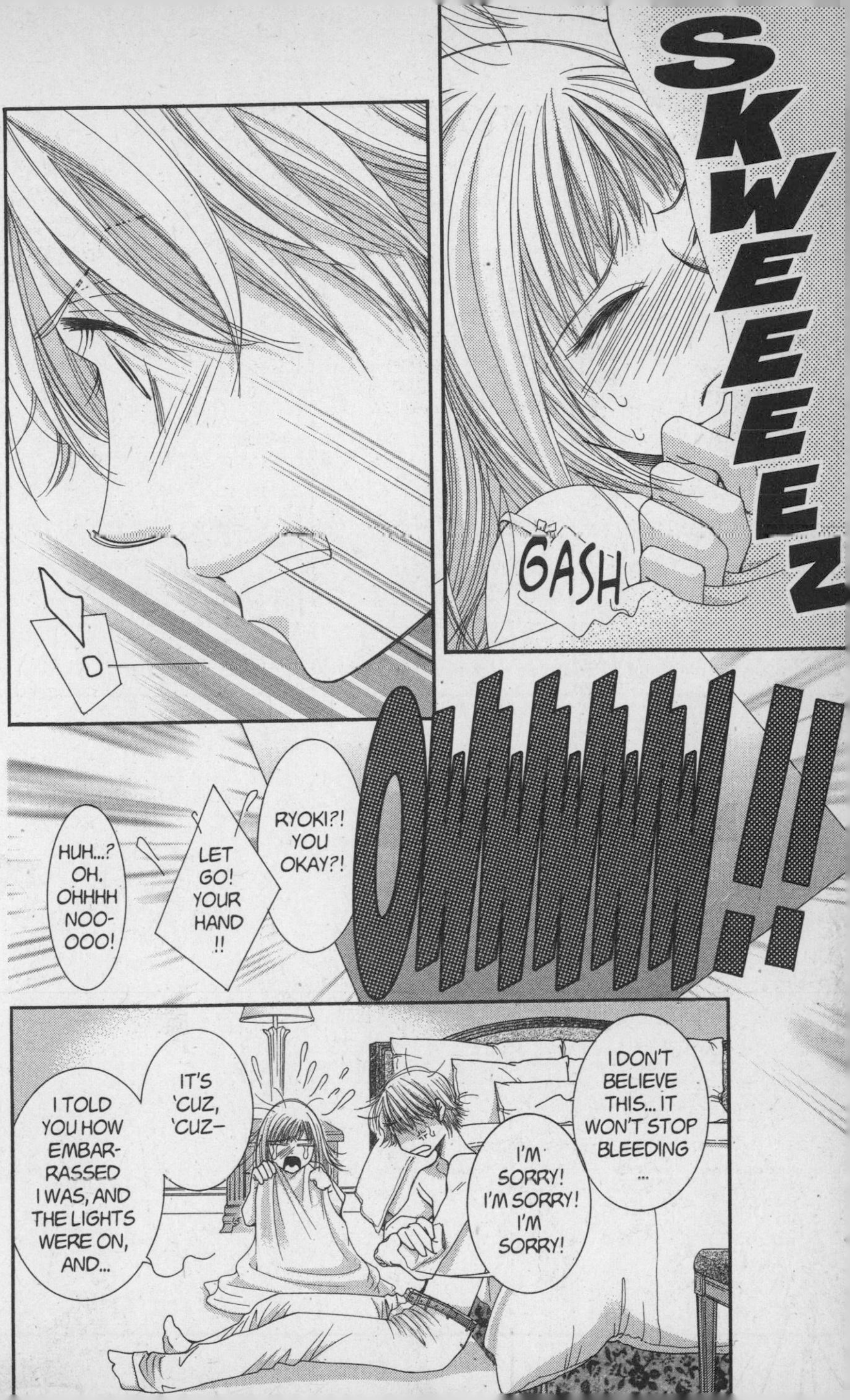
SKWEEEEZ
GASH
OWWWWW!!
RYOKI?! YOU OKAY?!
LET GO! YOUR HAND!!
HUH...? OH. OHHHH NOO-OOO!
I DON'T BELIEVE THIS... IT WON'T STOP BLEEDING...
I'M SORRY! I'M SORRY! I'M SORRY!
IT'S 'CUZ, 'CUZ–
I TOLD YOU HOW EMBAR-RASSED I WAS, AND THE LIGHTS WERE ON, AND...

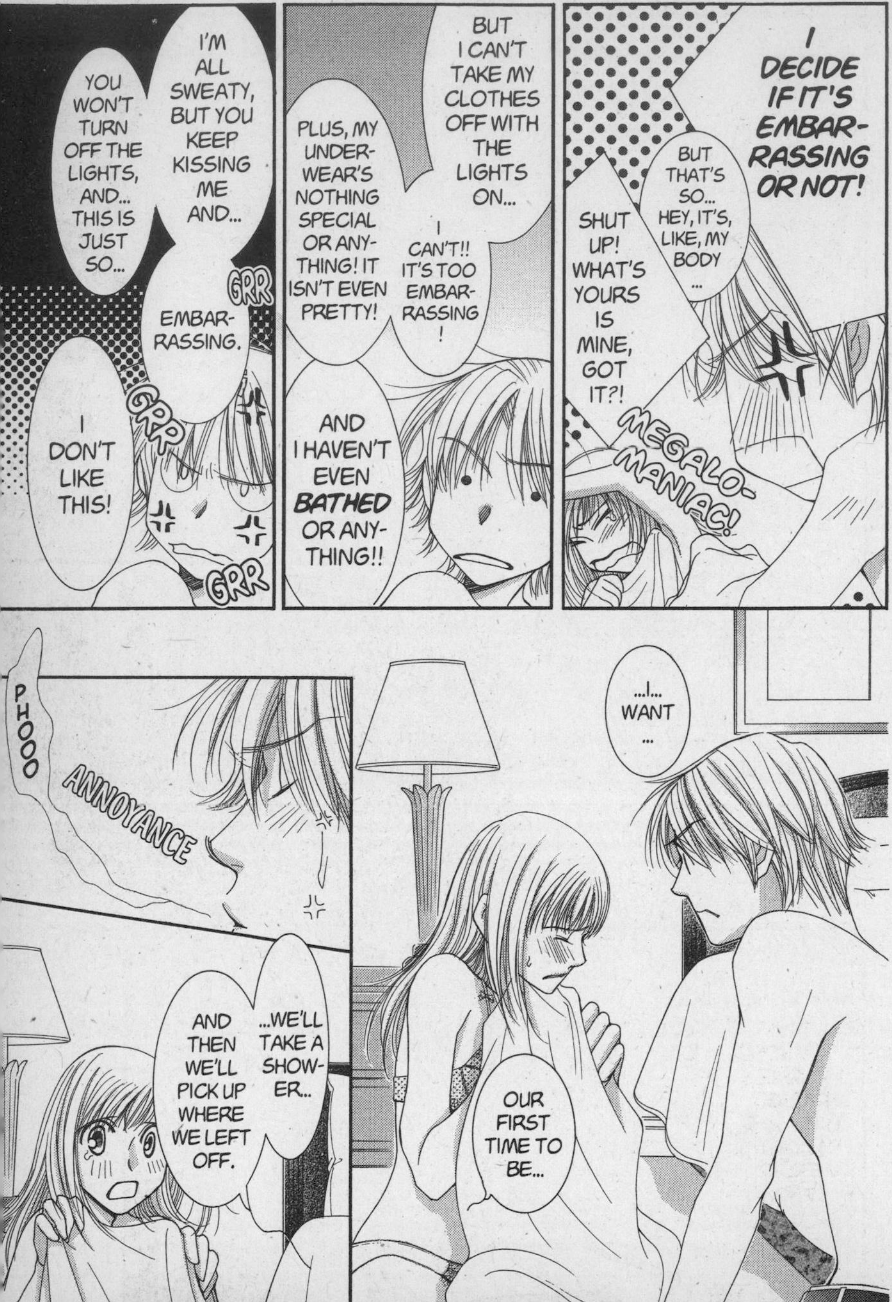
I DECIDE IF IT'S EMBARRASSING OR NOT!
BUT THAT'S SO... HEY, IT'S, LIKE, MY BODY...
SHUT UP! WHAT'S YOURS IS MINE, GOT IT?!
MEGALO-MANIAC!
BUT I CAN'T TAKE MY CLOTHES OFF WITH THE LIGHTS ON...
I CAN'T!! IT'S TOO EMBARRASSING!
PLUS, MY UNDERWEAR'S NOTHING SPECIAL OR ANYTHING! IT ISN'T EVEN PRETTY!
AND I HAVEN'T EVEN BATHED OR ANYTHING!!
I'M ALL SWEATY, BUT YOU KEEP KISSING ME AND...
YOU WON'T TURN OFF THE LIGHTS, AND... THIS IS JUST SO...
GRR
EMBARRASSING.
GRR
I DON'T LIKE THIS!
GRR
...I... WANT...
OUR FIRST TIME TO BE...
PHOOO
ANNOYANCE
...WE'LL TAKE A SHOWER..
AND THEN WE'LL PICK UP WHERE WE LEFT OFF.

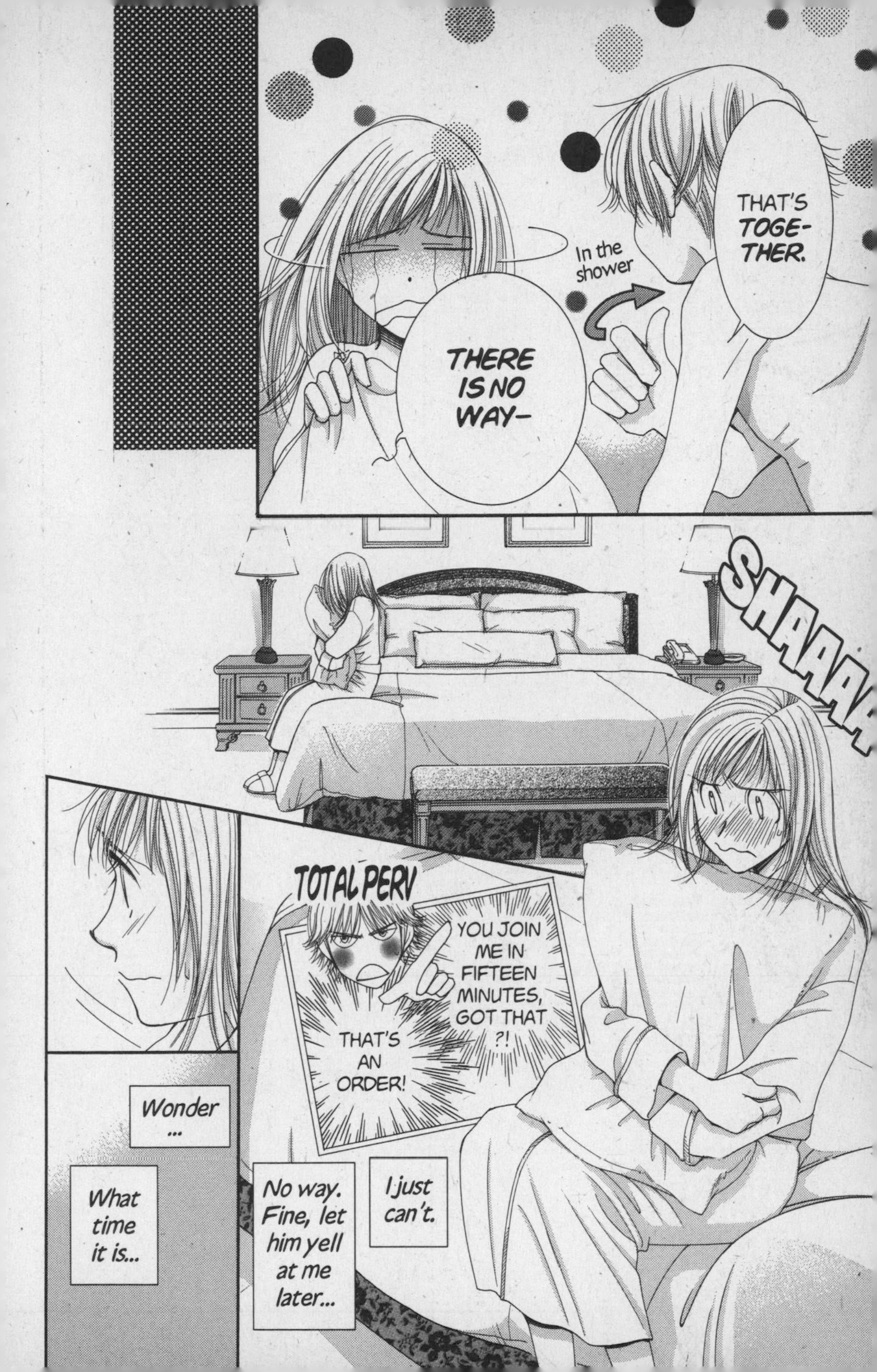
THAT'S TOGE-THER.
In the shower
THERE IS NO WAY-
SHAAAA
TOTAL PERV
YOU JOIN ME IN FIFTEEN MINUTES, GOT THAT?!
THAT'S AN ORDER!
I just can't.
No way. Fine, let him yell at me later...
Wonder...
What time it is...

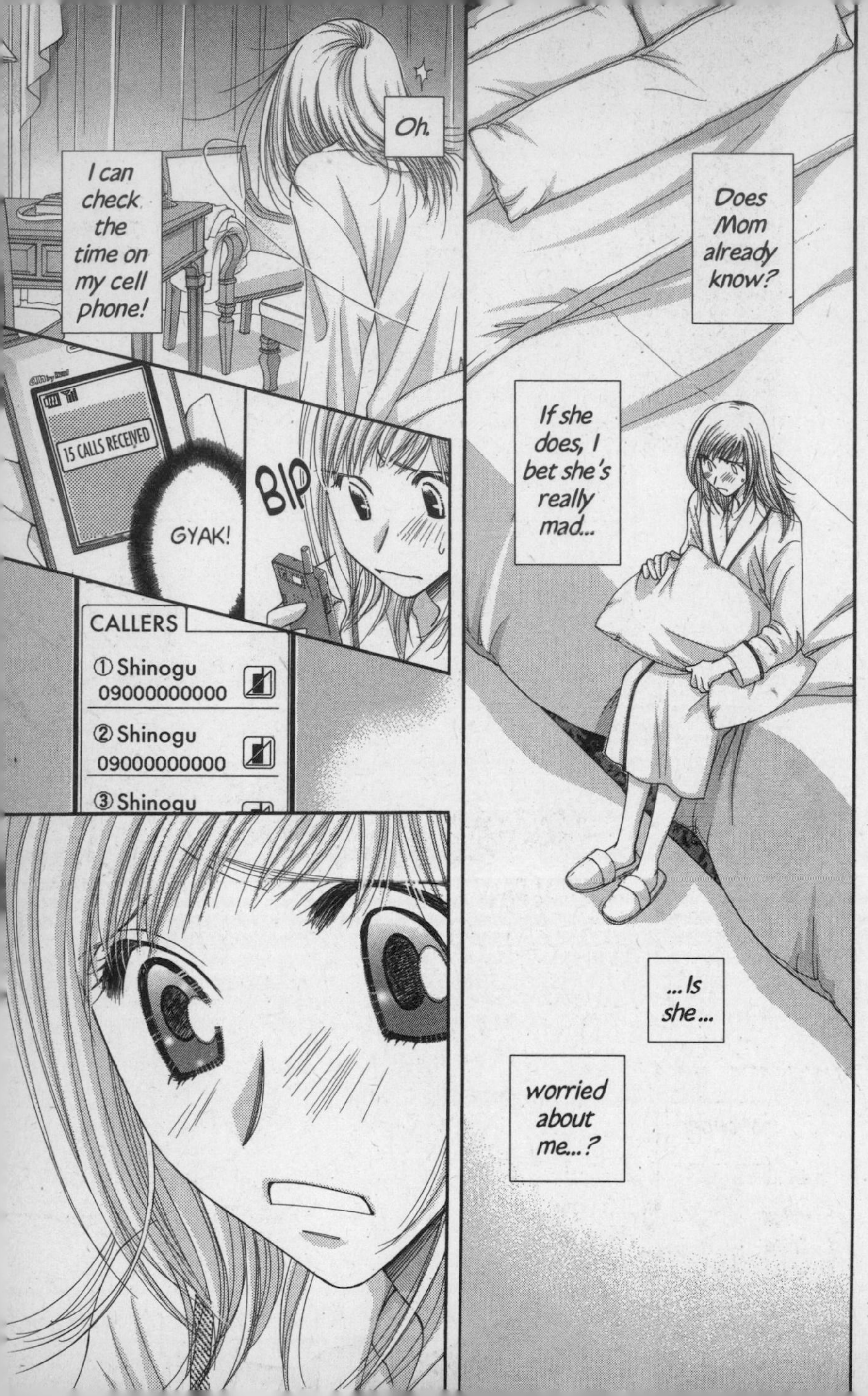
Does Mom already know?
If she does, I bet she's really mad...
...Is she...
worried about me...?
Oh.
I can check the time on my cell phone!
BIP
15 CALLS RECEIVED
GYAK!
CALLERS
① Shinogu 09000000000
② Shinogu 09000000000
③ Shinogu

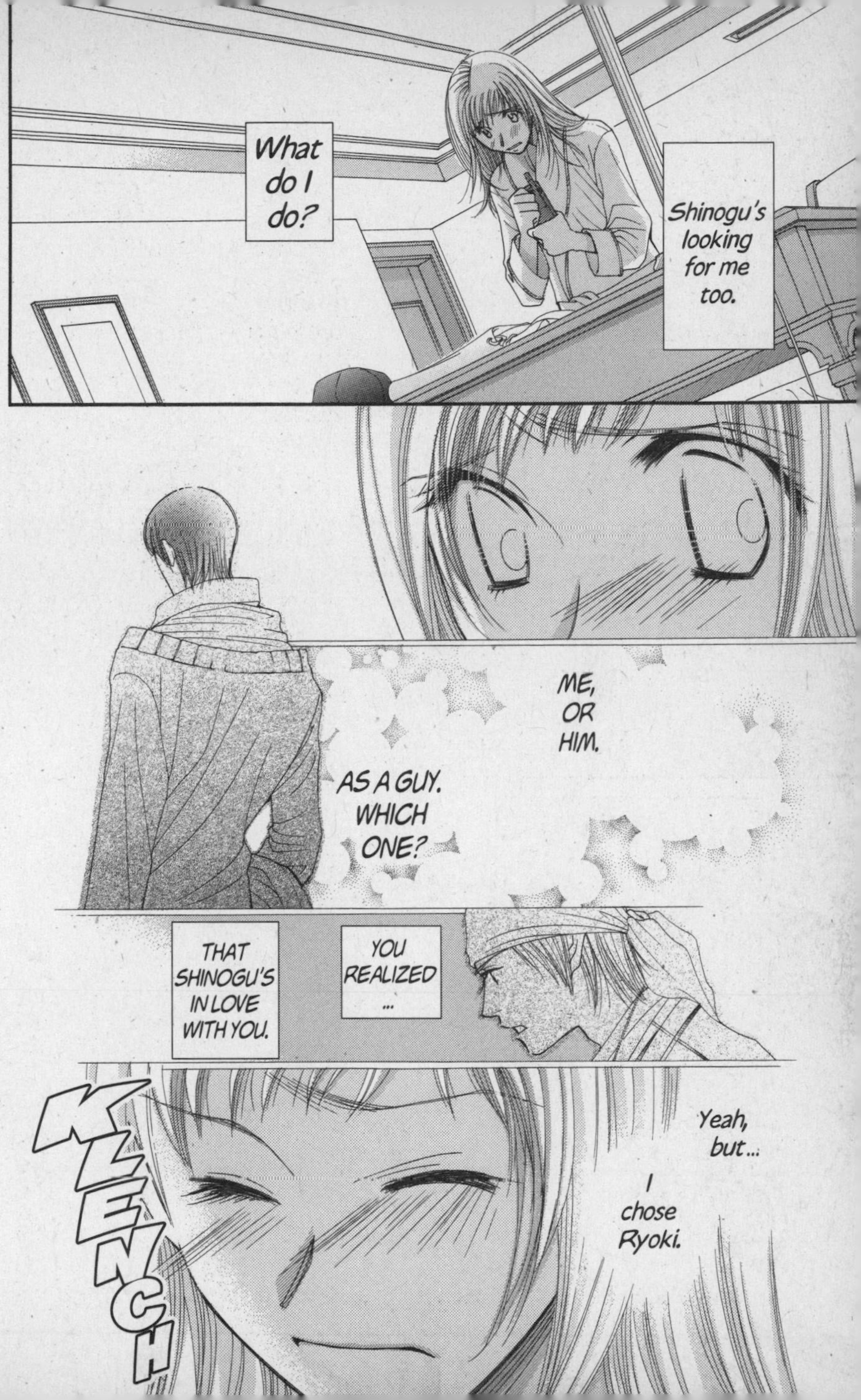
Shinogu's looking for me too.
What do I do?
ME, OR HIM.
AS A GUY. WHICH ONE?
YOU REALIZED ...
THAT SHINOGU'S IN LOVE WITH YOU.
Yeah, but...
I chose Ryoki.
KLENCH

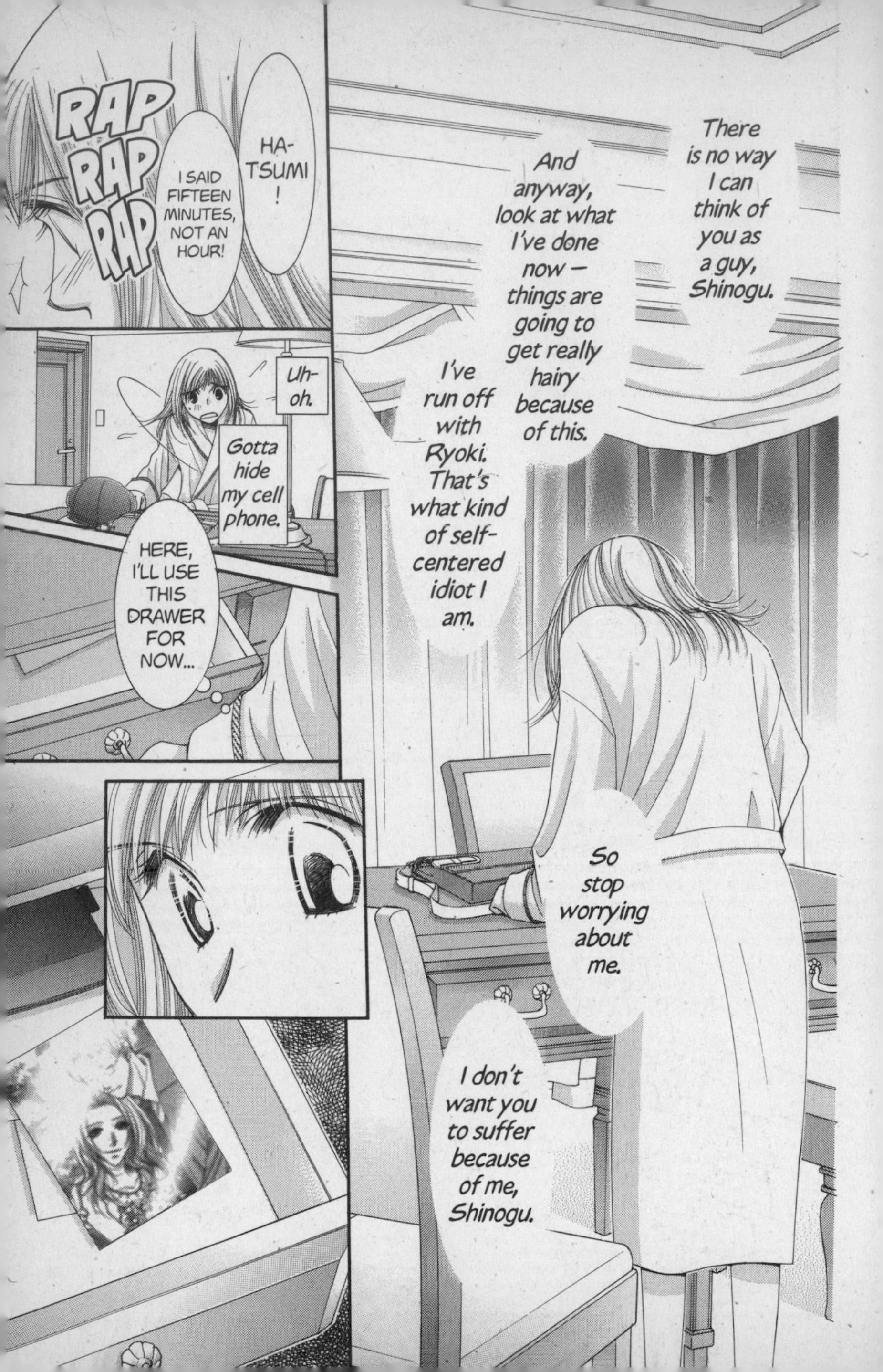
There is no way I can think of you as a guy, Shinogu.
And anyway, look at what I've done now — things are going to get really hairy because of this.
I've run off with Ryoki. That's what kind of self-centered idiot I am.
So stop worrying about me.
I don't want you to suffer because of me, Shinogu.
RAP RAP RAP
HA-TSUMI!
I SAID FIFTEEN MINUTES, NOT AN HOUR!
Uh-oh.
Gotta hide my cell phone.
HERE, I'LL USE THIS DRAWER FOR NOW...

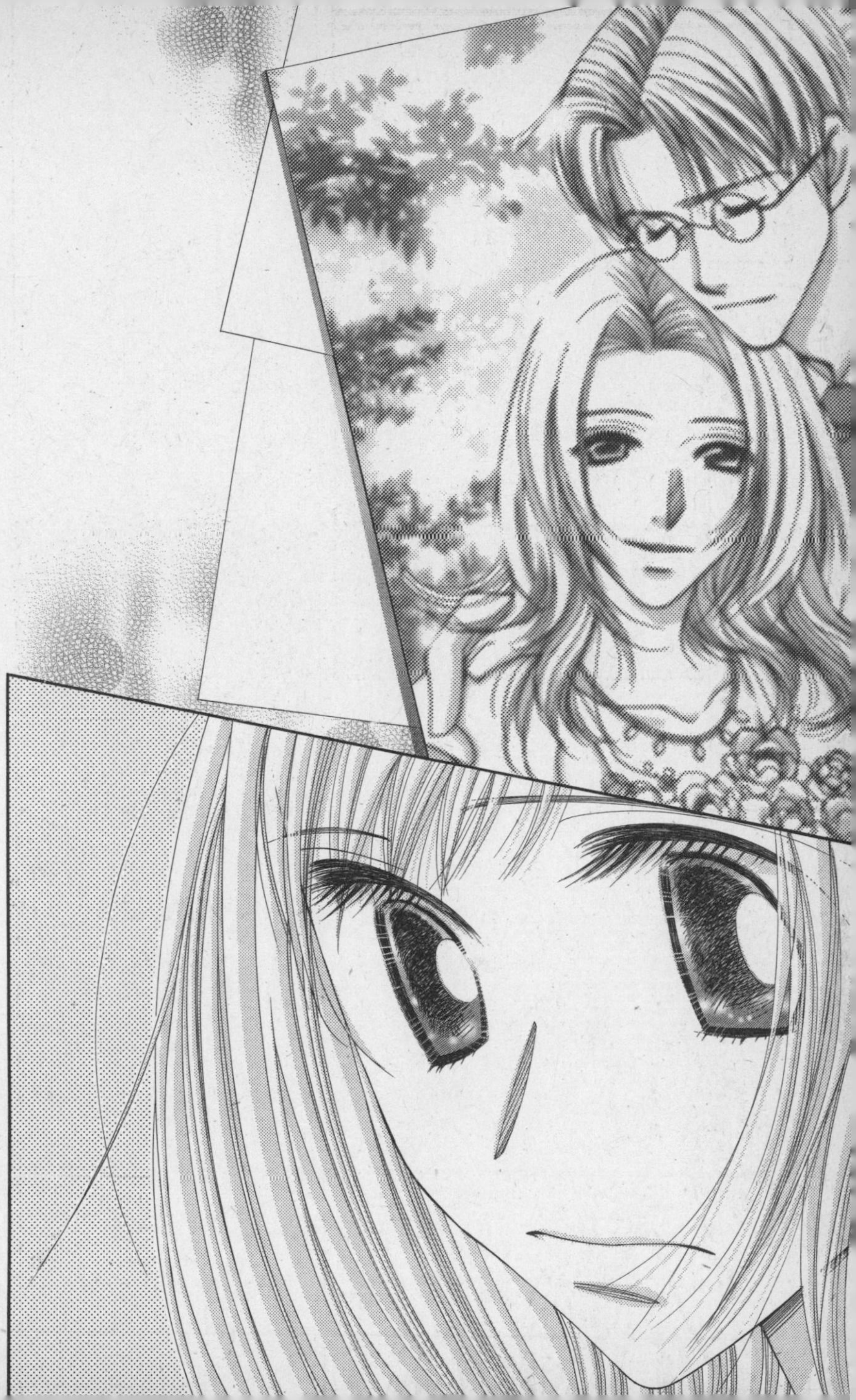

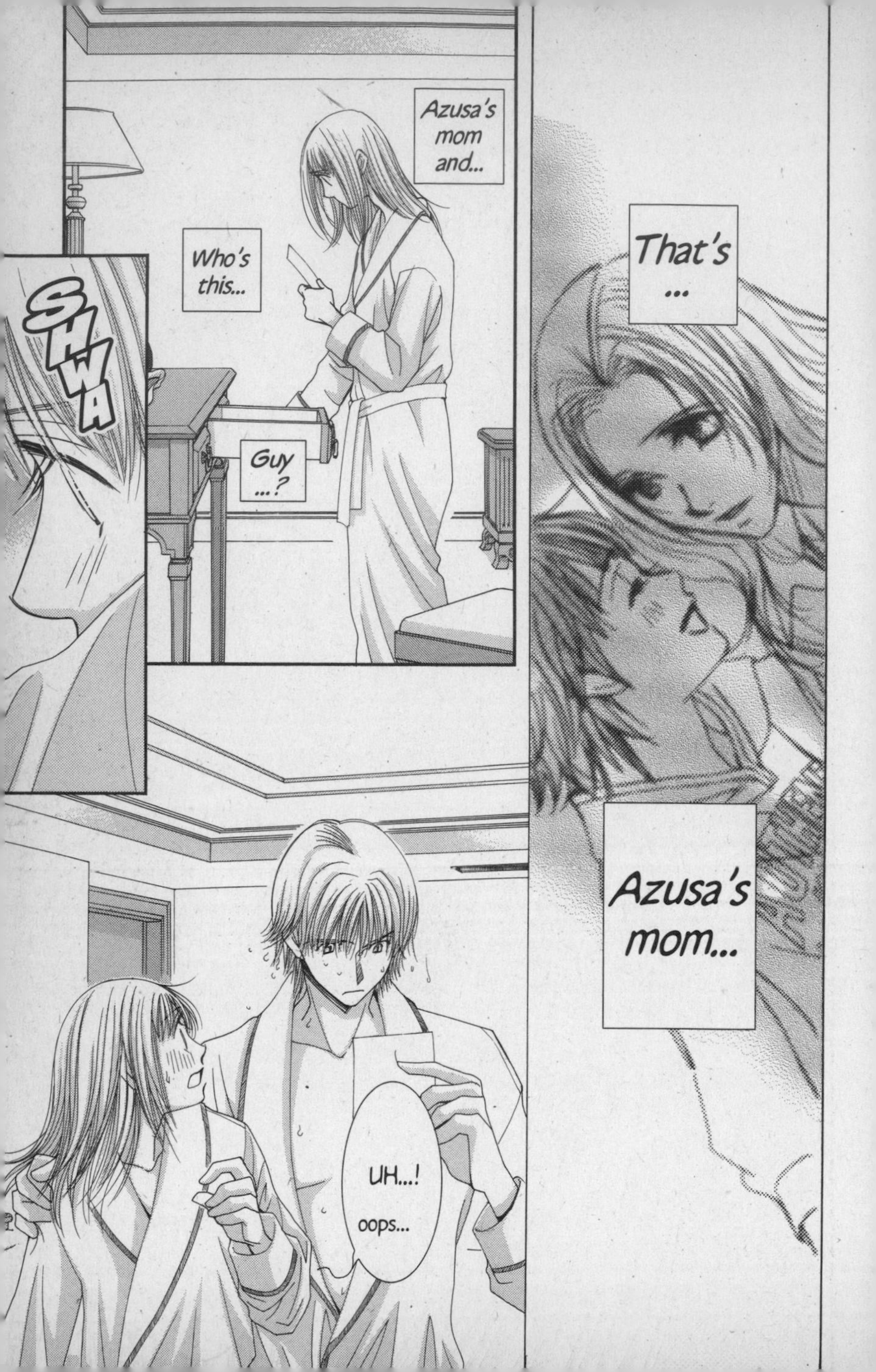
That's ...
Azusa's mom...
Azusa's mom and...
Who's this...
Guy ...?
SHWA
UH...!
oops...

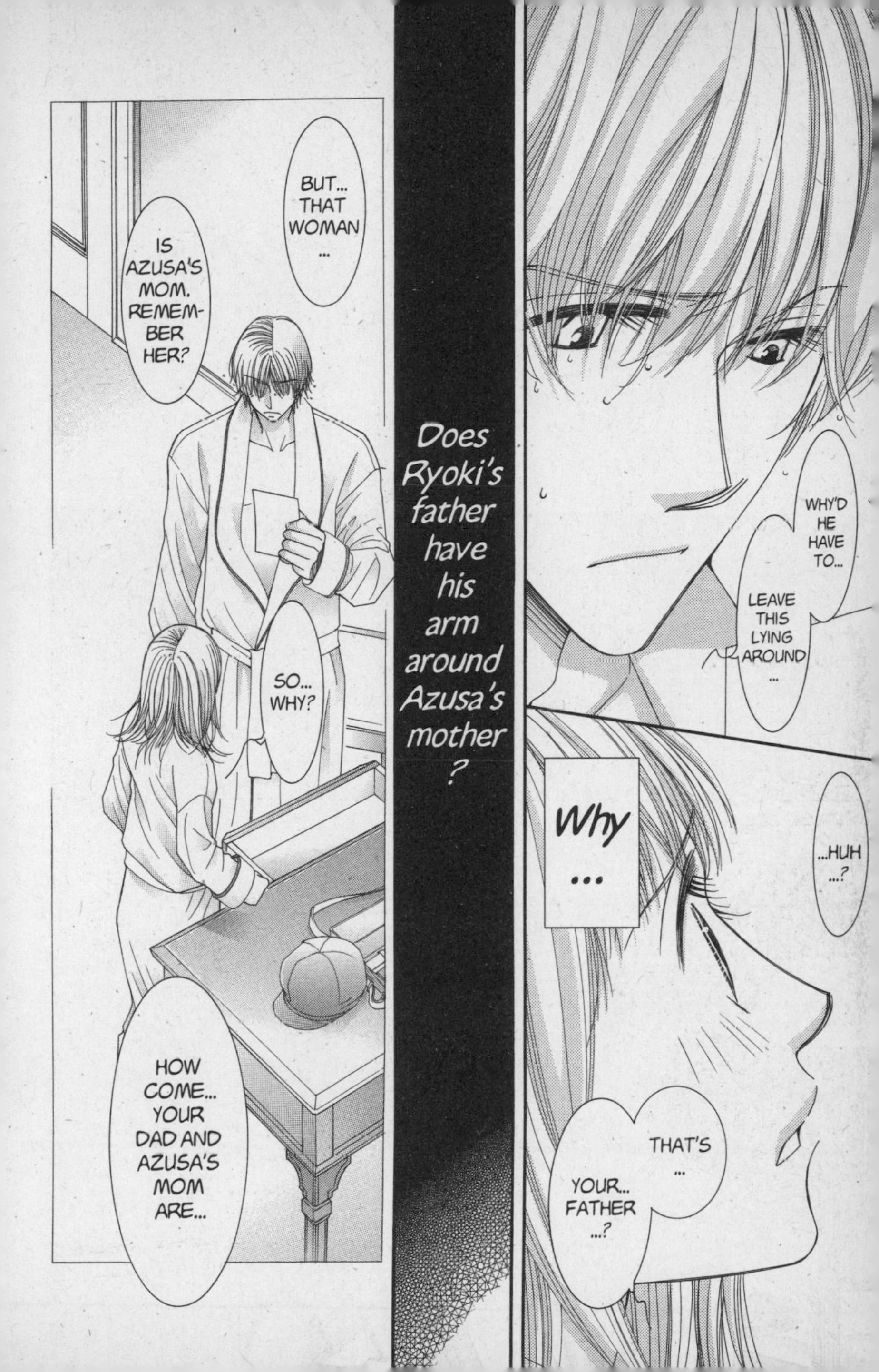
WHY'D HE HAVE TO...
LEAVE THIS LYING AROUND...
...HUH...?
Why...
THAT'S... YOUR... FATHER...?
Does Ryoki's father have his arm around Azusa's mother?
BUT... THAT WOMAN...
IS AZUSA'S MOM. REMEMBER HER?
SO... WHY?
HOW COME... YOUR DAD AND AZUSA'S MOM ARE...

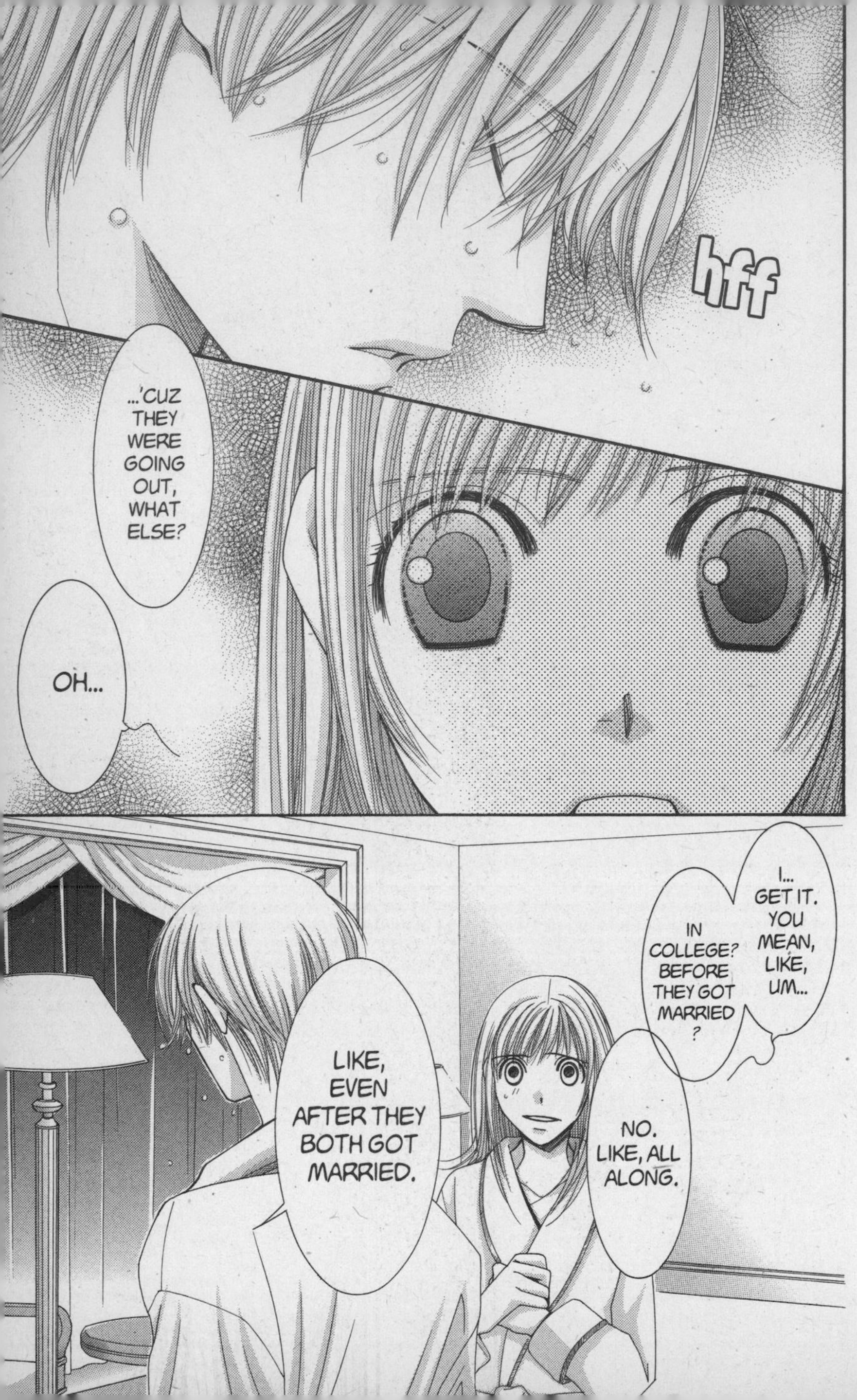
hff
...'CUZ THEY WERE GOING OUT, WHAT ELSE?
OH...
I... GET IT. YOU MEAN, LIKE, UM...
IN COLLEGE? BEFORE THEY GOT MARRIED?
NO. LIKE, ALL ALONG.
LIKE, EVEN AFTER THEY BOTH GOT MARRIED.

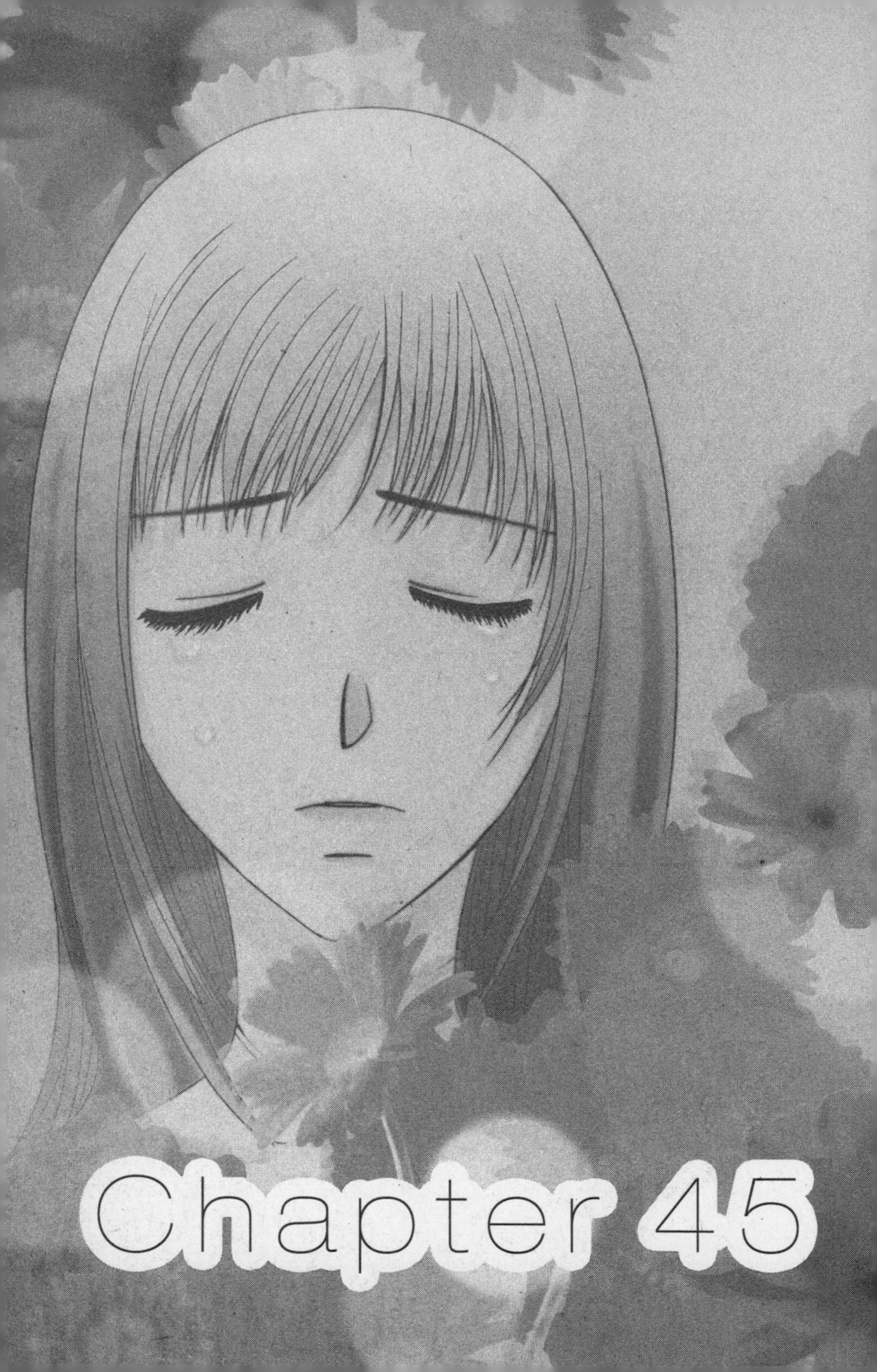
Chapter 45

hot gimmick

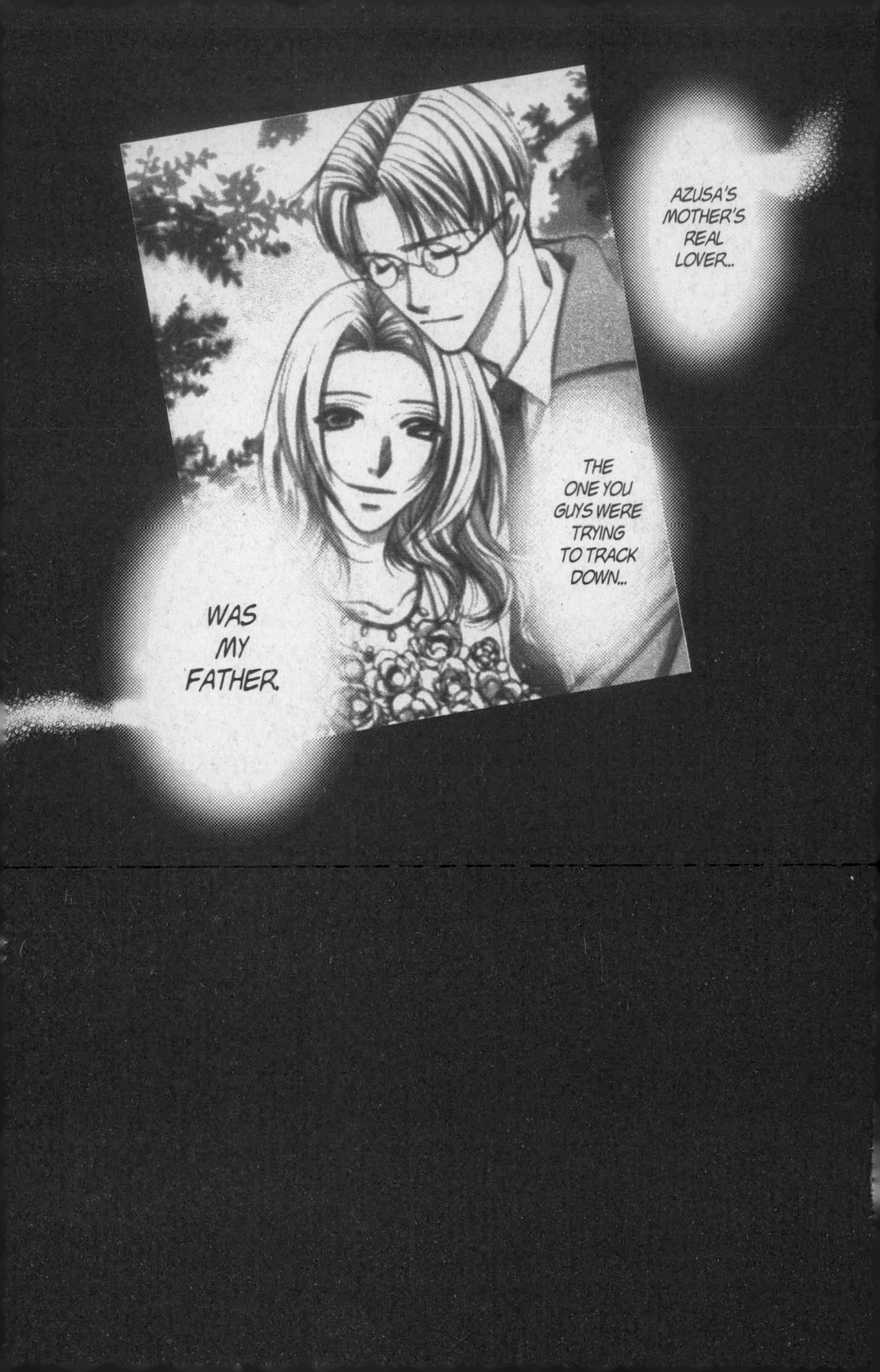
AZUSA'S MOTHER'S REAL LOVER...
THE ONE YOU GUYS WERE TRYING TO TRACK DOWN...
WAS MY FATHER.

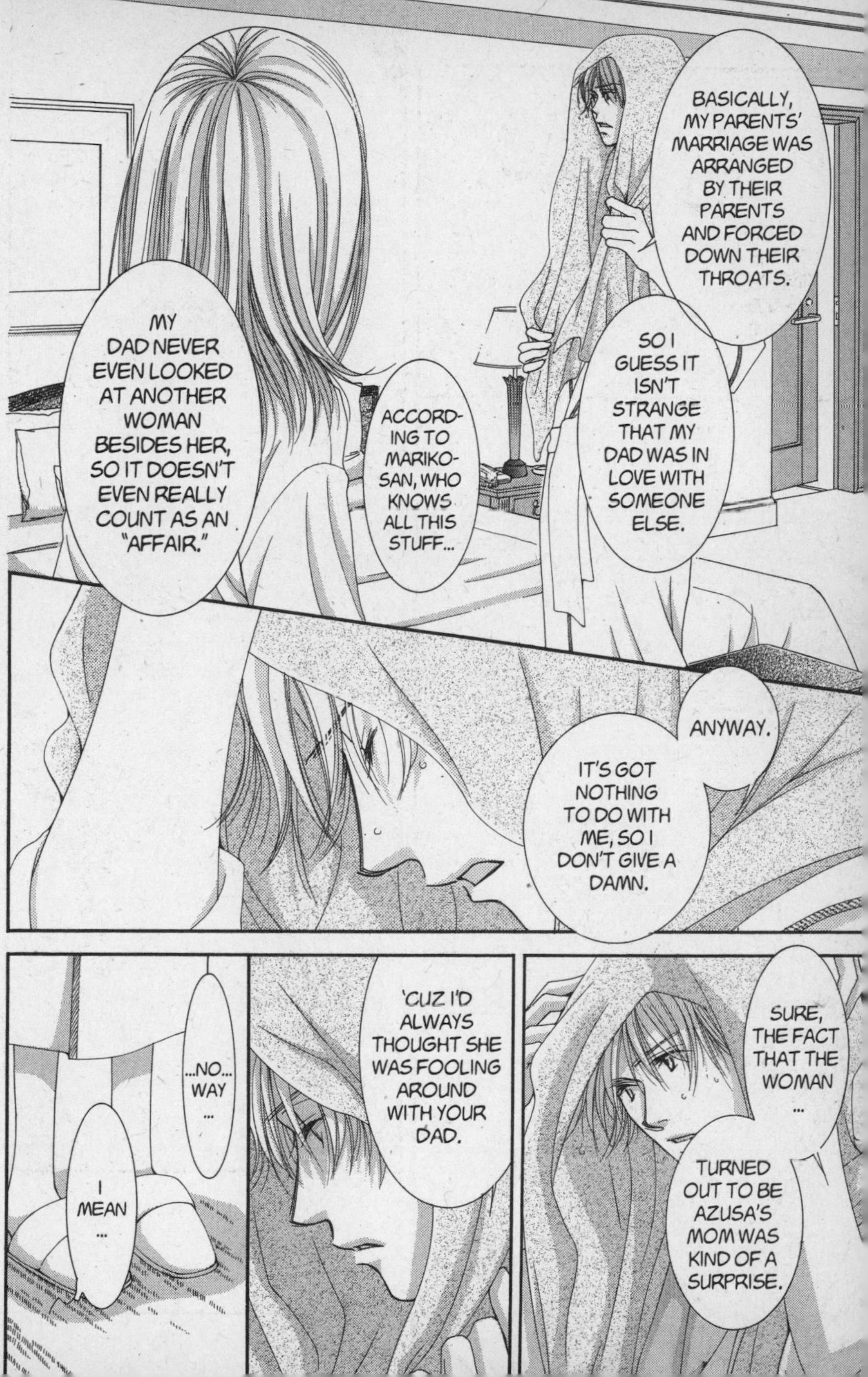
BASICALLY, MY PARENTS' MARRIAGE WAS ARRANGED BY THEIR PARENTS AND FORCED DOWN THEIR THROATS.
SO I GUESS IT ISN'T STRANGE THAT MY DAD WAS IN LOVE WITH SOMEONE ELSE.
ACCORDING TO MARIKO-SAN, WHO KNOWS ALL THIS STUFF...
MY DAD NEVER EVEN LOOKED AT ANOTHER WOMAN BESIDES HER, SO IT DOESN'T EVEN REALLY COUNT AS AN "AFFAIR."
ANYWAY.
IT'S GOT NOTHING TO DO WITH ME, SO I DON'T GIVE A DAMN.
SURE, THE FACT THAT THE WOMAN...
TURNED OUT TO BE AZUSA'S MOM WAS KIND OF A SURPRISE.
'CUZ I'D ALWAYS THOUGHT SHE WAS FOOLING AROUND WITH YOUR DAD.
...NO... WAY ...
I MEAN ...

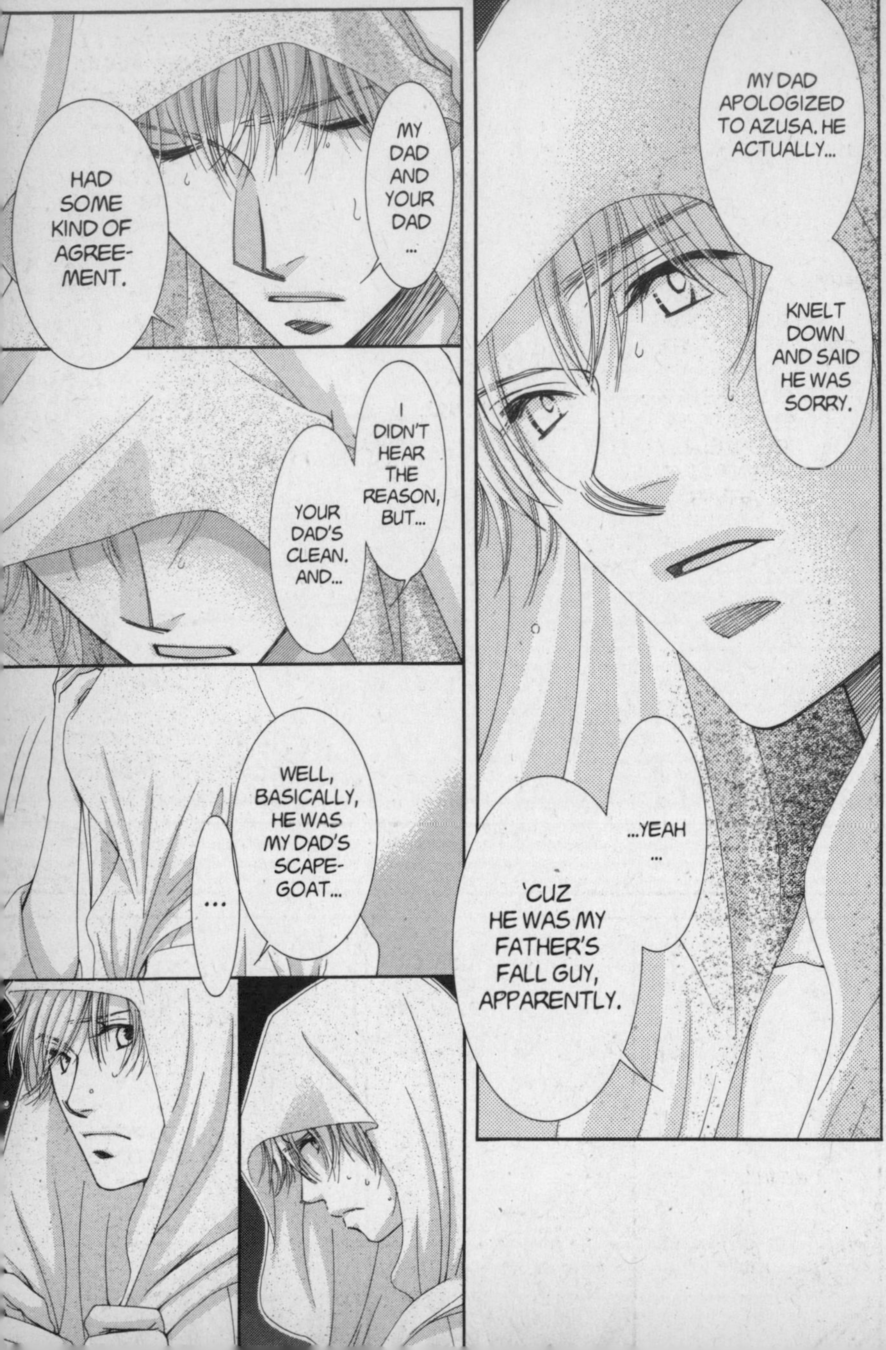
MY DAD APOLOGIZED TO AZUSA. HE ACTUALLY...
KNELT DOWN AND SAID HE WAS SORRY.
...YEAH ...
'CUZ HE WAS MY FATHER'S FALL GUY, APPARENTLY.
MY DAD AND YOUR DAD ...
HAD SOME KIND OF AGREE-MENT.
I DIDN'T HEAR THE REASON, BUT...
YOUR DAD'S CLEAN. AND...
WELL, BASICALLY, HE WAS MY DAD'S SCAPE-GOAT...
...

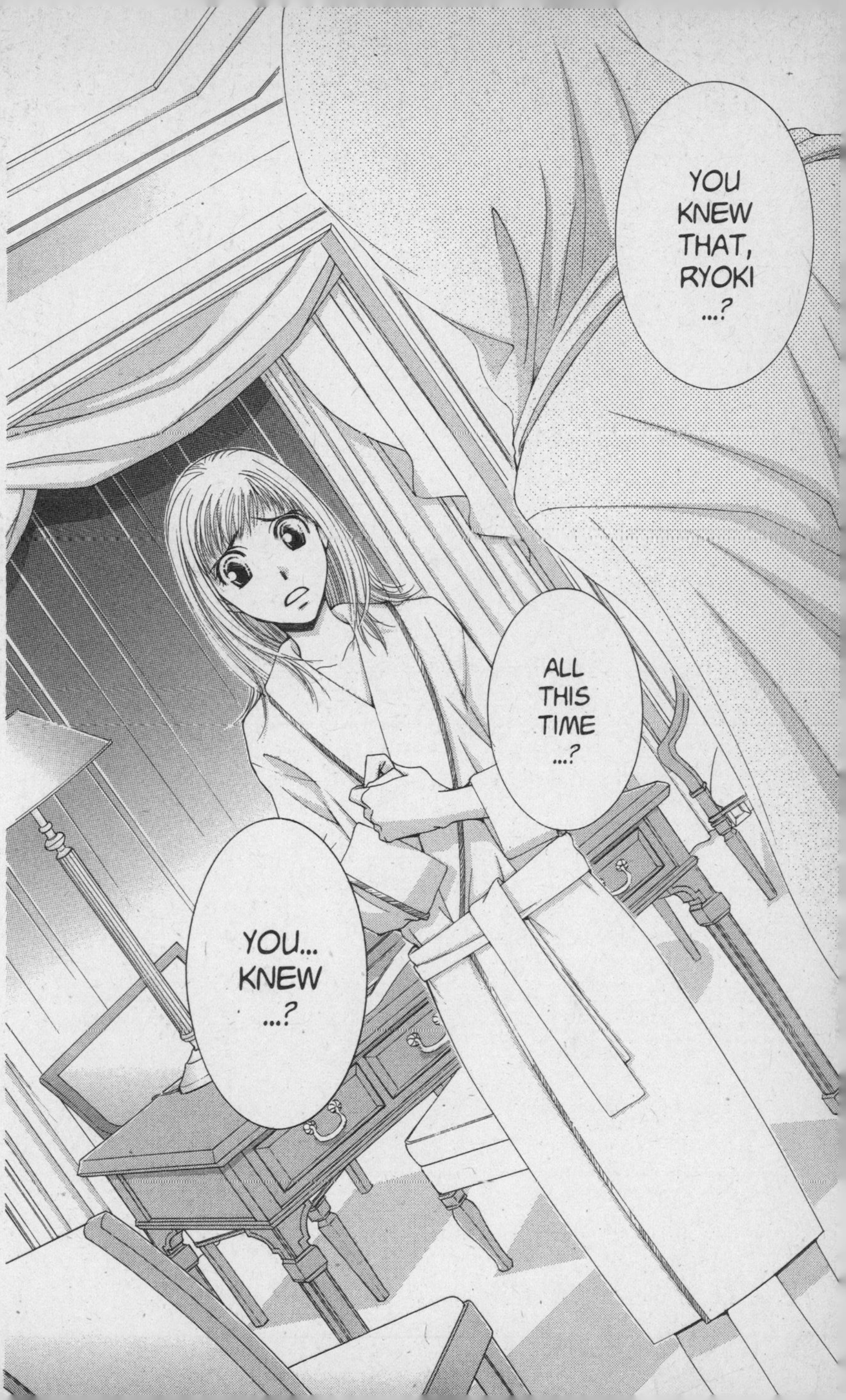
YOU KNEW THAT, RYOKI ...?
ALL THIS TIME ...?
YOU... KNEW ...?

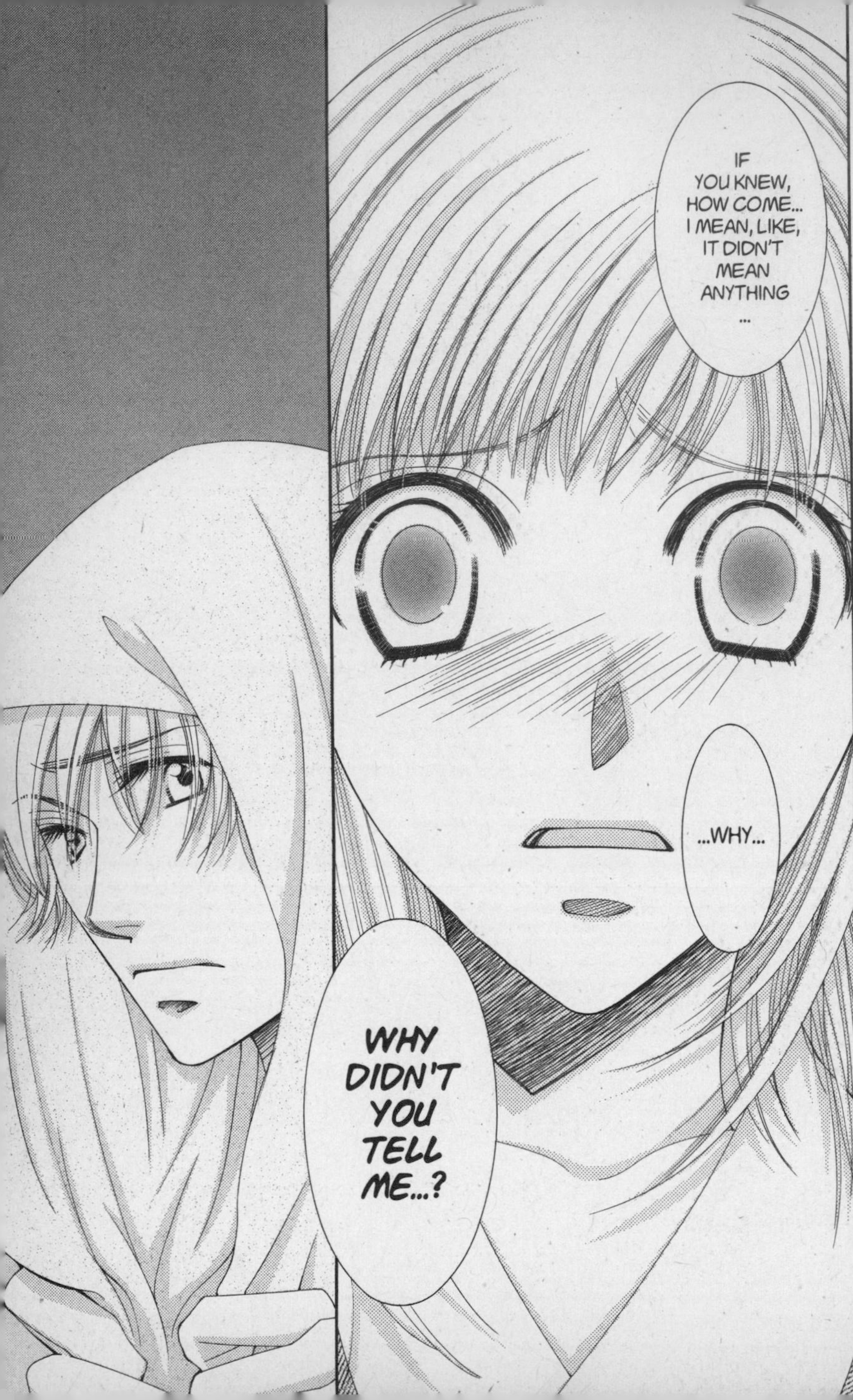
IF YOU KNEW, HOW COME... I MEAN, LIKE, IT DIDN'T MEAN ANYTHING ...
...WHY...
WHY DIDN'T YOU TELL ME...?

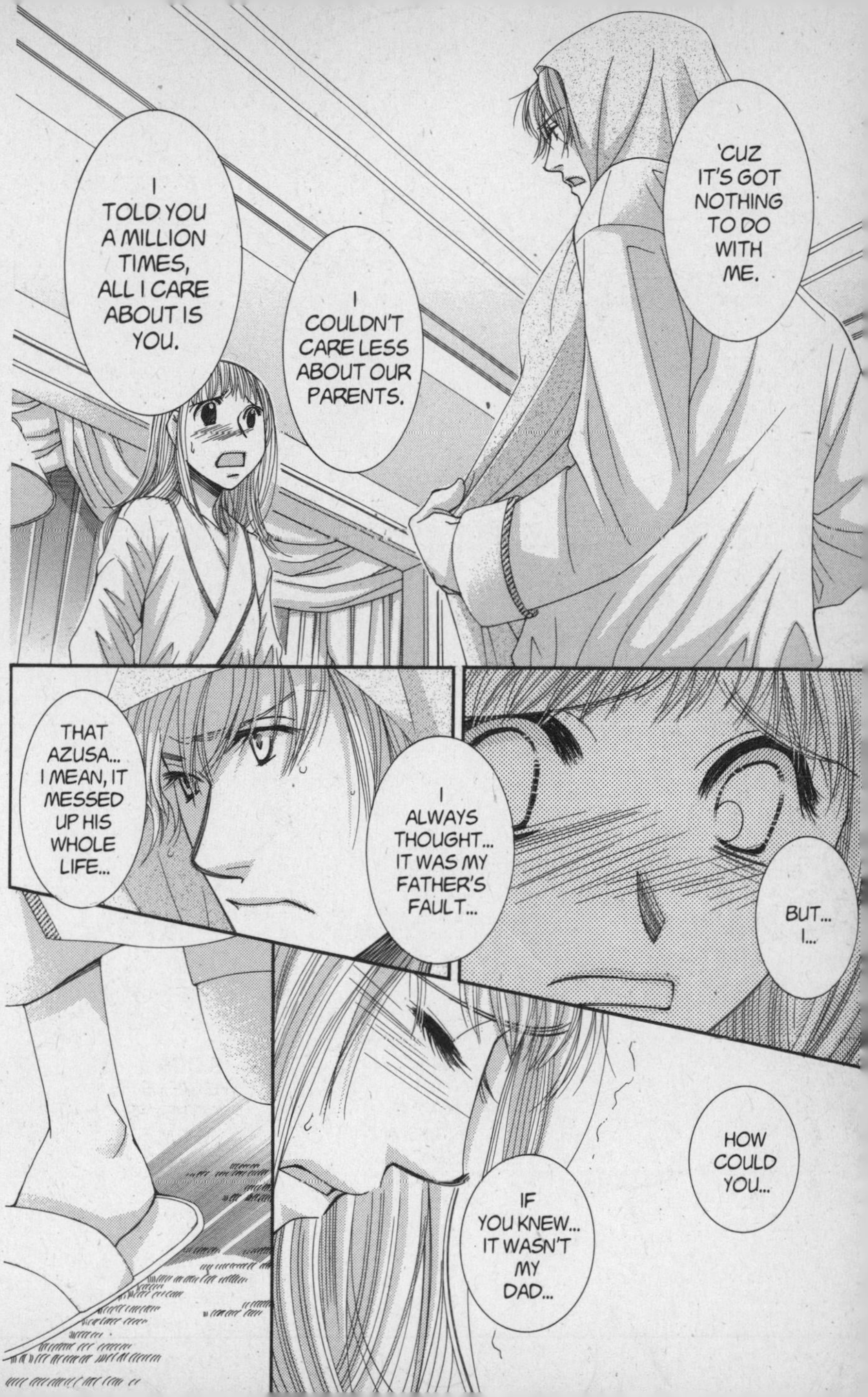
'CUZ IT'S GOT NOTHING TO DO WITH ME.
I COULDN'T CARE LESS ABOUT OUR PARENTS.
I TOLD YOU A MILLION TIMES, ALL I CARE ABOUT IS YOU.
BUT... I...
I ALWAYS THOUGHT... IT WAS MY FATHER'S FAULT...
THAT AZUSA... I MEAN, IT MESSED UP HIS WHOLE LIFE...
HOW COULD YOU...
IF YOU KNEW... IT WASN'T MY DAD...

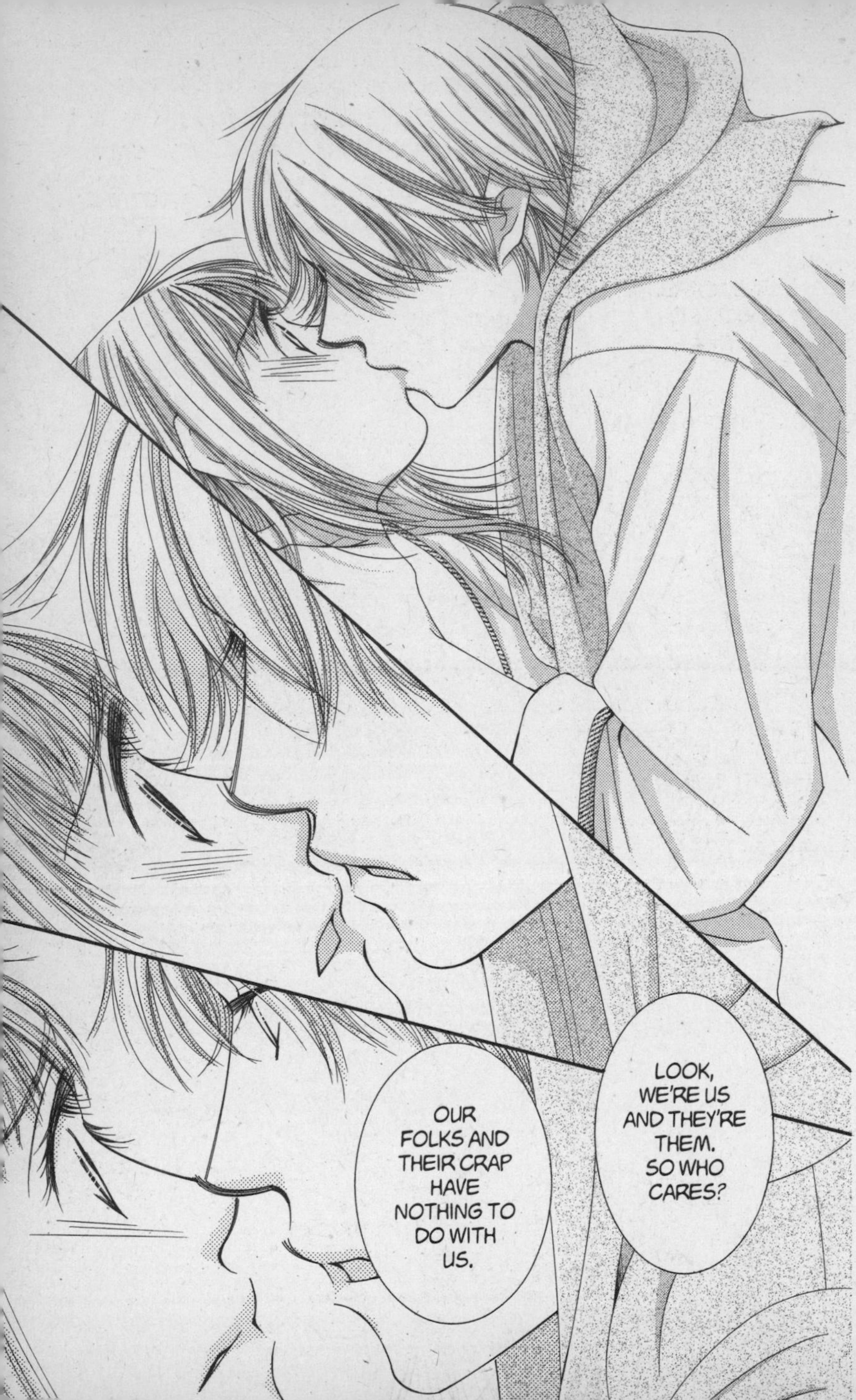
LOOK, WE'RE US AND THEY'RE THEM. SO WHO CARES?
OUR FOLKS AND THEIR CRAP HAVE NOTHING TO DO WITH US.

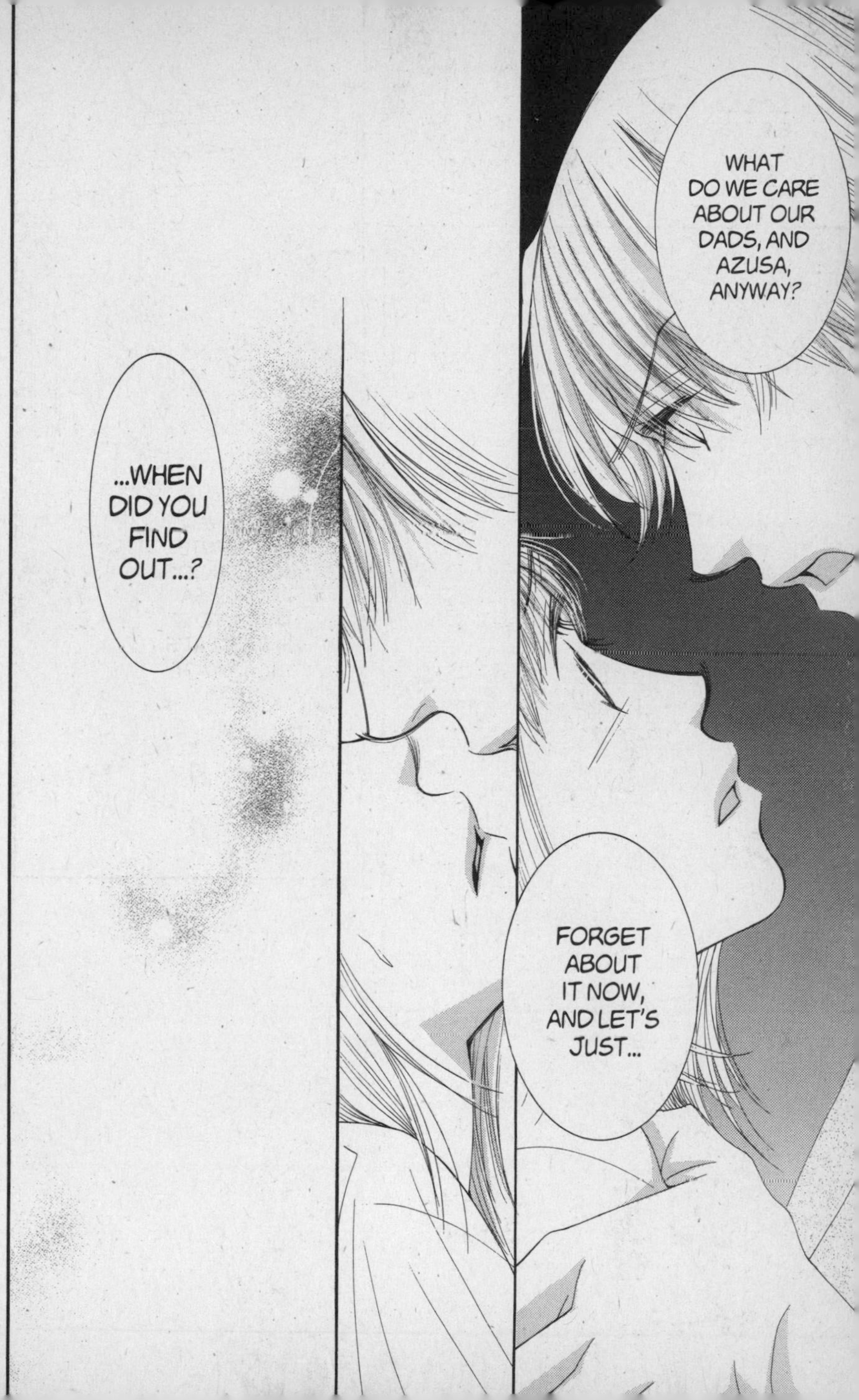
WHAT DO WE CARE ABOUT OUR DADS, AND AZUSA, ANYWAY?
FORGET ABOUT IT NOW, AND LET'S JUST...
...WHEN DID YOU FIND OUT...?

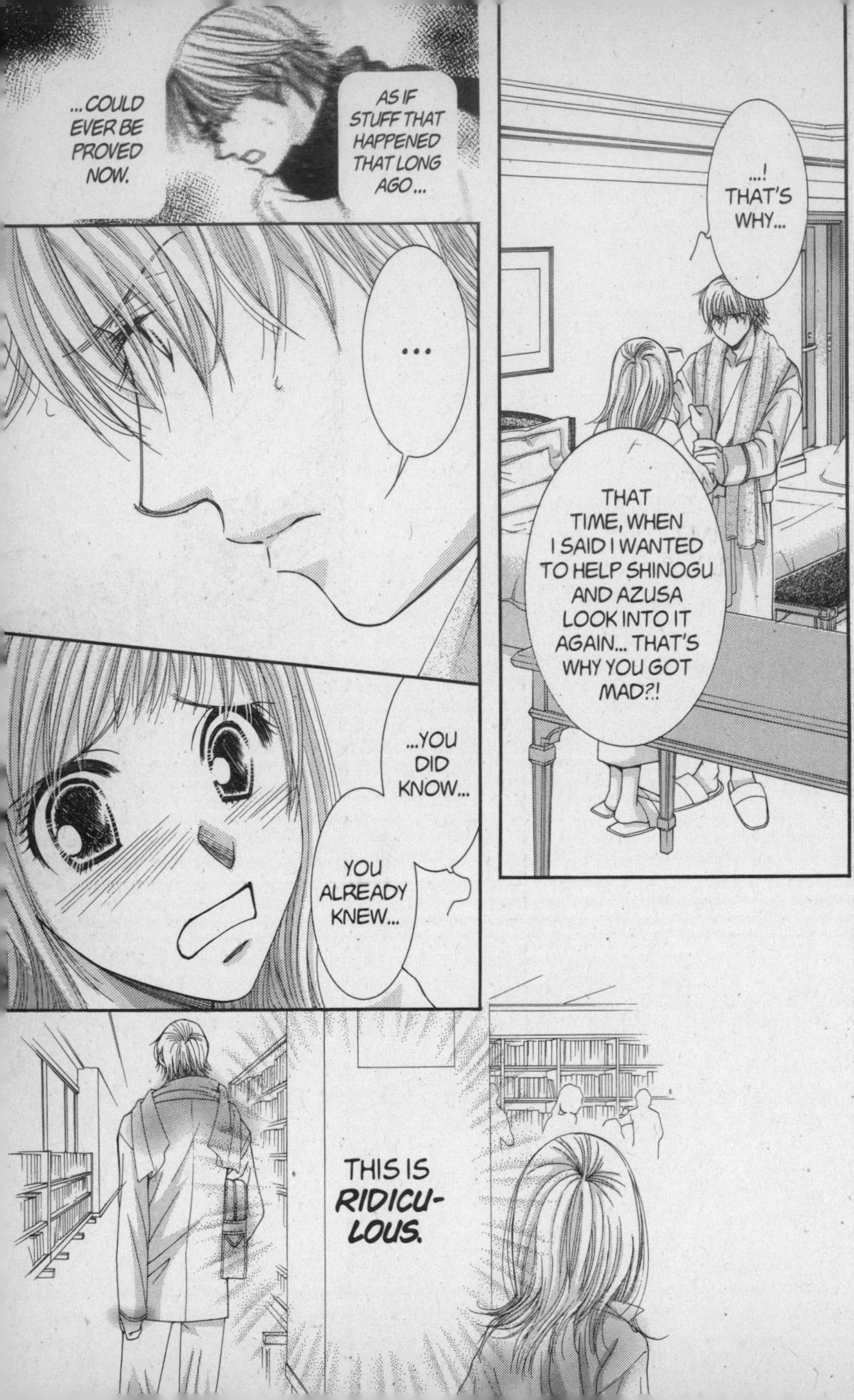
AS IF STUFF THAT HAPPENED THAT LONG AGO...
...COULD EVER BE PROVED NOW.
...! THAT'S WHY...
THAT TIME, WHEN I SAID I WANTED TO HELP SHINOGU AND AZUSA LOOK INTO IT AGAIN... THAT'S WHY YOU GOT MAD?!
...
...YOU DID KNOW...
YOU ALREADY KNEW...
THIS IS RIDICULOUS.

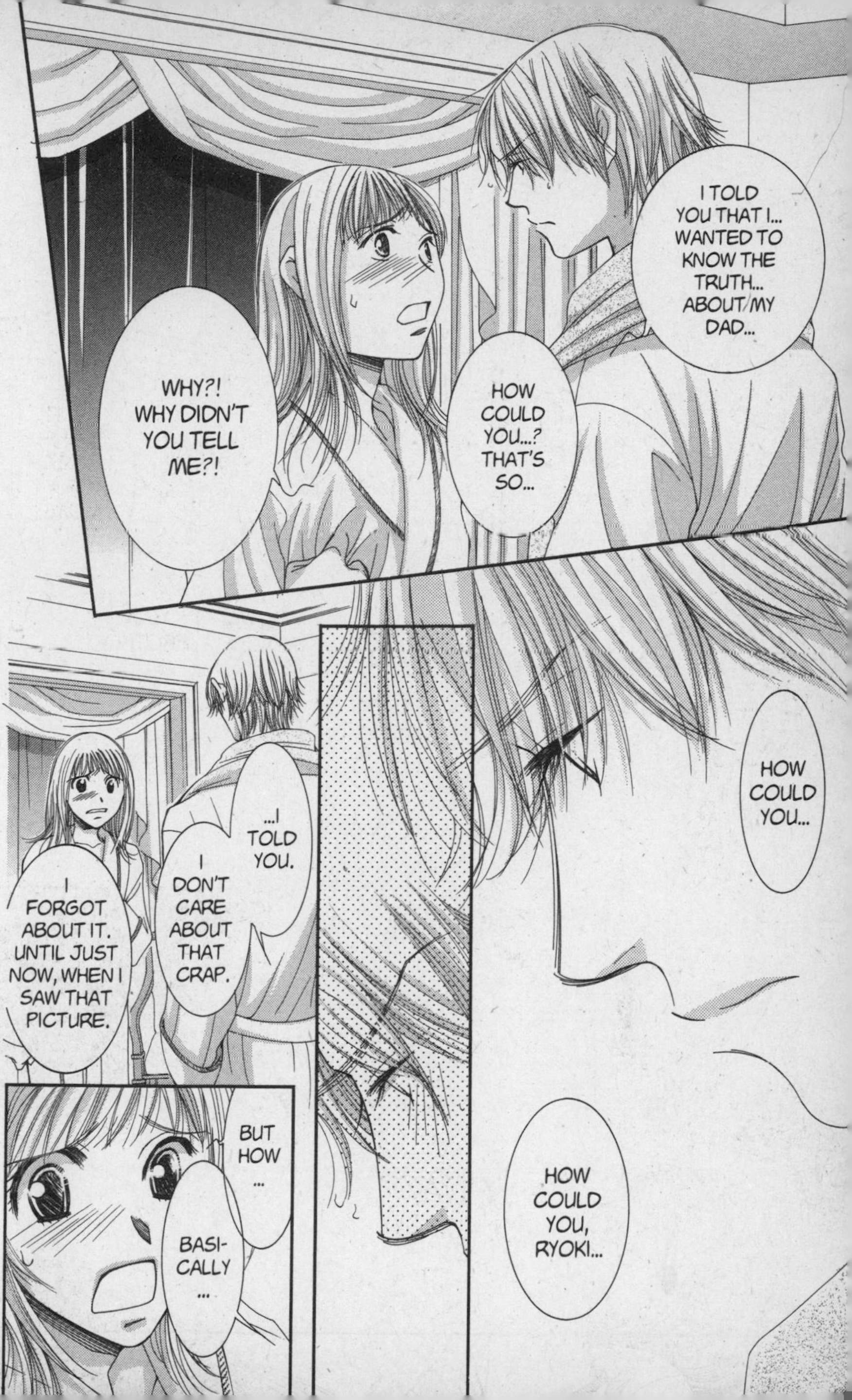
I TOLD YOU THAT I... WANTED TO KNOW THE TRUTH... ABOUT MY DAD...
HOW COULD YOU...? THAT'S SO...
WHY?! WHY DIDN'T YOU TELL ME?!
HOW COULD YOU...
HOW COULD YOU, RYOKI...
...I TOLD YOU.
I DON'T CARE ABOUT THAT CRAP.
I FORGOT ABOUT IT. UNTIL JUST NOW, WHEN I SAW THAT PICTURE.
BUT HOW ...
BASI-CALLY ...

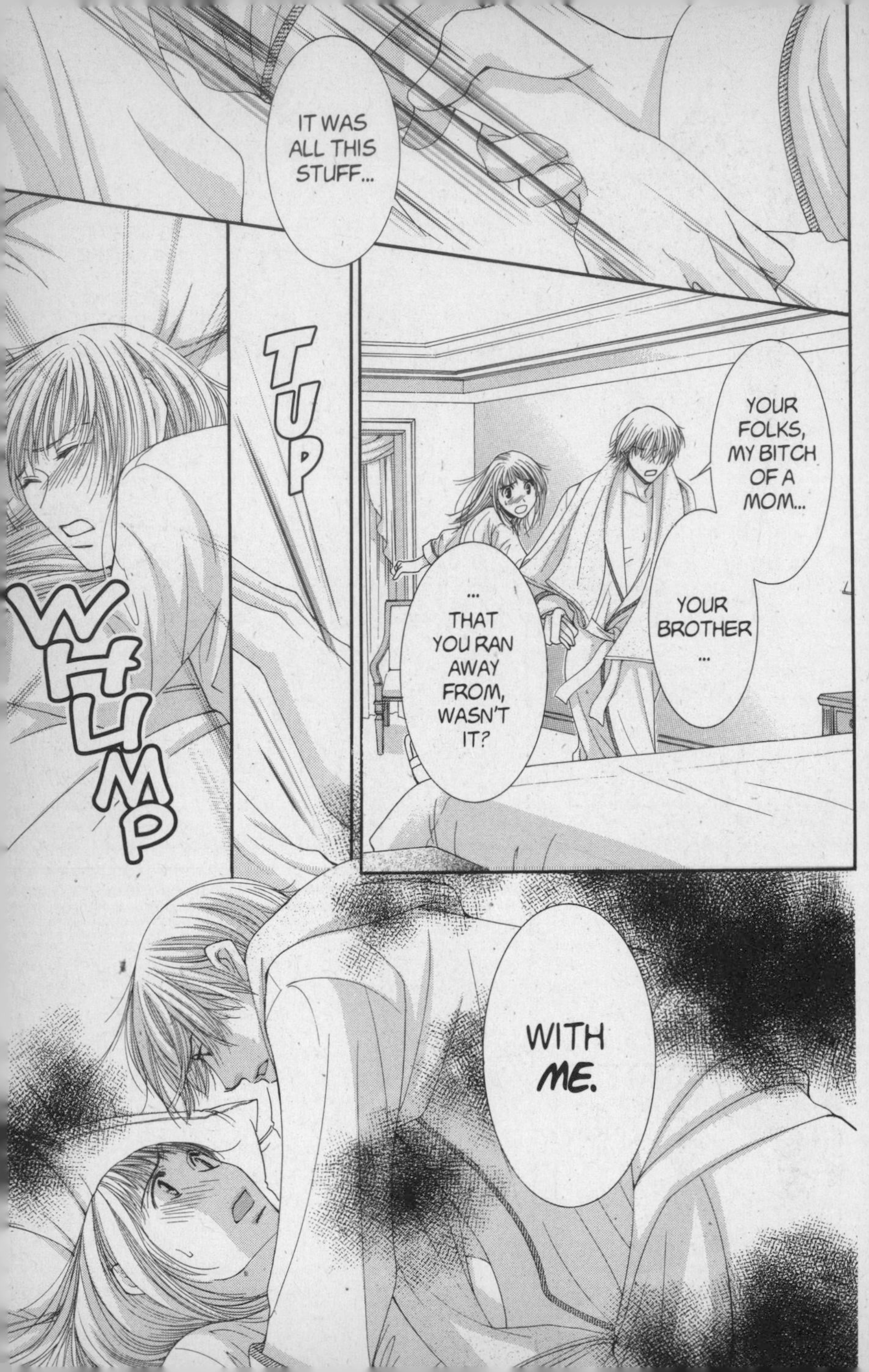
IT WAS ALL THIS STUFF...
YOUR FOLKS, MY BITCH OF A MOM...
YOUR BROTHER ...
... THAT YOU RAN AWAY FROM, WASN'T IT?
TUP
WHUMP
WITH *ME.*

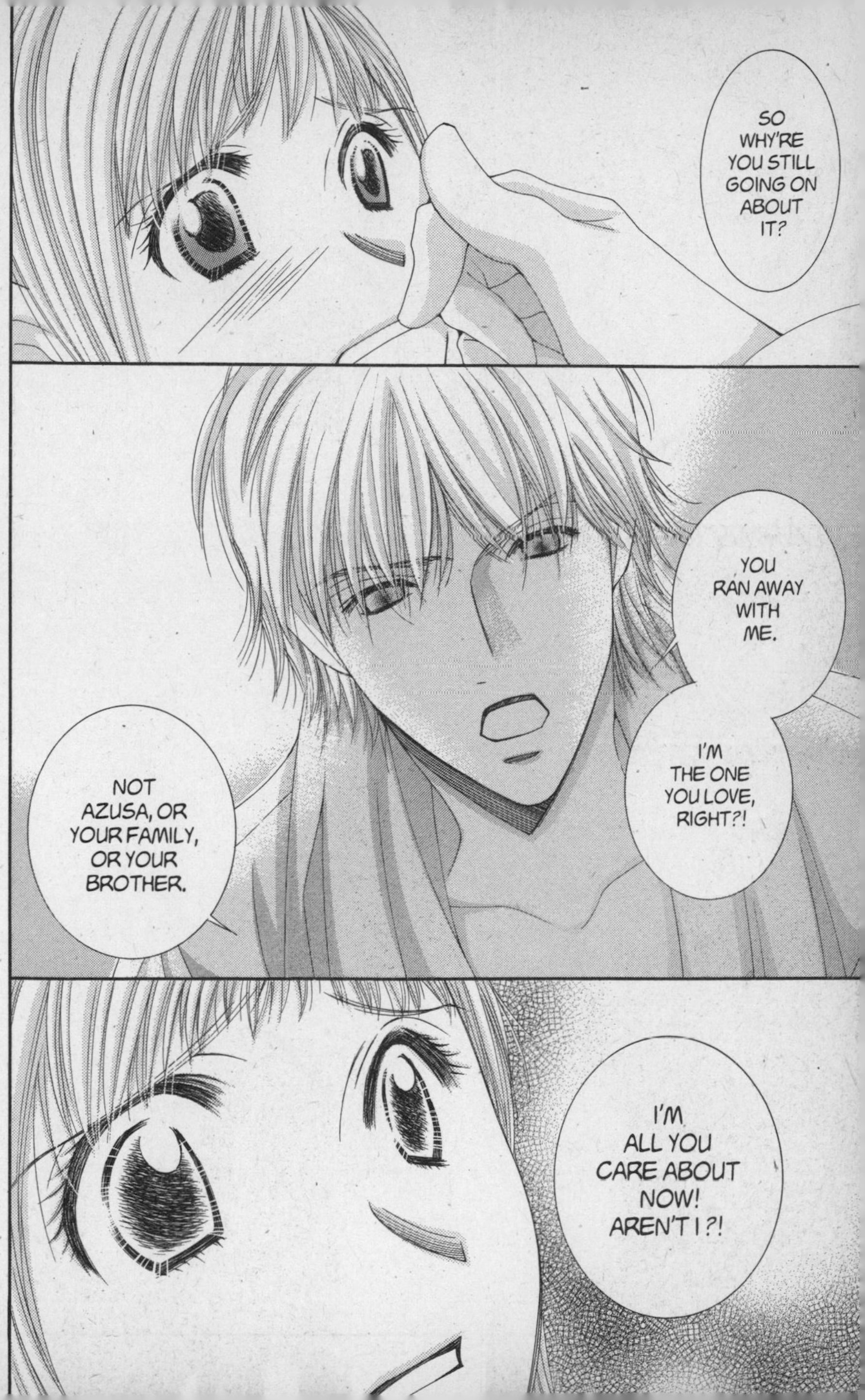
SO WHY'RE YOU STILL GOING ON ABOUT IT?
YOU RAN AWAY WITH ME.
I'M THE ONE YOU LOVE, RIGHT?!
NOT AZUSA, OR YOUR FAMILY, OR YOUR BROTHER.
I'M ALL YOU CARE ABOUT NOW! AREN'T I?!

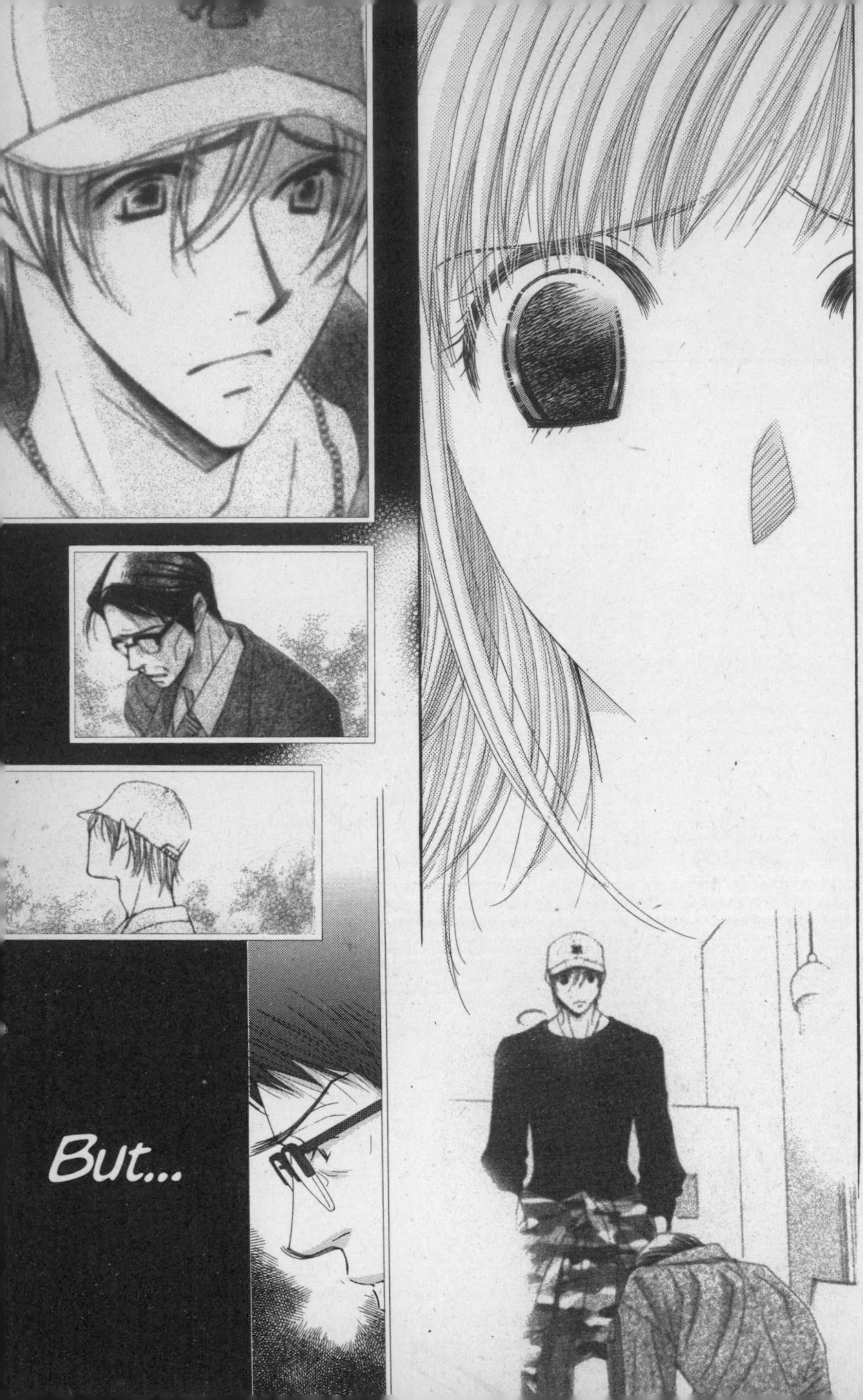
But...

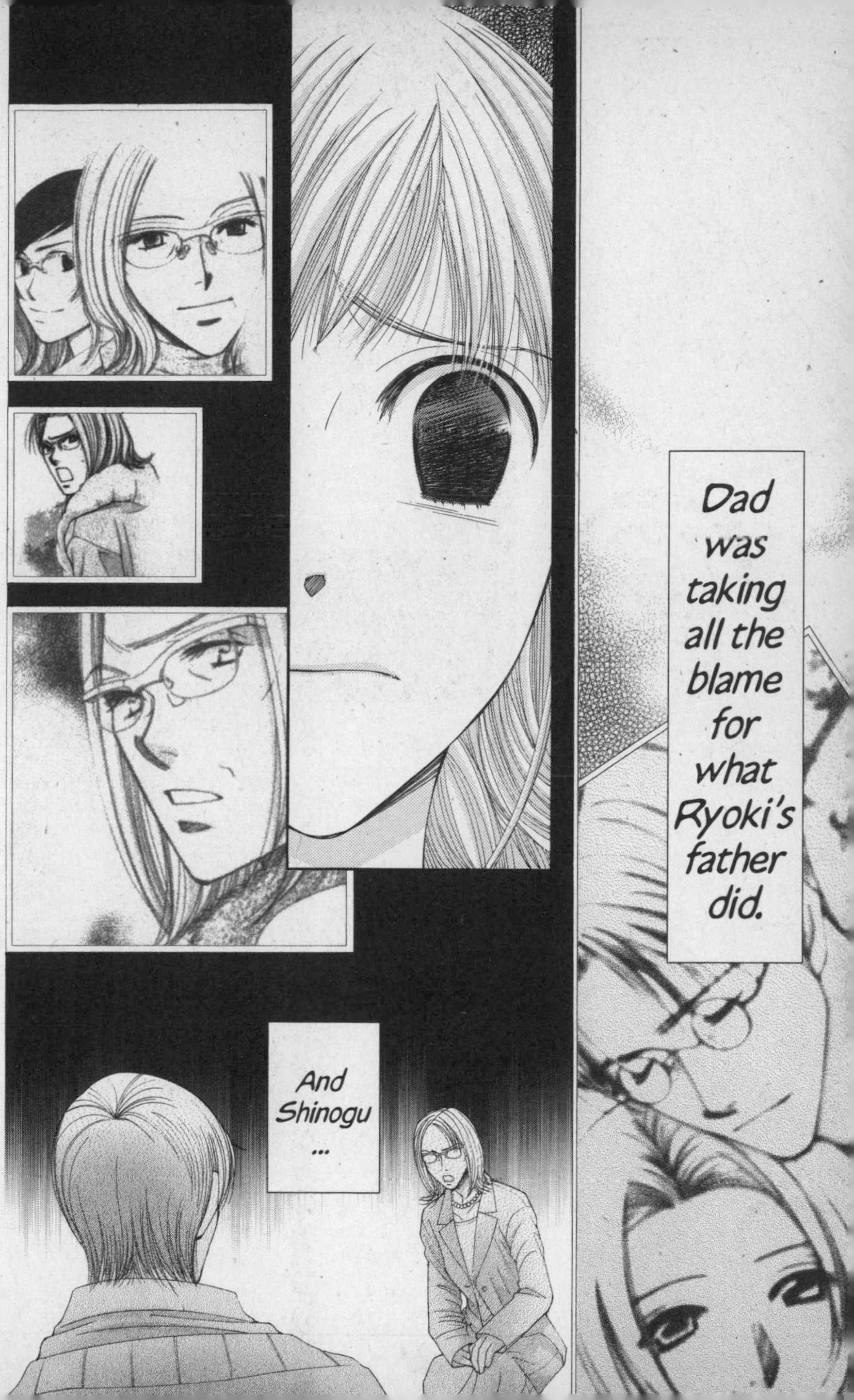
Dad was taking all the blame for what Ryoki's father did.
And Shinogu ...

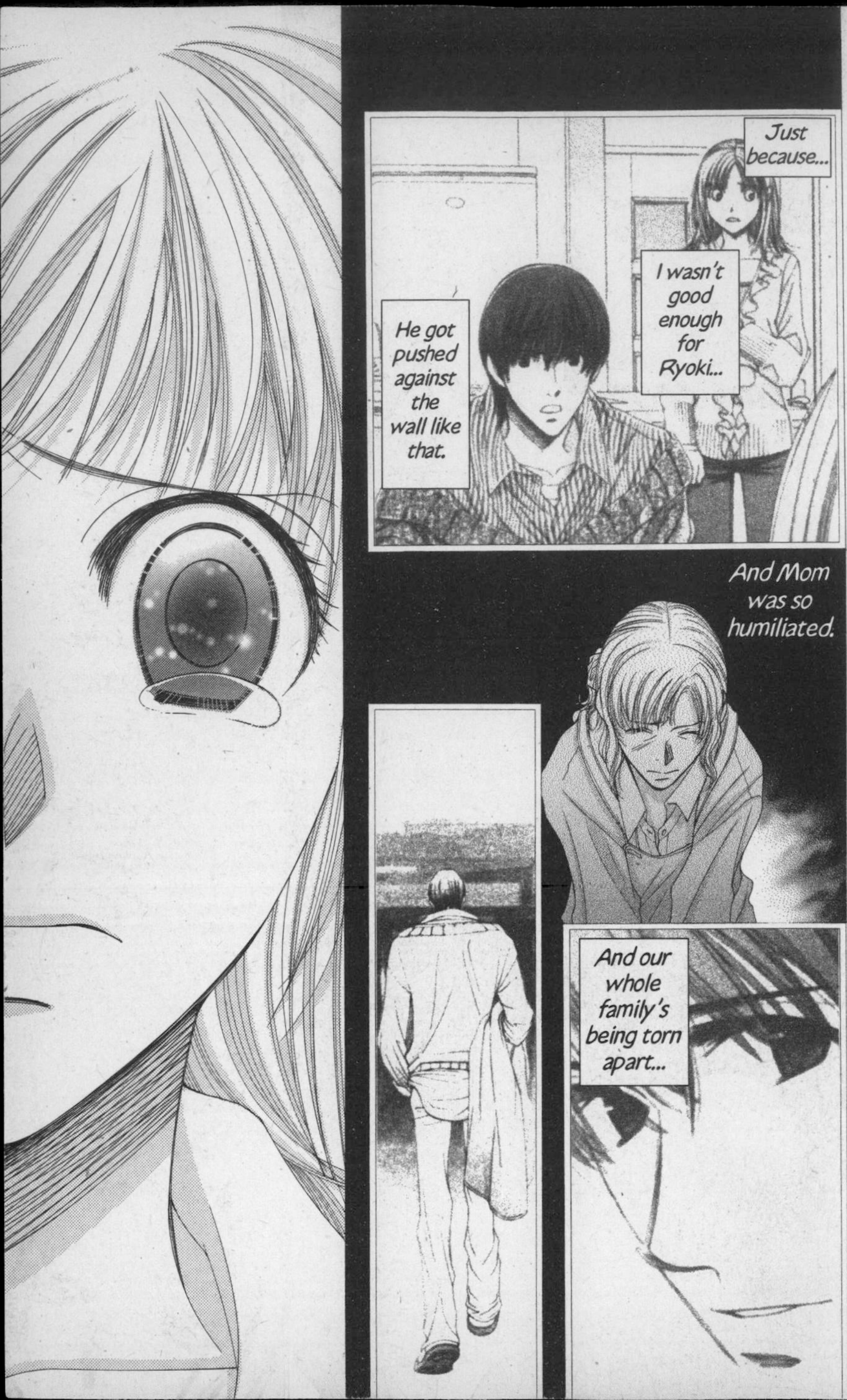
Just because...
I wasn't good enough for Ryoki...
He got pushed against the wall like that.
And Mom was so humiliated.
And our whole family's being torn apart...

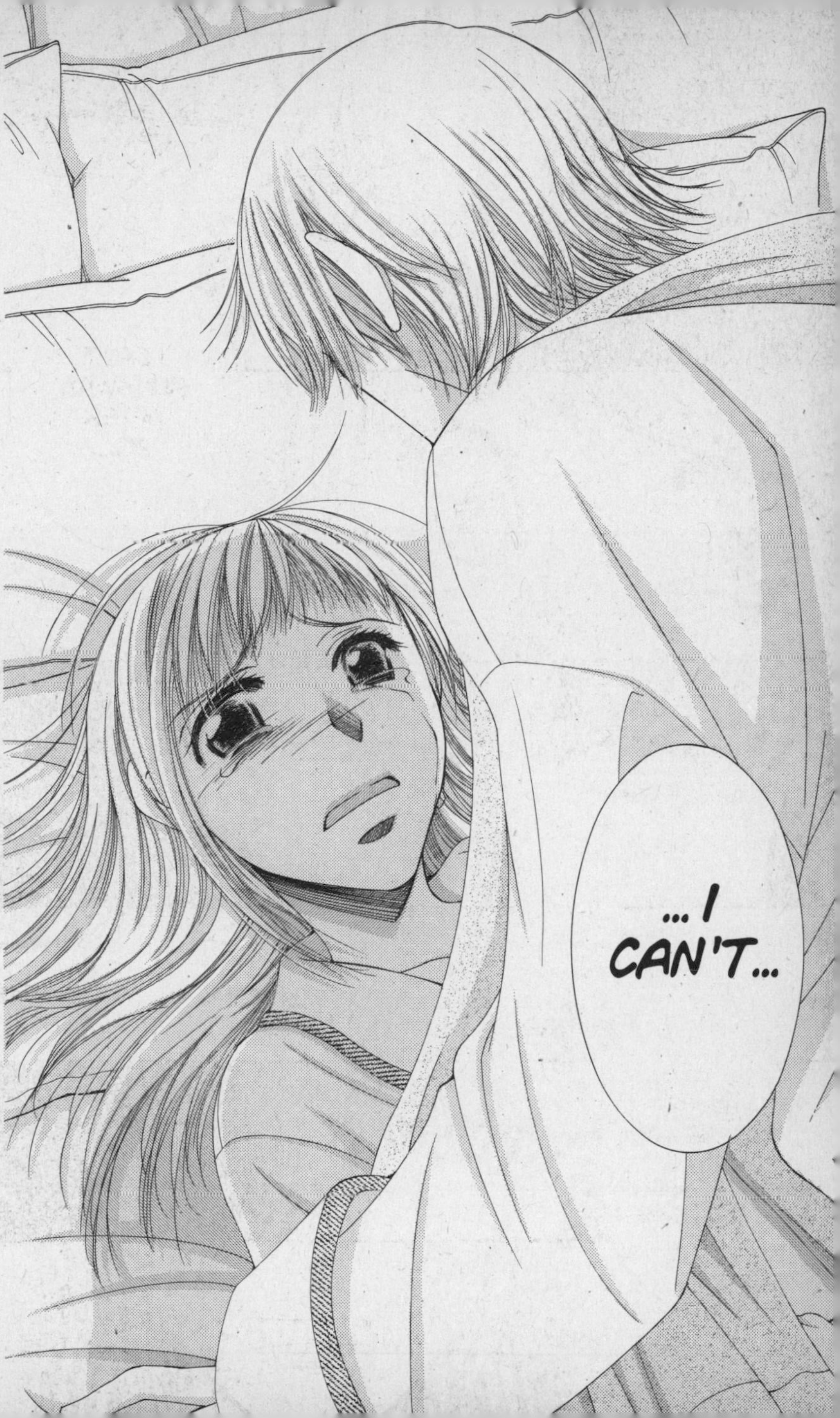
...I CAN'T...

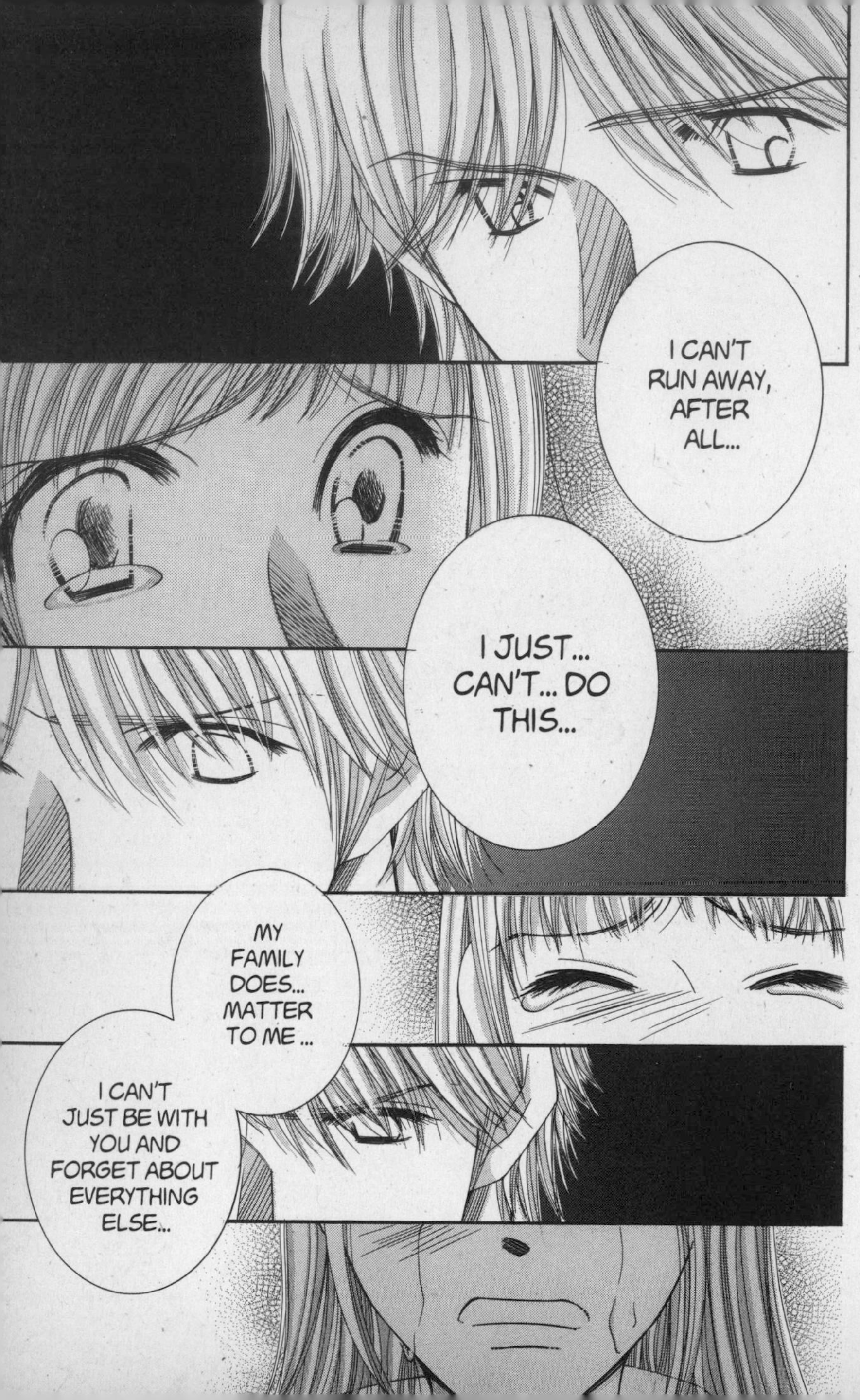
I CAN'T RUN AWAY, AFTER ALL...
I JUST... CAN'T... DO THIS...
MY FAMILY DOES... MATTER TO ME ...
I CAN'T JUST BE WITH YOU AND FORGET ABOUT EVERYTHING ELSE...

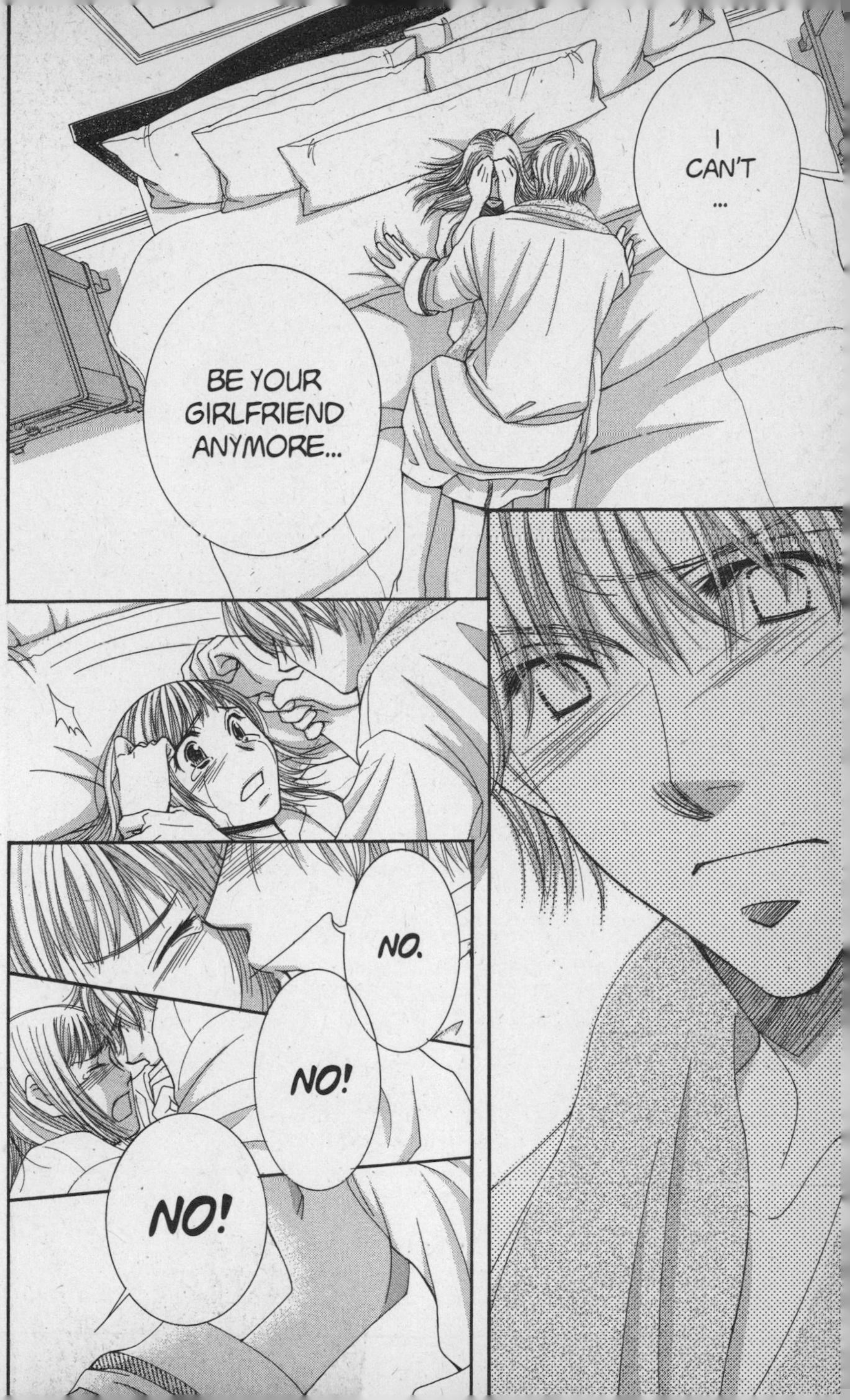
I CAN'T ...
BE YOUR GIRLFRIEND ANYMORE...
NO.
NO!
NO!

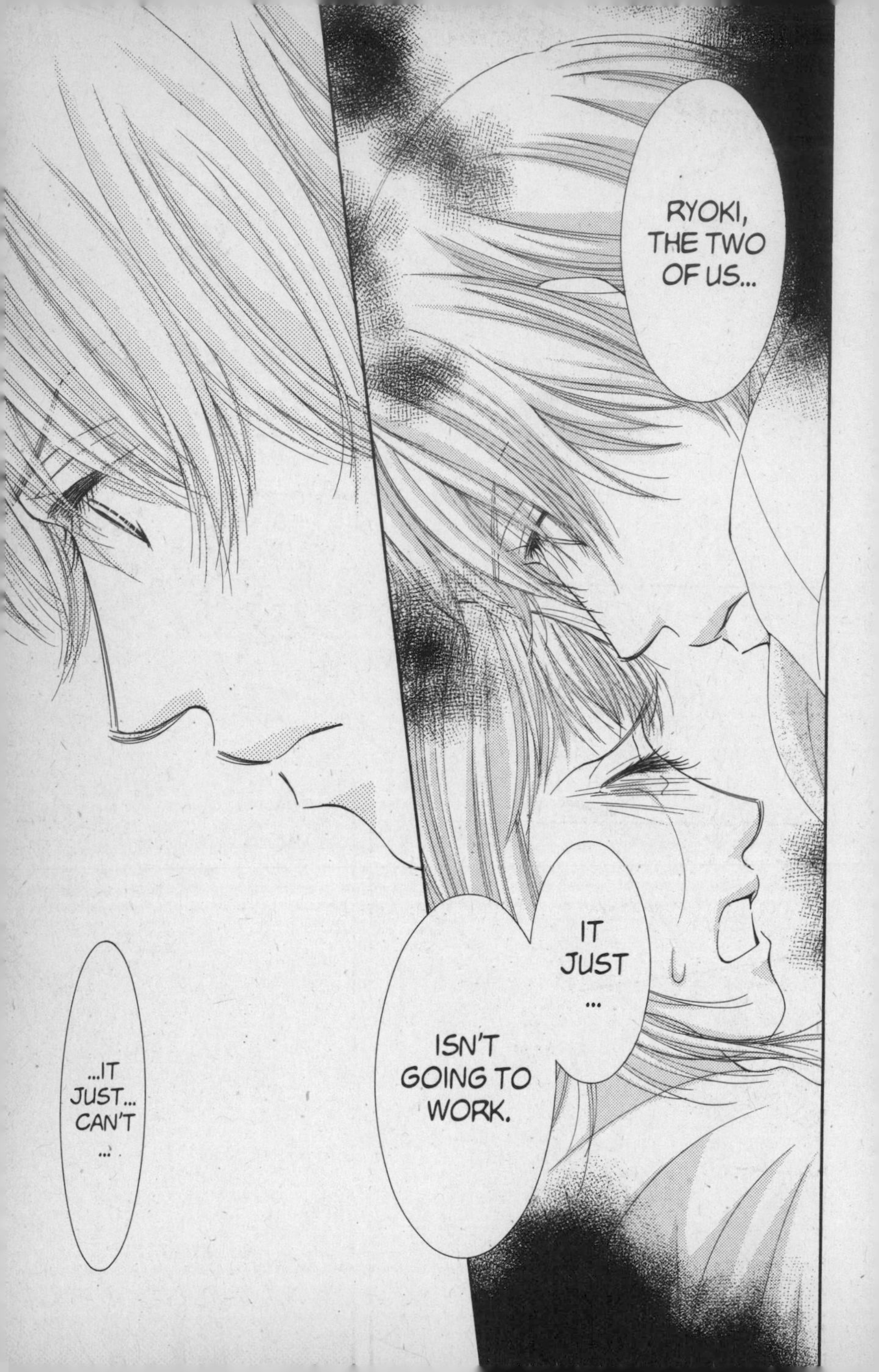
RYOKI, THE TWO OF US...
IT JUST ...
ISN'T GOING TO WORK.
...IT JUST... CAN'T ...

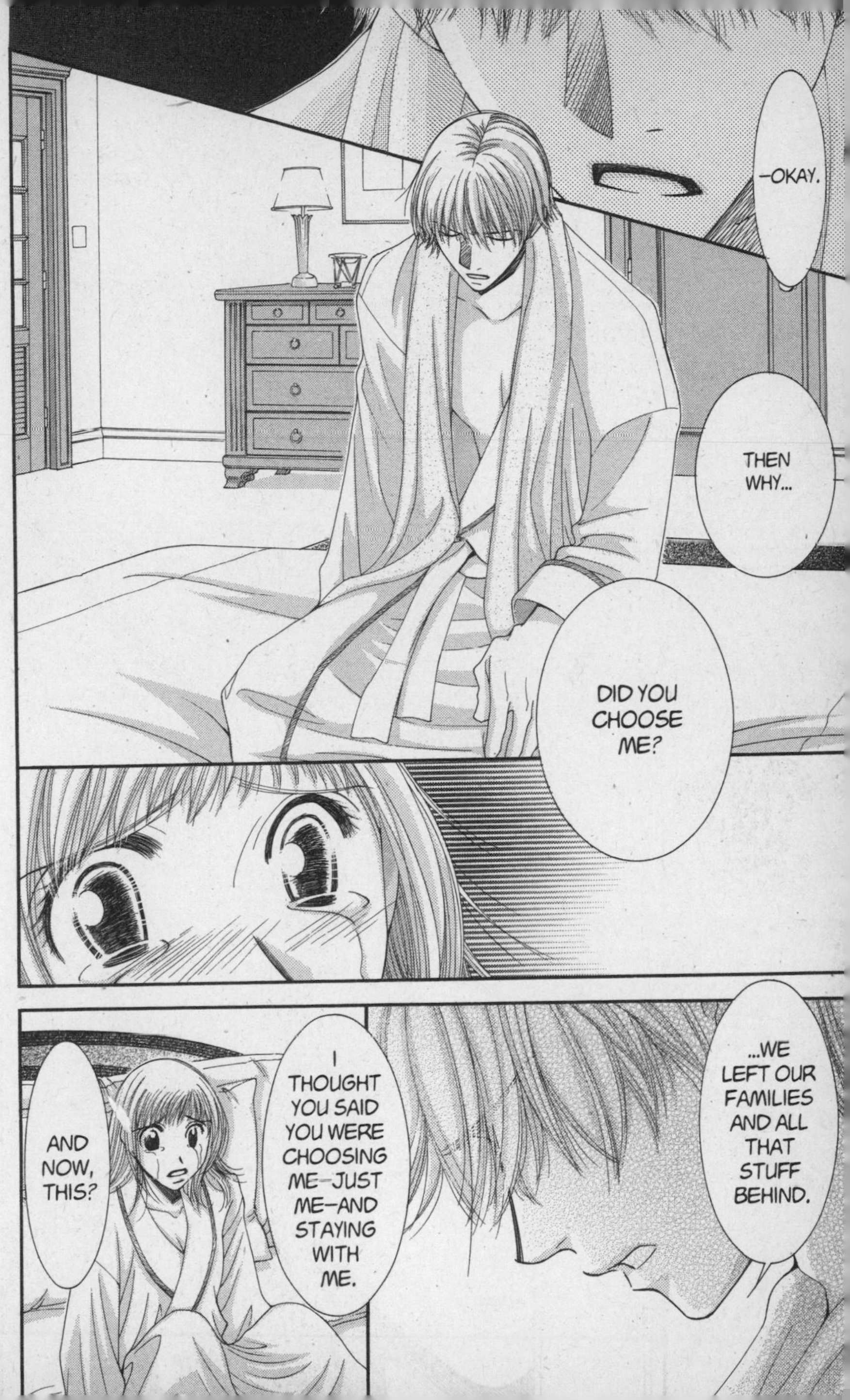
-OKAY.
THEN WHY...
DID YOU CHOOSE ME?
...WE LEFT OUR FAMILIES AND ALL THAT STUFF BEHIND.
I THOUGHT YOU SAID YOU WERE CHOOSING ME-JUST ME-AND STAYING WITH ME.
AND NOW, THIS?

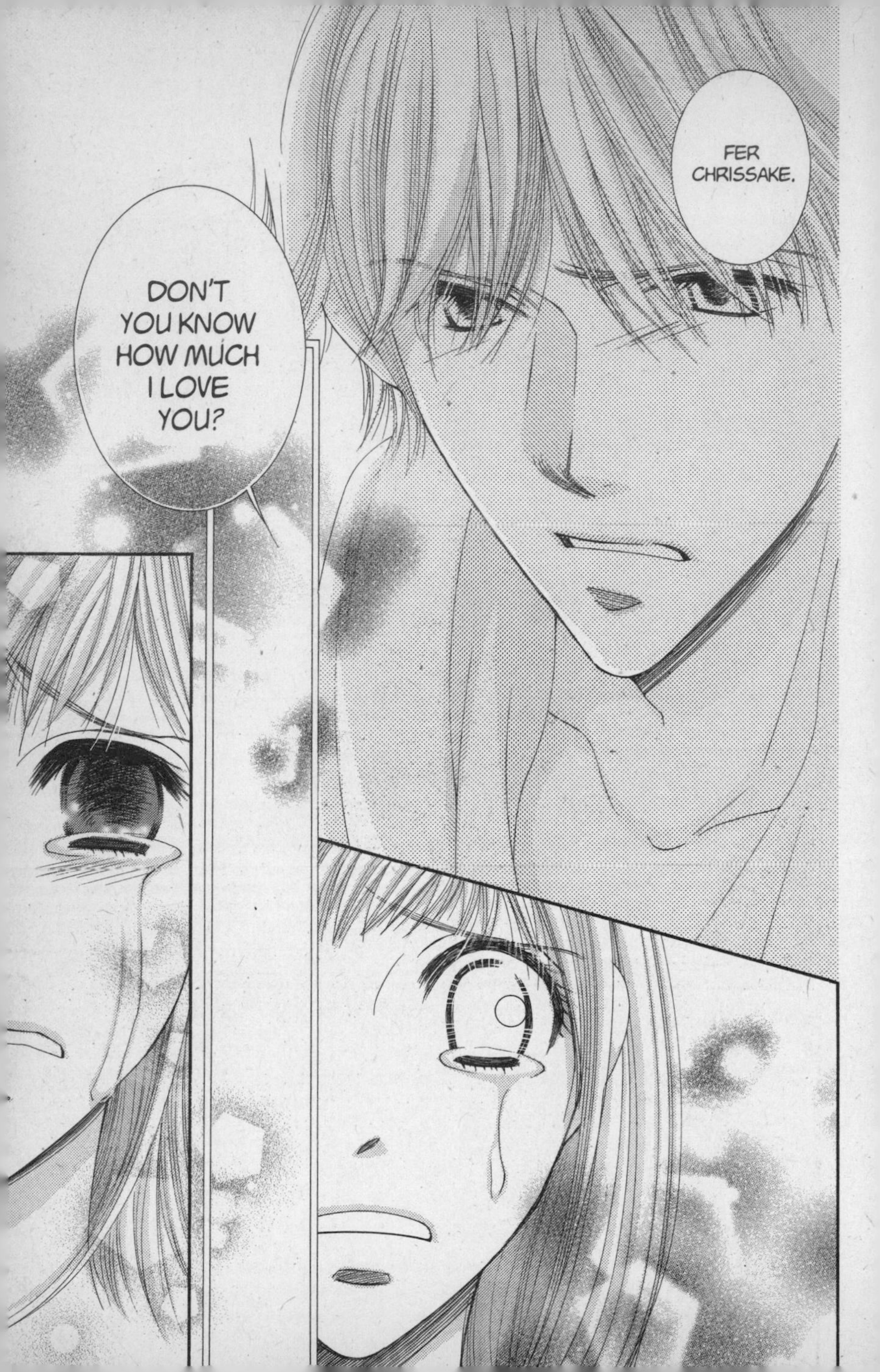
FER CHRISSAKE.
DON'T YOU KNOW HOW MUCH I LOVE YOU?

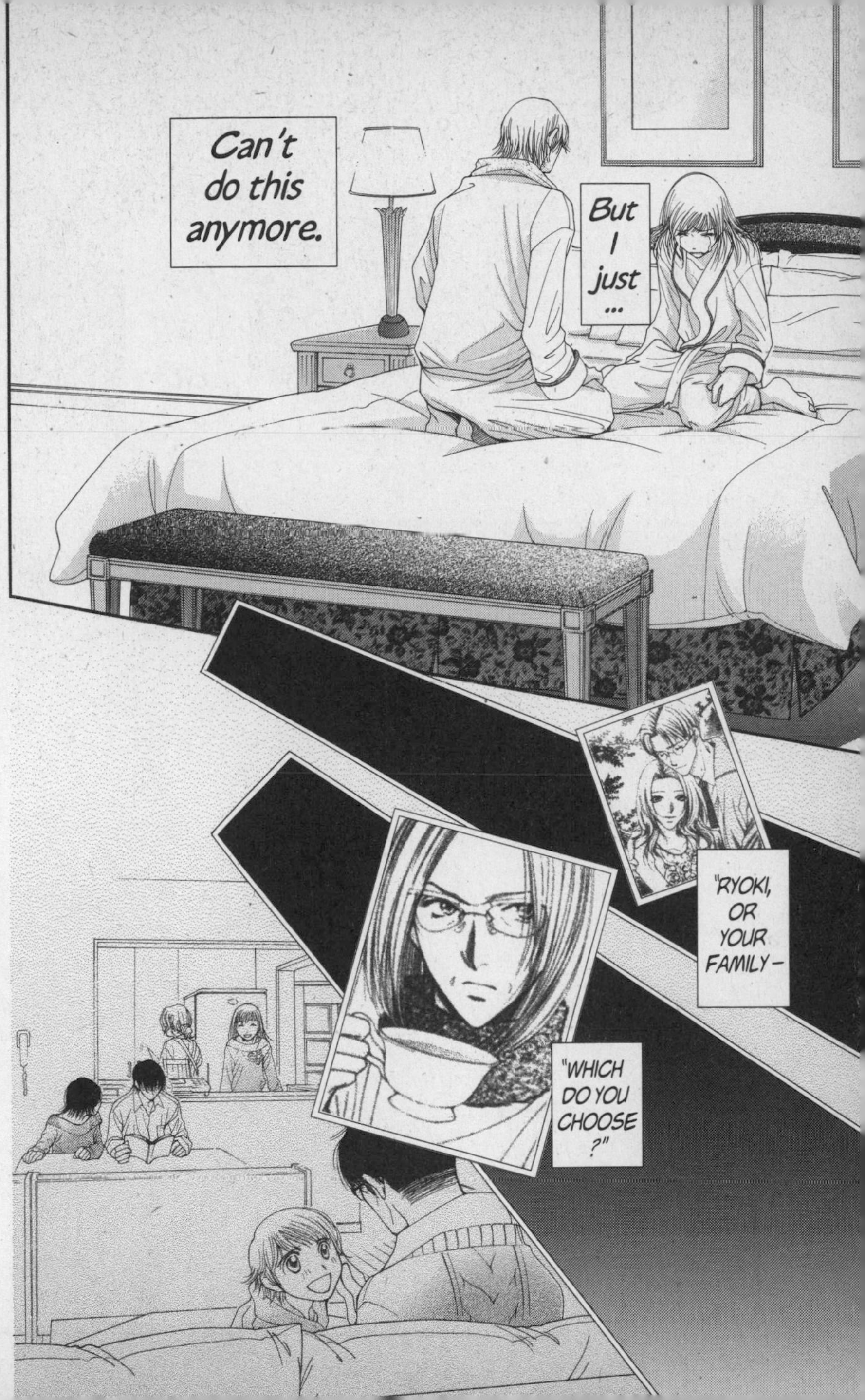
Can't do this anymore.
But I just...
"RYOKI, OR YOUR FAMILY—
"WHICH DO YOU CHOOSE?"

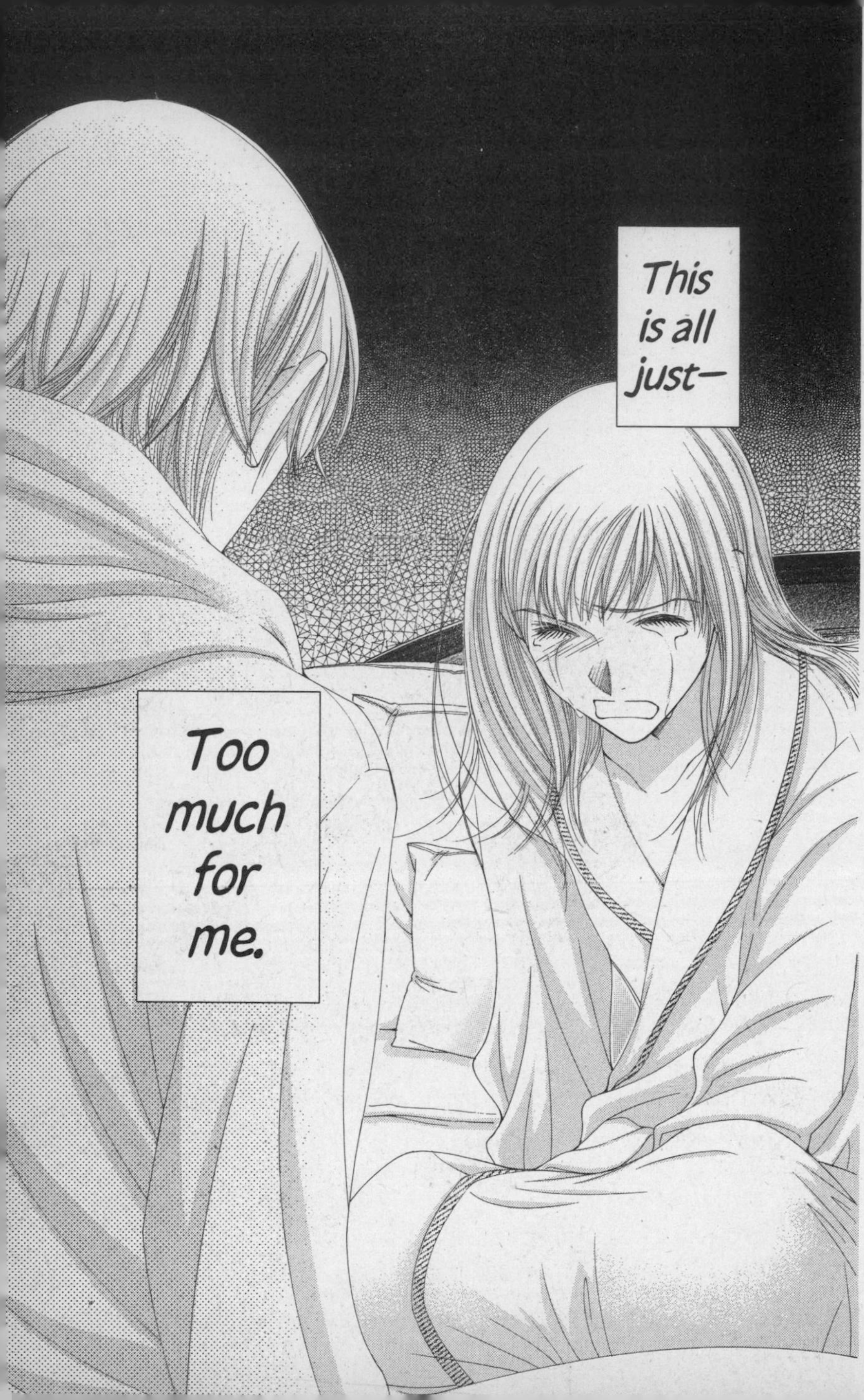
This is all just—
Too much for me.

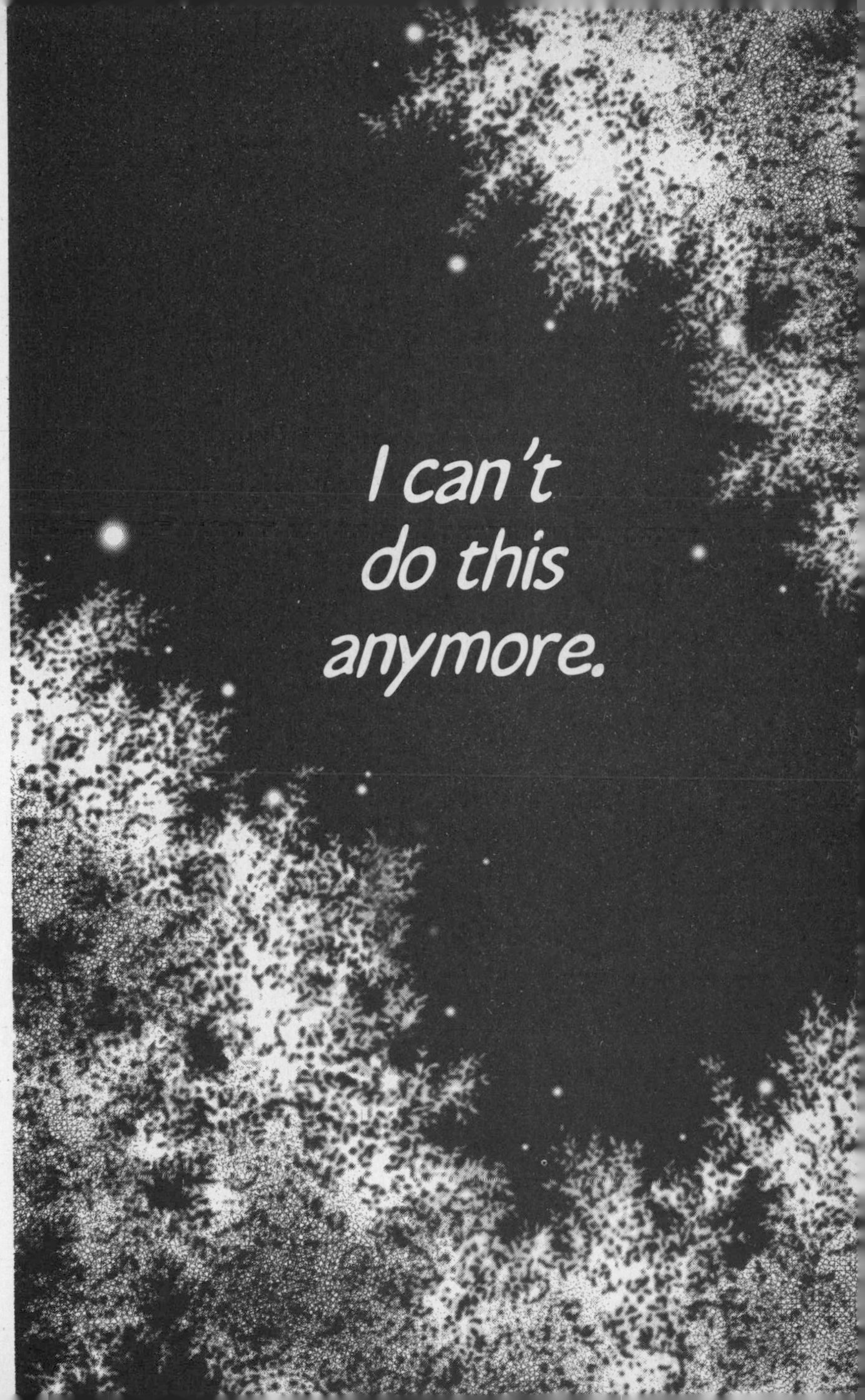
I can't do this anymore.

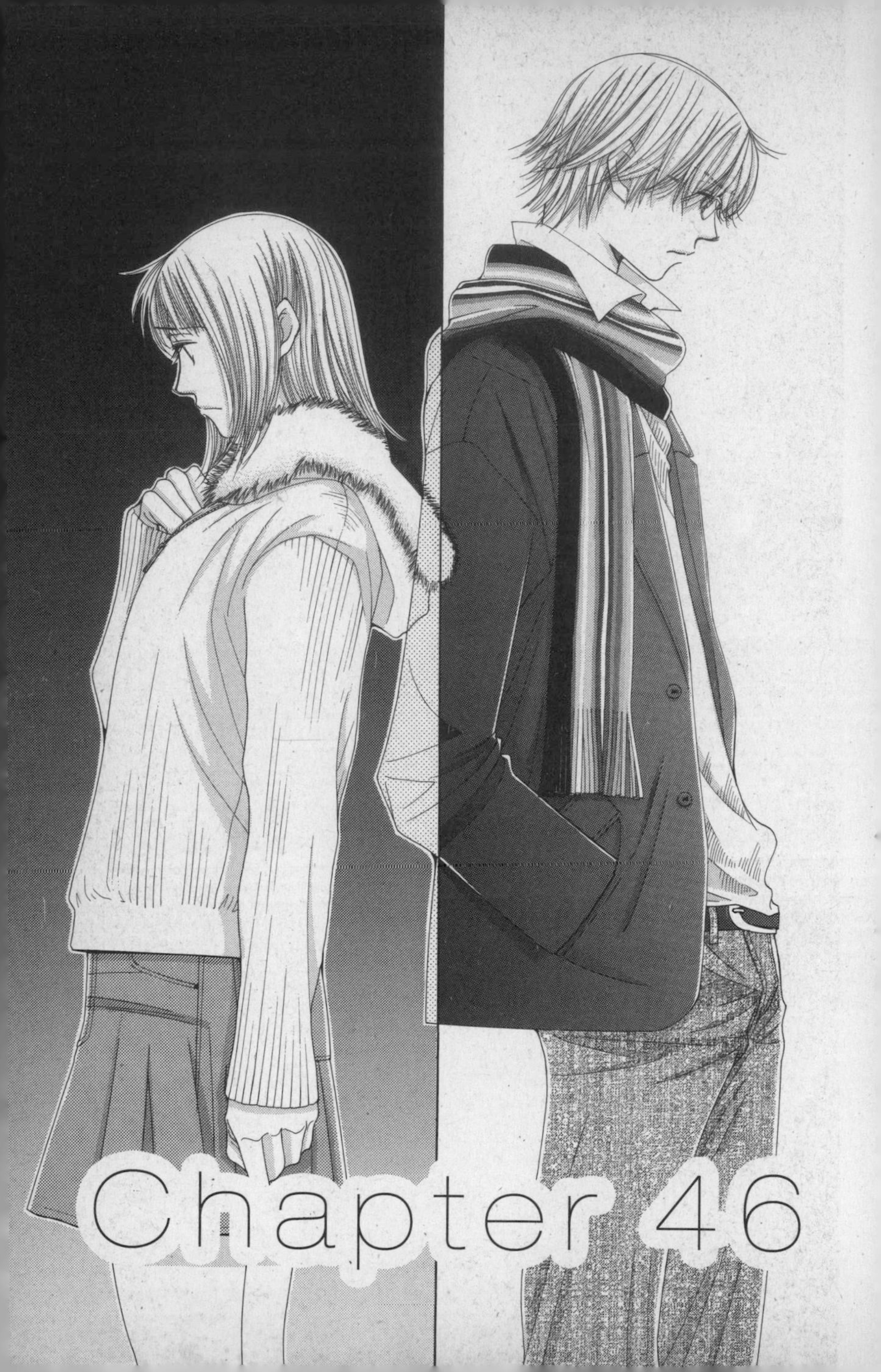
Chapter 46

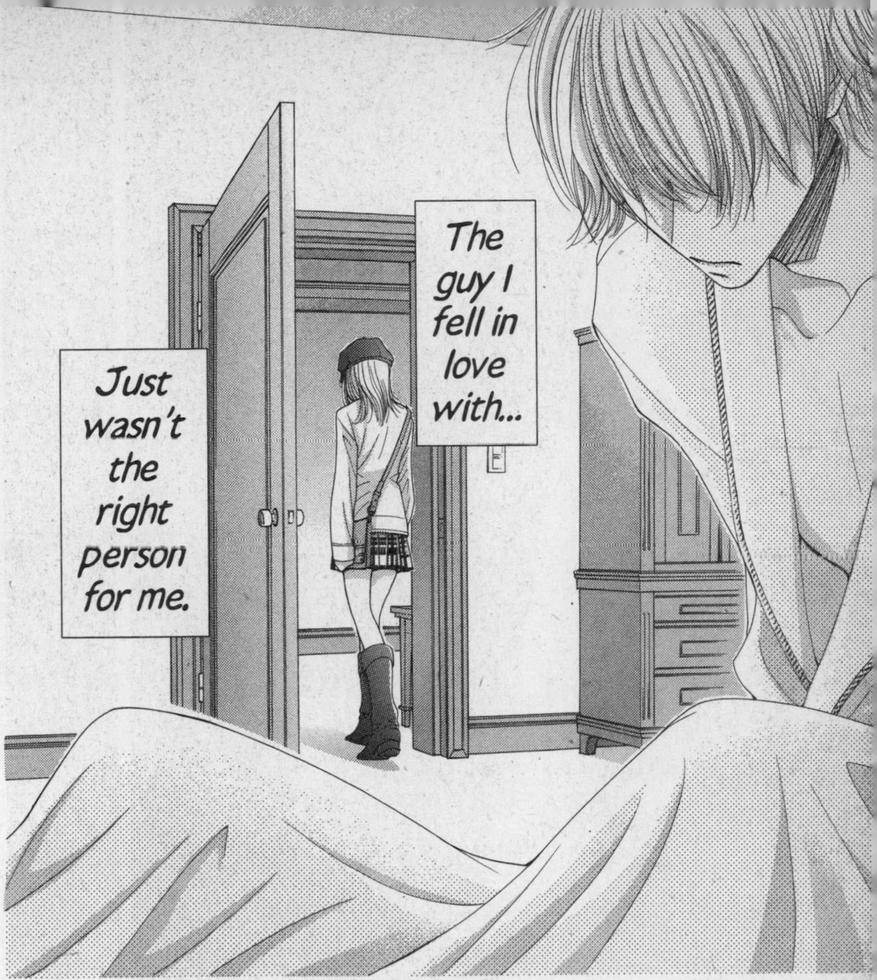
The guy I fell in love with...
Just wasn't the right person for me.

hot gimmick

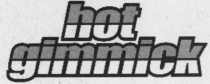

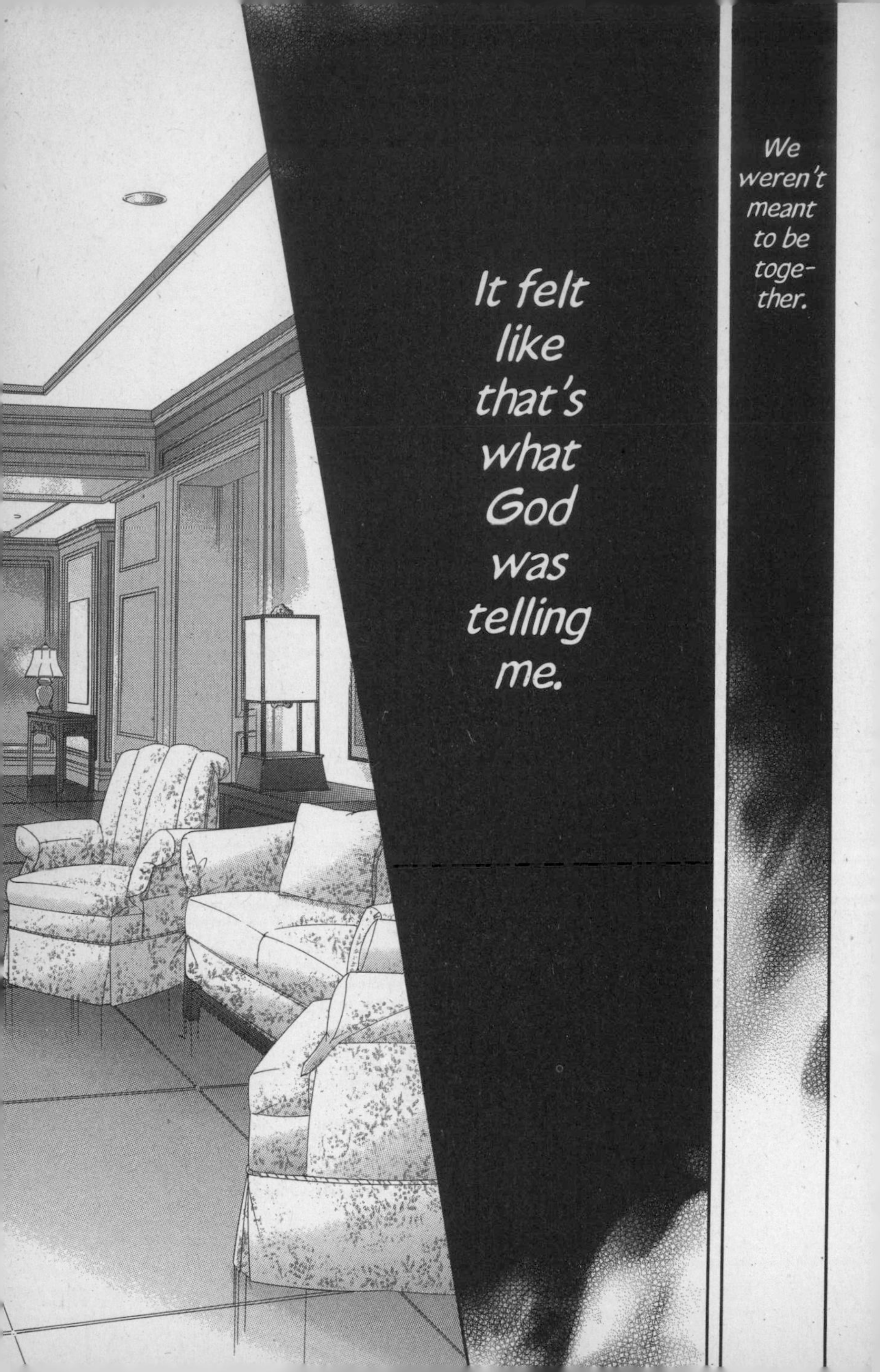
We weren't meant to be toge- ther.
It felt like that's what God was telling me.

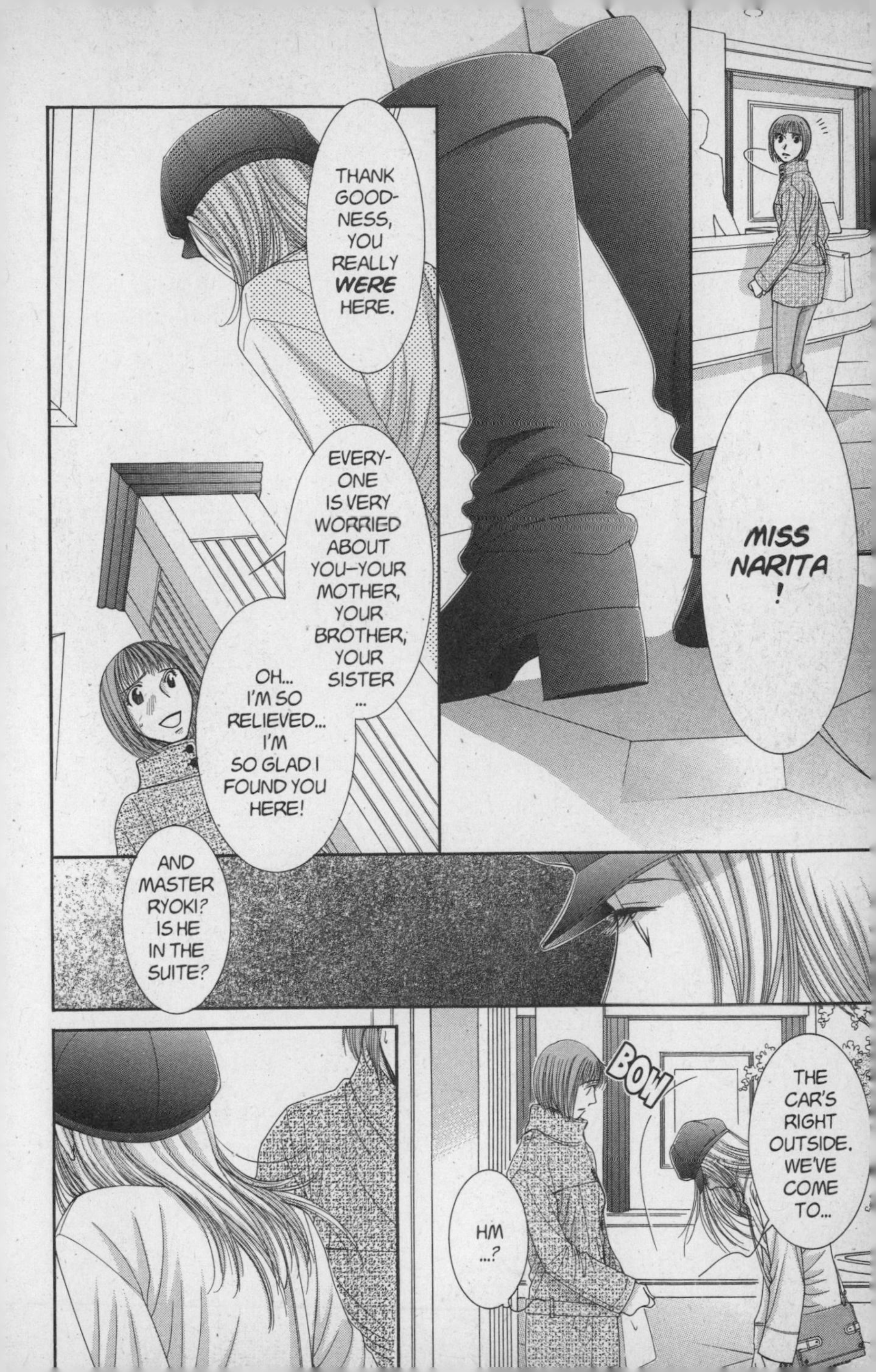
MISS NARITA!
THANK GOODNESS, YOU REALLY WERE HERE.
EVERYONE IS VERY WORRIED ABOUT YOU—YOUR MOTHER, YOUR BROTHER, YOUR SISTER ...
OH... I'M SO RELIEVED... I'M SO GLAD I FOUND YOU HERE!
AND MASTER RYOKI? IS HE IN THE SUITE?
THE CAR'S RIGHT OUTSIDE. WE'VE COME TO...
BOW
HM ...?

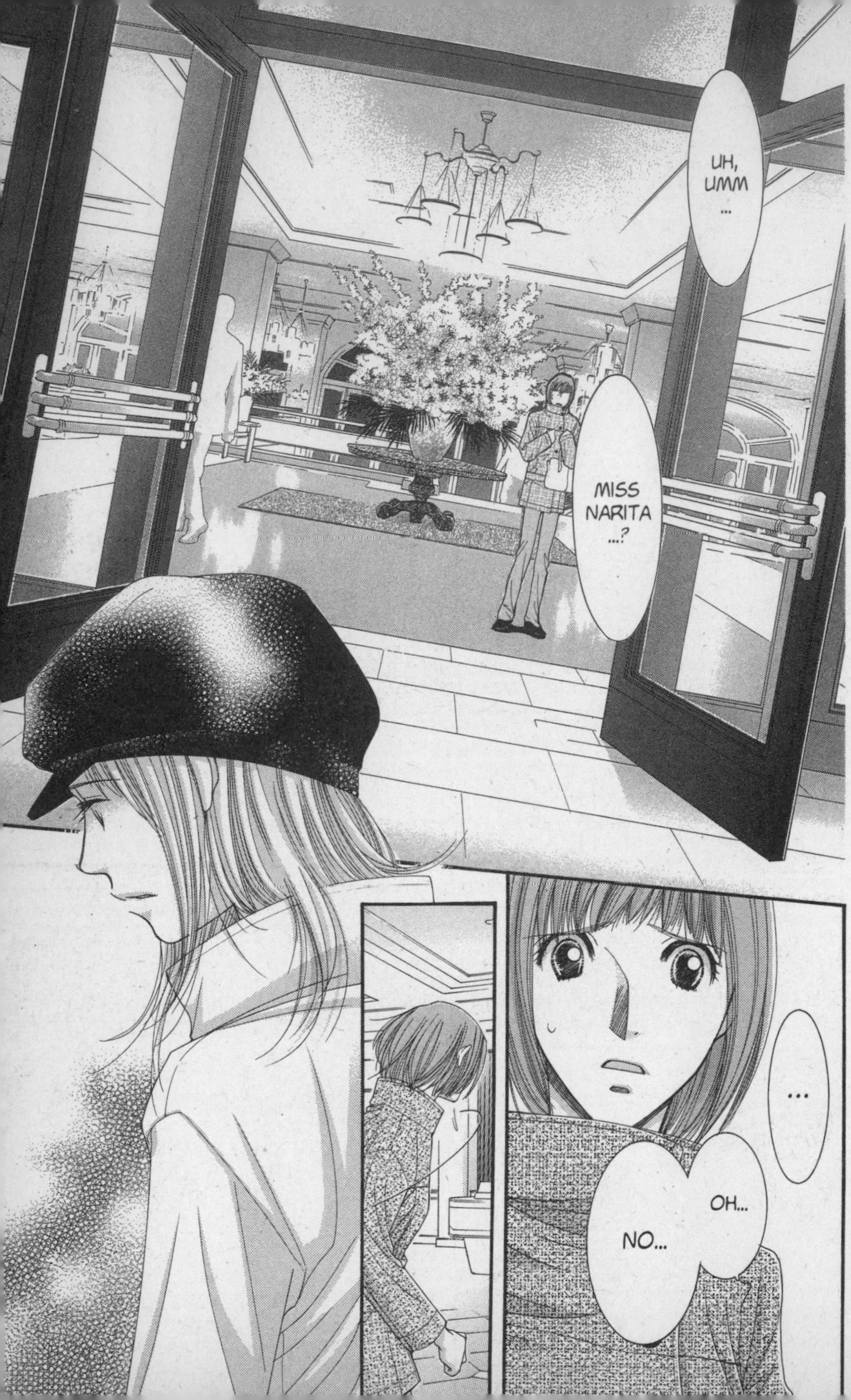
UH, UMM ...
MISS NARITA ...?
...
OH... NO...

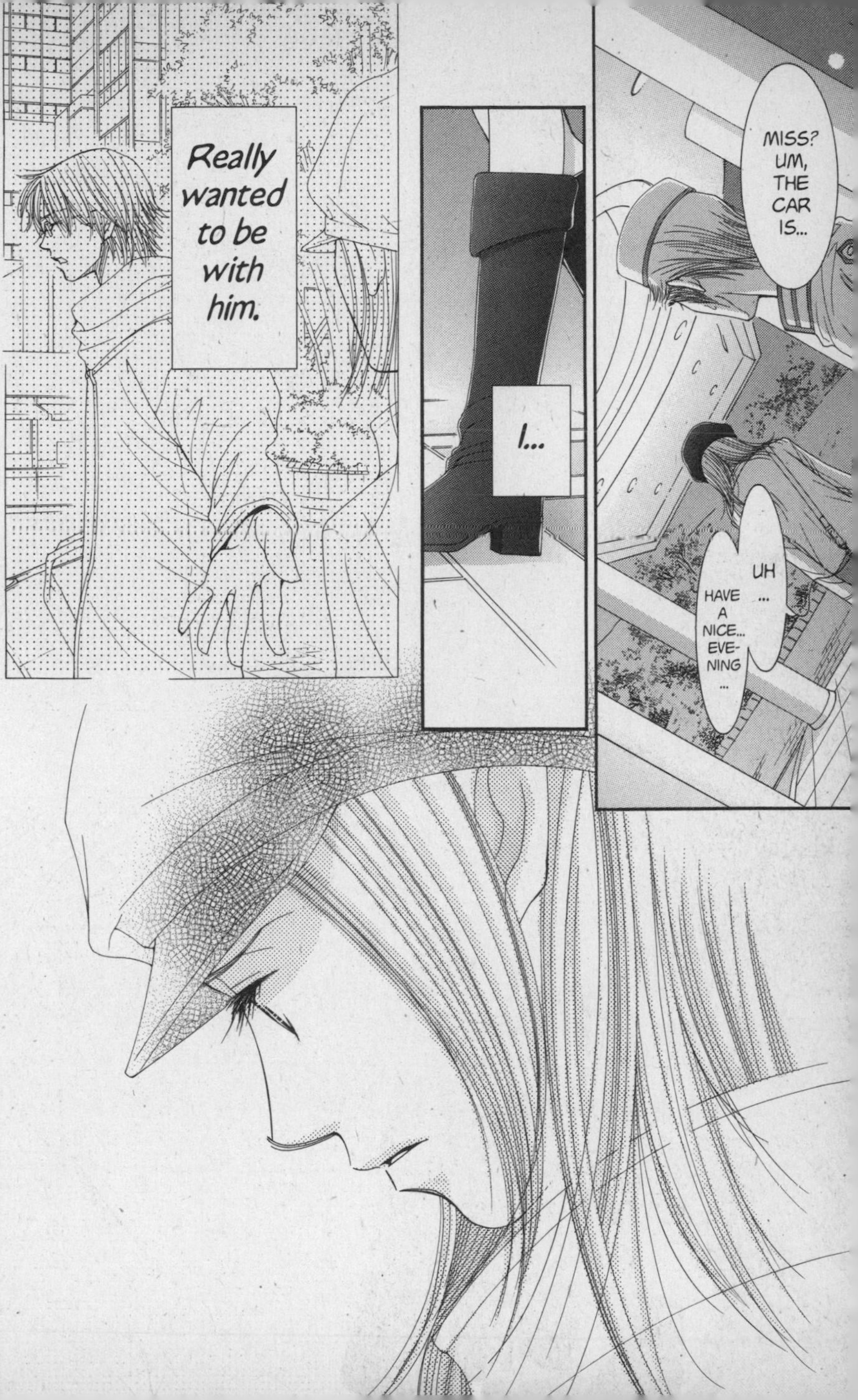
MISS? UM, THE CAR IS...
UH ... HAVE A NICE... EVENING ...
I...
Really wanted to be with him.

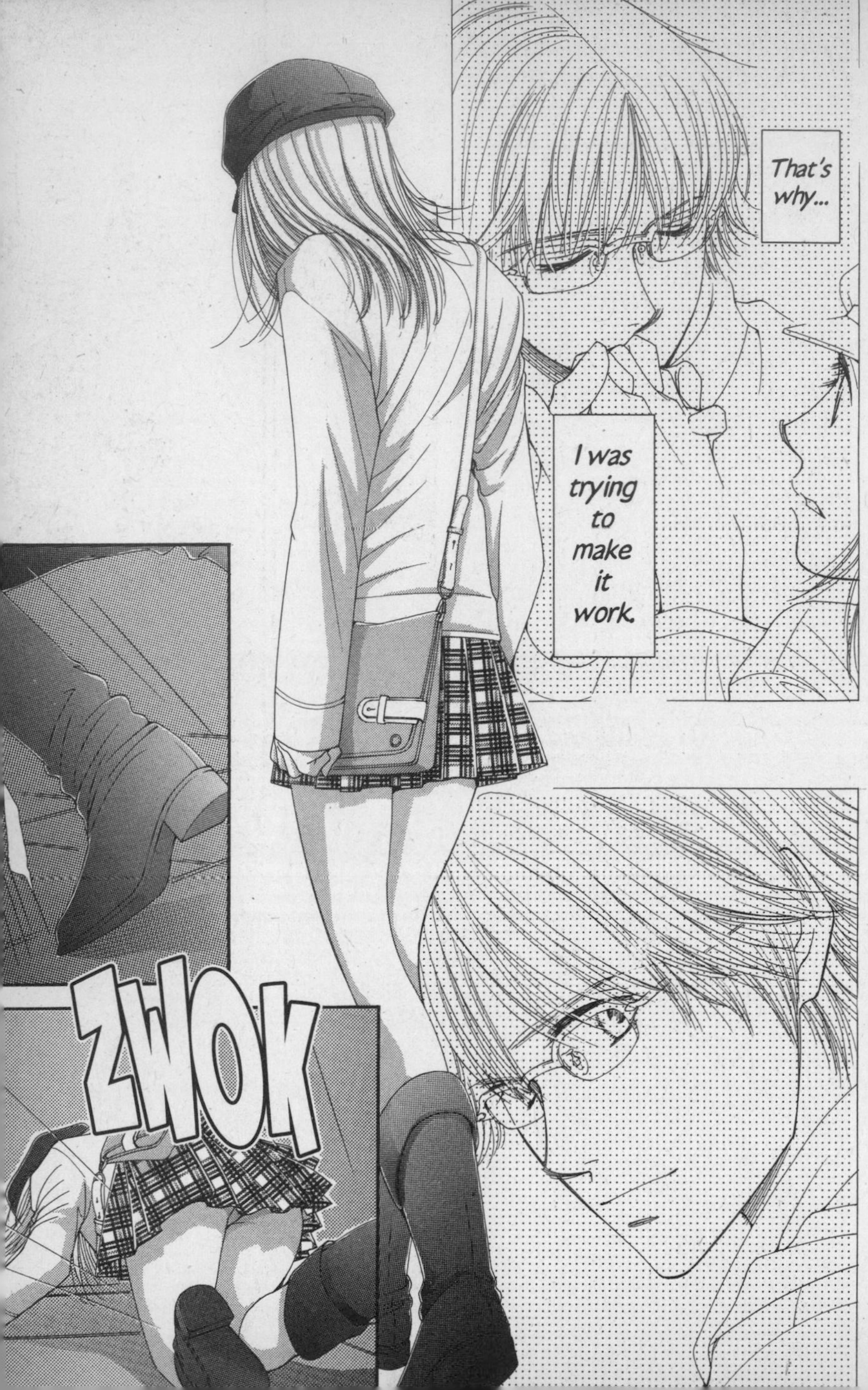
That's why...
I was trying to make it work.
ZWOK

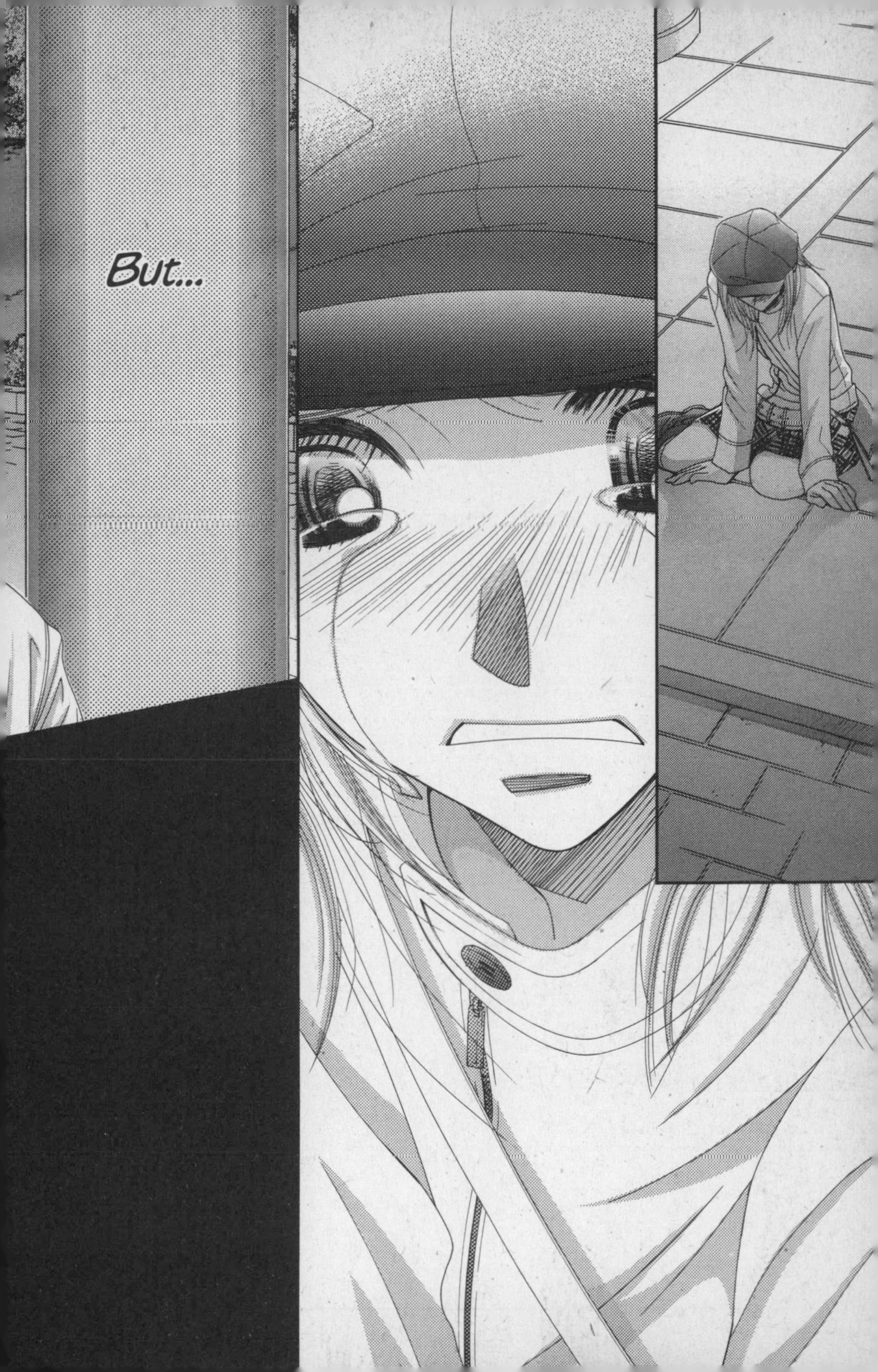
But...

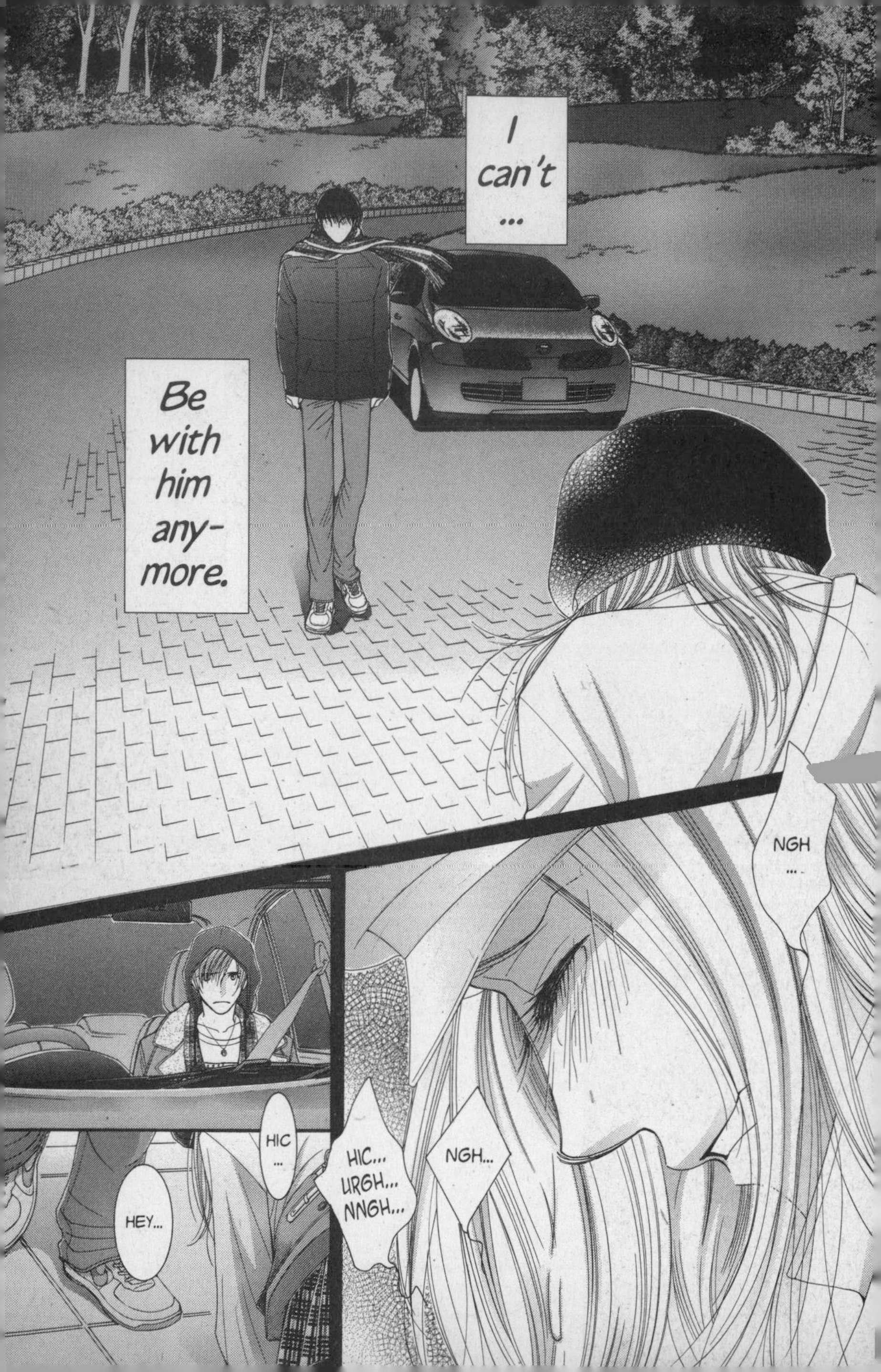
I can't ...
Be with him any-more.
NGH ...
NGH...
HIC... URGH... NNGH...
HIC ...
HEY...

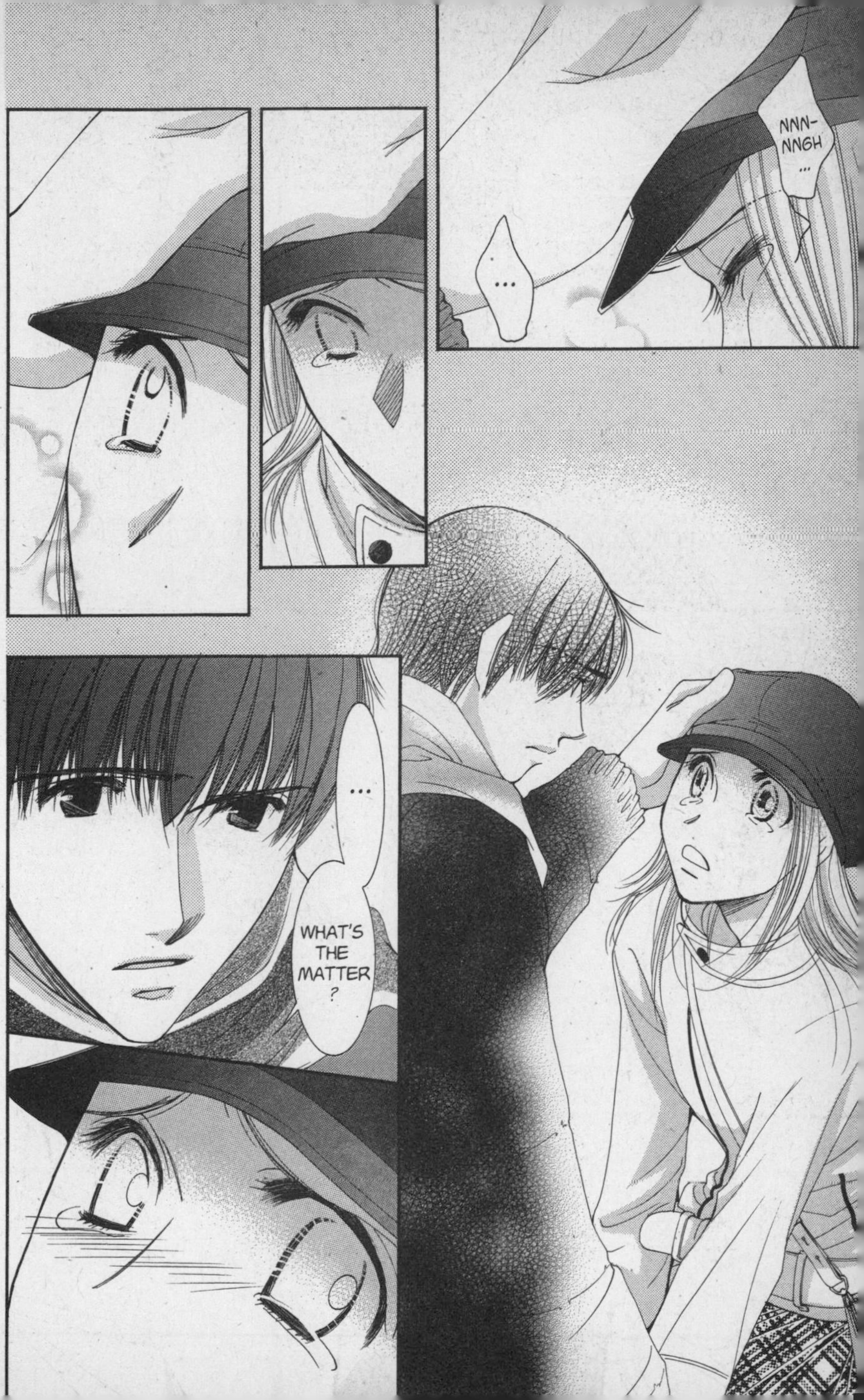
NNN-NNGH ...
...
...
WHAT'S THE MATTER ?

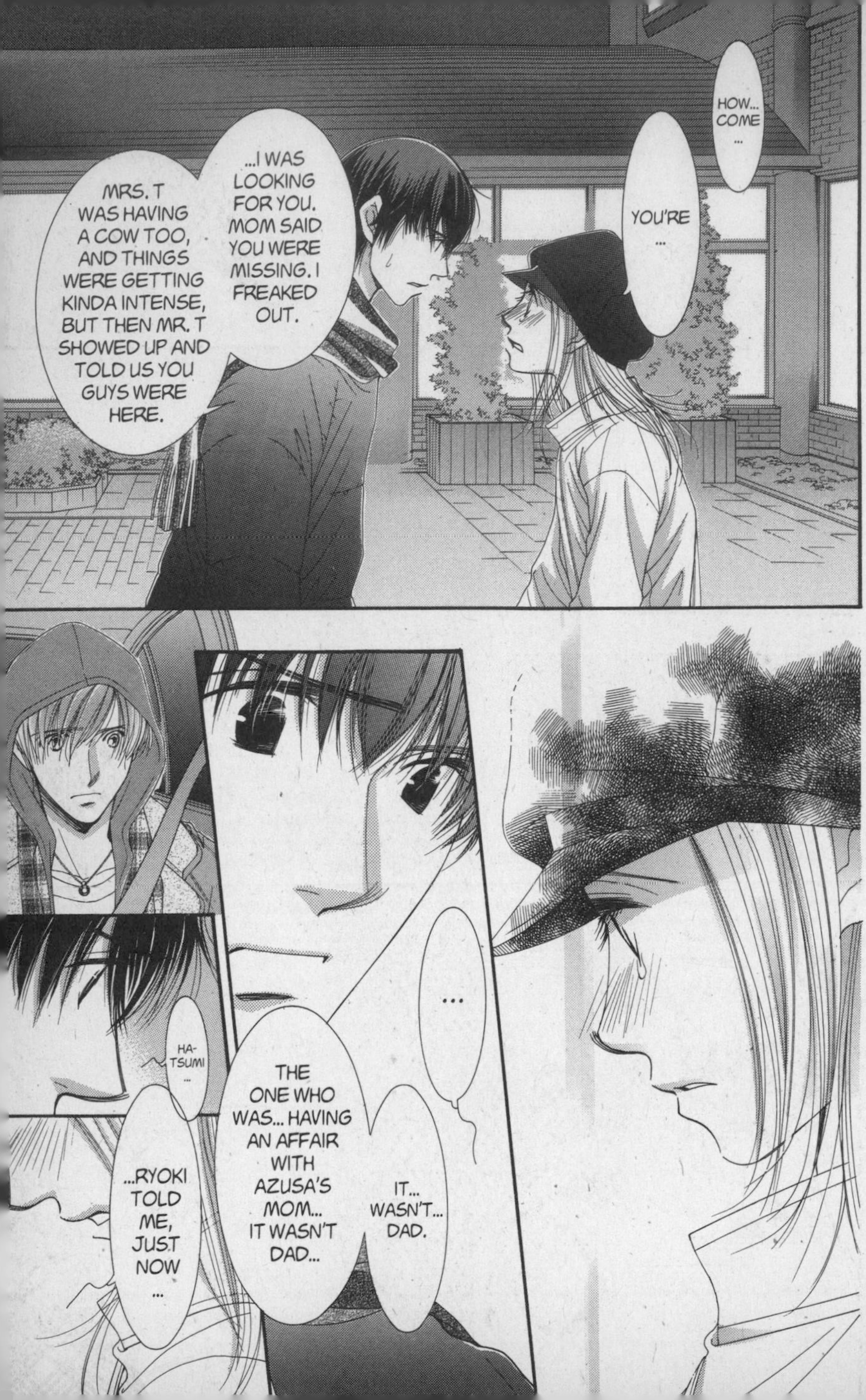
HOW... COME ...
YOU'RE ...
...I WAS LOOKING FOR YOU. MOM SAID YOU WERE MISSING. I FREAKED OUT.
MRS. T WAS HAVING A COW TOO, AND THINGS WERE GETTING KINDA INTENSE, BUT THEN MR. T SHOWED UP AND TOLD US YOU GUYS WERE HERE.
...
IT... WASN'T... DAD.
THE ONE WHO WAS... HAVING AN AFFAIR WITH AZUSA'S MOM... IT WASN'T DAD...
HA-TSUMI ...
...RYOKI TOLD ME, JUST NOW ...

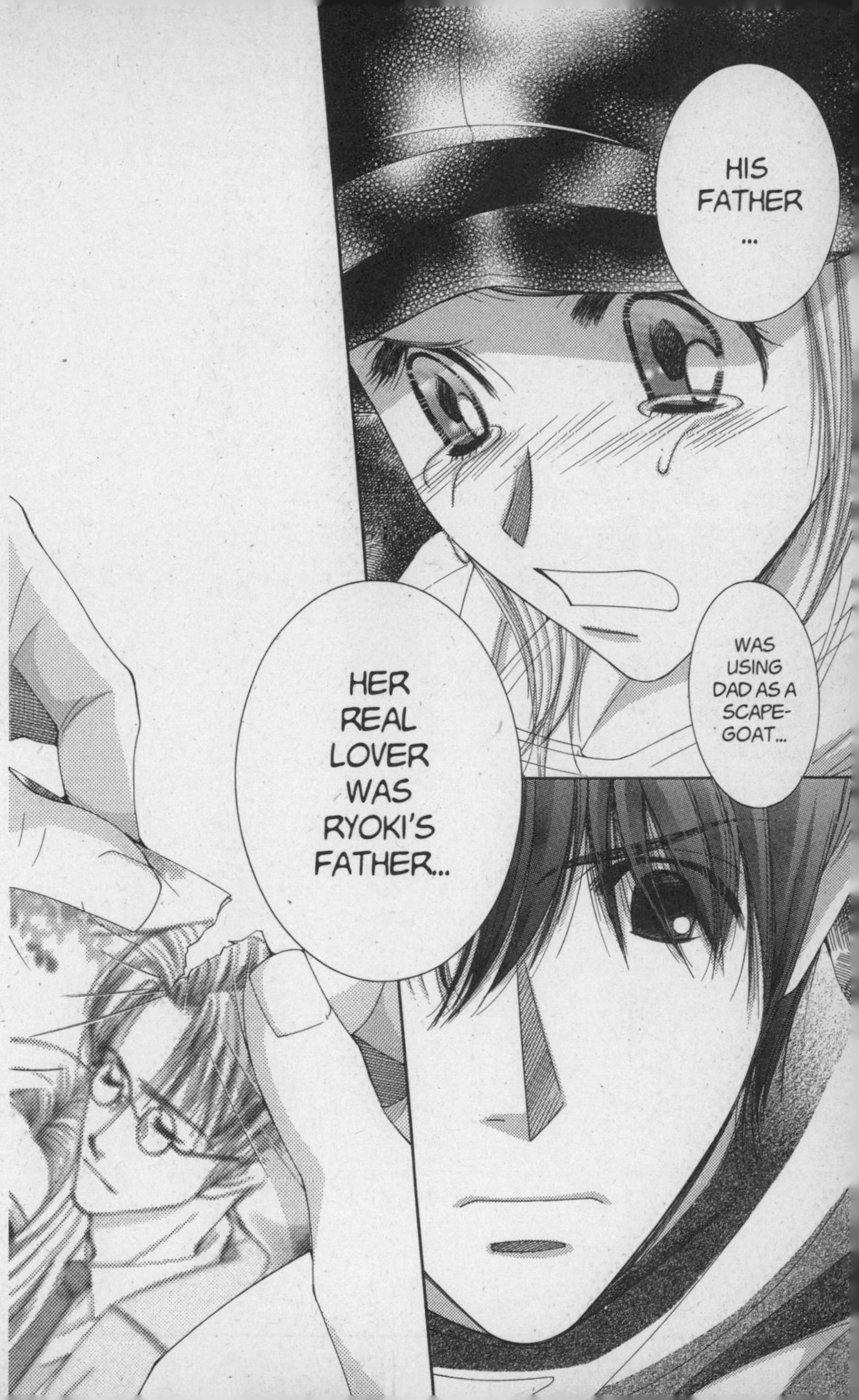
HIS FATHER ...
WAS USING DAD AS A SCAPE-GOAT...
HER REAL LOVER WAS RYOKI'S FATHER...

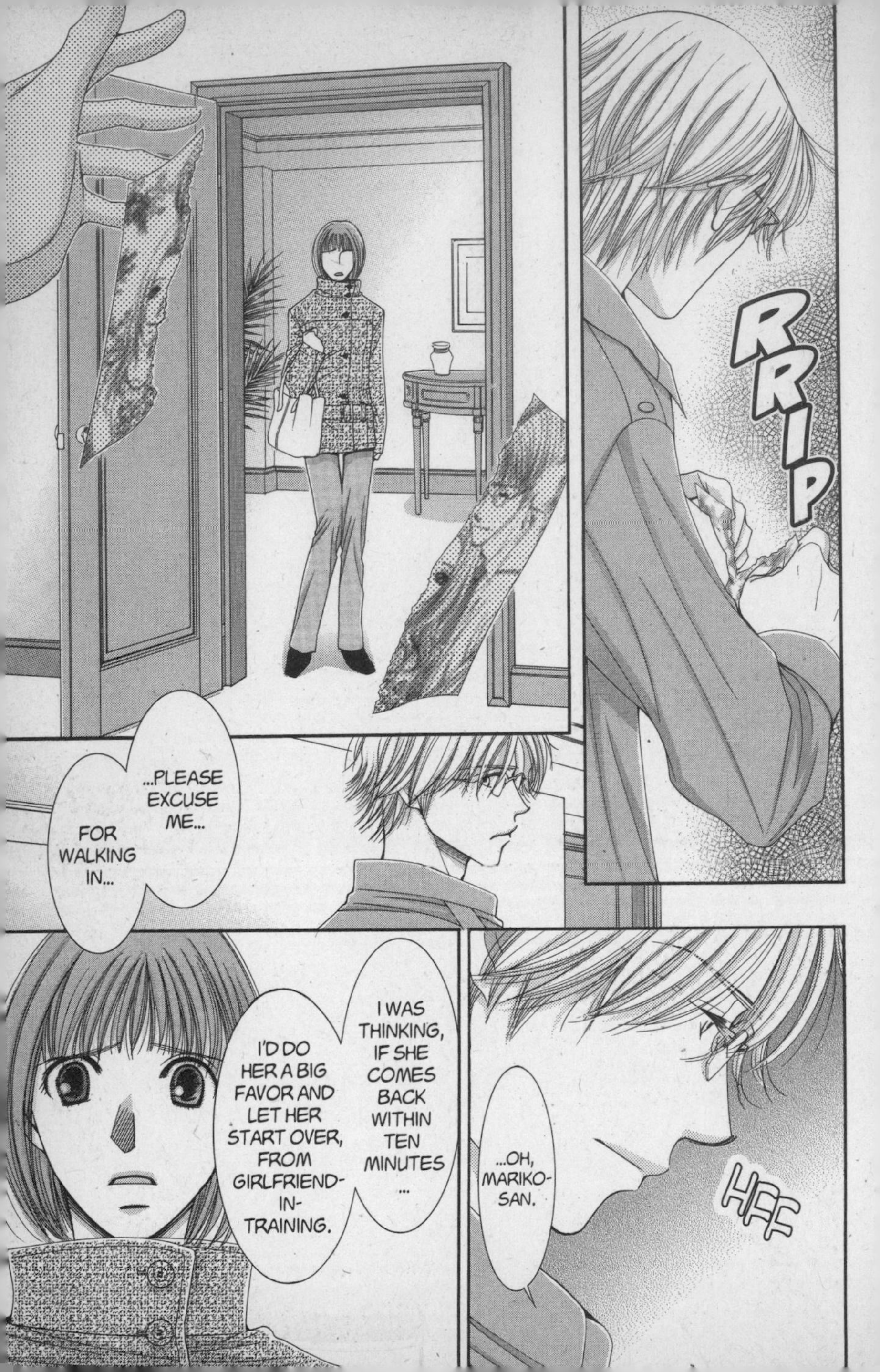
RRIP
...PLEASE EXCUSE ME... FOR WALKING IN...
HFF
...OH, MARIKO-SAN.
I WAS THINKING, IF SHE COMES BACK WITHIN TEN MINUTES ...
I'D DO HER A BIG FAVOR AND LET HER START OVER, FROM GIRLFRIEND-IN-TRAINING.

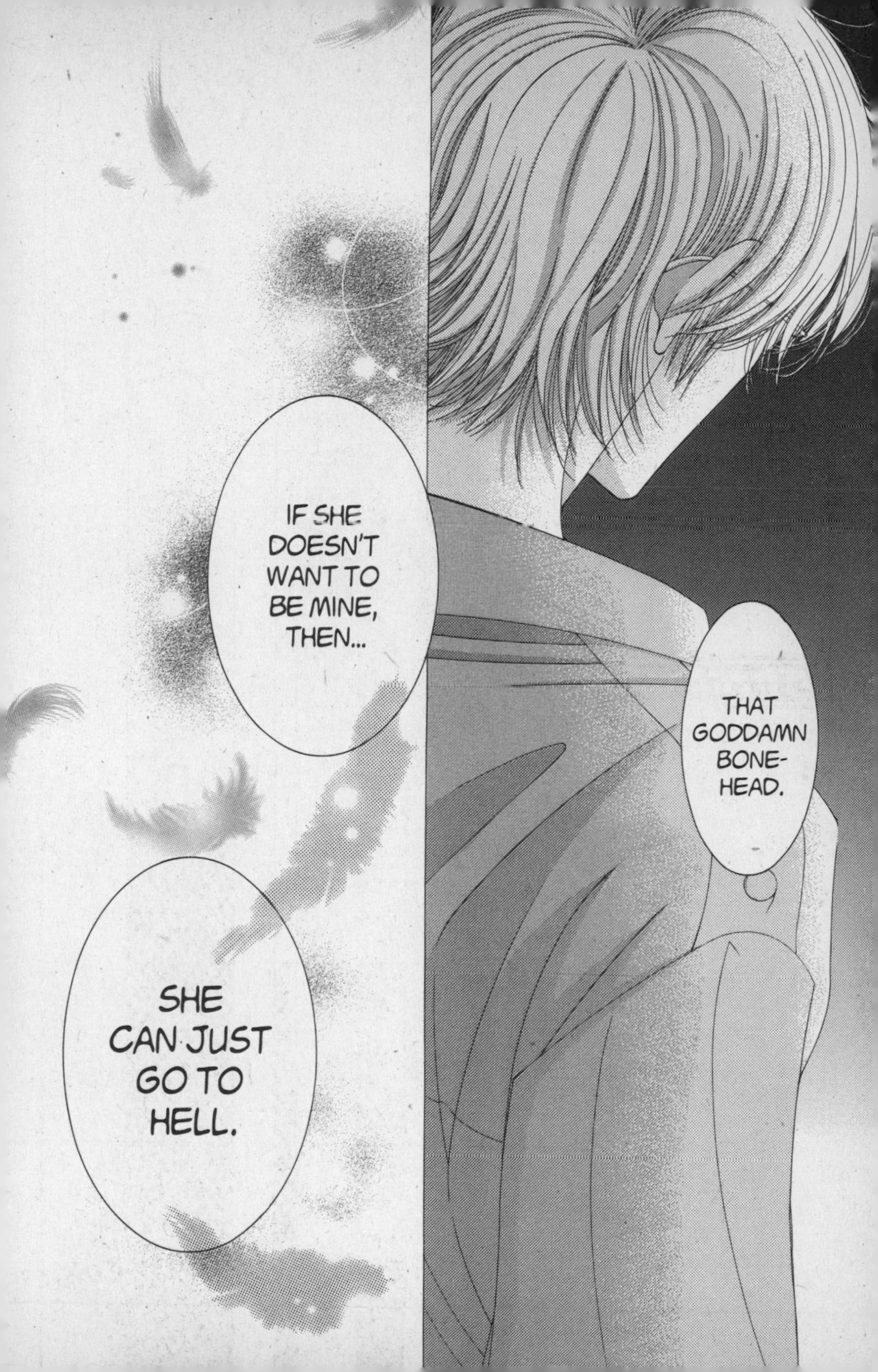
THAT GODDAMN BONE-HEAD.
IF SHE DOESN'T WANT TO BE MINE, THEN...
SHE CAN JUST GO TO HELL.

hotgimmick

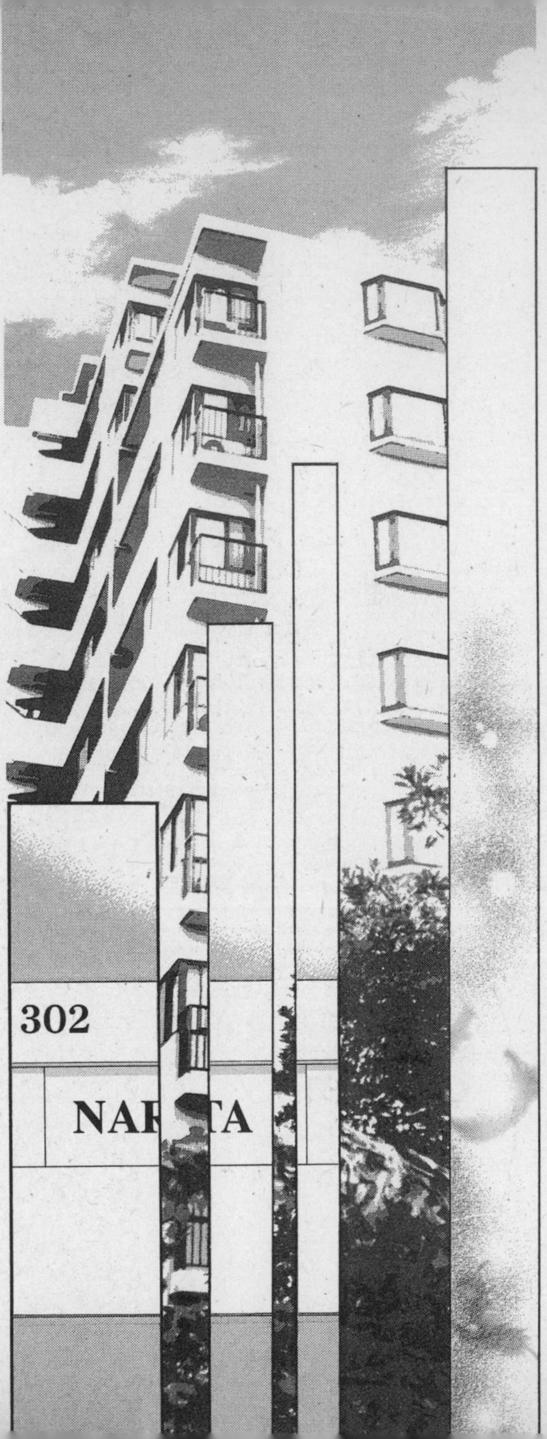
302
NAR TA

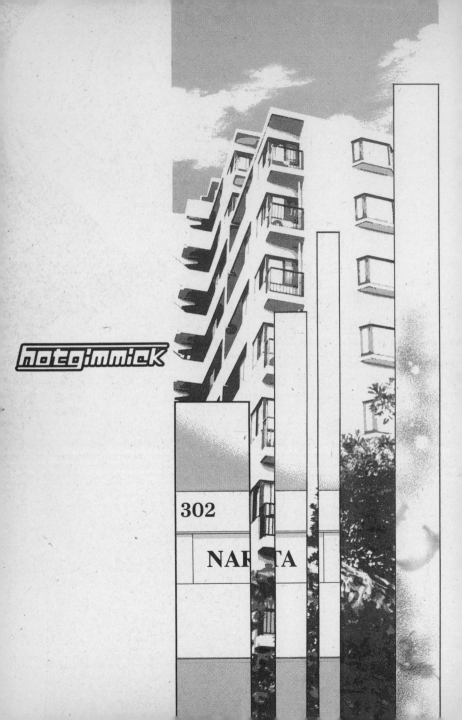

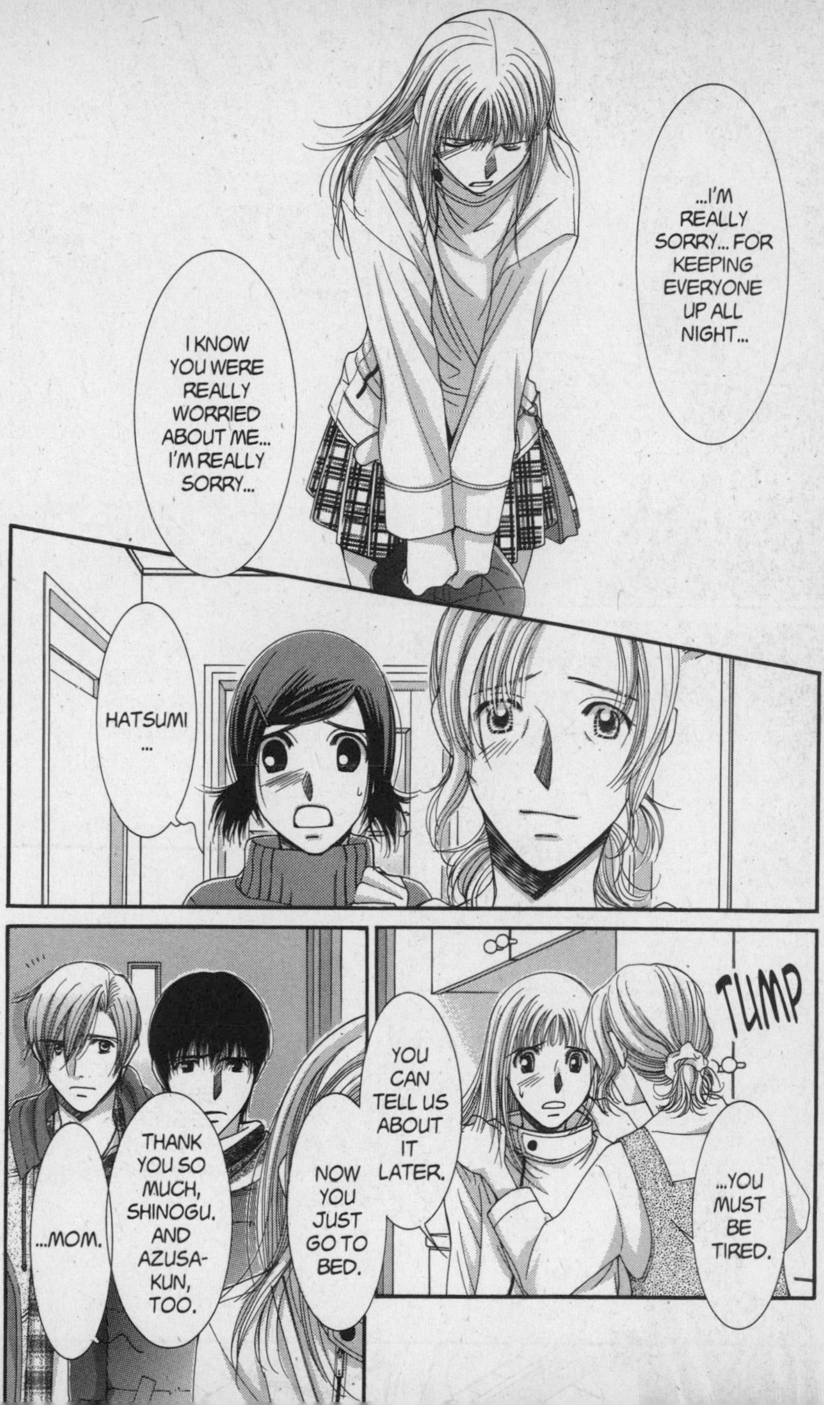

...I'M REALLY SORRY... FOR KEEPING EVERYONE UP ALL NIGHT...
I KNOW YOU WERE REALLY WORRIED ABOUT ME... I'M REALLY SORRY...
HATSUMI ...
TUMP
...YOU MUST BE TIRED.
YOU CAN TELL US ABOUT IT LATER.
NOW YOU JUST GO TO BED.
THANK YOU SO MUCH, SHINOGU. AND AZUSA-KUN, TOO.
...MOM.

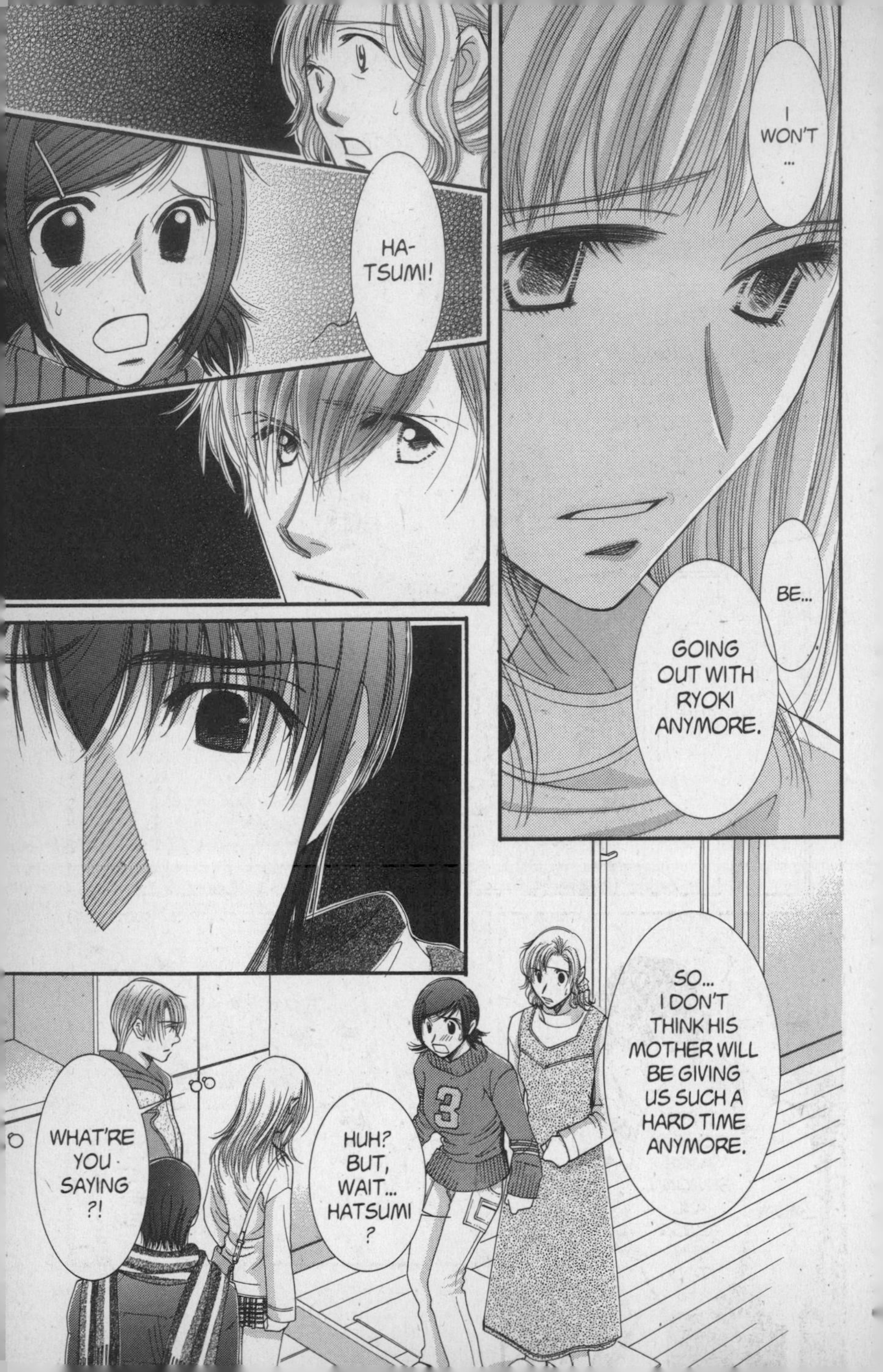
I WON'T ...
BE...
GOING OUT WITH RYOKI ANYMORE.
HA-TSUMI!
SO... I DON'T THINK HIS MOTHER WILL BE GIVING US SUCH A HARD TIME ANYMORE.
HUH? BUT, WAIT... HATSUMI?
WHAT'RE YOU SAYING?!

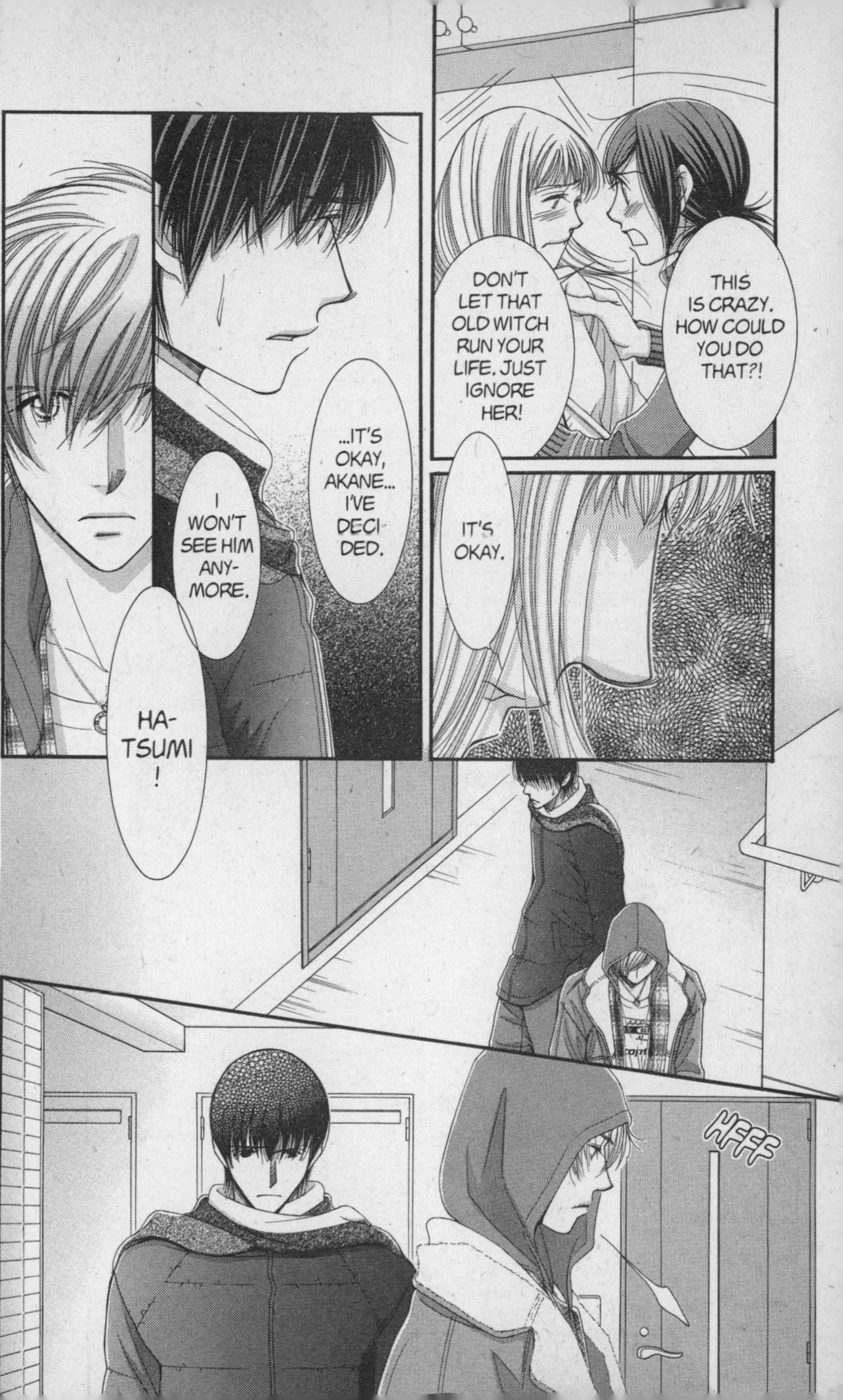
THIS IS CRAZY. HOW COULD YOU DO THAT?!
DON'T LET THAT OLD WITCH RUN YOUR LIFE. JUST IGNORE HER!
IT'S OKAY.
...IT'S OKAY, AKANE... I'VE DECIDED.
I WON'T SEE HIM ANYMORE.
HATSUMI!
HFFF

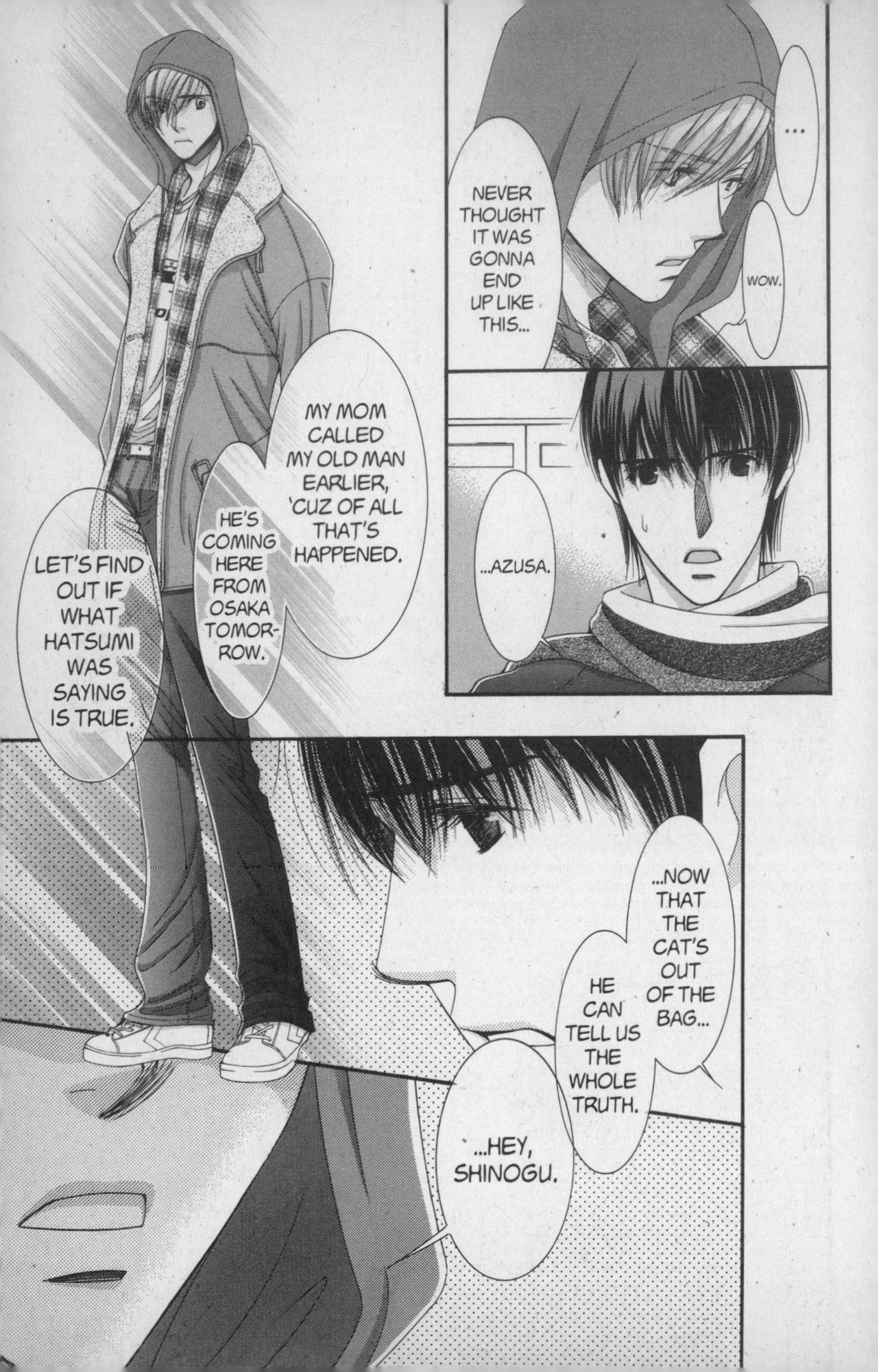
...
WOW.
NEVER THOUGHT IT WAS GONNA END UP LIKE THIS...
...AZUSA.
MY MOM CALLED MY OLD MAN EARLIER, 'CUZ OF ALL THAT'S HAPPENED.
HE'S COMING HERE FROM OSAKA TOMORROW.
LET'S FIND OUT IF WHAT HATSUMI WAS SAYING IS TRUE.
...NOW THAT THE CAT'S OUT OF THE BAG...
HE CAN TELL US THE WHOLE TRUTH.
...HEY, SHINOGU.

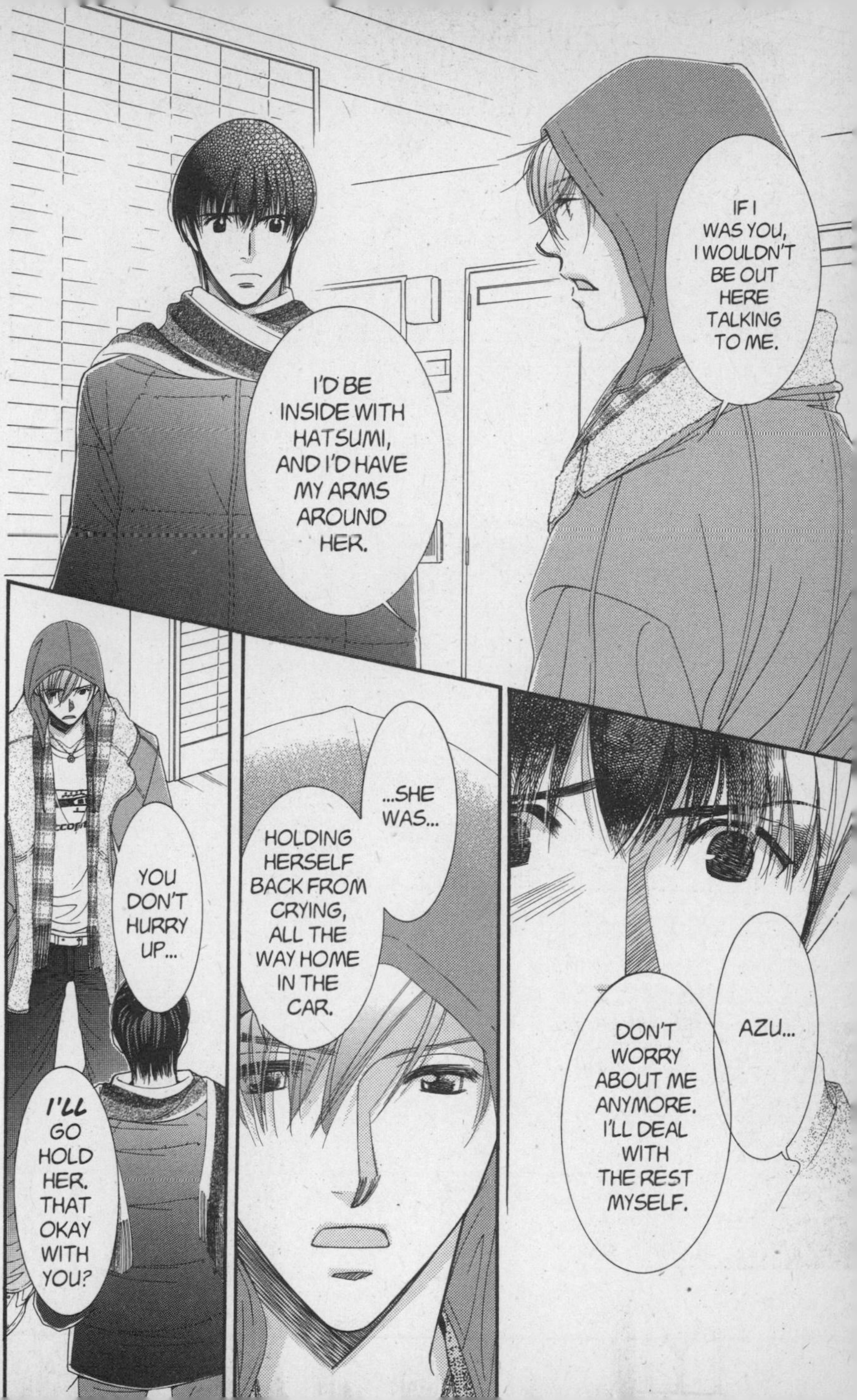
IF I WAS YOU, I WOULDN'T BE OUT HERE TALKING TO ME.
I'D BE INSIDE WITH HATSUMI, AND I'D HAVE MY ARMS AROUND HER.
AZU...
DON'T WORRY ABOUT ME ANYMORE. I'LL DEAL WITH THE REST MYSELF.
...SHE WAS...
HOLDING HERSELF BACK FROM CRYING, ALL THE WAY HOME IN THE CAR.
YOU DON'T HURRY UP...
I'LL GO HOLD HER. THAT OKAY WITH YOU?

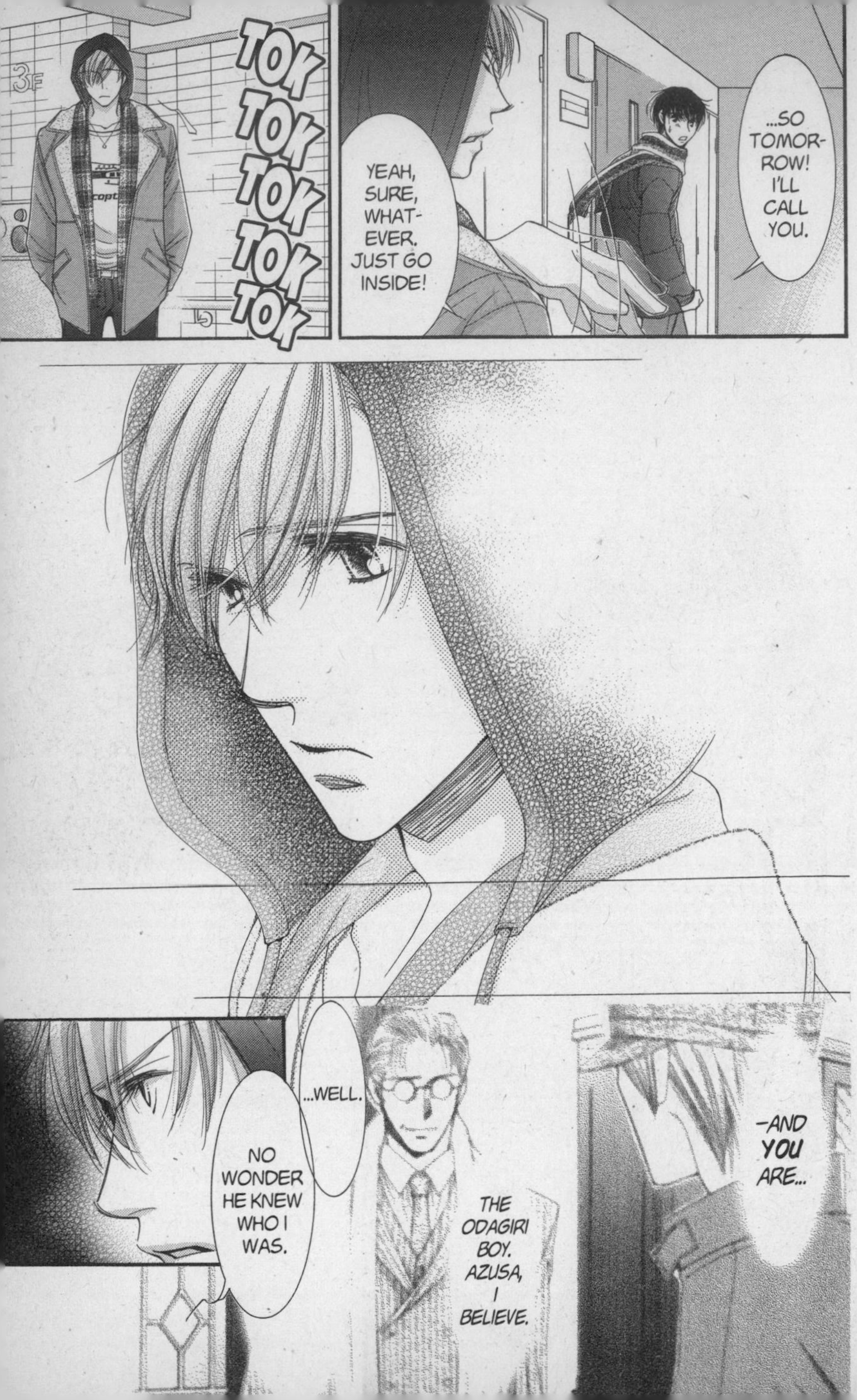
...SO TOMORROW! I'LL CALL YOU.
YEAH, SURE, WHATEVER. JUST GO INSIDE!
TOK TOK TOK TOK TOK TOK
3F
-AND YOU ARE...
THE ODAGIRI BOY. AZUSA, I BELIEVE.
...WELL.
NO WONDER HE KNEW WHO I WAS.

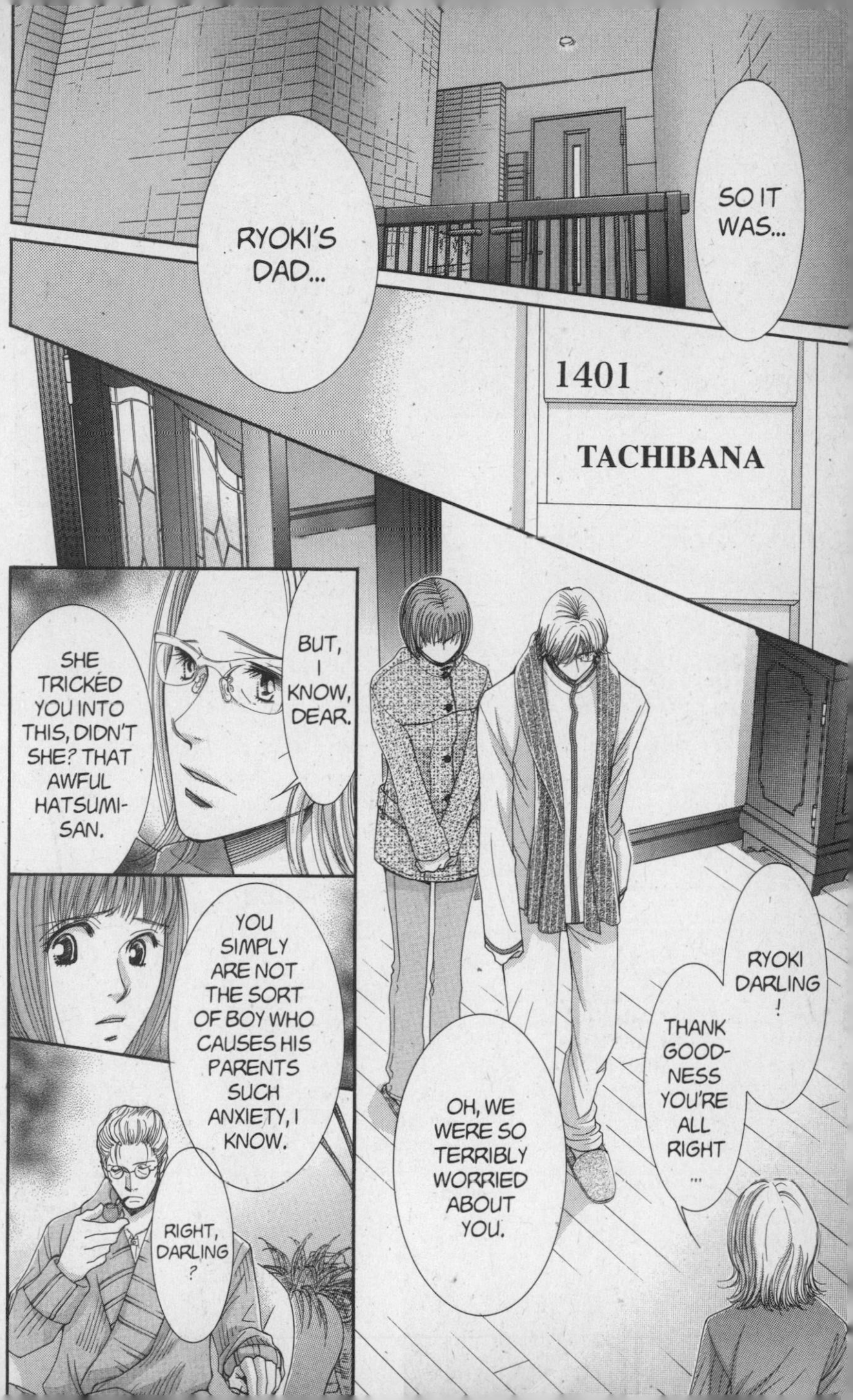

SO IT WAS...
RYOKI'S DAD...
1401
TACHIBANA
RYOKI DARLING!
THANK GOODNESS YOU'RE ALL RIGHT...
OH, WE WERE SO TERRIBLY WORRIED ABOUT YOU.
BUT, I KNOW, DEAR.
SHE TRICKED YOU INTO THIS, DIDN'T SHE? THAT AWFUL HATSUMI-SAN.
YOU SIMPLY ARE NOT THE SORT OF BOY WHO CAUSES HIS PARENTS SUCH ANXIETY, I KNOW.
RIGHT, DARLING?

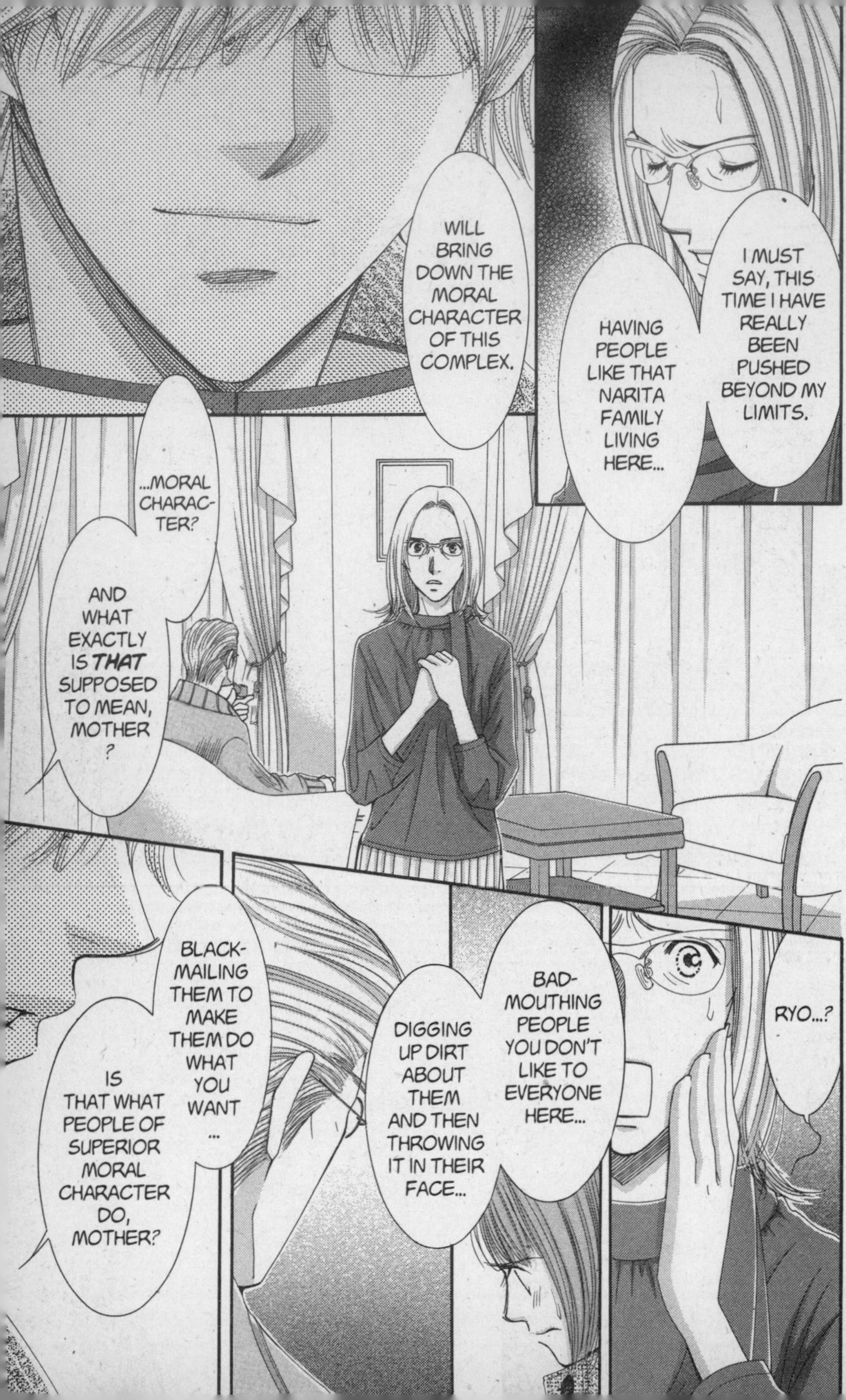
I MUST SAY, THIS TIME I HAVE REALLY BEEN PUSHED BEYOND MY LIMITS.
HAVING PEOPLE LIKE THAT NARITA FAMILY LIVING HERE...
WILL BRING DOWN THE MORAL CHARACTER OF THIS COMPLEX.
...MORAL CHARACTER?
AND WHAT EXACTLY IS ***THAT*** SUPPOSED TO MEAN, MOTHER?
RYO...?
BAD-MOUTHING PEOPLE YOU DON'T LIKE TO EVERYONE HERE...
DIGGING UP DIRT ABOUT THEM AND THEN THROWING IT IN THEIR FACE...
BLACKMAILING THEM TO MAKE THEM DO WHAT YOU WANT...
IS THAT WHAT PEOPLE OF SUPERIOR MORAL CHARACTER DO, MOTHER?

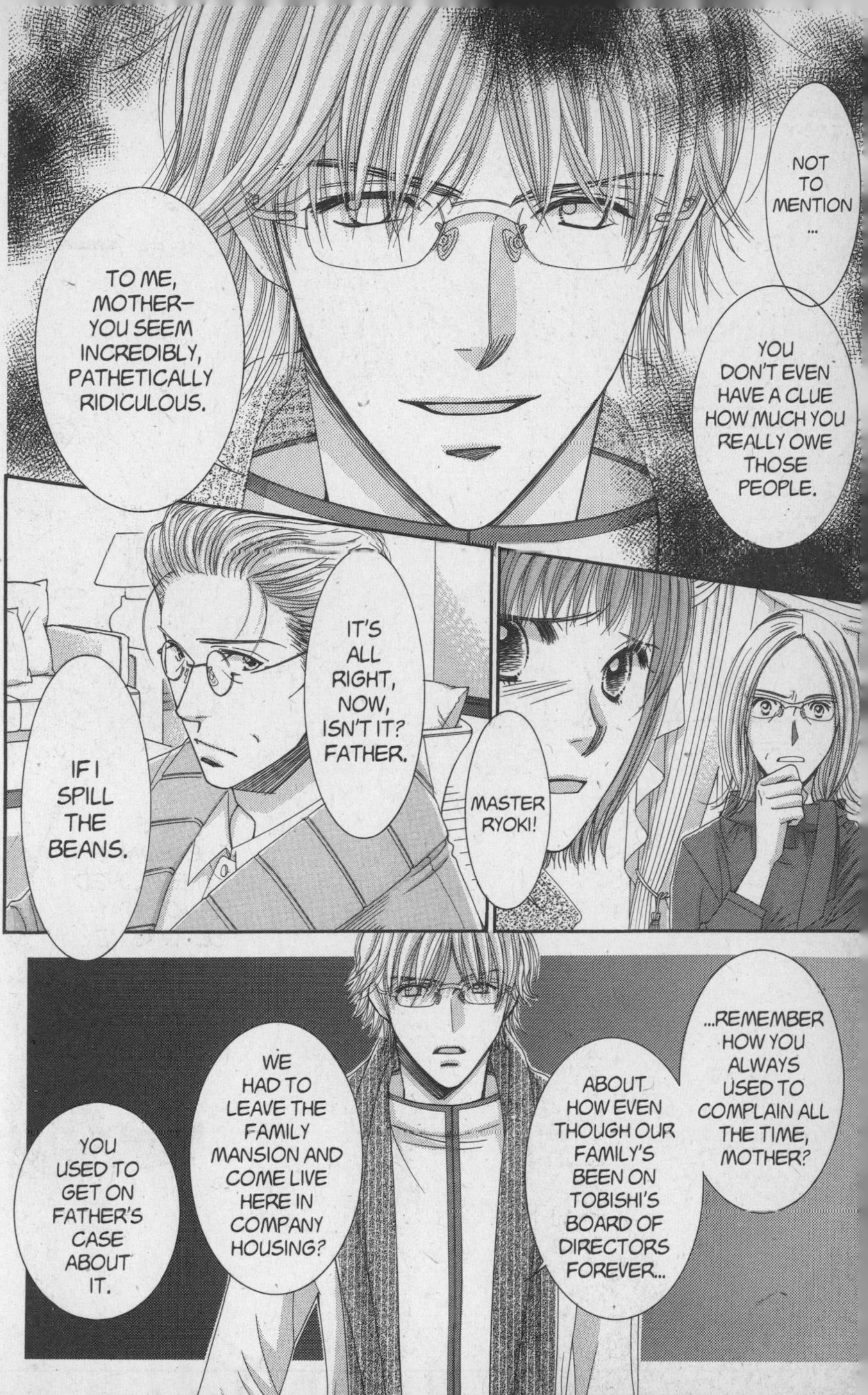
NOT TO MENTION ...
YOU DON'T EVEN HAVE A CLUE HOW MUCH YOU REALLY OWE THOSE PEOPLE.
TO ME, MOTHER— YOU SEEM INCREDIBLY, PATHETICALLY RIDICULOUS.
MASTER RYOKI!
IT'S ALL RIGHT, NOW, ISN'T IT? FATHER.
IF I SPILL THE BEANS.
...REMEMBER HOW YOU ALWAYS USED TO COMPLAIN ALL THE TIME, MOTHER?
ABOUT HOW EVEN THOUGH OUR FAMILY'S BEEN ON TOBISHI'S BOARD OF DIRECTORS FOREVER...
WE HAD TO LEAVE THE FAMILY MANSION AND COME LIVE HERE IN COMPANY HOUSING?
YOU USED TO GET ON FATHER'S CASE ABOUT IT.

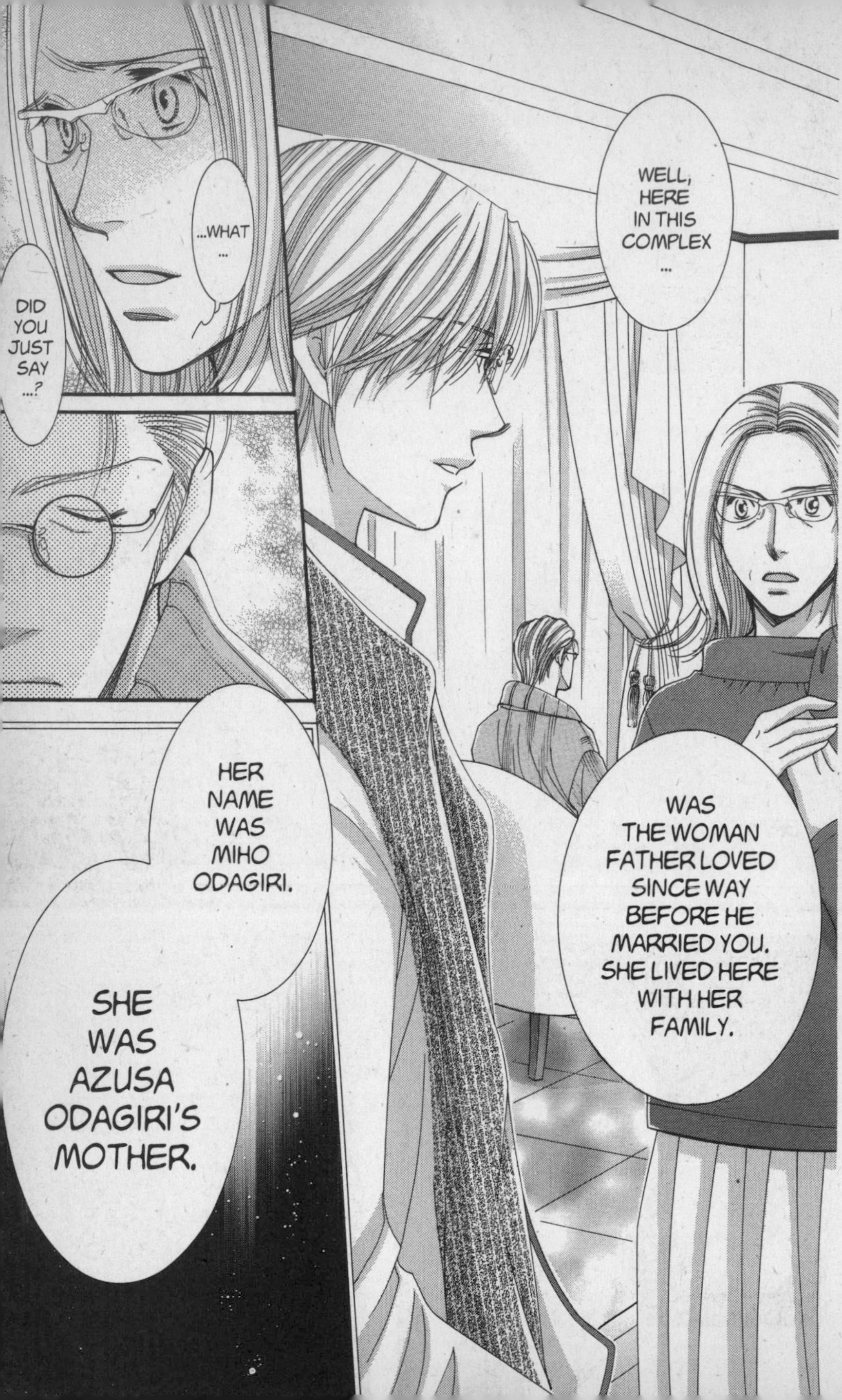
WELL, HERE IN THIS COMPLEX ...
WAS THE WOMAN FATHER LOVED SINCE WAY BEFORE HE MARRIED YOU. SHE LIVED HERE WITH HER FAMILY.
...WHAT ...
DID YOU JUST SAY ...?
HER NAME WAS MIHO ODAGIRI.
SHE WAS AZUSA ODAGIRI'S MOTHER.

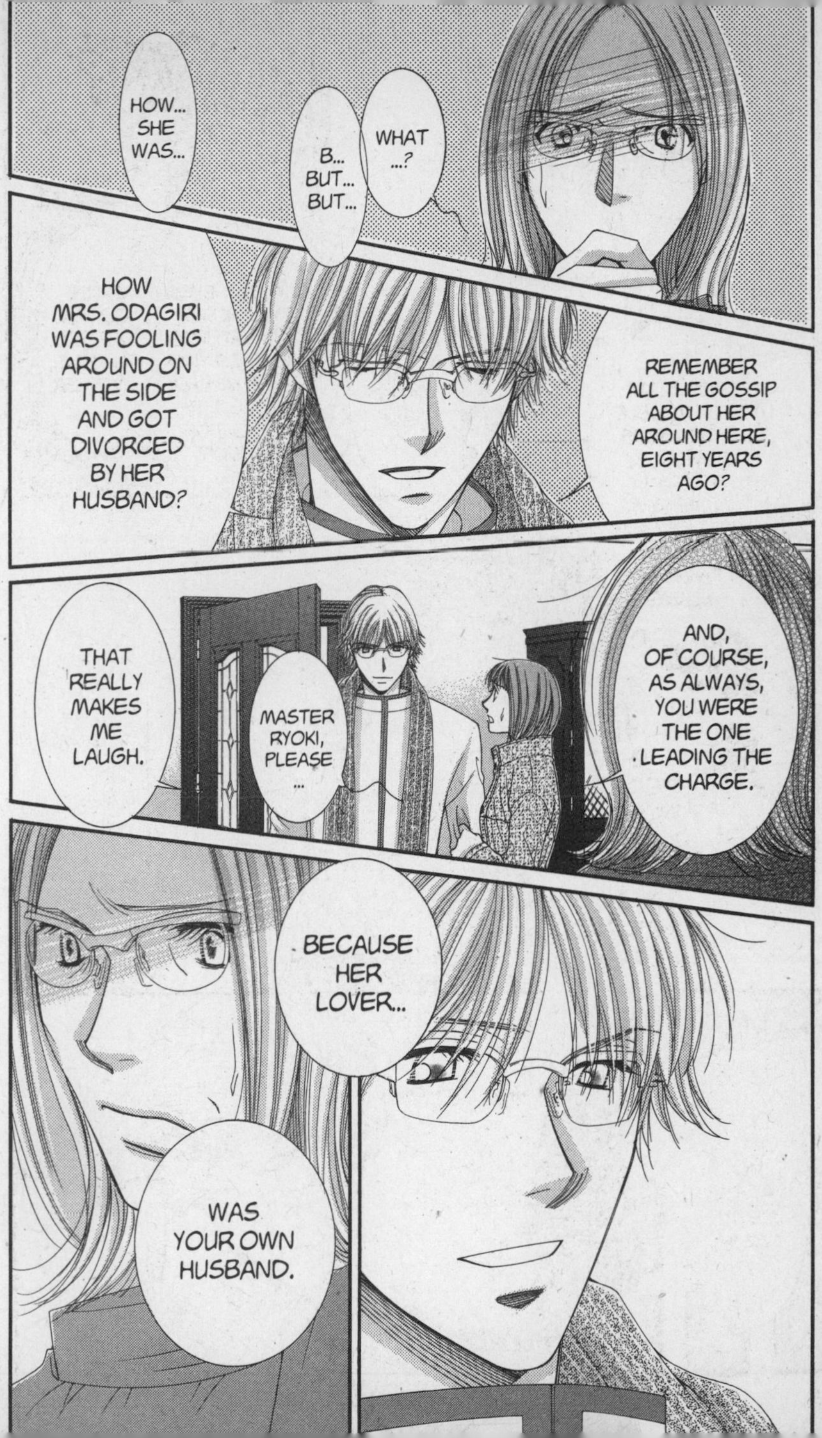
WHAT ...?
B... BUT... BUT...
HOW... SHE WAS...
REMEMBER ALL THE GOSSIP ABOUT HER AROUND HERE, EIGHT YEARS AGO?
HOW MRS. ODAGIRI WAS FOOLING AROUND ON THE SIDE AND GOT DIVORCED BY HER HUSBAND?
AND, OF COURSE, AS ALWAYS, YOU WERE THE ONE LEADING THE CHARGE.
MASTER RYOKI, PLEASE ...
THAT REALLY MAKES ME LAUGH.
BECAUSE HER LOVER...
WAS YOUR OWN HUSBAND.

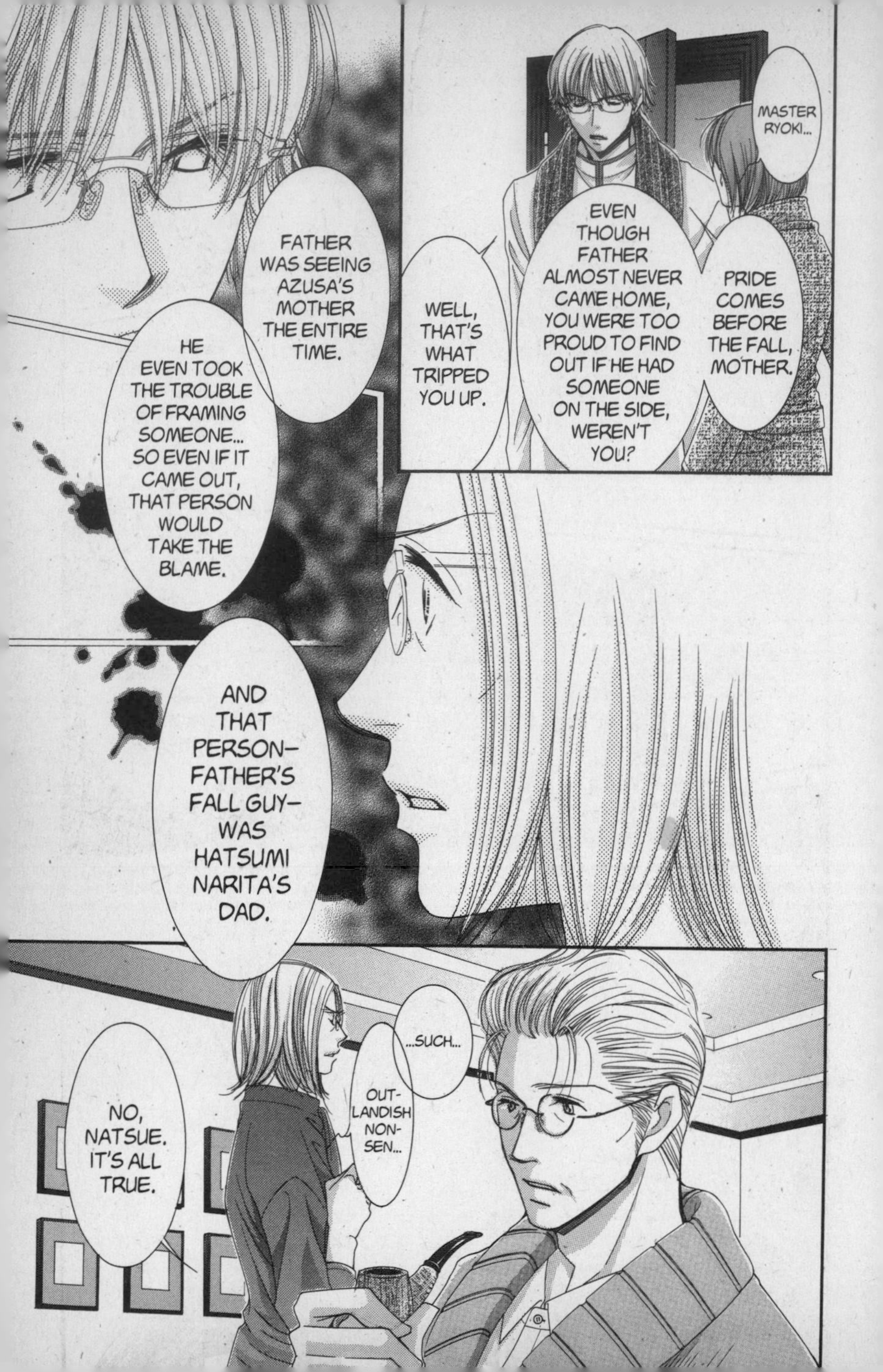
MASTER RYOKI...
PRIDE COMES BEFORE THE FALL, MOTHER.
EVEN THOUGH FATHER ALMOST NEVER CAME HOME, YOU WERE TOO PROUD TO FIND OUT IF HE HAD SOMEONE ON THE SIDE, WEREN'T YOU?
WELL, THAT'S WHAT TRIPPED YOU UP.
FATHER WAS SEEING AZUSA'S MOTHER THE ENTIRE TIME.
HE EVEN TOOK THE TROUBLE OF FRAMING SOMEONE... SO EVEN IF IT CAME OUT, THAT PERSON WOULD TAKE THE BLAME.
AND THAT PERSON—FATHER'S FALL GUY—WAS HATSUMI NARITA'S DAD.
...SUCH...
OUT-LANDISH NON-SEN...
NO, NATSUE. IT'S ALL TRUE.

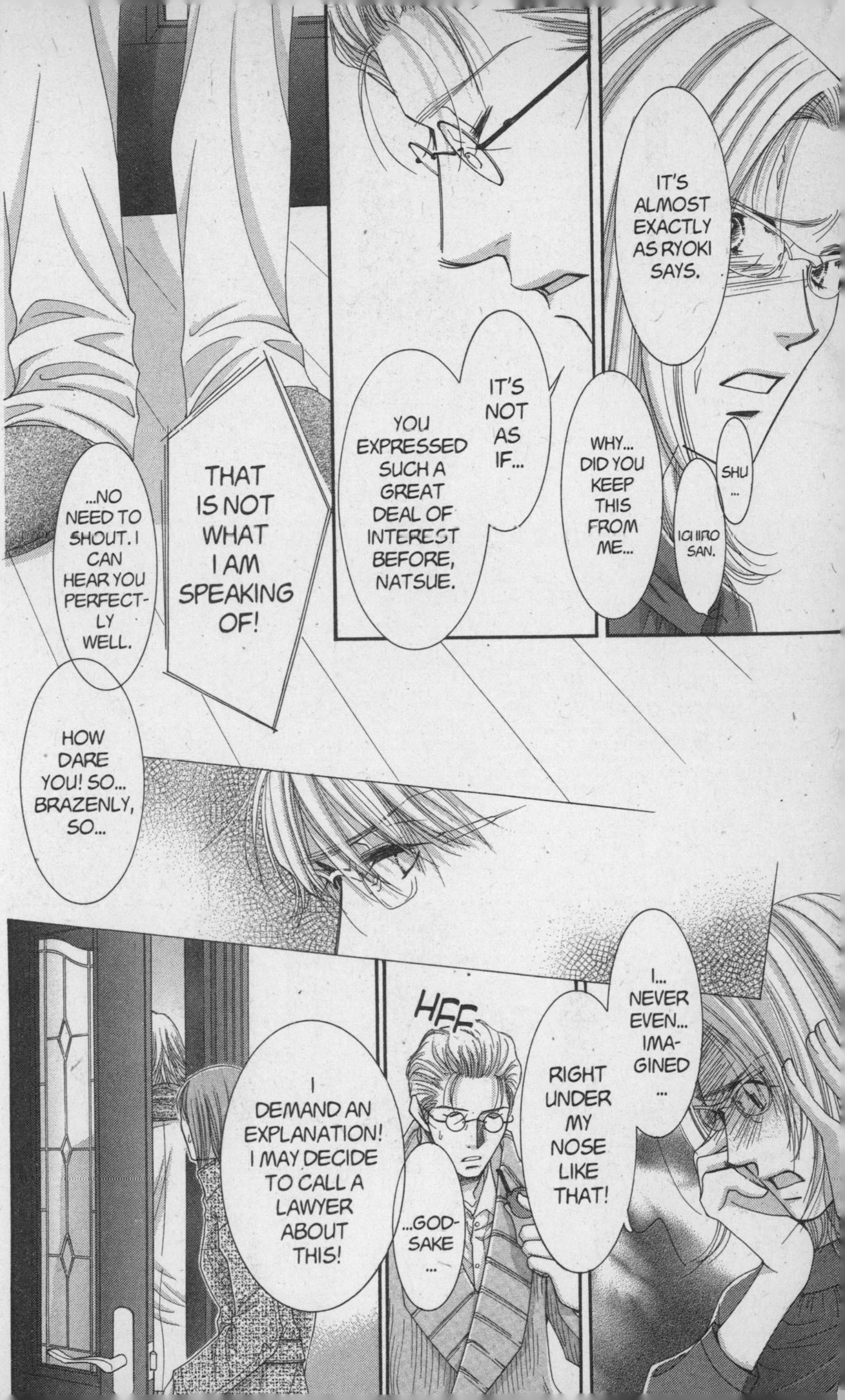
IT'S ALMOST EXACTLY AS RYOKI SAYS.
SHU...
ICHIRO SAN.
WHY... DID YOU KEEP THIS FROM ME...
IT'S NOT AS IF...
YOU EXPRESSED SUCH A GREAT DEAL OF INTEREST BEFORE, NATSUE.
THAT IS NOT WHAT I AM SPEAKING OF!
...NO NEED TO SHOUT. I CAN HEAR YOU PERFECTLY WELL.
HOW DARE YOU! SO... BRAZENLY, SO...
I... NEVER EVEN... IMAGINED...
RIGHT UNDER MY NOSE LIKE THAT!
HFF
...GOD-SAKE...
I DEMAND AN EXPLANATION! I MAY DECIDE TO CALL A LAWYER ABOUT THIS!

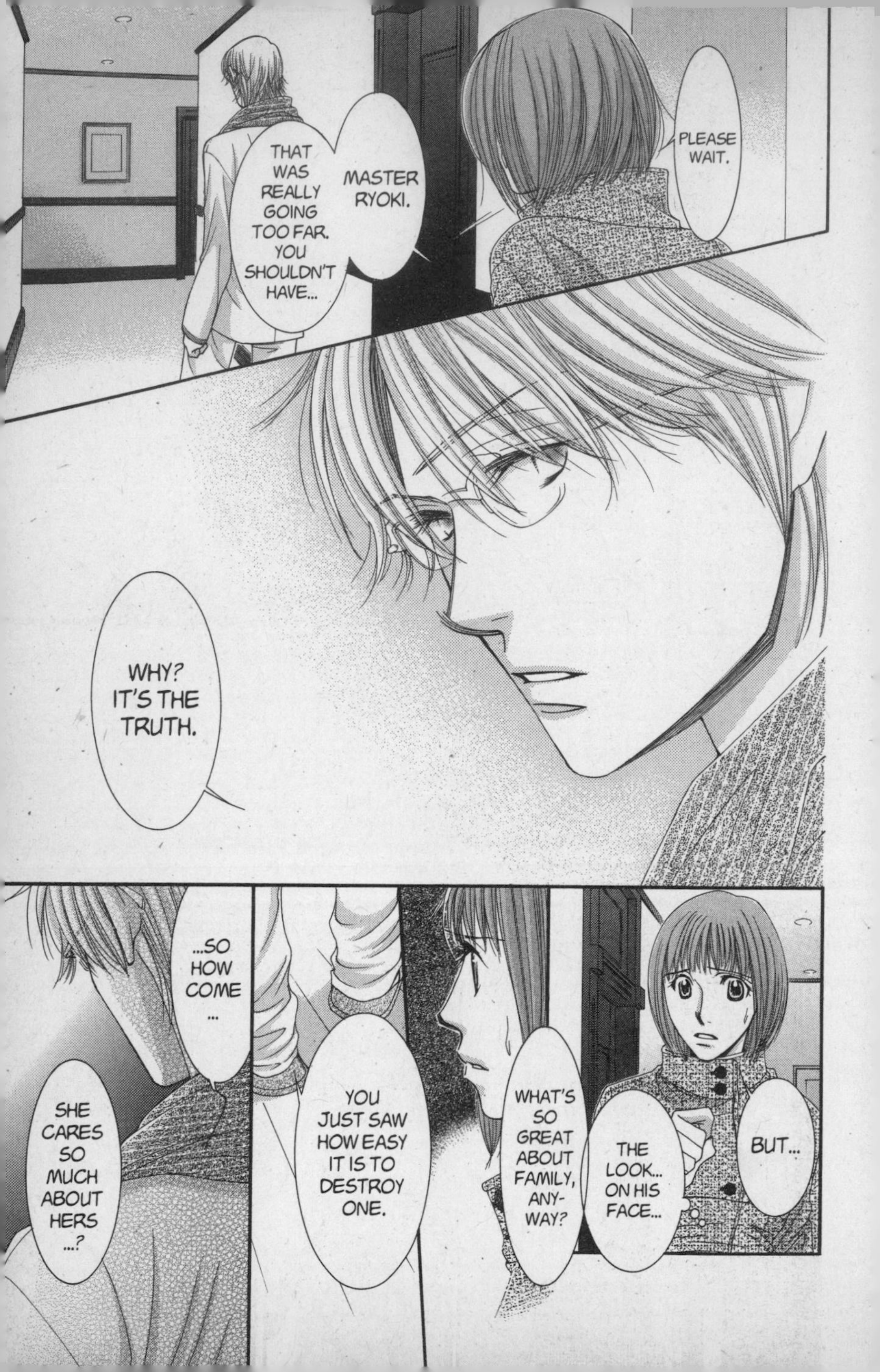
PLEASE WAIT.
MASTER RYOKI.
THAT WAS REALLY GOING TOO FAR. YOU SHOULDN'T HAVE...
WHY? IT'S THE TRUTH.
BUT...
THE LOOK... ON HIS FACE...
WHAT'S SO GREAT ABOUT FAMILY, ANY-WAY?
YOU JUST SAW HOW EASY IT IS TO DESTROY ONE.
...SO HOW COME ...
SHE CARES SO MUCH ABOUT HERS ...?

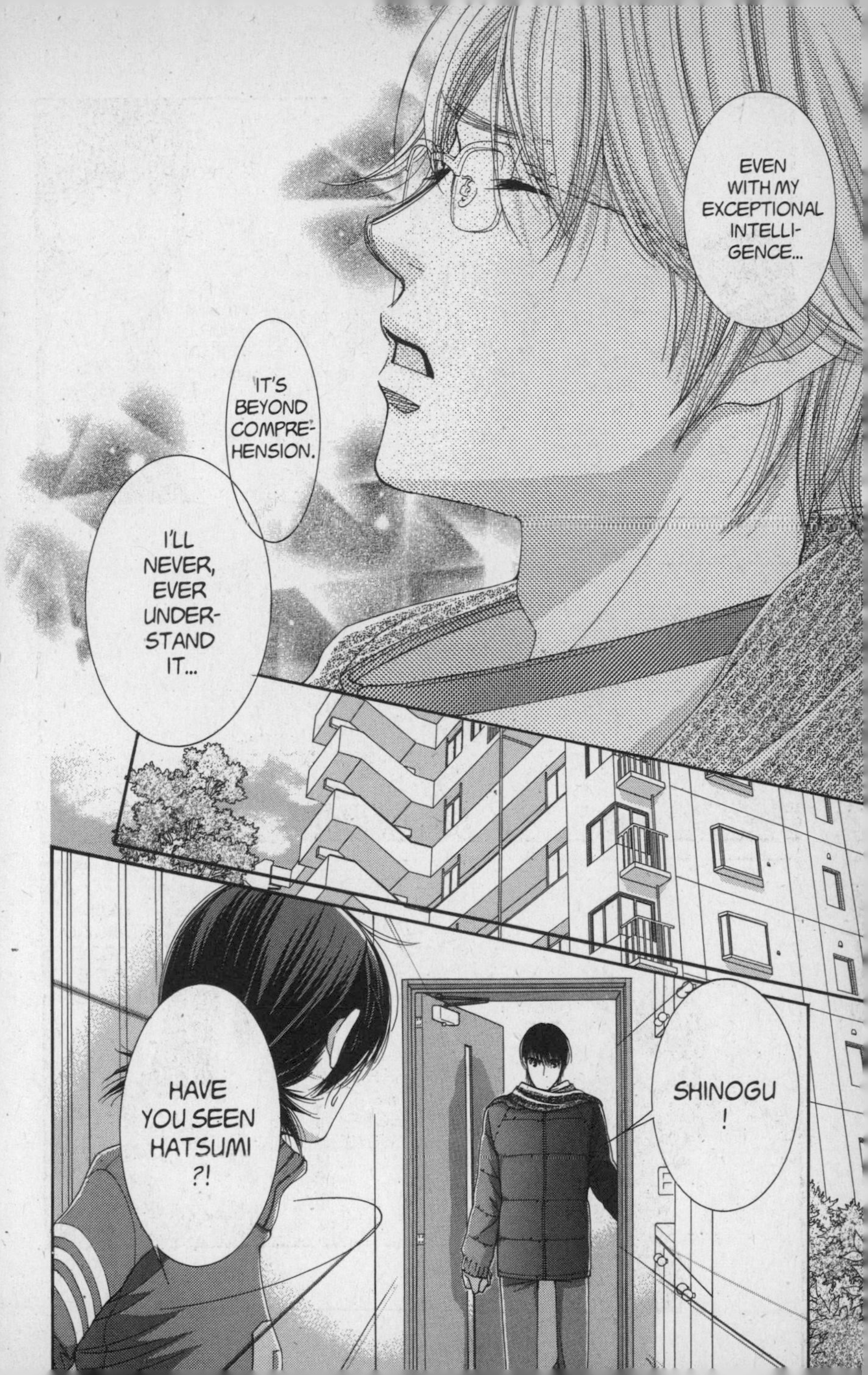
EVEN WITH MY EXCEPTIONAL INTELLI-GENCE...
IT'S BEYOND COMPRE-HENSION.
I'LL NEVER, EVER UNDER-STAND IT...
SHINOGU!
HAVE YOU SEEN HATSUMI?!

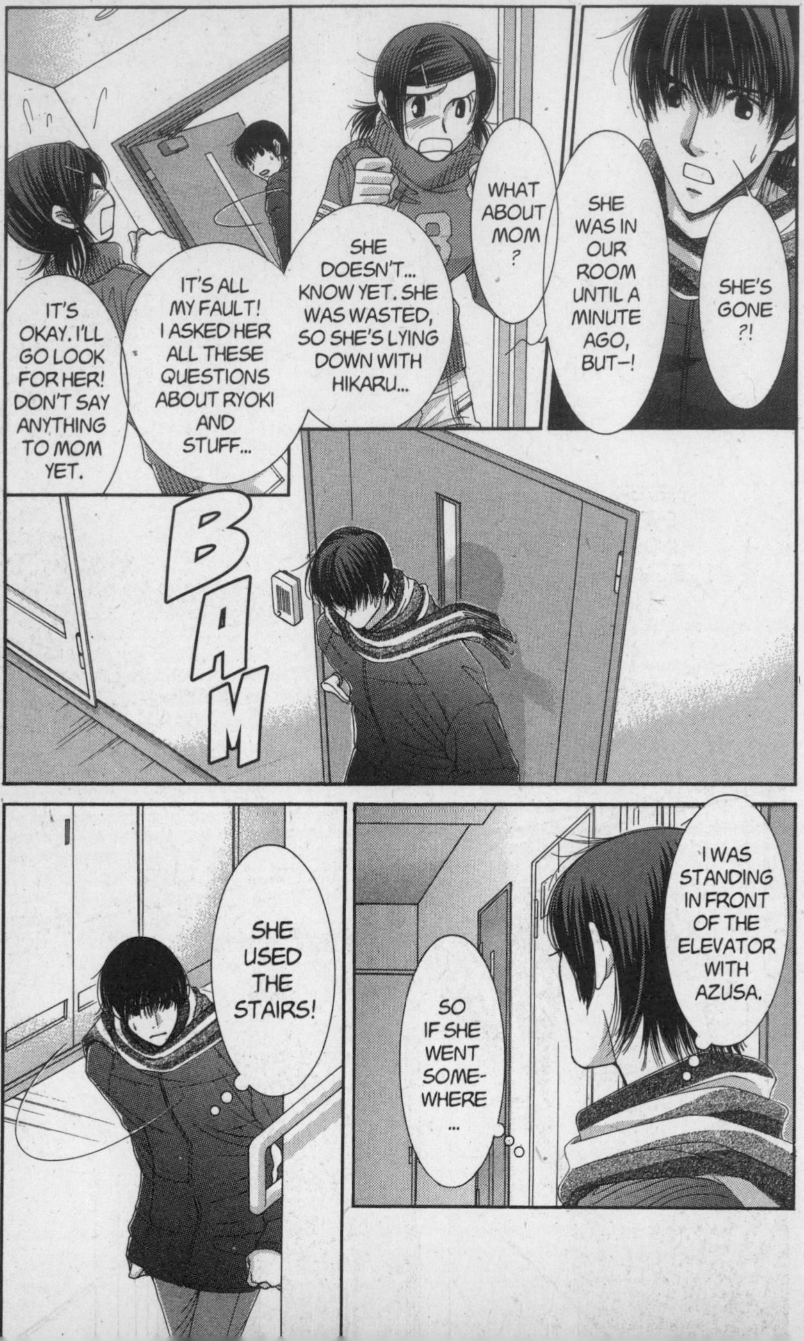
SHE'S GONE ?!
SHE WAS IN OUR ROOM UNTIL A MINUTE AGO, BUT—!
WHAT ABOUT MOM ?
SHE DOESN'T... KNOW YET. SHE WAS WASTED, SO SHE'S LYING DOWN WITH HIKARU...
IT'S ALL MY FAULT! I ASKED HER ALL THESE QUESTIONS ABOUT RYOKI AND STUFF...
IT'S OKAY. I'LL GO LOOK FOR HER! DON'T SAY ANYTHING TO MOM YET.
BAM
I WAS STANDING IN FRONT OF THE ELEVATOR WITH AZUSA.
SO IF SHE WENT SOME-WHERE ...
SHE USED THE STAIRS!

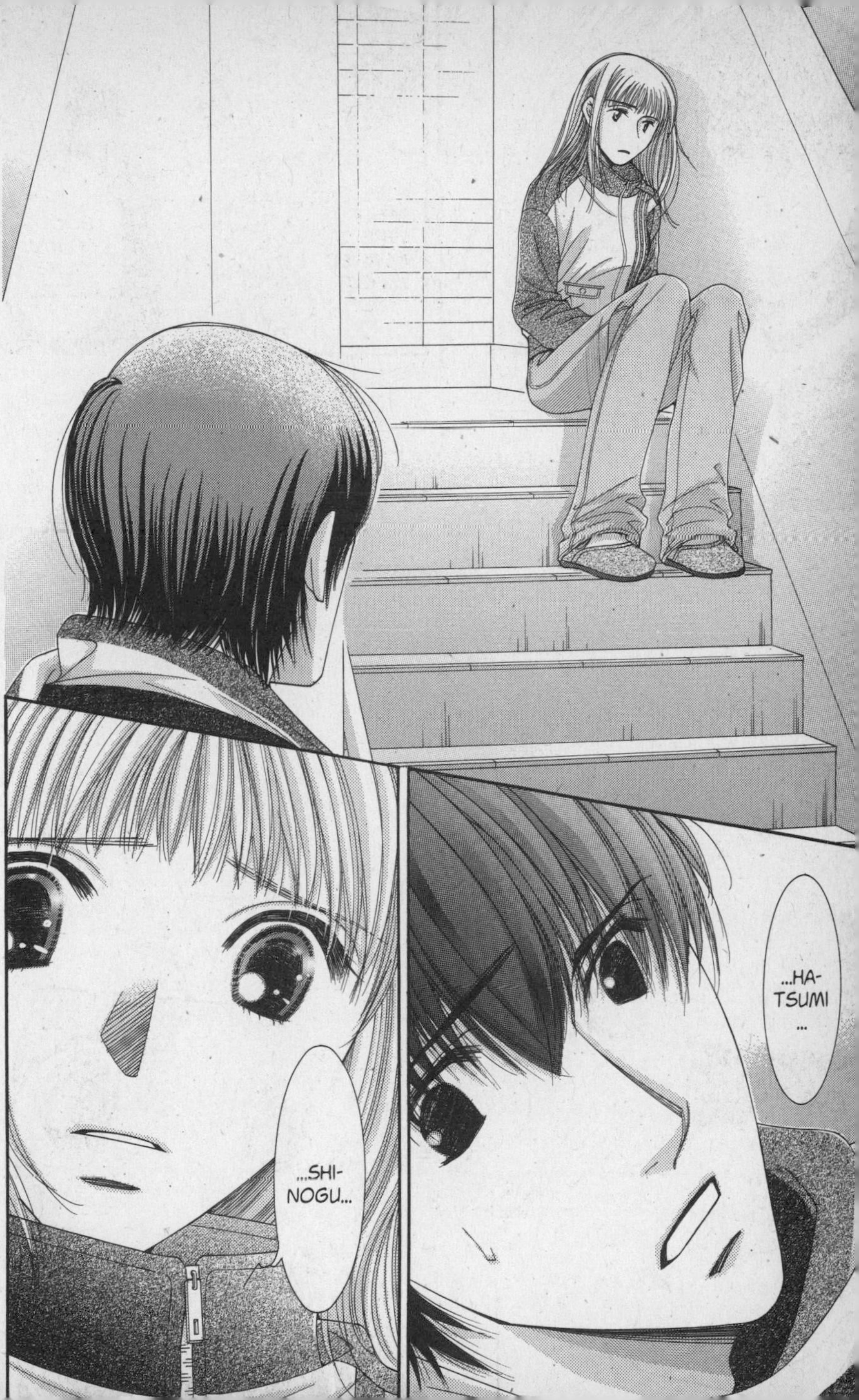
...HA-TSUMI...
...SHI-NOGU...

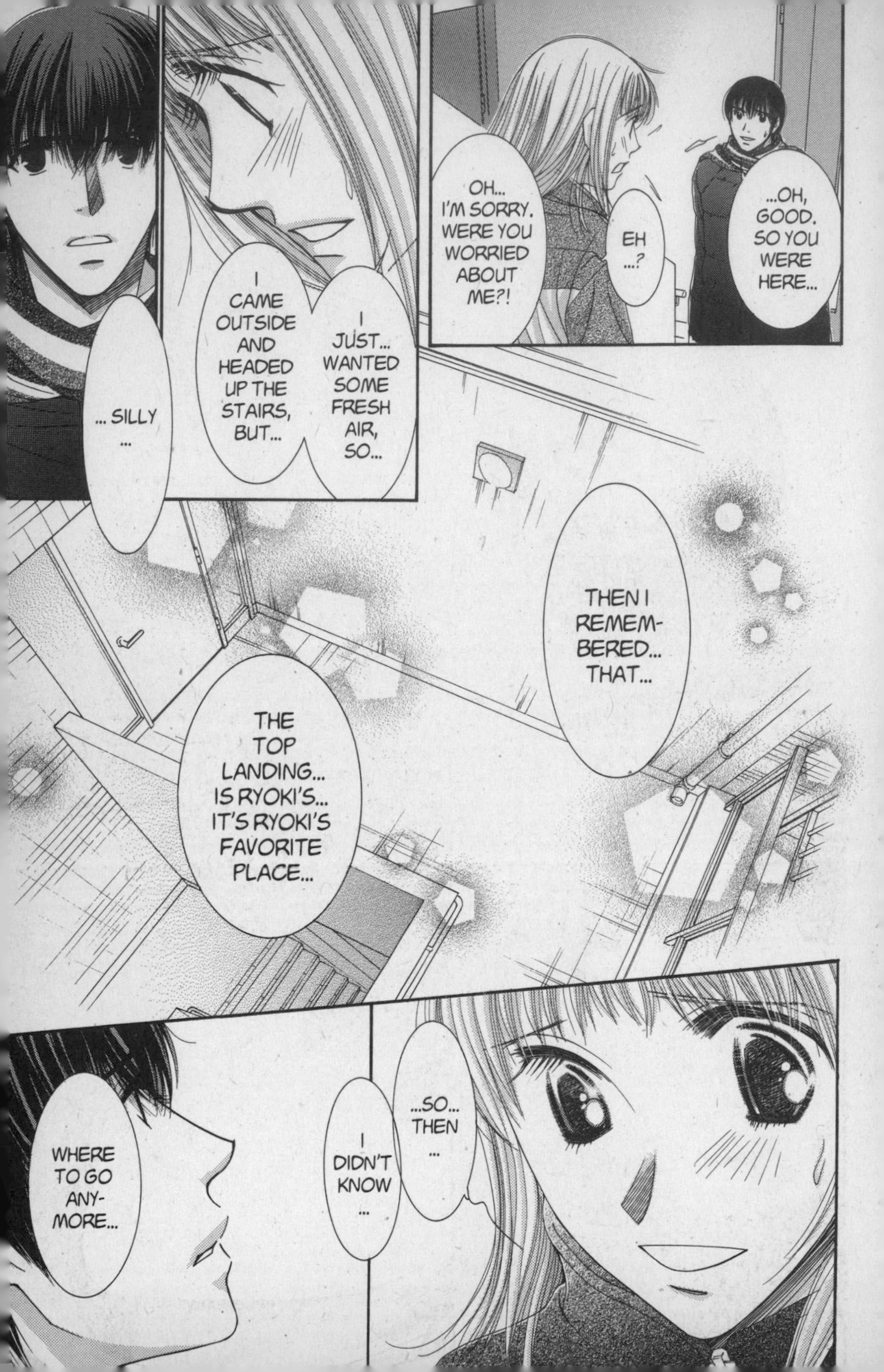
...OH, GOOD. SO YOU WERE HERE...
EH ...?
OH... I'M SORRY. WERE YOU WORRIED ABOUT ME?!
I JUST... WANTED SOME FRESH AIR, SO...
I CAME OUTSIDE AND HEADED UP THE STAIRS, BUT...
... SILLY ...
THEN I REMEMBERED... THAT...
THE TOP LANDING... IS RYOKI'S... IT'S RYOKI'S FAVORITE PLACE...
...SO... THEN ...
I DIDN'T KNOW ...
WHERE TO GO ANYMORE...

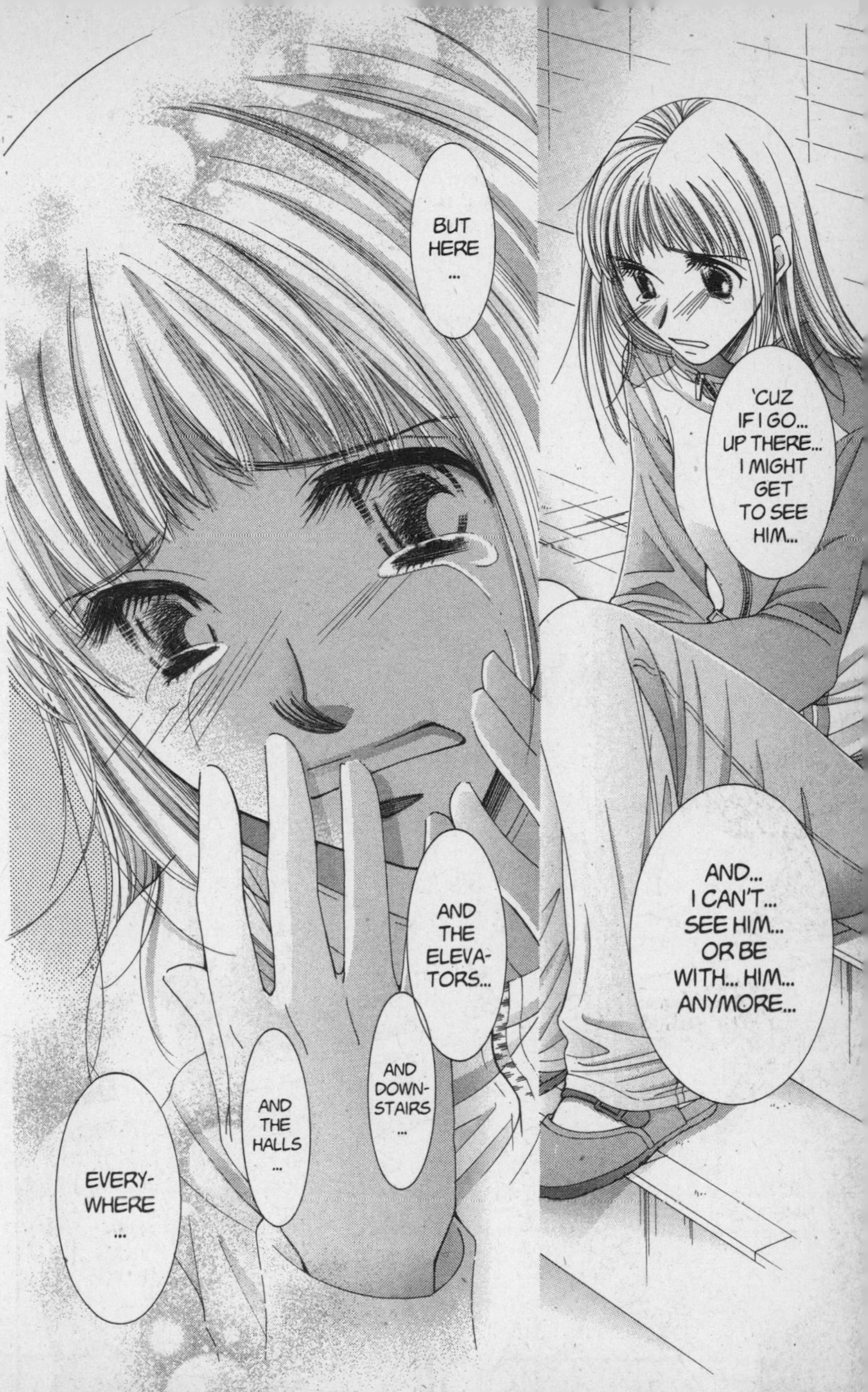
'CUZ IF I GO... UP THERE... I MIGHT GET TO SEE HIM...
AND... I CAN'T... SEE HIM... OR BE WITH... HIM... ANYMORE...
BUT HERE ...
AND THE ELEVATORS...
AND DOWNSTAIRS ...
AND THE HALLS ...
EVERYWHERE ...

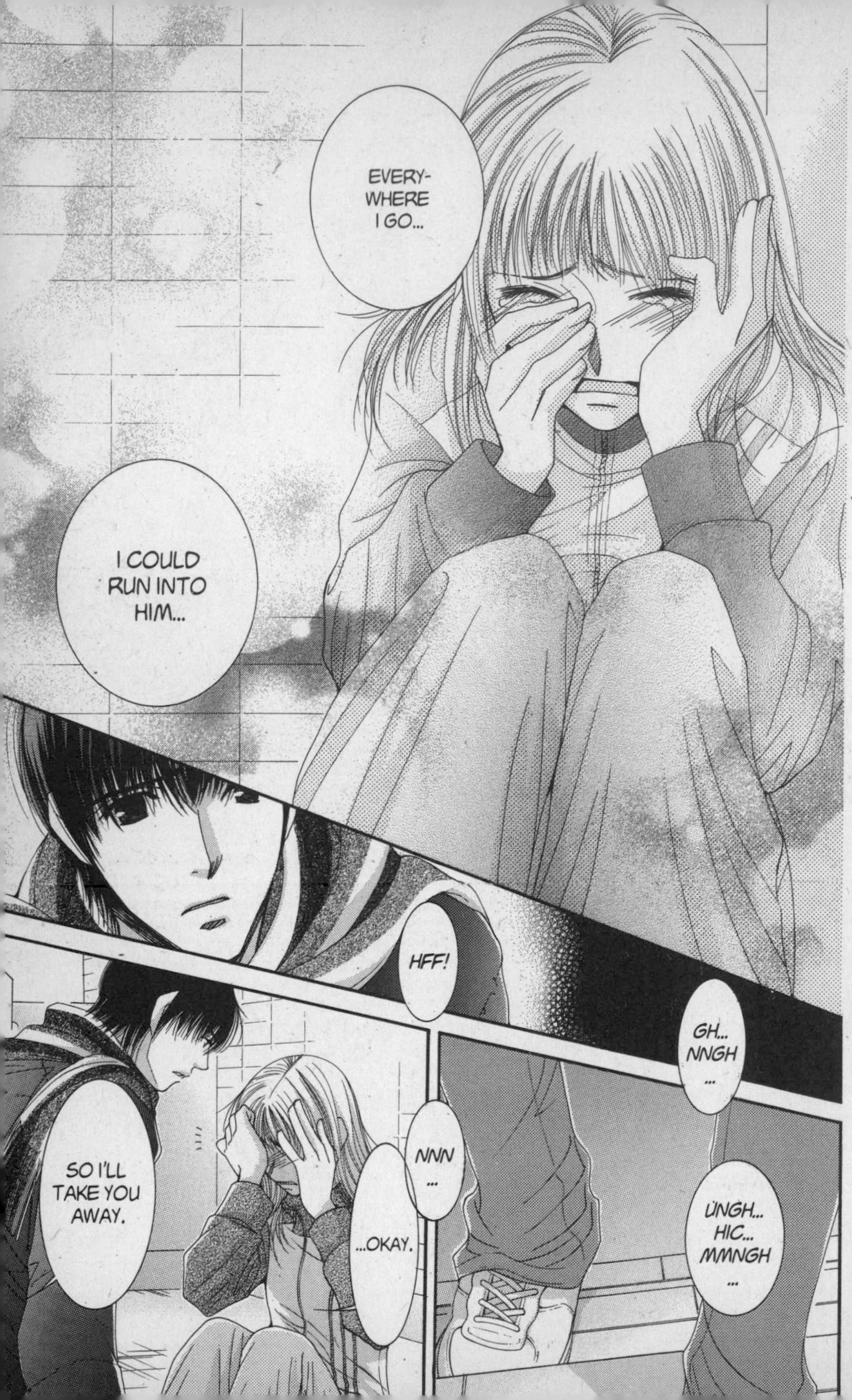
EVERY-WHERE I GO...
I COULD RUN INTO HIM...
HFF!
GH... NNGH ...
ÜNGH... HIC... MMNGH ...
NNN ...
SO I'LL TAKE YOU AWAY.
...OKAY.

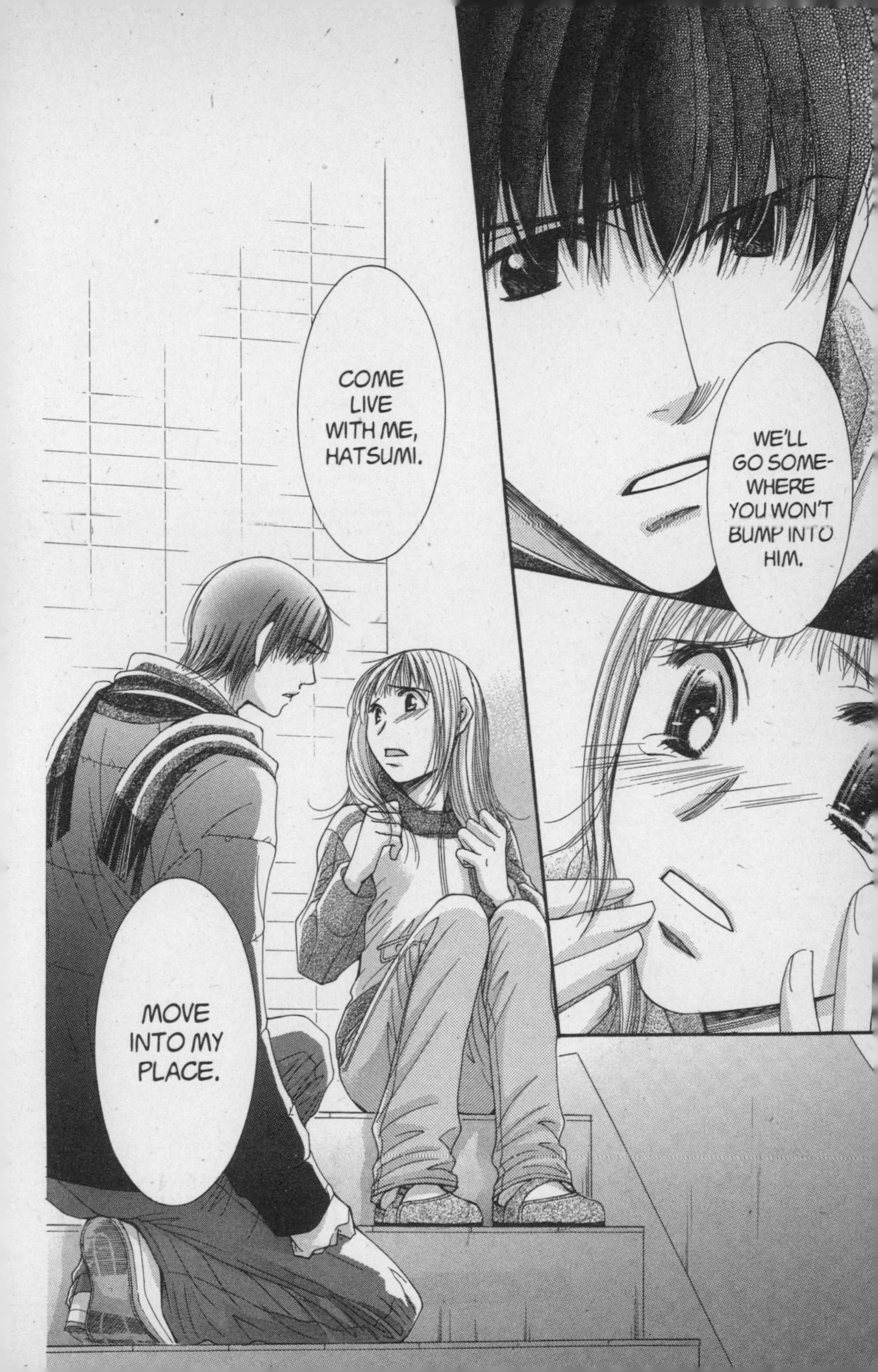
WE'LL GO SOME-WHERE YOU WON'T BUMP INTO HIM.
COME LIVE WITH ME, HATSUMI.
MOVE INTO MY PLACE.

To be continued

hot gimmick

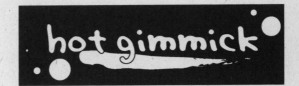

EXTRA!! GIMMICK

Thank you for buying Hot Gimmick Vol. 10.
My name is Miki Aihara.
Here, just for you graphic novel readers, is
more of that extra information that's so hard
to put into the actual story.
Read on!

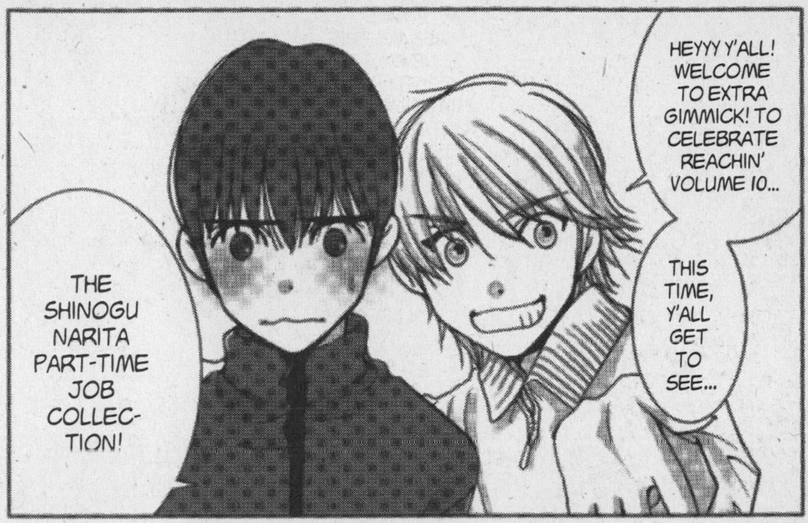
HEYYY Y'ALL! WELCOME TO EXTRA GIMMICK! TO CELEBRATE REACHIN' VOLUME 10...
THIS TIME, Y'ALL GET TO SEE...
THE SHINOGU NARITA PART-TIME JOB COLLECTION!

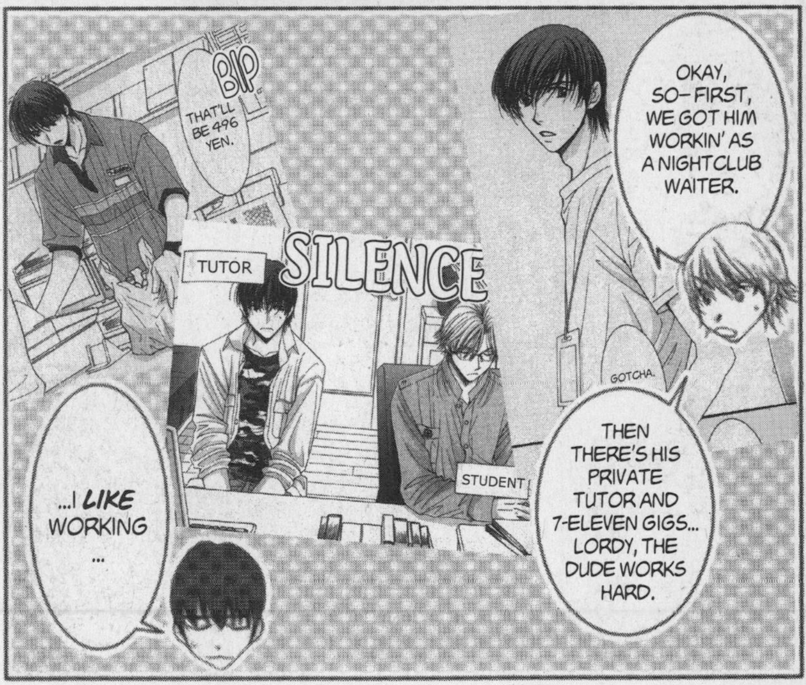
OKAY, SO— FIRST, WE GOT HIM WORKIN' AS A NIGHTCLUB WAITER.
GOTCHA.
THEN THERE'S HIS PRIVATE TUTOR AND 7-ELEVEN GIGS... LORDY, THE DUDE WORKS HARD.
SILENCE
TUTOR
STUDENT
BIP
THAT'LL BE 496 YEN.
...I ***LIKE*** WORKING ...

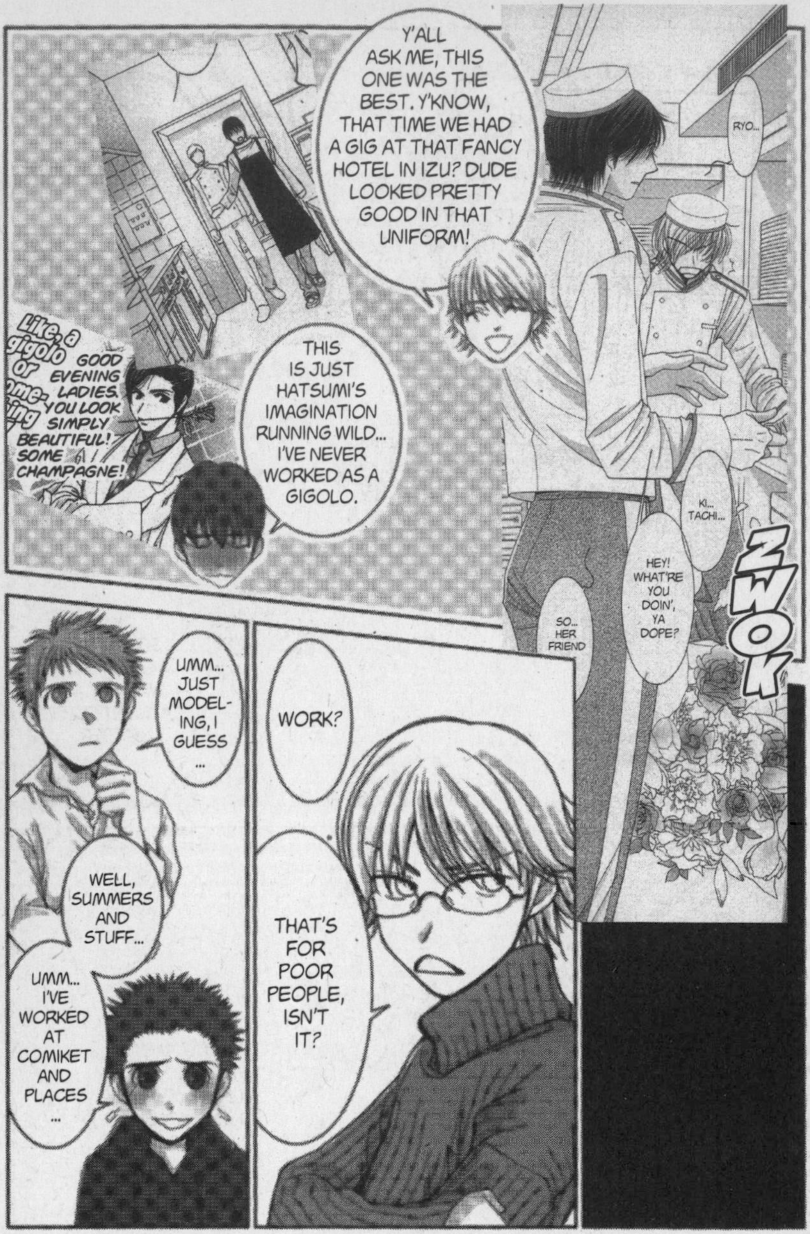
RYO...
KI... TACHI...
HEY! WHAT'RE YOU DOIN', YA DOPE?
ZWOK
SO... HER FRIEND
Y'ALL ASK ME, THIS ONE WAS THE BEST. Y'KNOW, THAT TIME WE HAD A GIG AT THAT FANCY HOTEL IN IZU? DUDE LOOKED PRETTY GOOD IN THAT UNIFORM!
THIS IS JUST HATSUMI'S IMAGINATION RUNNING WILD... I'VE NEVER WORKED AS A GIGOLO.
GOOD EVENING LADIES. YOU LOOK SIMPLY BEAUTIFUL! SOME CHAMPAGNE!
Like, a gigolo or
WORK?
THAT'S FOR POOR PEOPLE, ISN'T IT?
UMM... JUST MODEL-ING, I GUESS...
WELL, SUMMERS AND STUFF...
UMM... I'VE WORKED AT COMIKET AND PLACES...

HOT GIMMICK
Vol. 10

Shôjo Edition

STORY & ART BY MIKI AIHARA

ENGLISH ADAPTATION BY POOKIE ROLF

Touch-up Art & Lettering/Rina Mapa
Cover Design/Izumi Evers
Editor/Kit Fox

Managing Editor/Annette Roman
Director of Production/Noboru Watanabe
Vice President of Publishing/Alvin Lu
Sr. Director of Acquisitions/Rika Inouye
Vice President of Sales & Marketing/Liza Coppola
Publisher/Hyoe Narita

Printed in Canada.

Published by VIZ Media, LLC
P.O. Box 77010
San Francisco, CA 94107

10 9 8 7 6 5 4 3 2 1
First printing, November 2005

store.viz.com